Culture, Religion and Philosophy

Culture, Religion and Philosophy

Critical Studies in Syncretism and Inter-Faith Harmony

Edited by

N.K. DAS

RAWAT PUBLICATIONS
Jaipur and New Delhi

ISBN 81-7033-820-4

Published by
Prem Rawat for ***Rawat Publications***
Satyam Apts., Sector 3, Jawahar Nagar, Jaipur 302 004 (India)
Phone: 0141 265 1748 / 7006 Fax: 0141 2651748
E-mail : info@rawatbooks.com
Website : www.rawatbooks.com

Delhi Office
4858/24, Ansari Road, Daryaganj, New Delhi 110 002
Phone: 011-23263290

Typeset by Rawat Computers, Jaipur
Printed at Chaman Enterprises, New Delhi

Contents

Preface

This volume studies the phenomenon of syncretism, an unexplored and rarely studied aspect of culture, which has escaped the notice of conventional social science. Syncretism exists not only as a vibrant tradition but also as a coherent cultural reality in different parts of India. There are traditions and belief systems which are essentially based on a particular system of faith and worship. There are also syncretistic conventions and synthetically evolved belief systems which are based on combination of diverse religious traditions. Both views are seemingly correct in the Indian context. People often adhere to multiple religious traditions without necessarily drawing boundaries between them, even though they may affirm their overt allegiance to one religion. Such syncretistic religious practices, however, demonstrate regional variability. It may be argued that few religions are wholly immune from some degree of syncretism. Judaism, Christianity, Islam, Hinduism and Buddhism from their beginning combined many different religious ideas and rituals. Syncretism, as implied in this volume, signifies a belief in multiple religious assumptions, dogmas and doctrinal systems as also unification of different religious denominations, schools of thought and religious practices. Religious syncretism may occur on account of culture-contact or as a result of social protest or sectarian-reformist movement. Political instability and social pressures, in the past, often gave rise to reformist and messianic movements which resulted in development and spread of sectarian and syncretistic traditions in India. Many such movements attracted and involved sections of Hindu, Muslim, Dalit (scheduled castes) and Adivasi (scheduled tribe) communities. Propagators and prophets of such syncretistic traditions in different historical phases advocated the virtues of humanism and egalitarianism.

While globalization gains ground and people representing different faiths move from one place to another, most of the nations of the world have turned multi-cultural and multi-confessional. Interculturalism and blending of different religious traditions in vast parts of the globe have given rise to trans-cultural syncretism. In the present era of increasing cultural condensation, syncretism is a prevailing event. The globalized world has a vital stake in multi-confessional harmony. Syncretism as an important constituent of multi-cultural mainstream offers an opportunity to reinforce greater cultural homogenization. Today in India, varied notions of 'secularism' have created more problems than solving them. It is therefore worthwhile to arouse traditional modes of cultural synthesis and religious syncretism, which are fundamental sources of social tolerance witnessed in different parts of India for centuries. The contributors of this volume, belonging to disciplines of philosophy, history and anthropology, not only enthusiastically agreed to participate in this engagement, they affirmatively endorsed the original conceptual model of the editor. The editor is indeed grateful to each one of them. Here we are not constrained by familiar social science conventions and narrower models of Indian society, rather we have engaged ourselves in constructing an indigenous theoretical model by founding the analytic universal applicability of the concept of syncretism, with support of vivid empirical evidences. This book contains cases pertaining to adherents of all major and minor religions of India, including syncretistic faiths of the Adivasis and the Dalits. Several such cases, including the theoretical backdrop of this undertaking, are incorporated in the extensive introductory chapter of the volume. Thus, varied manifestations of syncretism and synthesized cultural formations are manifested in diverse experiences of people of India (Two cases dealing with Hinduism and Buddhism are drawn from the Philippines, Myanmar and other South East Asian countries). This book aims at providing a new perspective by challenging many popularly held beliefs about the rigidities of faith and by highlighting the glowing sphere of inter-religious harmony, which is the need of the era. In this pioneering work we have endeavoured to present syncretism not only as a viable way of life but also as a vigorous theoretical category.

November, 2002 **N.K. DAS**

Introduction

An Outline of Syncretism

N.K. Das

Interculturalism and blending of different religious traditions in vast parts of the world have given rise to trans-cultural syncretism. In the present era of increasing cultural condensation, syncretism is a prevailing event. Syncretism as an important constituent of multi-cultural mainstream offers an opportunity to reinforce greater cultural amalgam and multi-confessional harmony. The vast region of south Asia in general and India in particular symbolizes a remarkable confluence of cultural strands and cross-fertilization of religious ideas and ethnic/linguistic intermingling. Here cross-fertilization of sacred ideas and civil thoughts took place, in the midst of ethnic, linguistic and regional diversities, alongside growth of numerous religious cults and sects, in various historical phases. The sociologists and social anthropologists have thrown much light on the variety of religious forms through their studies of belief systems, rituals, symbols and meanings all over the world but they have not paid adequate attention to the phenomenon of syncretism, which represents a blend of multiple religious beliefs, in variegated degrees. In this regard Raymond Firth has rightly observed that the anthropologists have made only passing references to syncretism (1970:87). The concept of syncretism uncovers a remarkable dimension in the exploration of cultural reciprocation. It is unfortunate that this important dimension of contemporary culture has been dismissed as passing and trivial.

I

The sociologists and social anthropologists view religion as a universal phenomenon. Religions show enormous variety in terms of beliefs, rituals, spiritualism and symbolic imagery. Religion appears in several forms but there are three widely recognized religious forms. Along with Confucianism, Taoism and Shintoism, Buddhism is an *ethical* religion. It ascribes sacredness to moral principles rather than to a deity. On the other hand, Christianity, Judaism, Islam and Hinduism are *theistic* religions. Believers worship one or several gods. A third type is *animism*, in which followers believe that spirits can help or harm people but can be manipulated to serve human needs (Thio, 1989:369). Anthropologists agree that there is no society that is without some form of religion. In the nineteenth century, scholars were greatly concerned with the origins of religion and they looked to the so-called primitive societies for ideas about development of religion (Hendry, 1999:119–120). In a vast range of societies studied by anthropologists, concepts and formulations of gods, deities, supreme creator, guardian spirits and culture heroes have been applied profusely (Firth, 1996), but the debate over the term religion in anthropology and sociology remains unresolved generally. The sociologists and social anthropologists have expressed uneasiness with the word religion because of its vagueness (Smith 1962, Cox 1965, Evans-Pritchard 1965). S.F. Nadel comments that however the sphere of 'things religious' is defined, there will always remain a border zone of uncertainty (1954:7–8). Edward Tylor had proposed a minimum definition of religion: 'Belief in spiritual beings' (1903:424). This definition was subjected to criticism (see critique in Hamilton, 1995:12–13). A critical review of early debates and definitions shows that crucial problems centred on beliefs versus practices, character of religious entities or forces and the spiritual or supernatural realm. Even Durkheim's claim that religion has to do with the 'sacred' came to be challenged, as such terms coming from Western context are not applicable to non-Western societies. Goody found that no distinction is made between sacred and profane in a West-African society (Goody, 1961). The terms sacred and profane were found to be meaningless in the Azande society also (Evans-Pritchard, 1937). Emile Durkheim indeed identified the notion of sacred as the fundamental religious phenomenon. He regarded religion as a unified set of beliefs and practices relative to sacred things (1965:62). People everywhere in their myths and rituals have attributed misfortune and suffering to certain extra-human, extra-physical power and also related the same to divinity and the sacred. The structuralist concerns of Levi-Strauss, which have been very broad, have also subsumed the study of the 'sacred' under the forms of thought, modes of classification and mythologies. Even totemism is regarded as a mode of classification (1963,1966). Weber studied the preliterate as well as the world religions to explore the relations between religious beliefs and practices and also their 'secular domains'. Weber described mysticism as the attitude of abandoning worldly involvement. Anthropologists regard mysticism occurring in many religions as a form of assumed personal relation with a divine power (Firth 1964, 1996:173). The essence of a mystical experience is the search for or attainment of a sense of nearness to or unity with a transcendent power, usually God. This means an enhancement of the self, a heightened state of awareness, which seems to throw a new light upon the nature of reality for the mystic (Firth, 1996:173). A supernatural event or a miracle, according to Firth, is an unexpected performance resulting from supernatural power, exercised by direct divine intervention or through the agency of a divinely inspired person, such as a saint. The anthropologists and other social scientists have differently documented the status and role of the saint. Weber emphasized the social basis of varieties of theism, the role of prophets in society, different roads to salvation and 'universal love.' One of the central concerns of Weber's sociology of religion was the nature of human existence. He saw no future for religion but only its replacement by progressive rationalization and the decline of mystery, magic and rituals.

Anthropologists eventually turned from the origin issue to seeking explanations of religion within its social context. Thus religious rites were regarded as most crucial since they provided support to social structure (Hendry, 1999:119–120). Religious faiths and moral systems provided order and they socialized the individuals. The anthropologists gradually came to employ various approaches in the study of religion. Those employing the social approach generally saw religion as a 'reflection of social organization' and those using the cultural approach viewed religion as a 'conceptual system'. The anthropologists using such and other approaches however, undeniably projected the faith of a people, by and large, as a closed system and consequently the evolved anthropological definition of religion came to over-generalize the presumed 'unvarying' character of religious allegiance of people concerned, ignoring the veiled side of synthesized religious domain. As a matter of fact the religious beliefs of the people, as developed through extensive contacts and adoptions, were hardly ever rigid or sealed. People in most cases, as we intend to show in this book, often follow multiple religious traditions without necessarily drawing boundaries between them, even though they may affirm their overt allegiance to one religion at a given time. Here lies the analytic significance of the study of the concept of religious syncretism as an independent phenomenon.

In anthropological literature the Cargo cult has been described as a form of syncretism. Cargo cults are essentially syncretistic, blending the Christian doctrine with 'aboriginal beliefs' (Worsley, 1990). Cult members preached that masters would become slaves and slaves would become masters. Cult participation gave Melanesians a basis for common interests and activities and thus helped pave the way to achieve nationhood. The anthropologists have also included the blend of African, Native American, and Roman Catholic saints and deities in Caribbean 'voodoo' cults as instances of syncretism. In Haitian Voudun and other syncretic religions, the elements do not simply exist side by side, but are often merged in various ways. In Brazil, syncretic religions are an important element in the Black consciousness movement. According to David Levinson syncretism is also found in the economic system, in the diet, in kinship, and in politics (1994:226). Syncretism indeed is a poorly understood phenomenon. Of all elements of culture, religion and language are more open to syncretization. Though the process of syncretism provides an independent and demonstrative field of study, it was nevertheless ignored by the anthropologists, and when discussed it was included within 'the study of acculturation' (Kottak, 1991:407). Acculturation is an imperfect expression. Acculturation has been defined as including, "those phenomena which result when groups of individuals come into continuous firsthand contact, (with) subsequent changes in the original cultural patterns of either or both groups" (Redfield, Linton and Herskovits, 1936:149). The points specified here by these acclaimed anthropologists are 'contact' and 'subsequent changes'. Obviously, the concept of acculturation is least concerned with the survival question and perpetuation of pre-change religious and cultural beliefs and values, which ostensibly never die completely in any society. This notion of acculturation indeed is exclusively prejudiced in favour of supposedly accomplished culture change. There is no doubt that significant culture changes do take place but the pre-change culture traits and religious customs indeed survive in greater or lesser degree in many societies and therefore 'acculturation' persists in such societies only as an incomplete and partial process. Thus we witness the coexistence of dual religious beliefs and traditions, often prevailing determinedly and willfully. In due course, a course of syncretism automatically sets in which gets evolved in varied degrees depending on verve and impact of new beliefs and variegated intensity of contact amidst such societies.

Social scientists commonly aim to achieve a level of generality that would permit them judgments about social forms. In social sciences the term empiricism has broader meaning. Both the empiricist and the participant observer derive knowledge from their research experience. A researcher makes interpretations of data by concretizing and operationalizing his procedures. Two concepts, which are considered important in social research, are sensitizing and formalizing concepts. The latter may be illustrated by the 'ideal type', which Weber describes as a model. Meanings of sensitizing concepts, coined by Herbert Blumer, are not communicated by formal definitions. The sensitizing concept is flexible in its image and finds a certain virtue in its inexactness as elucidated by Bruyn (1966:33). The researcher must not interpret and conceptualize the mass of data in distinctive ways, he must also describe them both analytically and synthetically. Analysis and synthesis differ in the emphasis the observer gives to the general process. By synthetic process we mean discovering an element of unity or uniformity within disparate elements of data that relates them into a coherent whole (Bruyn, 1966:35). Joy Hendry (1999) has discussed this issue at length. Synthesis, according to Hendry (1999:144–145), takes place when one set of beliefs virtually subsumes another set of beliefs. Indeed there exists definite difference between synthesis and syncretism. Recent discussions pertaining to syncretism, which are very few indeed, have argued that all religions have drawn on different traditions over centuries (Stewart and Shaw, 1995).

It may be argued that few religions are wholly immune from some degree of syncretism. Even Judaism, Christianity, Islam, Buddhism, Hinduism and other major religions, from their beginning, combined many different religious ideas and rituals. Syncretism, according to Brandon, is to be found in all places where there has been contact between religions (1970). The term syncretism was originally used by Plutarch for 'fusion of religious cults' which occurred in the Graeco-Roman world, 300 BC-200 CE. Christianity, from its beginning, combined many different religious ideas and rituals (Gnosticism, hermetic and mystery religions).

Anthropology is a multi-paradigmatic enterprise. Multiple paradigms help us to see reality differently. They also help us to see different realities. Anthropologists have always followed diversified events in human societies. The different approaches of looking at social issues have led us towards more sophisticated methods. In this respect the model of syncretism indeed deserves the paradigmatic treatment. Anthropologists are well suited to the task of exploring the facet of 'religious syncretism' as it occurs at the level of everyday life in a wide diversity of settings. There is indeed need for a concerted effort in this direction particularly because this issue assumes significance in the contemporary context of the challenge thrown up by the 'deconstructionist strategy'.

II

The people of India came to know each other more intimately in the course of the freedom struggle. Integration, however, has been an ancient phenomenon. People visited sacred centres all over the country and thus a process of continuous interaction operated continually at the grass-roots level in all historical phases. Exchange and sharing of traits, thoughts and ethos contributed to cultural synthesis. One scholar has perceived Indian society as a 'honeycomb' in which communities are engaged in vibrant interaction, sharing space, ethos and cultural traits (Singh, 1992[2002]: 111). Between themselves the communities look more at commonalties than differences and they easily establish rapport. Thus a high correlation of traits is reported between Kerala and Lakshadweep. There is also a high correlation between Hindus and Buddhists at a wider level. The data set of *People of India* project suggests that people in the religious sphere share a high percentage of traits: Hindu-Muslim (97.7 per cent), Hindu-Buddhist (91 per cent), Hindu-Sikh (88.99 per cent) and Hindu-Jain (77.46 per cent). Other religious communities with a high percentage of sharing of religious traits are Muslim-Sikh (89.95 per cent), Muslim-Buddhist (91.18 per cent) and Jain-Buddhist (81.34 per cent). Other forms of traditional linkages are participation in each other's religious ceremonies and festivals. Such sharing, according to Singh (1992[2002]:111) includes performing actual roles in religious ceremonies. The proportion of such communities as Hindus, Buddhists, Sikhs and Jains visiting 'other religious shrines' vary from 80–92 per cent while 60–75 per cent of the communities following Islam, Christianity and other religions (mainly tribal) visit other people's shrines. Similarly participation in each other's festivals is common (81--91 per cent) for all categories of the population. About 15–22 per cent of people perform specific roles in festivals of other religions such as making images, dresses and ornaments for deities, organizing worship and processions, etc. (1992[2002]:112--113). These facts explain that despite contradictions and diversities, there exists vibrant sharing of cultural and religious traits. A basic sense of harmony prevails which dissolves our animosity and ultimately contributes towards shaping our unique homogenization.

Hendry (1999:12) has observed that in complex societies, people have come to live with apparently conflicting worldviews, and their cosmologies now include scientific, religious and even magical elements. In Japan, a sick person simultaneously consults a diviner as well as a doctor, and may also visit a shrine or temple to pray for recovery (Ohnuki-Tierney, 1984). Religious movements and a plethora of religious ideas, in varied historical phases, motivated the people and brought them closer towards numerous religious cults, sects, reform movements and diverse belief systems. The underlying assumption seems to be that people need solace and assurance about fulfilment of all their wishes ultimately; hence they solicit refuge and sanctification of their expectations through their trust on varied religious and sectarian dogmas. Mingling of numerous exogenous religious beliefs with pre-existing religious dogma of people may not be regarded as an aberration. It is also not a system within a system but the survival of multifaceted religious belief systems existing as a rational order. Syncretism as we have tried to show in this volume, is a matter of degree—some societies have blended prominent aspects of two religious dogmas, in others only certain aspects of the original or adopted religion/sect has been internalized. We have shown that syncretism pertains to a commingled religious sequence whose ill-defined frontier shapes its fundamental collective character.

III

Indian society is characterized by the caste system. It is a system of social hierarchy in which social groups are arranged in a rude order of ritual purity and pollution. Hence there prevailed immense space for dissent and reform within the society. Reformist groups and sects emerged from time to time as a result. Quests for equality, salvation and often a bit of mobility aspiration remained integral parts of reformist movements. Most of these movements that aimed at reorganizing the society in India were couched in religious terms. Social pressures had often encouraged adoption of new religious denominations and formation of sectarian and dissident religious orders in India. Religious orders such as the Sikh and Vira Saiva, according to Gnanambal (1970) have emerged as deviants from the orthodox Hindu religion. Sectarian-cultist orders had occurred as challenges to established doctrinal positions. New sects proliferate when the pre-existing religions fail to satisfy the need for meaningful interpretation of life problems (Toby, 1971). A sect is a religious group that rejects the social environment in which it exists (Johnson, 1963). Sects function to satisfy a society's needs. Some sects are savagely critical of secular society as well as of competing sects (Toby, 1971: 290). While a sect has a compulsory character and is characterized by the elective principle, the cult is a private personal religion of mystic type (Becker and

Weise, 1932; Sinha, 1970). Religious sects, in general, promote integration, homogenization and egalitarianism by calling attention to needs unmet by established religions. Sects also help to cope with problems of identity and meaning. Dumont and Renou agree that the pattern of sect development in India is unique in character (McCormack, 1963:61).

Led by their defiant gurus, reformist congregations emerged within the Hindu society from time to time. These rebellious saints were products of processes of dissent and reform. They reformed the rituals, de-emphasized the supremacy of the Brahman and preached egalitarianism. The leaders of several reform movements belonged to the lower economic classes and Dalit castes. Reformist leaders emerged among the Muslims and tribals also. They significantly advanced the homogenization process in their localities. It is observed that the original inspiration for social reform and religious transformation came from a charismatic mentor who drew devotees to his 'knowledge', his revelation of the true path---to eternal salvation. The mentor, either male or female, introduced reforms of religious practices in the shape of a fresh vision of eternal truths. New religious sects also arose to bring emotional satisfaction in the lives of marginalized and disadvantaged sections of society, sections not adequately served by established cultural institutions. In order to gain honour and privilege certain disadvantaged people such as the Dalits often sought alteration of their pre-existing societal status and thus embraced new religious-sectarian orders. Such people however could hardly ever give up entirely their primeval religious beliefs. It would be a travesty in the name of objectivity if we seek to subordinate these actualities and forms of consciousness to certain inflexible and shortened Western theoretical formulations such as acculturation.

Dissent has a long history in India. In the remote past intensive religious activity had taken place which aimed to overthrow the predominance of Buddhism and Jainism in peninsular India. In this period we witness even 'breaking of barriers of caste' inherent in the Vedic religion by admitting devotees even from 'untouchable' castes into the order of Bhaktas, thereby sowing the seed of Bhakti movement (Gnanambal, 1970). During the medieval period (thirteenth to seventeenth century) Hinduism underwent a drastic transformation. Focus was now on one god. The religious sect founded by Ramanuja (1017–1137 AD) was intended to propagate the Vishistadvaita school of philosophy. The followers of Ramanuja styled themselves as Shri Vaishnavas. Ramanuja propagated the doctrine of qualified *monism* in which self-surrender and grace (*prapatti*) formed the central theme (Gnanambal, 1970). While Sankara and Ramanuja had pan-Indian impact, the movement of Madhava (14th century) was confined to south India. Sankara, a metaphysician was not interested in the proselytizing of Hinduism or adding adherents. Ramanuja understood that to engage in a three-cornered fight against Buddhism, Jainism and the pure *monism* of Sankara, he had to simplify and liberalize the recruitment procedure. While the essentials of Advaita and Dvaita of Sankara and Madhava did not reach the masses, the Bhakti principle of Ramanuja appealed to all (Gnanambal, 1970). Ramananda (1400–70), a follower of Ramanuja, having settled down in Varanasi, established his own sect, Ramanandi. Ramananda strongly opposed the injustices of the caste system and opened his sect for all, and his twelve personal disciples are said to have included women, an outcaste and even a Muslim. The Ramanandi sect has great historical importance because of the growth of innumerable sects from within the Ramanandi sect. The Ramanandis paved the way for later sects like the Sikhs and Kabirpanthi. Kabir (1440–1518) started out as a disciple of Ramananda, but later developed his own characteristic eclecticism. Having been brought up in a Muslim home, Kabir remained a low caste weaver. According to Kabir, only personal bhakti could lead one to god. Vaishnavism, Hatha Yoga, Vedantic monism, and Sufism (Jordan, 1975) influenced Kabir's theology. Among the Saivites, the sect of the Lingayats was one whose influence reached several north Indian saints (Jordan, 1975). The Vira Saiva sect, led by Basava (14th century) came to be known as 'Lingayata', in common parlance, since the adherents wear a *linga* suspended on a string round their neck. Theoretically, the Lingayats cannot be called Hindus since they do not accept the differentiation of castes, the pollution of birth, death, menstruation, contact or look. The Lingayat women have equal ritual status with men (Gnanambal, 1970).

The religious sects and indigenous religious orders of India, such as Vira Saivism, Jainism, Sikhism and other orders began with a founder guru who preached a new faith. In fulfilling the new precepts the devotees separated themselves from established orders. The 1931 census of Punjab thus noted that a good many Hindus of 'lower jatis' were becoming Sikhs because they considered that "they gained status as soon as they ceased to be Hindus" (Mandelbaum, 1970:524). The founder Gurus generally emphasized the 'way of devotion' over 'scriptural knowledge', and propagated the dogmas which were generally based on egalitarian principles. The Jain devotees have practised their faith for more than twenty-five centuries. Mahavira and other sages stressed that personal acts, and not ascribed status, determined all that was important for the soul. Despite such long existence of a religious order, the Jains continue to worship Hindu deities, in lesser or greater degree, in different parts of India.

Like Kabir, Nanak identified himself with the most deprived sections in the society. Like Kabir, Nanak also denounced attachment to rituals (like prayer, fasting, bathing, image worship) and forgetting true faith in god. According to the main philosophy of the Sikh religion there is only one god. Guru Nanak taught that the Hindus, Muslims and people of all religious denominations are children of the same god. Influenced by the school of 'devotion' (Bhakti) of Ramananda, Kabir, Namdev and having assimilated the philosophy of Sufism and Islam, Guru Nanak gave a syncretistic form to his new religion. Uberoi (1994) has, however, observed that total human emancipation of religious man and not merely any ideal of a synthesis or reconciliation of Hinduism and Islam, was the faith and endeavour of Sikhism from its inception.

Both the Bhakti and Sufi saints had helped to recast and reorient the prevalent value system of the time. These saints propagated the fundamental equality of mankind. These saints patronized the *nirguna* theological stance, based on a notion that the divine is formless, 'without qualities'. A directness and unorthodoxy that was to give form to the priorities of new-sprung religious thought and practice typified the wave of Bhakti. Much as Bhakti did, Sufism de-emphasized the role of the clergy and elevated the love between a devotee and his god to ecstasy. Studies have revealed that the Pir and Darvez in different periods played a positive role in bringing about synthesis between the Hindu and Muslim cultures. The Fakir, Darvez, Qualandar and Baul are all known wandering mendicants of India. The Baul sect arose in Bengal with the coming of the Turks and then Islam, which was established in the thirteenth century (Sarkar, 1990). The Sufi movement had considerably coloured the Bengal Vaishnavism in the sixteenth and seventeenth centuries. The Islamic spirit of mystic songs has been deeply ingrained in the songs of Bauls and *Marfati*. The Marfati songs are significant in relation to Islamic spiritual heritage for the whole of humanity. They exemplify the syncretistic tradition in a unique manner. The Baul songs too are associated with the sects of both the Hindus and Muslims. A Baul is a wanderer. Spiritualism is his philosophy, he dances in ecstasy and sings in joy, longing for mystical union with the divine. Among the Bauls of Bengal we also find the continuity of the Sahajiya movement, a more systematized form of which is found in the Buddhist form of Sahajiya school (Sarkar, 1990). The Bhakti consciousness was more prominent in the impressive verses and songs of the saints whose *monism* found no room for Brahminical orthodoxy or the traditional stratification of Hindu society. Vernacular poetry found a new role in expressing sentiments and theologies of Bhakti. This saint tradition is most fully represented by the great mystic poet Kabir. He dismissed the dogma and external observances of both Hinduism and Islam, insisting that the true search for god must be an inner one, accompanied by contemplation on the divine name. Kabir found an easy method of spreading his ideas. Since his audience consisted of illiterates and being illiterate himself, his message could be spread only by word of mouth. Kabir's ideas were sought to be carried forward by Raidas (b.1415), a cobbler by profession. Following Kabir, Raidas and Nanak, all emphasized the concept of human equality. Dadu Dayal (b.1603) similarly asserted that all human beings had the same spirit derived from god and differences of religion are meaningless just as the water of a flowing river in different pots is the same. Regional Bhakti literary traditions help us to understand the growth and spread of humanitarian philosophies. The Kashmiri Bhakti literature begins with *vakh* poetry created by the ascetic poetess Lal Ded (1376) which combines references to Kashmiri life with the technicalities of Shaivite yoga, providing depth to her message of mystical devotion. Only Sheikh Nur-ud-Din (d.1438), founder of the heterodox Rishi order, whose verses are called shrukh, rivals Lal Ded's popularity. At the folk level, there evolved various forms of syncretistic blends of Islam with local cults, as reflected, for example, in the poetry of Sayyid Sultan of Bengal (sixteenth century). In his poem Nabi-Bagsa, he treated the major deities of Hindu religion such as Rama and Krishna as successive prophets of god, followed in turn by Adam, Noah, Abraham, Moses, Jesus and Muhammad. He identified and correlated the Muslim notion of prophet with the Hindu concept of avatar, an incarnation of god. Several elements of Bhakti tradition continue to survive even today in Indian consciousness, such as anti-clergy doctrine, humanism and human equality, human brotherhood, secularism, and non-discrimination between castes and sects. By the 1920s the immutable and extensive spirit of Indian religious and social reform movements had slowly diminished mainly on account of the advent of Mahatma Gandhi on the Indian landscape.

IV

On account of various levels of culture-contact, adoption and absorption, the tribes of India had often borrowed material, linguistic and cultural traits as also religious practices of various communities, sects and major religions such as Buddhism, Hinduism and Christianity. Cultural adoption, however, never occurred as a flawless event. The tribals perpetually adhered to many aspects of the original religion even after their adoption of a new faith. Pre-conversion native religious specialists also continued to operate in many societies. Indeed several reformist Bhagat movements and sects such as Mahima among the tribals could not erode their native religious beliefs. The tribal religions tend to be less systematized and less specialized than Hinduism, Christianity or Islam. The supposed 'assimilation' of tribal groups has gone on for a very long time. The tribes of the Gangetic plains, according to D.D. Kosambi, were 'conquered by and assimilated into' the kingdoms of Kosala and Magadha beginning in the sixth century BC (Kosambi, 1965:120). From the third century BC, there are references to tribes in the edicts of Ashoka (Basham, 1954:53). H.H. Risley noted in 1873 that the tribes all over India were gradually being transformed into castes. K.S. Singh, in his article included in this book, affirms that tribal religions always retained a great deal of internal autonomy, and that there is resurrection of pristine elements of tribal religion in many parts of India.

The religion of the tribespeople is generally defined in terms of animatism or animism. It is conceived that everything in this world has life and is animate whether plants, minerals, animals or the natural phenomena; or there are a number of souls sneaking around which are intangible and non-material spiritual beings which can influence and interfere in the life of the living persons. The term animism, according to Sahay (1998), was used to describe the exceedingly 'crude form of religion' in which magic remained the predominant element. The ghostly company of powers and elements, mostly impersonal in their character, surrounds people. Animism carried with it a belief in benevolent as well as malevolent spirits, which influenced the destiny of man (1998:129). It was J.H. Hutton, the British administrator-turned-anthropologist, who understood the analytic significance of 'tribal religion' and liberated it by segregating it from the notion of animism. In tribal societies, religion does not emerge as an independent phenomenon. In fact, it is closely tied with social structure. The tribal chiefs and headmen thus contain priestly functions and the political, economic and religious ties reinforce one another (Das, 1993: 128–132,2002). The chief ensures the mystical welfare of the tribe. Through access to spirits and/or medicine the chiefs emerge as rain makers or medicine men. Belief in a high god or a Supreme Being is present in all tribal societies. Moral issues are not inherent in tribal societies, though moral behaviour is mandatory (Das, 1988; 1989). There is hardly any temple of the tribal god and no formal worship. Shrines are few and priesthood is informal. The tribal deities are distinguished according to domains such as earth, sky, water and forest. There are many systems of divination and oracles that are consulted. Ancestor cults occupy an important place in tribal religious life. Great attention is given to funerals. At family, lineage and clan level congregations, elders function as religious specialists. In Naga society the will of the ancestors is made known through dreams and misfortunes. In some tribal areas the term indigenous faith has been emphasized. According to the Arunachal Pradesh Freedom of Religion Act, Number 4, 1978, 'indigenous faith' means such religious beliefs and practices, including rites, rituals, festivals, observances, performances, abstinence and customs as have been found sanctioned, approved and performed by the indigenous tribes and includes Buddhism (among Monpas, Kambas, Khamtis and Singphos), Vaishnavism (Noctes, Akas) and nature worships including worship of Donyi-Polo as prevalent among other indigenous communities of Arunachal Pradesh (Tamo, 1991).

The processes of sectarianism and syncretism have variously affected the tribes of India in different historical phases. There exists a religious cult among the Santals, called Sarna Dharma Semlet, which centres around the tribal deities. The rites of the cult emphasize and include the main features of tribal worship, besides worship in sacred groves, offering of rice beer, dancing and even sacrifice of cattle. Thus the tribal religion is being recast in a transcendental mold fashioned after the examples of Christianity and Islam as well as of Hinduism (Mandelbaum, 1970:615). This process of syncretistic religious consolidation is, however, called by Martin Orans 'rank concession syndrome' (Orans, 1965:123–1146). During 1870s a wave of culture change engulfed the Santal and Munda. These people thus rejected tribal symbols and embraced the rituals and symbols of encroaching religions such as Hinduism and Christianity. Borrowing from the Christian tradition, the tribal leader Birsa encouraged a belief in one god and inspired followers to give up sacrifices to Munda Bongas (Singh, 1966:44). Despite this confessional change, the Birsa followers continued to observe many tribal religious traits such as visits to ancestral places, adorning the forehead with sandalwood paste and wearing 'sacred thread'. The Santals launched a syncretistic movement called Kherwar movement towards the end of the nineteenth century. It embraced important elements of Hinduism. While studying the process of Christianization in tribal societies of Jharkhand at the inter-generation level, Sahay (1990) has brought to light the processes of combination, retroversion and indigenization at work. Some sections of the Christians seem to be apprehensive as they see the loss of vital elements of the Christian tradition in indigenization. In fact, 'syncretism', the watering down of what is distinctive to Christianity by admixture with beliefs and practices from other religions, is regarded as 'the most obvious danger' (Grant, 1961:41–42).

V

The Dalits, the previously untouchable communities of India, have often contested the religious oppression and rigid religious authoritarianism in different parts of India. In order to seek spiritual democracy in different historical phases, they often adopted several regional sects and religious orders such as Sikhism and Buddhism. There are Dalit castes such as Mahar and Balahi (Maharashtra and Madhya Pradesh) who have adopted Buddhism and Jainism respectively. The Balai (Rajasthan) have joined the Dadu Panthi sect. The sect shuns idolatry and believes in the unity of god. The Balmikis of Delhi are divided into several endogamous religious groups, such as Hindu Balmiki, Sikh Majhabi and Muslim Mussali (Singh, 1995:101–109). The Bazigars (Punjab) have adopted Sikhism. Earlier they venerated the Pirkhana. They now visit the gurudwara and also celebrate Holi, Diwali, Dashahra and Lohri (1995:200). The Banjaras (Himachal Pradesh) are divided into the Hindus, Muslims and Sikhs. The Hindus and Sikhs inter-marry, hence there has been a great deal of admixture between their religious life and practices (1995:130). The Beda Jangams are the Lingayats of Karnataka. They have five divisions based on different religious gurus. The disciples of these gurus (pithas or seats) avoid marital relations (1995:205). The census enumerators, during the 2001 operation, faced a piquant situation as all Lingayats insisted on being categorized as members of a separate religion 'Lingayat dharma'. Some Lingayats chose to be identified as Lingayat Hindu or Vira Saiva Hindu (*Times of India*, Banglore, February 16, 2001). The Bedia (Orissa), called Bedia Kudmi, profess both the traditional religion and Hinduism. They were participants of Medi movement of Orissa (Singh, 1995:211). The Bhangis of Gujarat consider Balmiki Muni as their god. They are also followers of Kabir, Ramananda and Nanak. The Chamars profess different religions and sects. In Himachal Pradesh, they are Ravidasis and also Nirankari Sikhs (1995:311). In Haryana, the Julaha are the followers of Kabir though some Julaha have adopted Buddhism, and some follow Sikhism and even Christianity. In Punjab, they are Ramdaasi Sikhs (Singh, 1995:315). The Jatav are one of the foremost of the Dalit castes whose struggle for emancipation continues through varied movements. They refuse to be called Chamar. Most of them have adopted Buddhism. A common blend of beliefs and practices of Hinduism, Buddhism and 'Ambedkarism' shapes their cultural life (1995:328). It has brought about a unique consciousness in every Jatav, notwithstanding an individual's formal affiliation to a particular faith. The Dhanak of Delhi profess Hinduism and Satnam dharma. They are also followers of Arya Samaj, Radha Soami sect and Kabirpanth sect. The Satnamis of Chhattisgarh state also refuse to be called Chamar and they regard Satnam-panth as a distinct religion (Das, 2000).

The Bhagat movement in south Rajasthan propagated vegetarianism and cleanliness and considerably influenced the Gavaria. It has also prompted them to give up bride-price, alcoholism and polygyny (Singh, 1995:535). The Dhanak of Delhi profess Hinduism and Satnam dharma. They are also followers of Arya Samaj, Radha Soami sect and Kabirpanth sect. The Dom and Dombara of Karnataka are followers of Hinduism, but the Lingayat Jangams are their sacred specialists. The Dom of Punjab are either Sikhs or Hindus. There are also Arya Samajis among them (1995:430--490). The Julaha of Delhi and Chandigarh are divided into two groups----Kabirpanthi and Julaha. The Kabirpanthi Julah have derived their name from Kabir's. The Hindu Juhalas also follow Kabir's teachings. There are both Hindu and Sikh among them. In Jammu and Kashmir, the Kabirpanthi are also known as Bhagats. The Khatik of Himachal Pradesh are divided into Hindu and Muslim, but in Haryana, they are also Sikhs. The Koli of Rajasthan follow Hinduism, Buddhism and Kabirpanth. A social reformer Veera Brahman raised the hopes of the Madiga of Andhra Pradesh. His sect came to be called Rajayogi. Many Rajyogis, however, became Christians. The Christian Madigas of Tamil Nadu observe pre-conversion Hindu lifecycle rituals and share water sources and burial grounds with other (Hindu) Dalits. The Mazhabi (Majhabi/Mazabi/Mazbi) of Punjab, Haryana, Himachal Pradesh and Uttar Pradesh follow Sikhism. Some of them have become Nihangs (Singh, 1995:923). The Hindu religious customs are also observed by the Mazhabis in Rajasthan. During the nineteenth century, the Matu Sanga, on the one hand and the Brahmo Samaj on the other, played important roles in uniting and uplifting the Namasudra of West Bengal. In Assam, they are followers of Damodardeo sect and Vaishnavism (Singh, 1995:980). The Koch in West Bengal, Assam and Tripura are Hindus. Many among them have become Muslims (1995:740). They are also known as Rajbanshi. The Rajabanshis of North Bengal have spread into the Brahmaputra valley of Assam. The Rajbanshi took part in the Tebhaga movement of 1946, and now they are involved in the Kamatapuri ethnic-separatist movement.

The Mahars of Maharashtra call themselves neo-Buddhists, after their adoption of Buddhism in 1956, under the leadership of Dr. B.R. Ambedakar, but elements of Hindu religion and caste system persists among them in entirety. The neo-Buddhists are also referred to as Nav Buddhist. They are found in Maharashtra, Uttar Pradesh, Karnataka, Gujarat, Andhra Pradesh and Punjab. They celebrate festivals connected with Buddhism and the birth anniversary of Dr. B.R. Ambedkar. In Karnataka they have converted from Mahar, Holeya and Madiga communities. But in Karnataka the neo-Buddhists celebrate most of the Hindu festivals and venerate Hindu deities (Singh, 1995:999). The Panchama, the Fifth One, has been described as 'avarnas' and 'untouchables', hence they are placed outside the four Varna schemes, and declare themselves as the fifth Varna. Panchama is a generic term. It includes many endogamous groups. In Andhra Pradesh many Panchamas have embraced Buddhism (Singh, 1995:1045). The Rehar of Himachal Pradesh are followers of a Saiva sect, but they believe in supernatural powers residing in forests, high hills and water sources. They employ sacred specialists from the Brahman and Sipi communities respectively (Singh, 1995:1117). The Sarera (or Sarde/Sorehara) of Punjab and Himachal Pradesh are mainly Hindus but Sorehara are Muslims. Again while some Sarera profess Hinduism, others are Sikhs. But they celebrate each other's festivals. The Sarera at Bungal worship Dadhani Baba and assemble there once a year. All religious communities of the region venerate the Baba (Singh, 1995:1167). The Thathiar of Himachal Pradesh are followers of Hinduism and Sikhism. Both the religious groups venerate Baba Achlecher Sahib and Kartik Rishi. The Shenva of Gujarat are Hindus, but many non-Hindu elements shape their religious life. The clan-deities are still worshipped during lifecycle rituals. They are also followers of Ram Dev Pir. The Sillekyathas of Karnataka are also affiliated to Muslim Pirs, though they remain Hindus (Singh, 1995:1223). They even accept water and cooked food from the Lingayats, Brahmans, Kurumbas and Muslims. The Adi Andhra of Tamil Nadu are also known as Thoti. They have been Hindus traditionally and they venerate the Hindu god Murugan. However a large section of Thoti have become Christian converts. But the Hindu and the Christian converts continue to marry each other and the Christian converts continue to observe the Hindu festivals (Singh, 1995:22). The Arunthatiyar of Tamil Nadu are Hindus. A section among them has adopted Christianity, but pre- change religious practices survive among the converts (Singh, 1995:47). The Badaik are also called Chik or Chik Badaik. The Badaik priests are called Pahan. These priests are drawn from the Munda and Bhuiyan tribes. The Badaiks, as observed in the field by this author in Orissa (Das, 1998) draw elements from both Hindu as well as local tribal religious practices (Das, 1998).

The above critique suggests that religious syncretism persists in an inconceivably vast number of tribal and Dalit communities of India, in lesser or greater degrees. We also noticed that mutual harmony exists between adherents of different religious dogmas and schools of thought and a definite process of homogenization is encompassing different ethnic and religious communities in all parts of India.

VI

In the study of religion in India, the major emphasis has been on a descriptive account of religious customs and their association with ethnic groups, the themes of purity/pollution in relation to caste system, descriptive concepts relating to religious phenomena and the modernization processes. More recent trend shows a departure from narrative recordings to reflective analysis of the Western discourse on Indian concepts used in Hinduism (Saraswati, 2000). In a review of literature, Saraswati refers to the nationalist and intellectual phases in the quest for indigenization or Indianization of anthropology. The latter phase developed in close alliance with Indology (Saraswati, 2000). He further argues that there should not be a single system of classifying information on cultures. Notwithstanding the difference in material culture and intellectual power, tribals and non-tribals share the same ideas and experiences of existence. If a new anthropology is to emerge then, he says, there is a need to give up the Western world-view, which has dominated Indian thought. Anthropologists in India and elsewhere in developing countries have been imitating their Western masters. What is imperative is to throw new light on the many aspects of indigenous cultures of Asia and Africa. A new cultural anthropology has to incline strongly towards cross-cultural perspectives in which the knowledge system, in a wider context, has to be examined and compared. No living culture is to be viewed as static.

Scholars belonging to different disciplines have contributed their valuable papers for this volume. Most of the contributors are, however, anthropologists. Suniti Kumar Pathak (Visva Bharati) and Bijayananda Kar (Utkal University), both philosophers, deal with the issues of the human immigration and cultural assimilation in a wider Indological perspective. Pathak reviews the contents of *Atharva-Veda*, and other old Sanskrit texts, in order to ascertain the primeval foundation of ethnic fusion as also the tradition of fire cult and occult practices from a syncretistic perspective. Kar illustrates the syncretistic character of the Mahima cult, which has assimilated the ideas and practices from several philosophical systems such as Vedantism, Buddhism, Visistadvaitism and Vaishnavism. Pathak has presented a philosopher's perspective of social formation and cultural interactions in Vedic era, encompassing even some cultures of central Asia. Pathak's paper is based on 'textual' analysis, while Kar combines textual interpretation with empirical evidence. Anoop Chandola of University of Arizona, USA has developed an ethical philosophy of 'contactism' (based on his theory of human contact, contactics) to understand the contact philosophy behind the conversion and universal acceptance of Buddhism. Buddhism like any religion exists in contactual reality. It spread globally through human inter-contact. The very notion of missionary religion starts with Buddhism. Christianity became a successful missionary religion because it also displayed contactism. He shows many similarities between Buddhism and Christianity. K.S. Singh disapproves the Orientalists who view the tribal religion in terms of a set of primitive values surviving within Hinduism. He says tribal religion retains a great deal of internal autonomy. He asserts that syncretism is visible in all civilizations, in day to day life, but it is concentration of forces or cultural homogenization which holds the key to power relations in society. T. Madhav Menon argues that the 'great tradition' did not always influence the 'little tradition' and that there has also been tribalisation of Hinduism by adoption of beliefs and deities of the tribals. He says that 'Hinduism' is not just one 'mainstream'; it has several 'streams' that ultimately inundate islands of difference within their catchments. Both tribal religion and Hinduism ultimately emerge as 'syncretistic agglomerations' of several layers of faiths and observances. K.G. Gurumurthy, a cultural anthropologist, has studied the presence of Hindu customs and manners among the Bagobo ethnic groups found in the Mindanao Islands of the Philippines, which are close to Malay and Indonesian islands. Kroeber, Beyer, Benedict and Manuel have also concluded that at one time in their history the Bagobo ancestors had direct contacts with the Hindus. Such transmission of culture traits of Hindu origin gave birth to a composite and blended culture of the Bagobo. M. Boisvert of University of Quebec, Canada, has studied the cultural parallelism in the Khmer, Sinhalese, and Thai societies that pursue Theravada Buddhism. Boisvert also compares certain institutions of Hinduism with Buddhist monastic life. M.K. Raha, in his anthropological study of the western Himalayan region has explored the dense synthesis of Buddhism and Hinduism in Kinnar society. Thus, the Kinnar simultaneously pursue local variants of Hinduism and Buddhism by alternatively engaging the Hindu priest and the Buddhist Lama for family rituals. In their paper on pluralistic Islamic traditions, which deals with the all-India situation, Shibani Roy and S.H.M. Rizvi have argued that Islam in various parts of India demonstrates the strong pull of original religious-cultural beliefs. They have shown the coexistence of pre-change religious beliefs with the adopted religious beliefs. The prevalence of the concept of 'ritual purity' (as amongst the Bohras) is an example of perfect synthesis of two counter-forces in the Indian religious scenario. History reveals that the abstract monotheism as preached by the Sufi saints and philosophers not only came to be accepted by the Hindu masses but also formed a bridge between the traditions of Hinduism and Islam. Akbar's Dine-e-Ilahi, Dara Shikoh's synthesis of Upanishadic monotheism with Islam, and Amir Khusro's linkage of Hinduism to the Islamic sphere gave rise to many a distinctive homogenizing literary works. In his study of the Rajabanshis of north Bengal, Rajatsubhra Mukhopadhyaya states that the process of Sanskritization started with their claim of membership in regional Hindu society. They adopted some Hindu deities and employed occasionally the Brahman priests, but they did not abandon their tribal deities whom they continued to worship by employing their tribal priests such as Adhikari. This 'accommodative' tendency as prevalent in the entire north-Bengal-Assam tribal belt, in the view of Mukhopadhyaya, may be similar to the somewhat controversial estimation made by Ghurye when he branded Indian tribes as an 'imperfectly integrated class of Hindu society' or what Verrier Elwin called 'Hinduized without being Hindus'. P. Venkata Rao has studied a Hindu-centric cult in a tribal belt of Andhra Pradesh. The cult called

Ollek is a local variant of the Mahima dharma of Orissa, whose philosophical foundations are described by Bijayananda Kar in this volume. Rao has described the prominent elements of Buddhism, Hinduism and Jainism, which are immersed within the Ollek cult. Suresh Patil has studied the Lingayat sect of South India. The adherents of the sect are divided into various castes, though Basava, the originator of the sect, established it as an anti-Hindu movement. Basava was able to synthesize most of the cultural differences between such disarray of castes and their individual ritualistic traditions and mould them into one single faith by introducing many uncomplicated principles. However, in course of time, the Lingayat adherents succumbed to the age-old principles of pollution and prohibitions based on old Hindu ideologies, though all major rituals of Lingayatism survived among them in a syncretistic style. The demands of emerging political situations prompted the elite among the Lingayats to launch a massive action to reorganize the scattered Lingayat community by invoking the egalitarian principles propagated by Basava. Their attempt in recent years has been to ensure internal unity so as to capture political power. What was achieved and lost by Basava is now being regained perhaps not because of the force of doctrines of Lingayatism but for the politics of coalition in order to consolidate political power.

Francis Kulirani has discussed the historical Jewish heritage, survival and continuity of Hindu-centric beliefs and customs, and perpetual cultural symbiosis between these traditions among the Syrian Christians of Kerala. The Jewish heritage of original vocation, many Jewish customs, the 'castes' (with caste endogamy), pollution after birth and death, reliance in Hindu astrology are all widespread. Hindu marriage customs of tying of tali, bridegroom rituals, Hindu rituals of lifecycle such as first formal feeding, first formal learning of alphabet, practice of dowry, manthrakodi (bridal veil), ceremonial receiving of the bridal couple with lighted lamp are all prevalent pre-conversion ceremonies. The church processions still resemble the Hindu temple processions in all their paraphernalia. R.K. Sinha and William Ekka have shown that the Bhagat movement among the tribal Patelias of Gujarat has divided the society into Bhagat and Nagad segments. The Bhagat Patelias claim a higher social status but establish marriage relationships with the Nagad. In Bhagat-tribal marriages, however, the religious customs of both segments are mixed and which is acceptable to both the segments. Nagad girls, who become Bhagat, after marriage, continue to adhere to old tribal customs.

Old tribal practices survive in the Bhagat segment and such blending of dual religious and cultural elements is not seen as an abnormality. Tamo Mibang, Pro-Vice-Chancellor of Arunachal University, has studied the Donyi-Polo religion among the tribes of Arunachal Pradesh. What is unique about this Donyi-Polo religion is that it has spread into several tribal communities in recent years such as Minyongs, Padams, Gallongs, Pasis, Paggis, Karkos etc. Those who profess this new religion, however, continue to adhere to their respective original tribal religions. There is no doubt that Donyi-Poloism has executed an integrative effect amongst diverse tribes and has helped in homogenizing divergent cultural traits in this high mountain region of the eastern Himalayas by shaping inter-ethnic harmony. Deimaphishisha Sun, a Khasi anthropologist, has shown that the Khasi-Pnar people of Meghalaya place the demands of matrilineal kinship system, which is an integral part of tribal religious order, above all other considerations. Hence the large-scale adoption of Christianity has proved to be incomplete adoption. Numerous Khasi tribal religious beliefs and conventions thus survive which include paramount precedence of the ancestress, respect for the departed soul, offering food to dead, and ritual-jural significance of the youngest daughter, who remains the custodian of all traditional matrilineal sacramental values, despite her adoption of Christianity. Anstice Justin belongs to the indigenous Nicobarese community of the Andaman and Nicobar Islands. Being a Christian Nicobarese, as also a cultural anthropologist, he has traced the trend of religious syncretism in his community. He observed that in spite of large-scale adoption of Christianity, the shaman-priesthood and several tribal animistic practices have survived among the Nicobarese. Sarit Chaudhuri, a cultural anthropologist, has observed clear instances of religious syncretism among the Sajolangs of Arunachal Pradesh. During fieldwork, the Sajolangs identified themselves as Buddhists, but while cross-verifying it was found that in day-to-day activities these people continue to observe several tribal rituals and festivals. Bibhash Dhar, a cultural anthropologist, has compared the syncretistic existence of Buddhism, Lamaism and Bon religion among the Monpas of Arunachal Pradesh and the Ladakhis of Jammu and Kashmir region, using first-hand and secondary source materials. S.A.A. Saheb, a social anthropologist, has traced the origin and spread of Sufism in India and describes the syncretistic practices observed in the Sufi shrine of Nagore-E-Sharif, located in Tamil Nadu, South India. The high praise for the saintly mystic powers and veneration by way of offering flags and lighting ghee lamps at the saint Nagore Andover's tomb by the local people particularly the Hindus and their corroboration by the Muslims shows the prominence of this dargah as a great homogenizing shrine. Samira Dasgupta and Amitabh Sarkar, both cultural anthropologists, briefly discuss Chhattisgarh's Bastar situation. Bastar kings exercised political control via imposition of Danteshwari cult, and by assimilating many tribal female deities and also tribal rituals in propitiation of the Danteshwari, which culminated in the annual celebration of Dashahra festival, involving Hindus, tribals and Dalits. The reformatory Baba cult and Mahima sect could not eradicate the strong bases of tribal Mata cults, though the tribals did amalgamate their tribal female deities with the centralized Brahmanical cult of Danteshwari, thus giving birth to a unique synthesized religious philosophy.

N.K. Das has observed that on account of multi-pronged cultural contact, the tribal religions of northeast India have been influenced, but the tribal cultures and religious traditions of the region are too strong to be obliterated entirely. He examines the impact of Hinduism, Buddhism, and Christianity in all seven states of the northeast and concludes that cultural transformation and religious conversions never eroded the essential tribal religious convictions and moral principles of tribals. Thus what we notice in most parts of the hills is a syncretistic coexistence of multiple faiths. In Assam plains, however, Shankar Dev's neo-Vaishnavism prompted the growth of numerous syncretistic cults, by incorporating the tribals. These Bhakti cults accommodated the cultural ethos and religious practices of tribals and initiated a bold process of homogenization. Basanta Kumar Mohanta, a Ph.D. scholar of Utkal University, has studied the Ho tribals who have adopted several Hindu deities, and worship them both by the local Hindu method and tribal method of worship, which invariably includes animal-sacrifices and rice-beer offering. Mohanta has also observed a strong tendency of linguistic syncretism among the Hos of Jharkhand and Orissa. The linguistic synthesis is noticed in terms of both the voluntary adoption and some time imposition of Hindu-centric attributes. Thus the phrase *'Om Ganesaya Nomoh'* is now found engraved at the top of the epitaph of the Hos, which is actually inserted by the Hindu engravers, without the consent of the Hos. Hinduized names are imposed by alteration of tribal names, mainly of students, by teachers. Enormous blending of religious elements is thus noticed. Though Bongaism has started loosing its charisma and authority, the Hos do not disregarded the capability of the

Bongas, and all major rituals, including elaborate mortuary rites, essentially involve propitiation of the main Bongas, though the Hindu procedures of veneration and idolatry have increased considerably.

This volume intends to develop a framework to comprehend the elusive and synthesized structure of Indian civilization, from the vantage point of syncretistic religious and cultural traditions of India. The case-studies and empirical evidences presented in this volume show how religious ideas and cultural traits mediate between diverse ethnic communities, religious communities, sects and cultural regions, and give rise to a complex unity. The complex cultural unity of India is built up through the protracted inter-relationship of the diverse cultural traditions, both literate and pre-literate. Our aim in this book is also to provide meaning to and draw certain conceptual linkages by focussing attention on empirical situations that reflect the phenomenon of religious and cultural syncretism in varied degrees. This book thus tries to establish, on the one hand, the falsity of the presupposed singleness of religious allegiance of the adherents, and on the other hand, highlights, the multiplicity of spiritual suppositions and confessional observances forged by amalgamation of distinct religious customs and beliefs, which ultimately sustain and maintain the syncretistic religious cosmos.

References

Basham, A.L. 1954. *The Wonder That Was India*. London: Sidgwick and Jackson.

Becker, Howard and L. von Weise. 1932. *Systematic Sociology*. New York: Academic Publication.

Brandon, S.G.F. 1970. *Dictionary of Comparative Religion*. London: Weidenfeld and Nicolson.

Bruyn, S.T. 1966. *Human Perspective in Sociology*. Englewood-Cliffs: Prentice-Hall.

Cox, Harvey. 1965. *The Secular City: Secularization and Urbanization in Theological Perspective*. New York: Macmillan.

Das, N.K. 1988. Tribal Priesthood and Shamanism in Chhattisgarh. *J. of Indian Anthrop. Soc.*23: 223--231.

----. 1989. *Ethnic Identity, Ethnicity and Social Stratification in Northeast India*. New Delhi: Inter-India Publication.

—. 1993. *Kinship, Politics and Law in Naga Society*. Calcutta: Anthropological Survey of India.

—. 1998. The Chick Badaik, Orissa. *People of India*. Calcutta: Anthropological Survey of India.

—. 2000. The Satnamis of Chhattisgarh. Mimeographed. Calcutta: Anthropological Survey of India.

—. 2002. Kinship, Headmanship and Jural Order in Naga Society. In *Studies in Anthropology in India*. Felicitation Volume in Honour of Professor Gopala Sarana. Ed. P.K. Misra. Mysore: Anthropological Association.

Durkheim, E. 1965 (1915). *The Elementary Forms of the Religious Life*. Trans. J.W. Swain. London: George Allen and Unwin.

Evans-Pritchard, E.E. 1937. *Witchcraft, Oracles and Magic among the Azande*. Oxford: Clarendon.

—. 1956. *Nuer Religion*. Oxford: Clarendon Press.

—. 1965. *Theories of Primitive Religion*. Clarendon: Oxford.

Firth, Raymond. 1964. Introduction, Malinowski as Scientist and as Man. In *Man and Culture*. R. Firth. Ed. New York: Harper.

—. 1964(1969). *Essays on Social Organization and Values*. London: Athlone Press.

—. 1970. *Rank and Religion in Tikopia: A Study in Polynesian Paganism and Conversion to Christianity*. London: Allen and Unwin. Boston: Beacon.

—. 1996. *Religion: A Humanist Interpretation*. London: Routledge.

Gnanambal, K. 1970. 'The Study of Mattas and Seats of Sanskritic Learning' in *Research Programmes on Cultural Anthropology and Allied Disciplines*. Ed. Surajit Chandra Sinha. Calcutta: Anthropological Survey of India.

Goody, Jack. 1961 (1967). *The Social Organization of the Lo Willi*. Second Edition. 1967. London: Oxford University Press.

Grant, J.W. 1961. *God's People in India*. Bangalore: The Christian Literature Society.

Hamilton, Malcolm, B. 1995. *The Sociology of Religion: Theoretical and Comparative Perspectives*. London: Routledge.

Hendry, Joy. 1999. *An Introduction to Social Anthropology*. London: Macmillan Press.

Hoebel, E.A., Jennings, J.D. and Smith, E.R. 1955. *Readings in Anthropology*. New York: McGraw Hill Book Co.

Johnson, B. 1963, On Church and Sect. *American Sociological Review*. 28:539–549.

Jordan, J.T.F. 1975. Medieval Hindu Devotionalism. In *A Cultural History of India*. A.L. Basham. Ed. New Delhi: Oxford University Press.

Kosambi, D.D. 1965. *The Culture and Civilization of Ancient India in Historical Outline*. London: Routledge and Kegan Paul.

Kottak, Conrad Phillip. 1991 (1996) *Anthropology: The Exploration of Human Diversity*. New York: McGraw Hill.

Levinson, D. 1994. *Ethnic Relations: A Cross-Cultural Encyclopedia*. California: ABC-CLIO.

Levi-Strauss, Claude. 1963. *Structural Anthropology*. Harmondsworth: Penguin.

---. 1966. Anthropology: Its Achievements and Future. *Current Anthropology*. 7: 124--127.

McCormack, W. 1959. The Forms of Communication in Vira Saiva Religion. *Traditional India: Structure and Change*. Ed. M. Singer. Philadelphia: American Folklore Society.

---. 1963. Lingayat as a Sect. *The Jr. of Royal Anth. Institute*: 93(1): 59--71.

Mandelbaum, D.G. 1970. *Society in India*. California: University of California Press (1972 Popular Prakashan, Bombay).

Ohnuki-Tierney, Emiko. 1984. *Illness and Culture in Contemporary Japan*. London: Cambridge University Press.

Orans, Martin. 1965. *The Santal: A Tribe in Search of a Great Tradition*. Detroit: Wayne State University Press.

Nadel, S.F. 1954. *Nupe Religion*. London: Routledge.

Redfield, R., R. Linton and M.J. Herskovits. 1936. A Memorandum on Acculturation. *American Anthropologist* 38:149--152.

Risley, H.H. 1915 [1969,1973]. *The People of India*, New Edition by W. Crooke. New Delhi: Oriental Books.

Sahay, K.N. 1990. A Theoretical Model for the Study of Christianization process among the Tribals of Chotanagpur. In *Tribal Transformation in India*. Vol.V Ed. B. Chaudhury. New Delhi: Inter-India Publishers.

---. 1998. *Dynamics and Dimensions of Tribal Societies*. New Delhi: Commonwealth Publishers.

Sarkar, R.M. 1990. *The Bauls of Bengal*. New Delhi: Gyan Publishers.

Saraswati, Baidyanath 2000. The New Anthropology. In *Contributions to Holistic Traditions: Anthropology in India*. R.K. Bhattacharya (Ed.) Calcutta: Anthropological Survey of India.

Sinha, Surajit. 1970. 'Complex Religious Institutions: Study of Sects in Hinduism' in *Research Programmes on Cultural Anthropology and Allied Disciplines*. Ed. Surajit Chandra Sinha. Calcutta: Anthropological Survey of India.

Singh, K.S. 1966. *The Dust Storm and the Hanging Mist: A Study of Birsa Munda and his Movement in Chotanagpur 1874--1901*. Calcutta: Firma KL Mukhopadhyay.

Singh, K.S. 1992 [2002]. *People of India: Introduction.* Calcutta: Anthropological Survey of India.

----. 1995. *The Scheduled Castes.* People of India Series. Calcutta: Anthropological Survey of India.

Smith, M.G. 1962. *Kinship and Community in Carriacou.* London; Yale University Press.

Stewart, Charles and Rosalind Shaw (Ed.) 1995. *Syncretism/Anti-Syncretism: The Politics of Religious Synthesis.* London: Routledge.

Tamo, Mibang. 1991. *Indigenous Faiths and Practices of the Minyongs in Religion and Society in the Himalayas.* Eds. T.B. Subba and K. Datta. New Delhi: Gyan Publications.

Thio, A. 1989. *Sociology.* New York: Harper and Row Publishers.

Toby, Jackson. 1971. *Contemporary Society: An Introduction to Sociology.* New York: John Wiley.

Tylor, E.B. 1903 (1958). *Primitive Culture.* London: John Murray, New York: Harper Torch Books.

Uberoi, J.P.S. 1994. 'Five Symbols of Sikh Identity' in *Religion in India.* Ed, T.N. Madan. New Delhi: Oxford University Press.

Worsley, Peter M. 1990. 'Cargo Cults' in *Anthropology: Contemporary Perspective.* Ed. Whitten, P. and D.E.K. Hunter. New York: USA: Harper Collins Publication.

1

The Mahima Dharma: A Confluence of Vedantism and Buddhism

Bijayananda Kar

The Vedas, composed in Sanskrit language, were not accessible to the common people. Moreover their emphasis on rituals and sacrifices was repellent to some thinkers who were moved by the consideration of piety. The sense of piety expressed itself in very vigorous forms in heretical systems like Jainism and Buddhism. It was manifested also in the anti-speculative schools where God was sought to be realized not through rigorous arguments but through simple devotion. In Orissa, however, we find a constant effort being made to bring about a synthesis of the above opposite forces of the Vedic tradition and the reactions against it. This spirit of synthesis is found in its maximum crystallization in the Mahima sect, a prevailing religious movement of Orissa, which has engulfed the caste-Hindus including the Dalits and the tribals, even beyond the borders of Orissa. The purpose of the present paper is to give a critical exposition of the philosophy of Mahima Dharma, in the specific context of the intermediation between Vedantism and Buddhism.

I

The Mahima religion has been in existence since the last hundred years[1]. Mahima Goswami was its founder. The life-history of Mahima Goswami, however, is shrouded in mystery. He is believed by his disciples to be God-incarnate. It is said that he used to travel around Puri in Dhabalagiri and Khandagiri areas during 1826. In 1838 he went to Kapilas hills and undertook severe meditation for about twenty-four years. Thereafter he became enlightened and in 1876 he passed away at Joranda[2] where we still find the monastery of the Mahima Sect.[3] His most renowned disciples are Gobinda Baba, Nrusingha Baba, Nanda Baba and Bhima Bhoi.

Like all great teachers of religion, Mahima Goswami preached his principles by oral instructions and his teachings were transmitted from generation to generation orally. One of his tribal disciples Bhima Bhoi has, to his credit, a number of treatises from which we get a good knowledge regarding the teachings of Mahima. Bhima has written mostly prayer-verses. These are *Stati Chintamani, Brahma Nirupana Gita, Bhajana Mala and Cautisa Madhucakra*. These are considered to be the first dependable literature of Mahima Dharma. In the present time, Biswanatha Baba is acclaimed as the most important exponent of Mahima philosophy. He has written one substantial book namely, *Mahima Dharma Pratipadaka*, in two volumes, and a short prayer treatise, *Sadhu Giti*.

II

The whole tradition of Indian philosophy is, almost in all cases, guided by a practical interest, an interest for purifying the heart, elevating the soul and achieving the sublime bliss of the Almighty, *Trividha duhkhatyantanivrtti*. The release from the threefold sufferings has been the aim of the Indian thinkers and philosophies, in order to achieve this religious end. "Philosophy in India did not take its birth in wonder or curiosity as it seems to have done in the West; rather it originated under the pressure of a practical need arising from the presence of moral and physical evil in life."[4] Religion and philosophy are mostly mixed and mingled in India. The philosophy of Mahima Goswami was no exception to this age-old tradition. His religious-philosophical position can be taken as orthodox in both the senses. He believes in the existence of God as the highest reality and also accepts the authority of the Vedas and the Upanishads. Preachers of Mahima repeatedly quote the authority of the *Srutis* in support of their teachings.[5]

Like most Indian systems, Mahima Goswami, too, acknowledges the threefold sufferings of the world. The individual, in his lifetime, realizes the insubstantiality of his own life and existence very often. The world, around him, is equally concealed with vagueness and ambiguity. The so-called pleasure, which is at times obtained, is not genuine but illusory. The more one clings to the worldly desires and passions, the more one understands their unreality and fruitlessness. Nothing of the world is noble, great, real and true. The essence of everything, that is there, is *Sunya.*[6] The word *Mahima*, which means the noble and the great is identified with the Sunya in Mahima literature. Reality is Sunya. This, almost sounds like Sunyavada of Buddhism. This conjecture seems to be more strengthened when we hear from Bhima Bhoi that Mahima Goswami is really the incarnation of Lord Buddha.[7] According to scholars like N.N. Vasu, the Mahima system is a modified form of Buddhism.[8]

But the contrast between Buddhism and Mahima is more distinct than their similarities. Mahima does not take Sunya as mere nothing or non-existent. It is also the Brahman in the Upanishadic sense. Sunya is identified with Absolute Soul or the *Advaita Atma.*[9] The highest soul is regarded as Sunya, because it is devoid of all worldly or empirical determinations, not because it is totally empty. It is described as attributeless (*nirguna*), formless (*nirakara*), indescribable (*alekha*) and absolute (*niranjana*). This implies that it is, largely, influenced by Advaita philosophy. Like Advaitism it not only asserts that ultimate reality which is otherwise called Mahima, is Brahman but also firmly maintains that the empirical world is the product of nescience. The individual being engulfed with nescience, cannot take notice of the Absolute and that is why it is subjected to suffering. As soon as there is the realisation of Mahima, the world-nature with all its duality and multiplicity dissolves into remote oblivion.[10] Like Advaitins the Mahimaites also describe their Mahima as *Nirguna.*[11] The Absolute cannot be grasped through sense-perception or any empirical way of knowing.[12] Because of all these significant similarities, A.B. Mohanty and many other scholars think that Mahima philosophy is yet another modification of the Advaita philosophy[13].

But in spite of these similarities, the differences between these two systems should not be overlooked. Unlike the Advaitins as well as the Sunyavadins, the Mahimaites contend that the Absolute (Mahima) is also Iswara[14]. Moreover, they maintain that the realization of the Absolute can be attained primarily by devotion (Bhakti)[15]. The *jnana* has a subsidiary place in Mahima philosophy. Besides these, the *jiva* is described as *Maya* or nescience, not in the Advaitin's sense that it is all due to magic or say it is not there but only appears; it is indeed Maya due to its transitory existence. That means the world of Jivas with all its duality and multiplicity does not exist for all times to come. It is actually produced out of Mahima and goes back to (the absolute) after dissolution. So this Mahima-Absolute creates the world of Jivas out of itself which means that this school accepts the theory of *Mahima-parinamavada* and not *Mahima-vivartavada.*[16] Even though the Mahimaites maintain that Sunya-Mahima, as the Absolute, is the only reality and there is nothing really (in the transcendental sense) existing apart from Sunya; yet they also seem to maintain that the Absolute, out of its own accord, creates the world of Jivas or the individuals and this effect, i.e., the world of Jivas remains distinct from the cause, i.e., Sunya Mahima for a temporary period (i.e., up to the time of dissolution). At dissolution (*pralaya*), the whole material world dissolves into *Sunya* and the empirical beings (*jivas*) realizing no genuine difference between them and the Absolute, merge with the Absolute as the rivers merge into the sea. *Jivatma* becomes united with *Paramatman* and thus it remains no more a separate being. By its own effort and good deeds it returns to its own eternal state (*sasvatavastha*) and is freed from the state of temporary distinctness. In other words, the Mahimaites, unlike the Advaitins, grant a separately created status, though ultimately of temporary nature, to the *jivas.* There is, of course, no absolute distinction between *jiva* and *Brahman* as we find in Ramanuja but a mere relative distinctness. Ramanuja believes in the realization of *Brahaman.*[17] The Mahimaites choose the middle path. They agree with the Advaitins so long as they maintain that by realizing the *Sunya* as the ultimate reality, the individual loses itself in the ultimate reality,[18] and thereby makes itself identified with the *Sunya.* Again, the Mahimaites go with the Ramanujaites when they contend that as long as *jiva* has not realized the ultimate reality, it is positively distinct from *Brahman*. Such distinction in fact actually exists, even though for a short while. But though with respect to the individual *jivas* it is seen that the Mahimaites seem to grant some reality, yet in respect of *Jagat,* the world of material forms, they are very near the Advaitins in admitting the *Vivarta* or the illusory character of it. The world is *Maya*, being the product of names and forms. The entire conception of space and time or the empirical phenomena is merely due to the confused nature of perception. This conception of Mahima almost sounds like Leibnizian where there is the admittance of the individual monads along with the rejection of the material world. But there is also an important point of contrast. The monad-like minds or *jivas* are not simply selected and admitted for actualization but are also created by the Supreme (The queen Monad or the Mahima).

The impact of *Bhakti* over Mahima thought is hugely noticeable. Devotion is the most pivotal path towards liberation. Knowledge and action play only the auxiliary roles. Even though, like all the mystics, the Mahimaites assert intuition to be the last means of liberation, yet they think that this intuition can occur through a series of rigorous steps of meditative devotion.[19] There is the acceptance of Yogic practices in this system of philosophy. Not mere practice of Yoga but along with it some flavour of actual and sincere devotion for the Absolute God should be present in the mind of the individual. Otherwise, all the success, attained through the path of work (*karma*) and knowledge (*jnana*), may be of no avail. Good and morally certified deeds may help man have sincere *Bhakti* towards God. Knowledge does not mean here the empirical knowledge of worldly things but the advice of the teacher (*Guru-ajna*)[20]. Biswanatha Baba has tried to establish the supremacy of the teachings of the teacher even above reasoning (*Tarka*). The teachings should be taken as the authentic scriptural sayings (*Apta-vakya*) and reasoning must not be insisted upon. *Sruti* or authority as a valid source of knowledge is accepted so long as it is in the form of teachings of the teacher and facilitates Mahima-realization. And lastly, not merely accepting what the teacher prescribes, but sincerely and devotedly following these sayings will lead one to ultimate realization.

According to the Mahimaites, God, who is not different from the Absolute can come to the world and can be in the form of living beings when the beings of the universe are either in distress or in confusion. This is the famous *Avatara* theory from the *Gita* where Lord Krishna speaks about his incarnation to Arjuna.[21] There is a difference between the individual *jiva* and this *Avatara*. The individual *jiva* has a particular body due to its activities in the previous life. But in case of *Avatara* no past activities determine the status of the present life. The individual, in order to gain release from the world of sorrows and sufferings must submit himself to Mahima. The truly religious consciousness is the self-surrender of *Jiva* to *Iswara*.[22] Mahima Dharma, like the traditional religions, prescribes a series of moral advice and religious conduct. Respect for religious and noble virtues and detachment from all types of vicious and sinful deeds are to be cultivated by each individual. *Ahimsa* is one of the key principles to be followed by all adherents of the Mahima dharma. The Mahimaites do not believe either in caste system or in any form of idol worship. Their radical disbelief for any form of idol worship even led to disclaim completely the Jagannath deity as the manifested form of the Lord.[23] The Mahimaites think that the householder (grhastha) as well as the monk or the supersocial man (Sannyasin) can perform meditation on Mahima. *Jivan-mukti* and *Videha-mukti* both are accepted in the system.

III

At the outset, it apparently seems that the Mahima philosophy has assimilated many ideas from other important philosophical systems like Buddhism, Advaitism, Visistadvaitism and Vaisnavism. We have already discussed the similarities as well as differences of thought between the Mahima school and the above-mentioned systems. It is true; the Mahimaites take great support from these systems for constructing their own philosophical position. But all these adoptions should not lead us to think of Mahima as a religion, as it does not possess any independent philosophical background of its own. The Mahima-Absolute is regarded as Sunya and again, is identified with Nirguna Brahman. Alekha (Absolute of the Mahima philosophy) is both attributeless and absolutely indeterminate (non-dual). The identification of Sunya with Nirguna Brahman implies that both Sunya-vada Buddhism and Advaita metaphysics do not essentially differ in their deepest philosophical speculation. Sunya-vada does not mean 'void' as a 'no-reality' doctrine but merely a 'no-view' about reality.[24] Any view framed on reality, is liable to fall short of it. That is why the Advaitins assert that Brahman is beyond all qualities and descriptions, since qualities of any number cannot exhaust Brahman and no description can adequately describe Brahman. The Mahimaites, somehow realizing the similarity in the logic of these two metaphysical systems have tried to bring a synthesis of the two views in their own philosophy propagating the Alekha Niranjana as *Sunya Nirguna.*

However, this is not all. They have also declared the Absolute as God and offer Him worship. Here a question arises. How can Brahman be the object of devotion or worship? Brahman, which is Nirguna, Alekha and Sunya, cannot be described again by the positive features so that God can substitute Brahman. The Advaitins, therefore, relegate the concept of God from the level of reality to mere appearance. Here, it is replied by the Mahimaites that the distinction of Jiva and Brahman is a practical or empirical one and so long as this practical distinction remains, the lower qualified Jiva should devote and meditate on the higher qualified Brahman. This devotion, though merely practical, leads to real realization. It should be remembered here that Samkara also maintains the distinction between Isvara and Brahman by the acceptance of Paramarthika and Vyavaharika (empirical) standpoints. According to him, Brahman, who is essentially Nirguna, can be taken as Saguna or God as long as there is no ultimate realization. So devotion or worship, etc., is also admitted by him. Samkara, in his Atmapuja pays regards to

Brahman.[25] But the point is, such worship by the Jiva to Brahman as 'God qualified' is not real at all, since neither Jiva nor God nor Saguna Brahman in fact actually exist. The Mahimaites do not, however, explicitly admit this concluding thesis of the Samktrites and have tried to remain away from them by giving some reality-status to the empirical happenings. The Absolute for them, is incomprehensible, intangible and indeterminable in the sense that no human way of knowing can properly estimate His being. That is why it is negatively described in the Advaitins' as well as the Sunyavadin's fashion as Nirguna and Sunya respectively. But all these negative descriptions of the absolute do not exclude the possibility of describing it as God since He is all powerful and can comprehend everything. This is why the Absolute is also described in the positive way as 'Mahima' or the greatest of all greats which implies nothing other than God or Almighty. Hence, the Absolute of the Mahimaites is a synthesis of both positive and negative descriptions. The Absolute is identified with God probably in order to satisfy the deep religious craving. God, being the starting as well as the ending point of all philosophy or religion, cannot be relegated to the level of appearance. To portray God as ultimately unreal is similar to giving an indirect death-blow to all types of religious consciousness. That is why the Mahimaites have identified God with reality seeking thereby a happy compromise between metaphysics and religion. They agree also with Ramanuja in rejecting the Vivartavada in preference to a theory of Alekha Parinama-vada. According to Mahima Goswami, the world is a creation of the Lord out of sport. It is not illusory, even though being transitory.

IV

It can also be pointed here that Mahima philosophy transcends all the above-mentioned schools (i.e., Sunya-vada, Advaita-vada, and partly Visistadvaita-vada) insofar as it accepts Bhakti or devotion as the only method of attaining bliss. It grants a subsidiary place to knowledge and action in the scheme of human life. In this respect, it is similar to the teachings of Sri Caitanya, but at the same time it is different from his teachings in respect of the concept of liberation. According to Mahima Goswami, the liberated soul completely loses its identity in the Alekha Brahman as the river loses its identity in the sea, whereas in Vaisnavism the liberation consists in the attainment of the Lord whose servants the souls are.

Though Mahima Goswami accepts the authority of the *Srutis*, he still rejects idol worship as the *Alekha Purusa* or indeterminate Absolute, which has no concrete determinate and limited forms. As long as the *Jiva* has not attained ultimate realization, there is nothing wrong in its praying and meditating the Lord. But for that no idol worship or ritual sacrifices need be performed. This shows that Mahima, as a religious philosophy is greatly the outcome of the contemporary situations of the country. Throughout the country there has been a great turmoil between the conflicting ideas of the East and West. The conservatives were insisting on the old practices, rituals and sacrifices whereas the West-influenced reformers[26] preach these as purely dogmatic and impractical prejudices. Reformative slogans were heard throughout the country from different corners in the 19th century. Mahima Goswami was no exception to this. He tried to bring reformation by dismissing the idol-worship and showing thereby that the Hindu can well appreciate the formless God. In addition, devotion to that formless Almighty can substitute the worship of idols or deities. In spite of these reformative trends, the Mahimaites keep themselves in close contact with diverse religious ideas, including Buddhism and Vedic ideas as described above. The Mahimaites thus sustain diversity amidst inner unity. This religious movement, therefore, is a wonderful attempt at synthesis. It synthesizes the Vedic tradition and the spirit of protest in advocating the worship of the 'Alekha-Niranjana', not in temples, not in front of images of the Lord, but in the sacred shrine of the human soul. In other words, the Mahima cult recognizes the necessity of prayer, not to any particular image of the Lord, but directly to the Lord Himself, the formless Absolute.

Acknowledgement

The author is indebted to Professor G. Misra for his critical and useful suggestions. In consultation with Dr. N.K. Das, the paper has been slightly modified, including its title, as per the requirement of the present volume, which is devoted to the discerning theme of religious syncretism. This paper was originally published in 1969 in Volume III of *Bharati*, the Utkal University Journal on Humanities.

Notes

1. C.R. Das, "Joranda Yatra" published in his own book, *Sila 0 Salagrama*, Jayanti Sahitya Samiti, Cuttack, p. 62.
2. It is a small village in the district of Dhenkanal of Orissa.

3. See the introduction by late Professor G. Das to the book, *Mahima Dharma Pratipadaka.* p.4.
4. M. Hiriyanna, *Outlines of Indian Philosophy*, London, p.18.
5. In this connection, please refer to *Mahima Dharma Pratipadaka* of Biswanatha Baba where different Sruti passages are cited in favour of the philosophical position of Mahima Dharma.
6. See, Bhima Bhoi. *Brahma Nirupana Gita,* p. 23:*Sunya Sunya Mahasunya boli Tahakuti kahi tanka uparaku bada nahim au kehi.*
7. See Biswanatha Baba: *Mahima Dharma Pratipadaka* p. 3 and also Bhima Bhoi: '*Cautisa Madhu-Cakra,*' p. 6 (29th stanza).
8. See N. N. Vasu: *"The Modern Buddhism and its followers in Orissa."* Calcutta. 1911, pp. 149–180.
9. See Biswanatha Baba: "*Mahima Dharma Pratipadaka,*" p. 74.
10. See Bhima Bhoi: *Bhajana Mala,* p. 68 (Both 77 and 78 stanzas).
11. Bhima Bhoi: *Brahma Nirupama Gita,* p. 25 (50th stanza).
12. Biswanatha Baba: *Mahima Dharma Pratipadaka,* p. 194.
13. Preface of late Professor A. B. Mohanty to *Cautisa Madhu Cakra* of Bhima Bhoi.
14. Bhima Bhoi: *Brahma Nirupama Gita* p. 3 and Biswanatha Baba: *Sadhu Giti,* p. 1.
15. Biswanatha Baba: *Sadhu Giti,* p. 7 (stanzas: 4 and 5).
16. Bhima Bhoi: *Brahma Nirupama Gita,* Pp. 67–68.
17. *Sri Bhasya,* (1.1.1.) "*Brahma bhavah na tu svarupaikyam*".
18. Bhima Bhoi: *Brahma Nirupama Gita* p. 127.
19. Bhima Bhoi: *Bhajana Mala,* (Part I), and p.7.
20. Here '*Guru*' commonly refers to Mahima Goswami.
21. *Gita: Janna-Yoga,* 7th verse.
22. Preface, by Professor A.B. Mohanty to Bhima Bhoi's *Cautisa Madhu Cakra,* p. 25.
23. It should be noted here in this connection that the followers of all religions, including the Buddhists of this part of India always acclaim Jagannath as their deity and worship the idol of Jagannath in the Puri temple. The author is thankful to Dr. N. K. Sahu, M.A., Ph. D., D. Litt, a well-known scholar on ancient history of Orissa for kindly communicating this point to the author. However, the Mahimaites are the only exception in this regard, as they never go to Puri temple to revere the idol of Jagannath.
24. Refer to Dr. T. R.V. Murti, *The Central Philosophy of Buddhism.* London: Allen and Unwin, p.313.

25. *Atmapuja*, pp. 8/10.
26. The Arya Samaj may serve here as an example.

References

Works in Oriya

Bhima Bhoi: *Brahma Nirupama Gita,* Prachi, Cuttack, 1951.

Bhima Bhoi: *Stuti Cintamani* Prachi, Cuttack, 1951.

Bhima Bhoi: *Bhajana Mala,* Prachi, Cuttack.

Bhima Bhoi: *Cautisa Madhucakra,* Prachi, Cuttack.

Biswanatha Baba: *Mahima Dharma Pratipadaka,* Prachi, Cuttack.

Biswanatha Baba: *Sadhu Giti,* Prachi, Cuttack.

Pt. Surya Narayan Das: *Odia Sahityara Itihasa*, Cuttack, 1963.

Chittaranjan Das: *Bhima Bhoi 0 Mahima Dharma,* Visva-Bharati Prakashana, Santiniketan.

Bijayananda Kar: Mahima Dharmara Darsanika Paryalecana, *Jhankar,* 21st year, Visuva Issue, Mesa, 1376, April 1969.

Works in English

Das, Pt. Nilakantha: Religious and Philosophical Developments in Orissa, *Journal of the Utkal University,* Vol. I, December 1961.

Misra, Ganeswar: Philosophy in Oriya, included as a chapter in the *Marathi Encyclopaedia of Philosophy.*

Mansingha, M.: *History of Oriya Literature*, Sahitya Academy, New Delhi, 1962.

Sahu, N.K.: *Buddhism in Orissa,* Bhubaneswar: Utkal University Publication, 1958.

Vasu, N.N.: *The Modern Buddhism and its Followers in Orissa.* Author, Calcutta, 1911.

2

Contactism: A Human Contact Philosophy and Buddhism

Anoop Chandola

Many years ago I bought a statue of the Buddha in a gift shop. He was seated in the lotus posture. His face was clearly the Japanese Amida or Amitabha type. But the skin colour was black. The statue was made by a male artist in Mexico. The gift shop was in the USA. The seller was a white American woman. The buyer was I, born and raised in India. The Buddha coming full international circle like this raises a question: What made the Buddha and his philosophy attractive internationally? For this purpose I will make a brief attempt here to evaluate Buddhist philosophy in terms of a philosophy of human contact that I call contactism. Why contactism? This real story of buying a Buddha statue is a story of long human contact that started some 2,500 years ago. I argue that a religious philosophy can be widely accepted as a whole or in part if it displays contactism. So before I talk about Buddhism's international appeal, I present a brief introduction of contactism.

Contactism

Contactism is rooted in contactics. Contactics is the science of contax which is a chain of one's conscious actions formed by a code. This code consists of eight elements which can be understood as eight basic questions: (1) What is the nucleus? (The activity); (2) Who does the activity? (The doer); (3) What are the means of this activity? (The instrument); (4) What is the aim of this activity? (The goal); (5) Who is affected by the activity? (The recipient); (6) What is the starting point of the activity? (The origin); (7) What are the time and place of the activity? (The base); (8) What specifies each of these questions? (The specifier).

The answer of each question above is given at its end in parentheses. The first letter of each answer makes an acronym for the code as ADIGROBS. When these questions organize a set of things in the brain, the set is called a situation. A situation can be expressed as a material expression or a linguistic expression. These two expressions combined make materialized linguistic expression. A situation is the internal representation of things selected arbitrarily. It is the minimum cognitive unit. What enters the brain in a fraction of a second is a situation consisting of images or roles of the things. The expressions are external representations of situations, hence actions. Put simply, a situation is our understanding of the things selected; a material expression is doing those things; a linguistic expression is saying of those things. The materialized linguistic expression is writing. What we understand, do, say and write is our contax.

Contax sounds like syntax. A chain of words put together by grammatical rules is syntax. In contax, things are put in contact by means of code, which I call conscious contact code, abbreviated as ADIGROBS. Contax includes all conscious experience and expression, emotional to intellectual, fictional to factual. The code is like the DNA that evolves situations uninterruptedly throughout the waking state. Only a few situations are expressed. Thus contactics, like genetics, is code-based and becomes a unique social behavioural science. It shows how we use things with an evolutionary process---things evolving into brain images or roles, and then into verbal and non-verbal action. We can consciously act with things only when we have decided on their roles. The things include animate, inanimate, concrete, abstract, imaginary, verbal (words) and non-verbal things. The easiest evidence for the underlying code is to observe any sentence or linguistic expression in which non-verbal things appear as verbal things. Here is an example:

(a) The monk slowly sprinkled water upon the floor with a green leaf.

Here the activity is 'sprinkling.' The doer of the activity is 'monk.' The instrument with which the activity is done is the 'leaf.' The goal of the activity is 'water.' The location or the base of the activity is 'floor.' In English grammar these items are also called verb, subject or nominative case, instrumental case, object or accusative case and locative case respectively. A past specifier, called past tense, modifies the verb. Another specifier for the activity is 'slowly,' called adverb. For the case nouns the specifiers are called adjectives such as 'green.' But in terms of the code, the activity and its seven other types of participants are like roles that are arbitrarily attached to the items or things by the brain owner, who puts things in contact, hence called contactor. Without these roles the brain owner cannot make any sense out of any thing. Examples of other roles are as follows:

(b) The monk gave the attendant a flower from his bag.

Here 'giving' is the activity, 'attendant' is the recipient or the dative-case noun, 'bag' is the origin or the ablative-case noun and 'his' belongs to 'pocket' as specifier.

Each person's contax is unique because each person selects things for situations arbitrarily. The things in each person's contax, therefore, are organized or contactualized uniquely. The same thing does not have the same image or meaning every time it is selected. Thus the sense of things we use is in flux. We change our views often because countless situations throughout conscious state cannot be managed consistently in terms of their images or meaning. This is why conversion is possible. The Buddha himself changed his views several times before he formed a set of situations and expressions as his contact program with which he converted his former friends. We are told that Vasubandhu changed his philosophical views to his brother Asanga's. Bodhidharma's views are different from Dharmakirti's. So we have international varieties of Buddhism. But all Buddhists hold that they follow the Buddha, who would be amazed if he were to see so many variations created and consumed internationally after his name. A major part of his contact program is known as *atthangika magga*, 'the eight-fold path'. A contact program is a set of expressions, which is used as a schedule, guideline, plan, protocol, etc. Contactors make it part of their contaxes, which means that they understand and do the things to match the program. A program or part of contax may lead to some unexpected side effects, which I call contaxic effects. Many differences about the eight-fold path of the Buddha are contaxic effects meaning the Buddha would never have expected them when he formed his contact program.

The idea of contax and other related terms as discussed above is influenced in part by Panini's *kriya-karaka* or activity-activator view (the verb-case view in grammar). A homogenous theory of action is possible only if it is based on its own organic components, namely, activity, activators and their specifiers. By considering contax we get a new unified theory of all human and non-human conscious action. That is, the code based on activity activators is observed in all verbal or non-verbal actions. For example, one can observe a monk doing non-verbally the things or items mentioned in sentences (a) and (b) above. Only humans have evolved saying (language) and writing. Non-human animals have only situations and material expressions in their contaxes. A contactor forms contax alone or with other contactors. When alone, her or his contax represents intracontact. But when two or more individuals come in contact, they represent an intercontact. Contaxes are made of things put in contact with a code, hence codified or contactualized. Because of the process of contactualization the things we understand, do, say and write exist in contactual reality, a created reality independent of the actual reality of the contactualized things. Any knowledge of the things represents their contactual understanding, never their actual nature in entirety. That is, individual consciousness is not designed to be omniscient.

Buddhism is human understanding and expression and thus, like any religion, exists in contactual reality. It spread through human intercontact. For example, the Buddha converted five men at Sarnath, and thus started the first missionary religion. Social scientists consider a conversion an act, which is an intercontact between the contactors, namely the converter and convert. The nucleus activity in this action is converting. The Buddha is the doer and the goal is those converts. And so on. We use the same eight code questions for the evaluation of any intercontact as follows:

(1) Is the activity of converting fair?; (2) Are the doers of this activity fair?; (3) Are the means or instruments of this activity fair?; (4) Is the goal of this activity fair?; (5) Are the recipients of this activity fair?; (6) Is the starting point or the origin of this activity fair?; (7) Is the base (time and place) of this activity fair?; (8) Are the specifics or specifiers of this activity fair?

These eight ethical questions define contactism. In simple words, two or more humans in contact for any purpose must consider each other's interest in a fair and egalitarian manner. Such a consideration in human contact is called contactism. This philosophy is a humanistic extension of contactics.

Discussion

Conversion is the action through which Buddhism became international. We can test the Buddhist conversion with the ethical questions of contactism using more simple words. Is the activity of giving Buddhism to others fair? Have the givers or the doers been fair to others? That is, were the converters invaders, traders, terrorists, despotic rulers and government officers with political or military authority? Were they discriminators against others because of social, cultural, ethnic, sexual, geographical and national differences? What were the means or instruments they used to convert others? Was conversion achieved with physical, economic, social, political and military coercion? In any good ethics the means must be as clean as the end. The goal was to give Buddhism to others. But was this goal appropriate or convincing to others? That is, why Buddhism instead of other religions? Did they try to explain the goal and its usefulness to others? The recipients were the converted. Was their acceptance of Buddhism fair? In giving them Buddhism were they treated nicely? Would it not have been better to leave them alone? Was the origin or starting point of converting others fair? Did the origin come from a power position? What and why were particular times and places selected to give Buddhism to others? Each of these questions is mixed with specifiers and cross-roles. But the point is fairness in the spread of Buddhism. If the answers to these questions appear fair then we can say that Buddhism spread with contactism.

In contactism, contactors consider common interests with a consensus. The Buddha had to display contactism in order to make his philosophy of *majjhima patipada* or the 'middle path" attractive to others. The 'otherness' had to be eliminated. People could be converted only on grounds that were common and open to all. For this purpose he created a new organization, the *samgha*. But in reality the new organization was a composite of many old and contemporary elements, a reorganized or contactualized religious order. In any missionary reorganization, only those religious and philosophical things have to be selected for contactualization through such situations and expressions that would present least conflict in the intercontact of conversion. Some of the old things could be kept intact while others have to be modified or totally replaced by the new ones. The following examples are intended to show this pattern in Buddhism.

The old background contained elements, for example, of Vedic traditions, Jainism and many other non-theistic traditions, as we know from the early Buddhist literature. In other words, the Buddha was in contact with the dharma complex used in his times. The foremost principle of conduct or *sila* known as *ahimsa* or noninjury was already established in the Upanishads and Jainism. Even the concept of *nibbaina* or nirvana could have come from the idea of *asat* or the original state of non-existence, as we find in the Rigvedic *Naisadiya Sukta*. The Samkhya tradition, not to mention Jainism and several materialistic schools, had already shown no belief in the existence of *Isvara* or God. The concepts of karma and *samsara* or rebirth were available to the Buddha in his ancestral heritage. Practice of Yoga, a vital part of Buddhism, may even be pre-Vedic. The *bhakti* or devotional element found already in the Upanishads was added eventually. He eliminated many well-established concepts, such as *atman* or 'self,' *Brahman, varna, yajna*, etc., to count a few. Nevertheless, he modified many old things in a new way and language. His replacement of Sanskrit by Pali was a step towards contactism. Later, Buddhist missionaries continued his policy: the use of people's language for communication and conversation. So we have a huge Buddhist literature from Chinese to English.

The foremost common ground is *dukham ariyasaccam* or "pain is the universal truth", i.e., we all experience and observe pain. Because of that truth, we all are in the same boat together. If there is a solution to eliminate the pain, then the question is whether it is available to all with no discrimination? The eight-fold path or the *atthangika magga* is the solution and is open to all. And yet everyone has the freedom to seek his or her own path---"Be your own lamp. Take refuge in yourself." The need for free or open contact must have motivated Buddhism to break the barrier of *varna* or class. Men born in low and poor classes and all women, who were barred from receiving the Vedic knowledge, found equal access to Buddhism. Vedic religion with its strong emphasis on social stratification could not display contactism, hence could not qualify as a missionary religion. The Buddha, on the other hand, wanted a missionary religion and philosophy without the contactual realities and contaxic effects created by his ancestral religion. These were the realities and side effects that produced socio-economic 'otherness' with no level playing field for everyone. Even though his church was reorganized or contactualized with several existing religious things. Any recognition of his ancestral religious things would have discredited his own church. In other words, he very well understood the lack of missionary appeal of his ancestral dharma.

Another important display of contactism in Buddhism is its policy to spread dharma with no coercion. Otherwise, it would be adharma or anti-dharma. Whenever a few deviations are found here or there, they could be considered unexpected effects or contaxic effects. Some criticize Buddhism for one of its major side effects: too much emphasis on 'unworldliness' such as nirvana, karma, samsara, etc., and less concern for the real existence in this world. Undoubtedly, such concepts are in the domain of 'beliefs'. But we can obtain many potential beneficial side or contaxic effects of Buddhist beliefs. For conversion, contactism is not the only necessary condition. Contactism increases the appeal of an intercontact. Otherwise humans are able to reason in keeping an intercontact if it has practical benefits here and now with or without contactism. Simply consider the social advantages of the five *silas* and yoga. The practice of non-injury, non-drinking, non-stealing, etc., is needed for reducing crime. Any civilized society attempts to regulate the actions of their members by adopting such principles through religion or law. Buddhism is responsible for the international propagation of meditation and other yogic practices. In yoga, we observe contactism; anyone can practise yoga anywhere. Those who practise it have been found relatively healthier physically and psychologically. Buddhism's emphasis on sharing *dukha* is not selfish. Otherwise, it could not have become a missionary religion.

As mentioned above, the very notion of international missionary religion starts with Buddhism. It is Buddhism's contactism that made it suitable for missionary purposes. Other missionary religions, too, became successful as they were able to reorganize the older traditions in such a manner that the emerging religion could display contactism clearly. Such a display meant social equality here and now, not for one party, but for all the parties. Christianity, for example, became a successful missionary religion because it also displayed contactism, which was partly due to reorganization. Most likely, Buddhism became the model for Christianity as we see so many similarities between these religions. Interestingly, some contemporary Christians have been international missionaries for Buddhism. In this respect Blavatsky and Col. Olcott, the founders of the Theosophical Society, are noteworthy. Even Swami Vivekananda followed the model of the Buddha and spread Vedanta to the West. These three great missionaries succeeded because what they selectively took from the Indian dharma complex is characterized by contactism.

Conclusion

I start my concluding remarks with a confession that I know very little about Buddhism. My fascination with Buddhism is because of its continuous international popularity. Any popular human phenomenon is about intensive and extensive human contact. So I chose my own theory of human contact, contactics, and its ethical philosophy, contactism, to answer my question why Buddhism as an Indian religion succeeded beyond its origin. My discussion above is meant to show that the inclusion and exclusion of some concepts and policies in the origin of

Buddhism created contactism as its side effect, helping its dissemination and acceptance later.

Contactism requires that in any human contact the contactors must consider each other's interests with fairness and equality. Democracy displays contactism at its best. For example, modern democratic governments are committed to protect religious freedom while refraining from the use of any religion to resolve modern problems. Ironically, some major problems today are due to religious conflicts and our world has been divided more by religions than by any other social-cultural phenomena. Nevertheless, all religions are our common human heritage and we still can utilize their ways to avoid human pain. Even in prosperous nations there is pain. For example, I often hear in America that, "Life sucks." That is what the Buddha said 2,500 years ago; life has *dukkha* or pain. But he also gave us a middle path for *sukkha* (pleasure) and warned us to avoid extremes. The path can be extended to achieve social *sukha*. A global economic middle path should lead to a global middle class. The Buddha himself renounced rulership. But a Bill Gates does not have to take the vow of poverty. Big businesses give millions of dollars' salaries and perks to a small number of the highest-ranked and lay off a large number of the lower-ranked employees. It does not display the principle of avoidance of extremes. This extreme craving for profit causes extreme pain for many. We need economic *ahimsa* to improve the quality of human contact.

I am not implying that the Buddha and his philosophy are perfect for fair human contact or contactism. In fact, in my novel, *Discovering Brides*, released recently in the USA, I have shown the Buddha not so fair to his young wife and infant son as he left them uninformed in the middle of the night. For my support, I have quoted in my novel the lines from the famous Hindi epic, *Yashodharai*, by Maithili Sharan Gupt. But then I have presented the Buddha not as a religious leader, but as a champion of contactism, who had the courage to cast away what was unfair in his ancestral religious background. He thought of greater good in his midnight flight, a flight to and for the world out there.

As the world economy is now more globalized than ever before in the history of humankind, we have begun to believe that there is very little chance for another world war. But how about international terrorism? We still need to practise *ahimsa* towards the members of our own human species. Anthropologists and other scientists have shown that humans evolved as one race and spread around the globe eventually. Many races are political fictions, one race is a scientific fact. The world to our human race came as one globe, not as many nations. Buddhism spread internationally because it ignored racial and geographical prejudices. This is what the Buddha statue story that I mentioned in the beginning symbolizes.

Reference

For contactism see the following works of Anoop Chandola, the author. *Book*: Contactics: Daily Drama of Human Contact (Lanhaxn, MD: University Press of America, U.S.A., 1992). *Book chapter*: "Ritualism and Contactism: Popularity of a Hindu Ritual." (*In* Nature and Function of Ritual, ed. Ruth-Inge Heinze. Westport, CT: Bergin & Garvey, Greenwood Publishing, U.S.A., 2000). This article was presented as a paper at the International Conference on Buddhistic Philosophy and Contemporary Issues, Roorkee, India (13th-15th November, 2000).

3

Fire Cult, Occult Practice and Ethnic Amalgamation: A Critique of Atharva Veda

Suniti Kumar Pathak

This paper discusses the process of syncretism as revealed in blending of cultural practices and also assimilation of ethnic groups of the Vedic era, by the second millennium BC. In this era the religious significance of the Vedas was not established. The author's main purpose here is to critically examine the contents of the *Atharva Veda,* which reveals multiple processes of cultural fusion, development of bands of *rishis*, origin of *gotras*, fire cults and occult practices.

The *Atharva Veda*

The Vedas are generally believed to be revelations experienced by numerous bands of *rishis* belonging to different ethnicities in different environments. In course of social amalgamation among the Vedic peoples, these *rishis* endeavoured to undertake *gotra* enumeration to establish separate ethno-descent identities in order to distinguish cult structures among the habitats of *Sapta sindhu,* referred to as *Hapta hindu* in the avesta of the Iranians. The geographic extension of Haptahindu (sapta sindhu) covering up to Anatolia in West Asia requires a separate discussion. Ethnonyms of those *rishis* though not always corresponding to descent or clan, leave room to support the idea of wide area of habitation of these people up to the Oxus Vakasu in Euro Asia. Whether the *Atharva Veda* represents such an old trend of extensive human migration, is a subject which demands further probing. Despite that, the

Atharva Veda preserves both older facts and the later evidences of the eastward migration of Vedic people's culture up to the Gangetic south belt (Bloch, 1965: 12).

Two renditions of the *Atharva Veda* namely Shaunaka and Pippalada, traditionally claim their multiple branches numbering either nine or fifteen. Numerous *rishis* were involved to develop a polygonal polytheist Vedic culture stratum.

Comparatively, the cult identity of some followers was distinct in the rishis fold. Their ethnic differences entered into a new form of cult distinctiveness through respective social processes, even though their economic growth, depended on mobile livelihood and that was tending towards temporary settlement in sympathetic congenial environment to live on. Vratya, the dejectable as a measure of differentiation, came in usage by the process of behaviourism when *medha* killing of living beings in socio-religious festive ritual *Yaga* was introduced among the fire cult *rishis*. Again, the latter distinguished themselves from raw meat eater ethnic groups, namely, *Pishaca*. A separate discussion is required again with reference to the broad ethnic enumeration of five peoples, *Pancajana*, in the *Rig Veda*.

The *Atharva Veda* is generally ignored for its emphasis on shamanic behaviours along with fire rituals, hence some traditional academicians claim, *Veca-trayi*, there are only three Vedas. The *Atharva Veda* is in its present form a metrical composition along with prose passages. It may be broadly divided into hymns for propitiation of cosmic luminous embodiments *deva* and into shamanic rituals with respect to the beings, earth inclusive of the underground world. The *Atharva Veda* is structurally unique from other three-metrical collections, *samhita;* e.g. the *Rig Veda* for recitation by specified reciters in ritual occasions, the *Sam Veda* for musical songs on relevant occasions and the *Yajur Veda* for the occasion of performing *Yajna* rites and propitiation ceremonies.

Fire was regarded as protector by them and accepted for cult identity. Agni, fire, derived from the verb root *ag*, to wind, to move tortuously or to go, is significant by the virtue of the fact that fire is one of the primary elements of this solar world. The followers of the agni-cult once became no less agile than those of the Indra-cult, when the Vedic civilization had been in cradles. That factor goes in support of the older antiquity of the *Atharva Veda*. The Atharvan, the Angirasa and the Bhrigu groups presumably claimed Agni in divination of the *deva* in spite of its manifestion both in blackness and in brightness. Smoke and smokiness out of fire refers to its dark passage Krisnavartman; while rays of fire are brilliant *arcisman.*

The genus for divination is popularly related with the sky, which is also believed to be heaven in theology. The sky appears bright in this solar world in spite of abundant dark cosmic space around the earth. Two verb roots *dyu* and *dyai* to construe *dyaus* for sky in the Vedic expressions are important. Among the five major ethnic groups in the early Rig Vedic period, the *Deva* were brighter in contrast to others like the *Gandharva.* That amounted to colour distinction, *varna*-bheda in the Indian classical texts, as was mentioned in the other three Vedas, *Rig Veda*, *Sam Veda* and *Yajur Veda*. Among the *rishis* involved in the *Atharva Veda*, three names are prominent—Atharvan, Angirasa and Bhrigu, who were in practice of preserving fire for their cult identities.

Fire Cult Identity

Angirasa was probably the pivot among those who had domination over fire. Fire has two aspects—blackness and brightness. The *Rig Veda* refers to the procedure of generating fire by rubbing two pieces of firewood (V.II.6). The similar verse is also read in the *Sam Veda* (Purva 108). Innovation of fire and its uses by mankind became the first step towards material growth. Fire is a power out of the alien nature around human beings. Angirasa, Dandhyan, Atharvan and Bhrigu who had been involved in using fire as cult identity marker, belonged to a separate ethnic status. Comparatively Zorasthra paid emphasis on preservation of fire, like the practice as followed by the Atharva-Angirasa and the Bhrigu-Angirasa units. Apri hymns in the Avesta invoke fire *ahura,* in Iranian, by different names.

In this connection the power divination of fire as *deva* in the Vedic fold is relevant. *Deva* is linguistically formed out of verb root *de* to protect, to cherish. Again the genera in maintaining ethnic colour distinction among the Vedic peoples may be traced to the hoary days of the past. Primarily superiority of the fair complexion led to a tendency of continuing 'genetic sanctification' and 'blood purity'. *Vratya* concept of the outcast, dejected or refused group amounted to rigid social segregation in the course of institutionalization of the later Vedic religious society, prior to the advent of Shramana culture facet by the sixth century BC, when the Buddha Gautama and the Jina Mahavira appeared.

Thematic Diversity

The *Atharva Veda* covers a wide range of behaviour patterns of the Vedic peoples in diverse contexts. A broad line of divergence may be located among the *Vratya* and the non-*Vratya.* The former usually paid no heed to the Vedic sacrificial rituals (Bhattacharji, 1984: 305). The former were distinguished by outward robe of black garment with turban. Some mentions of white woolen dress support the climatic conditions of their parental locality. They used to make the Vedic expressions, though not in a systematic manner. "Tandya Maha Brahmana (TMB), edited Bibliotheca Indica 1870–1874", twenty-five sections, appears to be a subsequent compilation in the Vedic literature paradigm. It preserves a unique status with a tendency of compromise or assimilation between the wider faction and the lesser one (Winternitz, 1927: 191). Presumably, *vratya* was a wanderer group and used to live on the donations of non-*Vratya* householders. The latter used to consider them holy by offering hospitality (TMB III. 1–3; 4–11; 4 XV, 11.1, 13.1).

In the spread of the *Atharva Veda* from westward to eastward along the Gangetic belt of North India, some tendency of syncretic socialization generated under the force of conditionality, when a wanderer group had become settler to some extent by circa 1000 BC. Occasionally two traditions are enumerated by a band of academicians. One is a great tradition and the other is little tradition, (Redfield, 1955:50). That may not be thoroughly applicable in the case of the *Atharva Veda* in the context of its acceptance of its less important *Yajna-cult* led by *Yajnavalkya* priestdom. *Vratya*, therefore, is a case of assimilation of the wanderer group with the settlers in spite of diversity in their normal ways of livelihood. Till their participation in Yaga, fire-festive ritual as *Brahma-vada*, branch of Vratya, their wandering behaviours and usual habits probably prevailed. A Vratya was honoured by a non-Vratya agriculture family as a respectable guest despite their suspended assimilation. Material basis of the Vedic people got priority among the *Atharvans*, *Angirasas* and the *Bhrigus* as the diverse oral traditions of the *Atharva Veda* preserved them more than those of the *Rig Veda*.

The following diversities in two *Atharva Veda* renditions are laid down.

(1) *Bhumi Sukta* in Mandala XII refers to the benevolent aspect of the Mother earth and the nature on the surface and the underground.

A pragmatic turn in the outlook of the Vedic *rishis* was emphasized in *Bhumi Sukta*, as the earth is the ground on which both animate and inanimate beings stand upon. Diversity of the mankind with ethno genetic peculiarities, unlike other animate beings on the earth was recognized by the seers in the *Atharva Veda*. The *Rig Veda* mentions diverse ethnicities referring to the geographic extent of lands, rivers, mountains and the other surroundings of the peoples concerned. Academicians attach such an area of the earth into which the Assyrians of present day Syria, the Mesopotamians (of Iraq), the Ionians (Cyprus), The Semitics of Yamen and Saudi Arabia and the Iranians (of Persia) were involved.

The earth thus becomes a resort of the human beings with no discrimination of ethnic distinction. Factually speaking, the Vedas refer to four categories of people involved in the pluralistic culture complex. Such as:

(1) *Asura,* Iranic *Ahura,* who had a parallel culture stratum as that of the *Devo* to which the rishi-cult belonged.

(a) Rishis who had been elevated either as the settlers or wanderers, established their separate *gotra* and their generic clan identity such as—Atri, Angirasa, Agastys, Kashyapa, Kanva, Gautama, Javala, Bhrigu, Bharadvaja, Vishvamitra, Shaunaka etc. Rishi hood was not always hereditary and that could be earned.

(b) Similar warrior clans like Anu, Krivi, Drahya, Trita Turvas, Puru, Bharata, Shrinja Rusma, Yadu etc. with their respective identities (Chanda, 1916:11).

(c) *Dasa* and *dashyu.* Were occasionally referred to as those (such as, Nisada, Pishacha, Raksasa of non-Vedic culture) who did not belong to the *rishi*-cult for Yajna fire ritual with medha sacrifice.

(2) Again seven *Atharva Veda* hymns captioned *Mrigara-sukta* in Mandala-IV, appear to be ethically motivated to formulate a social lien in spite of group identity.

(3) For survival of the humans during contest with the other animate beings on the earth, the local exigencies demanded to generate healing procedure out of nature and with her items accessible to the mankind, by the second millennium BC. The *Rig Veda* refers to the Atharvans, who might have been wanderers skilled in healing practice. The *Atharva Veda* mentions *Bhisk-Aatharvan* and *Carana-Vaidya* branches who might have been conversant in use of herbal plants like *kustha* (leprosy) along with the muttering of sono-jargonic recitations.

(4) The Angirasas, like the Atharvans played an eminent role in developing fire rituals under novel procedures of *abhicara* and *kritya* rites. The pilots of *Yajna-cult* like Gobhila, Khadira, Apastamba *rishis* did not approve malignancy in the usually prescribed ritual order.

The Asura cult is presumed to be experts in those occult practices and the Angiras group was also inclined to them. Two separate Vedas namely the Atharvan-Veda and the Angirs-Veda as mentioned in the *Shatapatha Brahman* (XI.5.6 4--8; IX.5.7.6,) leaves room to suggest a tendency of integration and that was co-ordinated by circa1500 BC when mantra-muttering by fire users became popular as a measure of healing and other social contingencies. Fire was not the only single feature utilized, the solar power, Surya in multiple epithets was propitiated in the *Rig Veda* and the *Atharva Veda*; the latter *samhita* laid emphasis on Aditya (II 81, II, 32) for skin-disease cure, conception and menstrual abnormality etc. The *Atharva Veda rishis* had a belief that malignant forces were led by the Asuars, the Pishacas, the Raksasas, who had been equipped with greater might than the humans. Abhicara rites and *kritya* deeds thus became the part of the *Atharva Veda* culture as the protective formula for mankind, in the course of developing Tantra fact popular in those days. These items were accepted to safeguard the humans and animals from the evils.

(5) The *Atharva Veda* shows how its *Brhma-Vada* and the *Veda-darsha* branches negotiated in the Vedicization of the fire rituals with mantra muttering for curative measures and as a safeguard from malignant forces, of the evil minded. In this regard *Kausitaki Brahmana,* otherwise the *Sankhayana-Brahmana* narrated the participation of the Atharvedic Brahmans in food sacrifice together with the *Yujur Veda* the *Sam Veda* and the *Rig Veda* priests like *adhvaryu, hota, udgata, ritvik* and others (Winternitz, 1927: 270).

Deductions

It is evident that the *Atharva Veda* preserves documents regarding the socio-cultural syncretism of the pluralistic ethnicity of the second millennium BC. During that period, Vedicism was in the process of institutionalization through the growth of the Brahmana literature. Two factions had been in contest despite multiple units and cults, as the Vedas mention. The *Ahura Mazda* of old Iranian source preserves a parallel column. Resultantly, the *Atharva Veda* shows two distinct lines in its early stratum, though in the course of changes in time, locus and conditionality, the opposition factions of the *rishi*-cult, the *Yajna* cult the *soma-cult* lost their distinction in many instances, as it is attempted to focus above.

Growth of the Atharva Veda in Oral Traditions
(An approximate time schedule)

Circa 4000 BC	3500 BC	The Atharvans explored Cura practice out of natural vegetation and animal bodies.
Circa 3500 BC	3000 BC	The Angiras established fire as their cult item. Early invocations restricted to the Sun, the Air and Water, extended to the fire.
Circa 3000 BC	1200 BC	Growth of *Atharva Veda* in multidimensions to meet the basic needs and emergencies for individual and society. Various cults led by other Vedic groups sprouted and extended.
Circa 1200 BC	800 BC	*Abhicara and Kritya Yagas* were challenged and denounced by *Veda trayi* supporters of *Yajna* cultists.
Circa 800 BC	400 BC	Nine or fifteen branches of the *Atharva Veda* sprouted under the then social forces. Shramanas like Gautama Buddha, Jina Mahavira and Ajivika exponents appeared with their institutions respectively to challenge the *Rishi* -- *ashrama* institutions. The *Atharva Veda* spread through the lower course of the Ganges up to the seacoast of Odivisa, present day Orissa.

References

Bhattacharji, S. *Literature in the Vedic Age,* Vol. I. *The Samhitas,*.K.P. Bagchi & Co. Calcutta, 1984.

Bloch, J. *Indo Aryan,* Paris, 1965.

Bloomfield, M. *The Hymns of Atharvaveda* (Selected) Sacred Books of the East Vol. XIII 1897.

Chanda, R.P. *Indo-Aryan Races,* Vol. 1 Rajshasti, 1916.

Chattopadhyaya, D.P. *Science and Society in Ancient India,* 1977 *Consciousness and Scientific Knowledge,* Indian Council of Philosophical Research, New Delhi, 2002.

Griffith, R.T.H. *Atharvaveda Samhita* (English tran.) Benaras, 1805–06.

Hopking, E.W. Gods and Saints of the Great Brahmana in *Transactions of the Academy of Arts and Sciences,* Vol. XV 1909, pp. 20--69.

Karambalkar, V.W. *The Atharvaveda and the Ayurveda,* Nagpur, 1961.

Keith, A.B. *The Kaysitaki Brahmana* (English tran.) Harvard Oriental Series, Vol. XXV, 1920

Lanman, C.R. *The Atharvaveda Samhita,* Harvard Oriental Series, Cambridge Mass, 1905 (edited. Whitney's edu.).

Lindner, B. Jena *The Kausitaki-Brahmana,* 1887.

Paranjpe, V.G. The Vedic Aryans, the RK-samhita and the Harappa Civilization, *Proceedings of the All India Oriental Conference,* XXIV Session, Varanasi, October 1968, Pub. 1972, pp. 235--238.

Pathak, S.K. The Atharva-Veda or the Indian Tantra in *Buddhism in India and Abroad,* Somaiya Publications, Mumbai, 1996, pp. 225--234.

Rahurkar, V.G. *The Seers of Rigveda,* Poona,1968.

Redfield, R. *Peasant Society and Culture,* Chicago 1955.

Renou, L. *Vedic India,* Calcutta, 1957.

Sharma, R.S. Class Formation and its Material Basis in the Upper Gangetic Basin, *Indian Historical Review,* Vol. II, No.I July, 1975.

Shende, N.J. The Rigveda and the Atharvaveda, *Journal of the Asiatic society of Bengal,* Calcutta, 1941.

Singh, Shivaji, Archaeological evidence on the pluralistic make-up of the Aryan culture complex. *Proc. of the All India Oriental Conference XXIV Session,* Varanasi, Oct., 1968, Pub. 1972, pp. 357--362.

Whitney, W.D. *The Atharvaveda Samhita,* Harvard Oriental Series, Vols. 7&8, Cambridge, Mass, 1905.

Winternitz, M. *A History of Indian Literature* Vol. 1, University of Calcutta, 1927.

4

Hindu Elements in Bagobo Traditions of the Philippines

K.G. Gurumurthy

One of the major features of the cultural history of the Philippines is the unusual character of the external influences, their bases, routes and media through which they reached the Philippine islands. These influences were drawn from India, China and Arabia and lately from Europe. European and Arabian influences reached the Philippines through religious spheres---Christianity and Islam. These two cultural contacts/influences were direct and powerful, and through their strength they were able to establish their colonial rule over the Philippines. So there is no doubt regarding their origin and media. Contrary to these, the Indian and Chinese contacts and their influences are indistinct but still they are deeply rooted in the Philippine culture, mythology, way of life and belief system. The Chinese influences, according to Manuel (1948) are more on the areas of trade and linguistic sphere—many Chinese words are found in the Filipino languages. To a certain extent, based on artifacts such as jars which are excavated from archaeological sites, the age of the Chinese influences can be determined. Nevertheless, estimating the age of Indian/Hindu influences, it is rather difficult.[1] Their penetrations are quite different from other influences; there are no signs of religious orders or political organizations to support them.

Among many scholars who have worked on this issue of the penetration of Indian influences in the Philippines, Kroeber (1944), Beyer (1921), Benedict (1913, 1916) and lately, Francisco (1960, 1963, 1964) are the leading ones. These scholars have studied Indian influences in the Philippines at three levels: (1) the presence of Hindu customs, manners, myths and folklore; (2) presence of Sanskrit words; and (3) archaeological excavations. A considerable amount of research has already been done on all the three areas and a great amount of credit goes to Prof. Beyer of the University of the Philippines. Today, Prof. Beyer's findings are questioned for reliability since there is no established evidence to show an exact and intimate physical contact between India and the Philippines. In the absence of these sources, scholars have taken to the study of neighbouring cultures, which probably might have served as the media of transmission. With regard to the presence of Hindu customs and manners, there are many evidences which are found in almost all the ethnic groups of the Philippines.[2] This influence, according to Francisco (1963) can be seen in their religious beliefs, consideration of omens, some of the native customs such as abstaining from worldly activities during special occasions and belief in concepts of purity and pollution.

With regard to the mythical and folk beliefs most of the ethnic groups show Hindu influences. Belief in a supreme god, more than one world, existence of the soul and heaven are all Hindu beliefs. The myths and folklores show Hindu influence and many parables are common in terms of ideas, but with native or local alterations in names and forms. Another significant influence from India is the treatment of time among Magindanao Moros of southern Philippines. The Moros divide the day into five parts, each of which is given a separate name: Maheshwara, Kala, Sri, Berma and Bisnu. These according to Kroeber (1944:200) are slightly altered names of Hindu gods. Regarding the Sanskrit words, Francisco (1960) who has discovered many Sanskrit words among the different Filipino languages and dialects, has discussed about their alterations and probable route of reaching the Philippines. It is also mentioned by Kroeber (1944) that most of the Sanskrit words referred to are names of Hindu gods and plants. In the archaeological findings, similarly, the Indian/Hindu influences are again evident in some of the excavations such as the bronze image of Hindu god Siva (1883), the golden image of Agusan (1917)[3] and the copper figure of Ganesa. It becomes very difficult to establish why there are so many ruined Hindu temples in Java and Borneo while there is absence of such temples in the Philippines, and yet there are strong Indian influences. According to Kroeber (1944:177) there must be some hidden evidence still waiting for excavation.[4]

The Bagobo are one of the ethnic groups in the northeastern province on the island of Mindanao, Philippines. With their nearness to Malay and Indonesian islands, Mindanao and Sulu islands show the greatest of Hindu and Islamic influences. This mixture of Hindu and Islamic influences might be due to the close tracking of Islam to all the places which had early Hindu influences. Islamic influence with its straight contact was able to suppress the Hindu manners and customs, at least among the people who embraced the Islamic faith. But a vast amount of Hindu influence is still evident among the ethnic groups who live in remote and far-off areas, away from the Islamic contacts. The Bagobo themselves are a good example of this phenomenon.

Benedict first studied the Bagobo culture in 1910s and later Prof. Manuel studied this culture in 1960s. Both the researchers have noticed plenty of Hindu influences among the Bagobo. Benedict has noticed some parallels in folk stories and mythical characters. She has also noticed a three-fold classification of Bagobo mythical stories which is similar to that of the classification made by Somadeva in his *Katha Sarit Sagara*, which is translated by Tawney (1926). The Bagobo three-fold classification of the folklore are: (1) Romantic tales about the mythical Bagobo, dealing with semi-divine, some of them possessing magical powers; (2) Demons known as Buso who haunt graveyards, forests and rocks; and (3) The myths associated with cosmogamy and natural phenomena. Tawney's (1926:197) observation in Somadeva's work is similar to this and are classed under these four groups: (1) Enemies of gods very rarely visiting the earth; (2) Servants of gods frequently coming in contact with mortals; (3) Independent super-humans often mixing with mortals; and (4) Demons hostile to mankind.

Apart from this parallel element, there are some more common beliefs among the Bagobo and the Hindus. Bagobo believe that Diwata created the sun, the moon and the stars, the river, the sky and the earth. The term Diwata, according to Benedict (1913:15), is used more as a collective term than as a specific one referring to a particular god; it refers to the gods in general, or to any of them. This collective belief is more similar to that of Hindu advaita belief in one god—Saguna Brahman, who created the universe out of himself. This meaning can be read from such Sanskrit words *Aham Brahmasmi* (I am Brahman), *Tat Tvam Asi* (It is me in it) which gives an understanding of the fact that the Brahman is omnipotent, omnipresent and omniscient. A similar type of belief system is also given by Benedict (1916:14), where one is led to infer that Diwata cares for the rice, watches over the sun, the moon, the stars and all the people, that Diwata is a good Manobo who lives in the sky, that Diwata is the highest god, etc. Even the Pamulak Manobo's belief that a human body is made of earth is also a local version of a Sanskrit rendition. The Bagobo belief that Diwata made the great eel (*kasoli*), a fish, that is like a snake in the river and which is coiled around the globe, is also similar to the Sanskrit belief of a giant snake Adishesha, who carries the globe on his head and whose shaking causes earthquakes. The Bagobo also have a belief that the writhing of the eel, whenever the great crab bites, results in earthquakes.

The Bagobo mythological belief that the sun and the moon are in the human form, is similar to the Hindu belief. The Hindus believe that the sun is hot and so do the Bagobo, and that the moon is cooler than the sun and it is a dark place. The Bagobo explanation of eclipse is similar to the Hindu one, according to which, the planets are devoured by a snake—Rahu. According to Bagobo belief, a monstrous bird—Minokawa swallows the planet and on these occasions the Bagobo strike gongs, shout and cry for help and try to scare the bird so that it will release the planet soon. This is because, according to Benedict (1916:19), the Bagobo believe that after devouring the planets the bird will also eat them.

There are many Sanskrit words in the Bagobo vocabulary; also there are many Bagobo words, which are similar to Sanskrit words. Some of them are slightly altered or added with one or more letters. For example, a Bagobo word 'Pamulak Manobo' means the creator. In Sanskrit literature, Manu is regarded as the originator of Manava (mankind) and the Bagobo word 'Manobo' might be the altered form of Manu. Another word 'Tigyama' is a name given to the god who is the protector of Bagobo houses. In Sanskrit belief, Yama is the god of death, and one goes to Yamapuri after one's death. The Bagobo words 'Stara Bümi' stand for the god of corps. A Sanskrit word 'Sthira' also means earth. Another Bagobo word 'Dios ka tana' (1916:18) means the place on which one lives or stays. The Bagobo word 'Mardegar' means a good person. An Indian word (Kannada) 'Madi' means ritually clean or pure. A 'Madegara' literally means a washerman and in certain contexts it also means a person with clean habits.

Tagamahalinga is one of the supernatural beings of Bagobo who is associated with mountains. Linga in Hindu tradition is used to refer to Siva, one of the major gods of Hindus, who was incarnated on earth in the form of Mahalinga—the great lord. This Mahalinga is also associated with a mountain and he lives on top of it. This is also similar to the Bagobo belief (1916:24) in another god—Mandara Rangan, the god of the sky who lives on Mount Matutan. For the Hindus, Mandara Rangan means lord of a particular mountain Mandara Giri. Bagobo women, according to Benedict (1916:25), also have a goddess in the sky called Daraga. According to Hindu belief, the women mostly worship Durga, other name of Kali (both refer to Parvati, the wife of Mandara Rangan). Two other names which are recorded by Prof. Manuel (:429) owe their origin to *Ramayana*, one of the two great epics of Hindus. They are Kusilaw and Wali. These names, according to Manuel, are the names of the Bogobos' ancestors. In India, even today, it is a common custom to name children after mythical heroes such as Lawa and Kusha.

According to a belief among the Indians, seeing an animal (hare) in the dots of the moon is called *Sasi* and *Mriganga* (Somadeva, 1880:109), one who is having an animal in his body. But Bagobos (Benedict, 1916:48) see a white monkey sitting on the branch of a tree in the dots of the moon. Though both the Indians and the Bagobo see different animals, the identification of an animal by both is important from the point of view of belief system.

In the field of literature and especially in similes, the Bagobos show much Indian influence. A good number of them were noticed in the *Tuwaang* epic recorded and published by Prof. Manuel (1957). In Bagobo myths and folklore, a frequently mentioned item is the coming down of a golden Sinalimba (1957:496) to carry back the mythical heroes to the heaven, which is described as an 'air boat', something floating in air. This belief is similar to Puspaka *vimana* which is frequently mentioned in *Mahabharata* and *Ramayana*. Another element noticed in the Bagobo culture is the significance of betel chewing. In the Indian culture the betel has ritual, social and moral values attached to it. We can notice this in the *Tuwaang* epic of the Bagobo where betel-chewing has a significant place. Throughout the epic, we can notice exchange of betel-nut containers. Even today among the Bagobo, it is a custom to give betel to the visitors as a sign of hospitality and respect. All these values attached to the betel are similar to those we witness in the Hindu culture.

Conclusions

The presence of Hindu elements in numerous customs and traditions of the Bagobo naturally made researchers like Kroeber, Beyer, Benedict and Manuel conclude that at one time in their history, the Bagobo ancestors had direct contacts with Hindus. But other scholars are of the opinion that there were no Hindus on the Philippine soil at any point of time as there are no established religious institutions or structures built by the Hindus. So they concluded that the Hindu influences found in the Philippine culture are due to secondary contacts, established through Hindu modeled Indonesia and such other Southeast Asian cultures which show much Hindu influence even today. Some others like Francisco (1963:177), even go to the extent of saying that these possible Hindu influences may not be really Hindu/Indian and might be a result of independent existence or might be derived from a common source which might have been cut off due to still more powerful historical factors. But the mystery remains unsolved to a great extent since we are not confident whether the cultural traces we call Hindu are really Hindu. If they are, then another question arises, how did they reach the Philippines, through diffusion or by way of direct culture-contact? There is urgent need for detailed ethno-historical study not only of the Philippine culture but also of neighbouring cultures which might have served as intermediaries for transmission of culture traits of Hindu origin, which gave birth to the composite and blended culture of the Bagobo.

Notes

1. The author expresses his thanks to Prof. A. Manuel and Dr. Juan R. Francisco, University of the Philippines, and Dr. P.B. Desai, Department of Ancient Indian History and Culture, Karnataka University, Dharwar for their help in preparing this paper. This is an abridged version of a paper published in The Journal of the Karnataka University. The paper is modified to suit the themes of homogenization and syncretism pointedly emphasized by Dr. N.K. Das, editor of this volume.
2. There is no tribe in the Philippines, no matter how primitive and remote, in whose culture of today elements of Hindu origin cannot be traced. See Kroeber, 1944:11.
3. The year of excavation.
4. Had not the Philippines been so remote that the first force of Indian contact was spent before their shores were reached, we should undoubtedly find ancient 'stone buildings' here also. See Kroeber. 1944:177.

References

Benedict, L.W., 1913, "Bagobo myths." *Journal of American Folklore*, XXVI: 13–63.

Benedict, L.W., 1916, "A Study of Bagobo Ceremonial, Magic, and Myth." ANYAS, V. 12, 1–308. New York: Published by the *Academy, May 15,* 1961.

Beyer, H. O., 1921, Philippines before Magellan. *Asia,* XXI: 86–92.

Beybr, H. O. and Jaime C. Deveyere, 1947, *Philippine Saga.* Manila: Capital Publishing House Inc.

Francisco, Juan, R., 1960, Indian influences in the Philippines; with special reference to language and literature. Ph. D. thesis submitted to the University of Madras, India. Mimeographed.

Francisco, Juan, R., 1963, "Analogous customs, beliefs and traditions in India and the Philippines". *Historical Bulletin,* VII: 2: 143--177.

Francisco, Juan, R., 1964, "On the Date of coming of Indian influences in the Philippines." A paper read in International Conference on Asian History, Hong Kong. (Mimeographed).

Kroeber, A. L., 1944, *Peoples of the Philippines.* Second and revised Edition. New York: American Museum of Natural History.

Manuel, Arsenio E., 1948, *The Chinese elements in the Tagalog; with some indications of Chinese influence on other Filipino languages and-culture, and an excursion info Austronesian linguistics.* Manila: Philippines Publication.

Manuel, Arsenio E., 1957, "The Maiden of the Buhang Sky: A fragment of the Bagobo epic cycle." *Philippine Social Science and Humanities Review,* XXXII: No. 4.

Somadeva, 1880, *The Katha Sarit Sagara.* (Translated by C. H. Tawney). Vols. 1, 2 & 3. London: Chas J. Sawyer Ltd., Grafton House, W.I., 1926.

5

Cultural Parallelism in the Khmer, Sinhalese and Thai Societies: Burmese Buddhist Rituals in Perspective

Mathieu Boisvert

In the pages that follow, we will analyze the temporary admission of young monks to the Burmese Buddhist monastic order, together with the ritual ceremony that frames this important act and the socio-cultural context in which it is set. Further, we will look at the educational role played by the Buddhist monasteries (*kyaung*). We will see how some have historically transformed themselves, through colonialism, into *prahita* to cater to children who cannot afford to attend public schools. This will enable us to circumscribe the impact of colonial influence on the initiation ceremony. Finally, we will review the contemporary situation for young girls with respect to the admission ceremony. In order to circumscribe the Theravada Buddhist context, we will make connections to the ancient Pali texts that still govern the Burmese Buddhist tradition and we will also, from time to time, draw parallels with surrounding Buddhist societies, Sinhalese, Khmer and Thai.

* * *

Anyone who goes to the Union of Myanmar (Burma)[1] soon notes the vibrant presence of the Theravada Buddhist tradition. The vast majority of the population are in fact Buddhists and the religion plays a predominant role in daily life; people go regularly to the temple to make offerings, to pay homage to the monks and to meditate. At first sight, what appears to distinguish the Union of Myanmar from the other Theravada countries including Sri Lanka, Thailand, Cambodia and Vietnam, is the impressive number of young, even very young, Buddhist monks. This article presents the results of a study that we carried out in the spring of 1999 on these young Burmese monks of the Theravada tradition. In the pages that follow we will analyze the temporary admission of young monks to the Buddhist monastic order, together with the ritual ceremony that frames this important act and the socio-cultural context in which it is set. Further, we will look at the educational role played by the Buddhist monasteries (*kyaung*). We will see how some have transformed themselves into *prahita* to cater to children who cannot afford to attend public schools. Finally, we will review the contemporary situation for young girls with respect to the admission ceremony. In order to circumscribe the Theravada Buddhist context, we will make connections to the ancient Pali texts that still govern the Burmese Buddhist tradition and we will also, from time to time, draw parallels with surrounding societies, Sinhalese, Khmer and Thai.

The novitiate admission ceremony, *shin pyu*, is by far the most important Burmese ritual. As the term signifies (from the Burmese: to make, of the layman, a novice[2]), this ceremony makes a boy into a novice within the monastic tradition. To begin with, we must clarify the distinction between novice (Pali: *samanera*) and monk (Pali: *bhikkhu*). The novice need respect only ten precepts, while the monk must rigorously observe 227. It is usually required that one be a novice before becoming a monk.[3] Further, one cannot be ordained a monk before the age of twenty. This means that, according to Western criteria, the postulant would have to be nineteen, since Buddhist tradition calculates age from the moment of conception and not from the day of birth.[4]

In the Union of Myanmar, as in Thailand and pre-Khmer-Rouge Cambodia, every man was required to become a novice for a period of time varying from one week to his whole life. Although contemporary Thailand, like the Union of Myanmar, celebrates a traditional novitiate admission ceremony, it takes place much later in the life of the young man, usually not long before marriage (Lévy-Ward, 1997:228). However, before the public school system was instituted in Thailand, Thai children became novices much earlier so that they could have access to an education (Tambiah, 1976:270). This contrasts with Sinhalese tradition, in which joining a monastic community as a novice or monk is considered a lifetime commitment. Hence we find far fewer young monks in Sri Lanka. If all male children had to become novices and then monks for life, the Sinhalese population would disappear after one generation.

The contrasts are even more striking when one compares Theravada Buddhism to the Hinduism of the *sashtras*. Here the individual could not in theory become a monk (*samnyasa*) before fulfilling the conditions associated with the three preliminary stages of life (*ashrama*): student (*brahmachariya*), householder (*grhastha*) and forest dweller (*vanaprastha*).[5] By contrast with the prescriptions in the ancient law codes, contemporary Hindu practice is much more flexible; could this be because people are now more familiar with the doctrine of reincarnation and might assume that a young boy had fulfilled the conditions for the three preliminary stages in a previous life? Like the Hindu *upanayana* ceremony, in which the 'twice born' (*dvija*)[6] are officially admitted to their social class (*varna*), the *shin pyu* is a rite of passage that fosters integration into Buddhist society.

A variety of criteria set the minimum age for becoming a novice. According to canonical tradition, the young boy must either have reached the age of fifteen, or be big enough to frighten away the crows.[7] This final criterion lowers the minimum age for becoming a novice considerably. Nevertheless, contemporary Burmese tradition does not admit boys until they have reached their seventh year. Until the total repression of religion carried out by the Khmers Rouges in 1975, the Khmer tradition had been very close to the Burmese, with young boys between seven and twelve years of age being encouraged to join the monastic life temporarily as novices and to later rejoin as monks, before getting married (Martin, 1997:316).[8] The admissibility of a young candidate was determined, according to *La Vie du paysan khmer*, by his ability to "touch his left ear with his right hand, passing his arm over his head"[9] rather than by his capacity for chasing off crows.

In addition to being seven years old, the future Burmese novice must be able to correctly pronounce the Pali sentences required for admission. He must also have obtained his parents' permission, for reasons we will turn to shortly. Once he has become a novice, it is in theory up to the boy to gauge the opportune moment for his return to the lay community, if there is such a moment. Although a minimum age is set, there is no age limit for becoming a novice. For the parents, though, it is important, if not crucial or even imperative, that each of their sons become a novice before they die. It is likewise unthinkable for a man to marry before having been a novice. The *shin pyu* ceremony, and the novitiate experience that follows it, allows each Burmese boy to experience the ideal life that monasticism represents in the Theravada countries, at least for a while.

Shin pyu is the most meritorious ritual that can be carried out in Burmese society. To begin with, the boy must scrupulously follow the ten Buddhist precepts: he must abstain from killing, stealing, sexual misconduct, lying, taking intoxicants, eating after noon, dancing, singing or playing a musical instrument, adorning himself with garlands, perfume or other form of make-up, using an elevated or luxurious chair or bed and, finally, handling silver and gold (and by extension, using money). This moral conduct (*sila*) ensures an incommensurable acquisition of merits (*punna*) for the boy. Apart from the enormous acquisition of merits through his moral practice, each novice has the opportunity to learn the *paritta* (protective verses), to familiarize himself with the major canonical texts and to learn the fundamentals of meditation practice. If the boy remains a novice for a prolonged period, the nature of his education will be determined by the monastic lineage within which he is ordained; he will receive either a more academic training (*pariyatti*), or a more rigorous training in meditative practice (*patipatti*). Whether the boy decides to stay in the monastery or not, the accumulated merits are immense. They will assure him, at the very least, an excellent condition in his future life; at best, his monastic practice will allow him to realize Buddhism's highest ideal, *nibbana*.

In addition to the benefits for the boy, the *shin pyu* ceremony is extremely meritorious for the parents, as is also the case in Cambodia and in Thailand.[10] M.E. Spiro points out that the Burmese candidate traditionally must remain a novice for three lents, that is to say three years; the merits associated with each of the years are transferred respectively to the mother, the father and the boy (Spiro, 1970:236). The karmic force of these merits is so strong that it even ensures that a 'sinner' not be born again in hell, even though by his profession he contravenes the first Buddhist precept of not killing.[11] The *shin pyu* is a source of merit for the parents to the extent that it is associated with the act of charity (*dana*). The road that leads to *nibbana* is often represented by the noble eightfold path (*ariyatthangikamaggo*), itself divided into three sub-categories: morality (*sila*), concentration (*samadhi*) and wisdom (*panna*). At the same time, it is often specified that lay people must develop charity before being able to master the three sub-categories of the noble eightfold path.[12] The financial investment that the novitiate admission entails is the occasion for parents to manifest charity. To begin with, a copious meal is offered to the entire monastic community (*samgha*) that is receiving the newcomer, a community that may contain a considerable number of monks. Furthermore, robes, begging bowls and other necessary goods are offered to the majority of the members of the *samgha*. Nevertheless, the financial contribution is infinitesimal considering the fact that the parents are offering the monastic community their most precious possession: their son.

A few canonical episodes demonstrate the importance attributed to the son. There is of course the legend about the admission of Rahula, the son of Buddha, in which the child is represented in a negative manner, as a source of attachment and, by extension, of suffering (*dukkha*). After Rahula had been admitted to the monastery, his grandfather Suddhodana demanded that the Buddha formulate the rule of parental consent. According to Suddhodana, the affect felt for a son is far from being superficial; it pierces the skin, the muscles and the bones to lodge in the depths of the marrow. Thus it is desirable that parents agree to the admission of their son, lest entry into the monastic order abolish parental ties.[13] Another example illustrates the renunciation of Siddhattha Gotama. This episode holds a primordial place in Buddhist hagiography. Following the announcement of the birth of his son Rahula, Gotama is said to have become aware of the constraining power of emotional ties to a son; he is then said to have decided to break the ties at once, before they could become too strong.[14] Together with the 'four sights',[15] this is taken to be one of the principal motivations behind Gotama's renunciation.

Although we certainly do not need the foregoing hagiographic episode to convince us that the ties that bind a son to his parents are strong, the incident nevertheless highlights the traditional Buddhist view of the subject. Returning to the *shin pyu* ceremony, we may affirm that in agreeing to let their son become a novice, Burmese parents are, literally, offering him to the *samgha*. This constitutes a high act of abnegation, the most meritorious gift a lay person can give, in that parents are renouncing, even though usually in a temporary way, the parental ties that bind them to their son.

In many traditional Asiatic societies, sons are responsible for looking after their parents in their old age. We may think in particular of the Indian model, where parents live in the family home until they die; when the oldest son marries, he becomes the master of the house. Daughters leave when they marry and are replaced by the daughters-in-law who come to join their husbands. Burmese society is very different.[16] Women do not automatically leave the family home to join their husbands. After they marry, depending on their financial situation, the couple may either set up an independent household or stay with the parents of either the husband or the wife. Women tend to take care of elderly parents. Nevertheless, men are in no way exempt from this responsibility; the

Buddhist texts stress the importance, for the son, of taking care of his parents. As the text that describes the beatitudes of lay life stipulates: "To take care of one's father and mother, cherish one's wife and children, have a peaceful occupation; this is the highest beatitude."[17] In offering their son to the *samgha*, parents are renouncing the security that he could offer them at the end of their lives. This double renunciation, of the filial tie and of security, is interpreted as an act highly productive of merits and, therefore, the act of charity par excellence.

Two other, more contemporary, examples highlight the meritorious aspect of the admission ceremony. During our stay in Myanmar, a Burmese man confided in us that his mother's deepest regret was that his father died before he became a novice. His father was not able to gather the merits associated with the admission of a son into the Buddhist community, and his mother was overcome with grief.[18] This attitude is corroborated by the commentary of Hla Maung which stipulates that Burmese parents cannot allow themselves to die before their son's *shin pyu* has been accomplished (Hla Maung:14.). It also happens that a relatively well-off couple who have no sons may sponsor the *shin pyu* of a poor boy or an orphan. By symbolically adopting the child (*katimatha*), the couple acquires the same merits as though they had sponsored the ordination of their own son (Khaing, 1996:49). These two examples confirm that the giving of a son to the *samgha* is understood to be a highly meritorious act.

Preparing for the admission event begins at least one week before the ceremony.[19] The whole of the extended family is involved, since a large part of the village population is invited to the ceremony. We note a clear hierarchy. The wealthiest invite members of inferior social strata to the ceremony, mainly in order to acquire extra merits; the poor, on the other hand, restrict themselves to a smaller number of guests. The quantity and quality of food required to invite higher class families and social strata is a drain on financial resources. The number of guests is directly linked to the social status of the parents. Several days before the ceremony, the women of the house begin to prepare the dishes that will be served first to the members of the monastic community, then to the guests, once the monks have finished their meal. New suits are prepared and ceremonial costumes pressed. The candidate goes to the monastery to learn how to pronounce the Pali formulas required for his admission and to prepare himself mentally for the drastic changes that will soon take place. The monks teach him the daily schedule that he will have to follow and the different rules he will have to obey.

On the day of the ceremony, a procession is organized to accompany the young man across the village before taking him to the monastery. The boy wears a royal costume and a parasol (the South Asian symbol of monarchy) is placed above his head. Although traditionally boys from rich families were transported by elephant (another symbol of royalty), boys from the majority of families are carried on horseback, or on a chariot pulled by a water-buffalo. Children from poor families are carried on their father's shoulders. Usually the father follows behind his son carrying the monastic robes and bowl, that is, if his son is not on his shoulders; in the latter case, the uncle would carry these articles. The mother carries other goods necessary to monastic life: soap, sheets, etc. A fanfare enlivens the procession. In urban centres today, i.e., Yangon, Mandalay, Taunggyi and Mawlamyine, it is more common for the child to travel in a motorized vehicle. A procession of cars led by a pickup truck on which the future novice is enthroned, moves at high speed through the streets of the capital. The fanfare is replaced by loud speakers on one of the vehicles.

When they arrive at the monastery, the parents and the boy are presented to the community. A monk is designated to shave the candidate's head, thus symbolizing dispossession and rupture with the boy's lay personality. While the shearing is taking place, the candidate must meditate on the ephemeral character (*anicca*) of existence and the non-attractiveness (*asubha*)[20] of the thirty-two parts of the body, the hair being one of these. Having asked for and received permission to join the order, the boy offers the community the articles every novice needs (*parikkhara*): a begging bowl, monastic robes, a belt, a razor, a pin and a seive. Next he asks the community to return these items to him and to confer initiation upon him. The boy then removes his royal robes, puts on the monastic robe and formally asks permission to enter the *samgha*; the request is repeated three times. If none of the members objects, the boy promises to follow the ten precepts and take refuge in the three jewels: Buddha, *dhamma* and *samgha*. A preceptor is named to supervise him. Finally, the newly admitted novice pays homage to the community as a whole. Thus the admission ceremony officially comes to an end.

To the foregoing are added a few important elements. In Buddhist societies, each of the three jewels commands a profound deference. To this inescapable threesome, Burmese culture adds parents and teachers.[21] While the child must always demonstrate unconditional reverence towards his parents, a role reversal follows the *shin pyu*; thereafter it is the parents who prostrate themselves before the novice, this individual who has just acquired a very new status, one well above that of his parents. In fact, the novice is no longer considered to be the son of his parents; he has become a son of the Buddha. Next comes the meal that takes place in silence and in great simplicity, even though the dishes are more refined and more numerous than for everyday fare.[22] After the meal, each guest returns home; the novice remains with the monks, within the confines of the monastery, until he decides to reintegrate into lay society.

The majority of admissions to the novitiate take place in April, during the Burmese new year (*thingyan*), at the end of the school year. This makes it possible to remain a novice until the beginning of the new academic year and thus not compromise on the school program. This is not a strict rule, since it is possible that a boy may want to remain a novice, sometimes even against the wishes of his parents.[23] It is equally important to stress that because the *shin pyu* and the consequent state of being a novice are considered to be highly meritorious, and that the novitiate is not perceived as an unpleasant experience, it often happens that the same individual has admitted himself into the monastic community more than once in his life.

We are of the opinion that the *shin pyu* ceremony has played a crucial role in maintaining the vitality of Buddhism in Burma.[24] We can envisage three reasons for this impact. First, the ceremony maintains and strengthens the societal links woven around the monastic community. Second, the *shin pyu* encourages each boy to have a personal experience of the monastic tradition. The novice thus comes to develop profound respect for a way of life that he will henceforth know to be arduous and worthy of homage. Third, and in our view most importantly, the *shin pyu* brings the hagiography of Siddhattha Gotama, the Buddha, to life. Carrying the candidate to the novitiate across the village on a palanquin, replays, by analogy, the renunciation scene of prince Siddhattha.[25] The symbolic presence of Siddhattha in the village reinvigorates the religious fervour of lay and monastic communities. In the hours that follow, this young man will renounce royalty,[26] symbolized by the clothes he wears, the parasol and the palanquin, to involve himself in a search that will bring him to the supreme awakening. This scene reminds us of a passage in the *Dhammapada*:

> Come, look at this world, adorned like a royal chariot;
> While it swallows up the ignorant, the wise are in no way attached to it.[27]

This symbolic staging of hagiographic passages from the life of Siddhattha Gotama is not the sole preserve of the *shin pyu*, far from it! As

Guy Ménard emphasizes, the purview of a rite is exactly to 're-present' the myth, to portray its gesture or setting (Ménard, 1999:75ff.). We find this *ritual* need in the majority of religious traditions.[28] The *shin pyu* allows every Burmese Buddhist family whose son joins the *samgha* to have among them, symbolically, the individual who has become a Buddha.

This presentation would not be complete without a brief discussion of the social functions of the young boys' ordination. Like Catholicism in Québec at the beginning of the century,[29] Burmese Buddhist monasticism played a significant role in the education of boys before 1885 when the colonial period began.[30] The Burmese term for monastery is the same as the one used for school (*kyaung*). The monastery was the village school; the young boy left the family home and became a novice in order to acquire the knowledge that would be useful to him in adult life. During his stay in the monastery, the young boy learned to read and write; he was also taught the doctrinal and practical foundations of his religion, the rudiments of the history of his country and sometimes, mathematics.[31] Obedience and respect for authority were also qualities acquired during a stay in the monastic environment. Burmese and Thai parents did not seem to want to take on the rough disciplinary function, preferring to leave it to the monks.[32] Some monasteries (*pwè-gyaùng*) with essentially intellectual vocations, took in monks and novices who wanted to deepen their studies. As N.R. Ray points out,[33] these monasteries were true university calibre institutions of learning; an analogy with certain medieval Christian monasteries could easily be drawn.

Before the installation of a non-confessional educational system by the British, the *kyaung* offered the same education to all boys, rich and poor, urban and rural. A parallel structure also seems to have existed for girls (Bagshawe, 1998:278). As Cady has noted, the monastic schools were important agents of social equalization: "The sons of princes and fishermen enjoyed the same status at the monastery, for entrance was open to all alike and all were subject to the same discipline" (cited by Spiro, 1970:326, n.). It was nevertheless true that the manpower needs of poor, often agrarian, families, could quickly shorten the education of a young boy. Equally, the same family's lack of food could force the endless lengthening of their child's 'education'.

When the British arrived in Burma, the education system took a totally different turn. On the one hand, the rural environment preserved their traditional Buddhist schools (*kyaung*) and a free education, monastic as well as secular,[34] was offered in the monasteries to all the novices.

Parallel to the *kyaung*, the first government-subsidized public school system was created, known as the national school or the Anglo-vernacular school. It was present in both rural and urban settings. In addition, the few urban centres saw the development of new educational structures; totally private, Christian schools, founded by European missionaries,[35] with only Western teachers, and semi-private schools, partially subsidized by the government, directed by Burmese, in which only Burmese taught.

In 1965, the private schools were nationalized. The entire school system had to respect the policies of the Revolutionary Council Government of the Union of Burma, except the *kyaung*, which belonged to the religious sphere. Burmese became henceforth the language of instruction and it was forbidden to teach in English.[36] Teachers' salaries, set by the government, barely covered subsistence needs; the number of disciplines taught in the schools was limited. The quality of education deteriorated quickly. At this point there emerged a parallel, underground, black market in education, designed to circumvent the constraints imposed by the government of the day.[37] We therefore find today a free national educational system, theoretically accessible to all,[38] an 'underground' educational system, accessible only to children from well-off families, and finally, the system of the *prahita*, replacing the *kyaung*, whose contemporary vocation, as we will see below, appears to be essentially humanitarian.

In Burmese monasteries today we find a double educational structure. On the one hand, religious education is present in all the monasteries. As we mentioned above, the novices in the monasteries learn specific Pali texts, *parittas*, or protective verses, meditation and all that constitutes the foundations of a monastic education.[39] Other monasteries, known as *prahita*, offer the same education for novices, while also offering a secular curriculum. The *prahita* teach two programmes: one follows the monastic curriculum and is for novices only; the other follows the government curriculum and is for novices, boys and girls. Today, lay people who attend the secular educational programme at the *prahita* are from poor families, unable to feed their children or to meet the subsidiary costs associated with the national public schools. Young girls cannot live in the monastery, since this is strictly a male establishment. Nevertheless, some *prahita* have built shelters beyond the confines of the monastery where girls can stay. Other monasteries take in lay people during the day, but they must bring their midday meal with them and return home in the evening. It is to be understood that the functioning of the *prahita* varies from one monastery to another. There are nevertheless a few elements that remain the same and are omnipresent. The *prahita* are absolutely free and school supplies are distributed to the students. The students must participate in the upkeep of the monasteries, which are generally in a pitiful state.

As an example, let us examine the Phaung Taw *prahita* on the outskirts of Mandalay. The place is relatively small. New construction has gone up on adjacent plots, which had formerly been garbage dumps. The classrooms are open spaces measuring 15 x 20 metres, covered by a roof. They can accommodate thirty to forty students, all seated on the ground in the traditional manner. Very few have a blackboard. The student body is made up of 200 novices and 1,750 lay students, the majority of them girls. The *prahita* has 30 teachers, only three of them monks, for the entire student body, yielding a ratio of one teacher for every 65 students. The young lay students bring their midday meal, and return home when the school day is over. All the subjects from the government curriculum are taught, which is to say Burmese, English, mathematics, applied sciences, geography and social sciences. By contrast with the majority of *prahita* that only offer the first five years of primary schooling, the Phaung Taw *prahita* teaches upto the eighth grade.

Less than two kilometres from this *prahita*, we find A Ye Mon, a similar structure, founded in 1948, but for girls exclusively. It plays the role more of an orphanage than of a monastery, since it is directed by a *silavin*, a woman endowed with a status similar to that of a monk but with significant differences, to which we will return shortly. The young girls who live there are orphans, or children whose families cannot support their subsistence or their education. They receive boarding and lodging there. The *silavin* teach them prayer and contemplation of the thirty-two parts of the body referred to earlier, but not the *pariyatti*, the study of Buddhist texts, since they are not authorized to do so. This establishment did not receive any government subsidies to begin with. Currently, the government provides rice for all the children, as well as a modest sum of 60 kyats per month per boarder, or the equivalent of about twenty US cents per month. As far as education is concerned, the girls travel by bus to different schools in the region of Mandalay, the neighbouring city. Transportation costs, school books and clothing are totally paid for by the orphanage, which subsists thanks to lay donations.

At present, young boys from well-to-do families rarely become novices in order to get an education, since better quality schooling is available in the public system. The contemporary functions of the novitiate are: (1) to make it possible for boys and their parents to acquire numerous merits, (2) to maintain and preserve a very important ancestral tradition and (3) to be initiated into the fundamentals of Buddhism. These aspects of tradition and of merits are found among poor families, but then they are often associated with financial motives as well.

The *shin pyu* ceremony is a ritual for all Burmese boys, but what about the young girls? Because the order of Buddhist nuns disappeared and has not been there for the past several centuries, it is impossible for a young girl to become a novice.[40] Nevertheless, a parallel order exists in the Theravada countries, within which women follow the ten Buddhist precepts and wear ochre, crimson or pink robes. These women are called *silavin* in Myanmar (*dasa sil matavo* in Sri Lanka; *Mae-chii* in Thailand). They live like nuns, even though they do not have the social status of monks.[41] Nevertheless, they have the advantage of not having to submit to the eight entrance conditions demanded of nuns, conditions which would make them dependant and submissive to male monastic authority. However, women who become *silavin* before marriage are rare.

Traditionally, young Burmese girls have their own rite of passage; *narthwin*, or ear piercing. This independent ceremony, even though it forms part of the *shin pyu* itinerary, takes place just before the boy goes to the temple. The young girl takes advantage of the propitious occasion created by her brother's *shin pyu* in order to have her ears pierced. This rite of passage does not necessarily imply that the young girl has reached marriageable age, but rather that henceforth she may 'dress like a woman.' It is nevertheless imperative that she accomplishes this rite of passage before she marries. It may happen that the date of a younger brother's *shin pyu* be advanced in order not to delay unduly his older sister's *narthwin*. By contrast with the *shin pyu*, the *narthwin* is an essentially social ritual, since no religious connotation is associated with it.

This article has attempted to show the importance of the *shin pyu* within Burmese tradition. Comparing the *shin pyu* with similar rituals in Cambodia, Thailand, Sri Lanka and Vietnam has led us to engage diverse themes, such as traditional (pre-colonial) and contemporary schooling within monastic institutions. We have noted that traditionally the monasteries (*kyaung*) in Burma and other Buddhist countries, offered all young boys a secular and religious education, encompassing the learning of reading, writing and sometimes arithmetic. Other, much more specialized monasteries (*pwè-gyaùng*) were true intellectual centres where diverse secular disciplines flourished; these were abolished between 1853 and 1878. Today, the monasteries continue to offer religious education for novices. Secular education has been moved into the public school system, set up at the beginning of the century. In addition, very few monasteries (*prahita*) look after the secular education of children from poor families. Finally, we have attempted to situate young Burmese girls with respect to the *shin pyu* ceremony. In doing so we also referred to the nuns in other Buddhist countries in order to draw cultural parallels.

Acknowledgement

I would like to thank the Barre Centre for Buddhist Studies, for offering me a propitious environment in which to write this article. This research was made possible with the help of Social Sciences and Humanities Research Council of Canada and of the Fonds du Conseil d' Aide a la Recherche of Quebec.

Notes

1. The country has changed names several times over the past sixty years. Prior to independence in 1948 it was called Burma, or British Burma because of its colonial status; from 1948 to 1974, the Union of Burma; from 1974 to 1988, the socialist republic of Burma; from 1988 until now, the Union of Myanmar. In this article, we will use the name that corresponds to the period being referred to.
2. Not "white elephant," as might be suggested by the expression "*hsin hpyu*," which is phonetically similar to the Western ear.
3. We find in the texts that regulate monastic life, in particular in Chapter 28 of the *Mahavagga*, the possibility that an individual might be ordained a monk without having been a novice; Chapter 30 of the same collection insists, however, on the necessity of having been previously admitted as a novice.
4. For more information on the characteristics of Buddhist monastic life, see the article by Boisvert, "Early forms of Buddhist and Christian Monasticism."
5. As Édith Parlier-Renault points out ["L'image de l'enfant" p. 24], a number of bas-reliefs from the Gandhara period(2nd to 7th centuries) show the Buddha himself inviting young boys to join the monastic order. These iconographic representations suggest that the Buddha was positioning himself against the Hindu prescriptions of the epoch.

6. The term *dvija* makes reference to the members of the first three Hindu social classes (*brahmana*, *kshatriya* and *vaisya*) who have access to initiation (*upanayana*) and to the sacred texts that constitute the *Vedas*; the fourth class (*shudra*) could neither read nor hear the sacred writings. The age for this initiation ceremony varies according to the class of the candidate: eight years for a *brahmana*, eleven years for a *kshatriya*, and twelve years for a *vaisya*.
7. V.I,79.
8. See also note 12.
9. Freely translated citation from the article by M.A. Martin, p. 319; it is odd that M.A. Martin specifies neither the author of this book, nor any bibliographic details.
10. In Cambodia, custom has it that the boy must be ordained twice before officially entering adult life. According to M.A. Martin, the first taking of the robes as a novice (*nên*), between seven and twelve years, aimed to acquire merit for the mother; the second ordination, as a monk (*phiku*), taking place not long before marriage, aimed to acquire merit for the father. [M.A. Martin, p. 316; see also Solange Bernard-Thierry, "Enfances khmères", p. 338]. In Thailand, the novitiate is a way of transferring merits to deceased parents or grandparents. [Tambiah, p.269–270]
11. It is interesting to note the animal hierarchy implicit in the apportioning of Burmese professions. In the Union of Myanmar, the raising (and slaughtering) of pigs is done almost exclusively by the Chinese (who generally are Confucians); of cows and sheep, by the Chinese and by Muslims (of Indian origins). The Buddhists can only be fishermen, since fish are an animal species inferior to mammals. Even though killing a fish is a lesser evil, this act still carries a heavy negative karmic charge (*akusala*).
12. We think, among others, of the *Vessantara Jataka*; this text tells the story of one of the previous lives of the *Bodhisatta*, where the future Buddha gradually sacrifices all his goods, his children, his wife, and even his own life in order to acquire the necessary merits that, in a future life, will allow him to become a Buddha. Prince Vessantara has become the very ideal of generosity (*dana*). The importance attributed to this text among laymen shows very well how they perceive the act of *dana*. On this subject, see the book by R. Gombrich and M. Cone, *The Perfect Generosity of Prince Vessantara*, Oxford: Oxford University Press, 1997.
13. V.I,82.

14. DhA.I;85 [see the translation, *Buddhist Legends* I, p. 195]. In fact, the text specifies that after this realisation, Gotama was ready to renounce the world. Returning to the palace, he heard the song of his cousin Kis_ Gotam_: "Happy [*nibbuta*] this mother, happy [*nibbuto*] this father; happy [*nibbuta*] indeed the wife of such a husband." It is, then, thanks to Kisa Gotami that he realised that happiness [*nibbutapada*] was to be found with his wife and son. It was only later, stretched out on the royal couch and disgusted by the bodies of the sleeping dancers in front of him, that Gotama decided to give up worldly life. A nuance. On the basis of the foregoing, Buddhists say that Rahula was the cause of Gotama's renunciation; after all, doesn't Rahula, mean "fetter"?
    An interesting play on words slips subtly into the text of the *Dhammapadatthakatha*. The term designating the family happiness [*nibbuta*] that Gotama becomes aware of shares the same root as the word *nibbana*; *nibbuta* designates the one who is satisfied, whose desire is fulfilled; it is used regularly to qualify individuals who have attained *nibbana*. One may well ask which happiness, or rather which nibbuta, the text is referring to.
15. See note 30.
16. The situation of women in Burma is privileged compared with that of women in neighbouring countries, notably India. Burmese women could engage in economic activity outside the family home, could dispose of their goods as they saw fit, could defend themselves, prosecute and even be head of the village. As Tilak said, Burmese society was characterized by "freedom of religion, education of women, late marriages, widow remarriage, a system of divorce",... (Ram Goppal, *Lokamanya Tilak*, New Delhi, 1956, pp. 220; cited by Aung San Suu Kyi, *Freedom from Fear*, p. 92.) See also Mimi Khaing, *The World of Burmese Women*, and Marie-Hélene Cardinaud, "Femmes et contes en Birmanie", in *Études birmanes en hommage à Denise Bernot*, p. 385.
17. *Mangalasutta, Sn*.II,4.
18. In Cambodia, during funeral ceremonies, the son would often become a novice at the cremation site in order that the dead person benefit from the merits of this act. [Solange Bernard-Thierry, p. 338] This practice does not appear to be present in the Union of Myanmar.
19. Spiro gives a detailed description of the *shin pyu* [pp. 234–247]; we are therefore limiting our discussions to selected points that we judge to be important. This being said, we note important differences between Spiro's descriptions and our observations. A number of reasons could be put forward; let us simply mention that his field study took place almost

forty years ago, and that the ceremonies that he observed seem all to have been carried out in relatively wealthy settings. Ours come mainly from relatively poor, rural environments. Most of our data were gathered in Tihanshwe, on the outskirts of Taunggyi (Shan state); we have also gathered information based on ceremonies observed in the two main cities, Yangon et Mandalay.

20. For further information on the meditative practice of "non-attractiveness," see the Boisvert's article, "*Maranasati*".

21. [The Three Jewels] "were transformed into an authoritarian framework of total deference and obedience by adding the two other secular personalities of parents and teachers. In fact, these five authorities are considered to be five omnipotent and supreme objects of veneration equal in status and rank, although it is not certain that Buddha himself had mandated this ranking". [Mya Maung, *The Burma Road to Poverty*, p. 12–13].We note a similar attitude in Sri Lanka, where the children "adore" the feet of their parents. As Elizabeth Bopearachchi points out, "Les deux stances que l'on récite pour honorer ses parents sont les premières récitations qu'apprend l'enfant. En disant 'j'adore les pieds de ma mère', il récite *matu padan namami*' [sic], en disant 'j'adore les pieds de mon père', il récite *pitu padan namami* [sic]. Les enfants adorent les pieds de leurs parents en posant leur tête sur leurs mains jointes posées sur le sol." [*L'Éducation bouddhique*, p. 237].

22. Spiro mentions that the meal for monks and guests takes place before the *shin pyu* ceremony; however, in the *shin pyu* ceremonies that we observed, the meal always came after. [Spiro, p. 239].

23. Several years in the monastery can, in the contemporary context, endanger normal progress in secular education.

24. We do not contest Spiro's data [p.284]. They demonstrate a clear decline in the number of monks and novices in the Burmese tradition. We are nevertheless of the opinion that the *shin pyu* is one among numerous factors, among them of course government policy, that have considerably attenuated the decline of the tradition.

25. Before his renunciation, Gotama did a "tour of the town" during which he witnessed the four sights that incited him to leave worldly life: old age, sickness, death and finally, an ascetic.

26. E.M. Mendelson is rather of the opinion that this association with the symbols of monarchy demonstrates that the initiation is not an activity that helps the individual integrate into the society, but rather one that allows him to exclude himself, temporarily, from the norms of reciprocity, from the omnipresent exchange, that social life implies.

According to Mendelson, the king constantly commits crimes against the rules of reciprocity. The Buddhist novice would then be in a sphere of anti-reciprocity, as for example when his parents come to pay hommage to him after his admission. ["Initiation and the paradox of power".]

Since Buddhist tradition represents the gift of the dhamma (*dhammadana*) as the most important, one can, contrary to Mendelson's thesis, see the teaching monk as being always active in the system of exchange. At the same time, from a purely Buddhist perspective, the monk must also be above all forms of karmic exchange: even though he receives, he must not derive any pleasure from it; even though he can give, he must do it without waiting for anything in return. From a theoretical and purely karmic perspective, Mendelson's argument prevails; in practice, it is another thing.

27. Freely translated by the author. [Dh.xiii,5]
28. Take for example the Christian Eucharist that re-plays the Last Supper. Or the Jain collective pilgrimages (*tirthayatra*) in which couple who are the primary sponsors of the journey, at the moment of reaching the pilgrimage destination, is placed on a superb chariot in the heart of the procession. For the assembled pilgrims, this man and this woman represent the parents of the *Tirthankara*. The group pilgrimage is possible thanks to the gifts given by these two individuals, just like reaching liberation for the Jain hero was possible thanks to the parents who brought him into the world. [The term *tirthankara* is the attribute Mahavira, founder of Jainism. It means "maker of the ford," the bridge that links the riverbank of *samsara* to the farther shore of liberation.]
29. Without going back so far into the past, we might mention that the confessional status of the school boards on the Island of Montreal was only withdrawn in 1997.
30. We note as well that in Cambodia the monastery schools practically wiped out illiteracy [Solange Bernard-Thierry, p. 339]
31. Mimi Khaing, p.2. Monasteries that put the emphasis on secular rather than religious education were known by the name of *lawkatat*. In rural Thailand, such monastic establishments were practically the only place for schooling before the 1960s [Cf. Annick Lévy-Ward, p.228]; the same phenomenon was present in Cambodia, but only up until the establishment of the French protectorate [Solange Bernard-Thierry, p.339].
32. Mimi Khaing specifies that the Burmese parents "whose hearts suffered too much at the thought of inflicting any punishment themselves now handed them [the children] over to the monks with the plea that they

would teach them to be good and obedient, and chastise them severely if they did not obey" [*Burmese Family*, p.2]. A.W. Graham notes that the Thai child also installs very early " un régime de tyrannie dans la maison. Sa mère, son père et les autres membres de la famille sont tous ses humbles esclaves, son moindre désir est une loi et il est gâté et choyé par tous les visiteurs" [*Siam: A Handbook of Practical, Commercial and Political Information*, London: A. Moring Ltd. 1912, p. 149--150; cited and translated by Annick Lévy-Ward, p. 227.]

33. "[T]here in the darkness and solitude of the library hall of the monastery generations of monks strove hard, day in and day out, to master the sacred texts of their religion and other works most suited to their lines of study. No subject was too unworthy for their pursuit and attention; and though naturally Buddhism in all its various aspects and branches demanded the most serious and careful attention, subjects like grammar, logic, medicine, astrology, astronomy, philosophy, polity, law, prosody, metres and even military science claimed their time and labour, grammar of course being one of the most important and favourite." N.R. Ray, *An Introduction to the Study of Theravada Buddhism in Burma*, p. 259. Unfortunately, these monasteries oriented towards the secular and intellectual were abolished under the reign of King Mindon [1853--1878].
34. Secular education was confined to learning to read, to write and to do mathematics, the traditional "3 Rs".
35. This kind of school began not long before the start of the official colonisation of Burma. On this subject see the article by L.E. Bagshawe in which he discusses, among others, the vain attempt of the East-India Company to use the *kyaung* to promote the kind of education the British wanted, i.e. to train manpower for the East-India Company.
36. It was only in 1980 that English was once again allowed to be taught in the public schools, and used as a medium of instruction.
37. For more details on the Burmese educational system, colonial and post-colonial, see the article by U Kaung, "A Survey of the History of Education in Burma before the British Conquest and After;" see also Mya Maung (1991), pp. 37--38, 106 and 181--188.
38. Nevertheless, supplementary costs associated with schooling, including books, uniforms, transportation, etc., prevent some children from attending public schools.
39. M. Spiro describes in detail the monastic education that still takes place within the monasteries [p. 360--361]. During our observations in a monastery in Taunggyi we noticed, contrary to Spiro's observations, that discipline and motivation were definitely present among the young novices.

40. The order of nuns cannot be re-established because in order to ordain new nuns, a quorum of five monks and five nuns is necessary, and there are no more nuns... For more information on the situation of women in Therav_da Buddhist monasticism, see Mohan Wijayaratna, *Les Moniales bouddhistes*; Tissa Bartholomeusz, "The Female mendicant in Buddhist Sri Lanka" and Ingrid Jord, "Bhikkhuni, Thilashin, Mae-chii: Women who renounce the world in Burma, Thailand and the Classical Pali Buddhist Texts".
41. By citing J. Crawford ("The profession of a nun is not much respected by the people, and in general may be looked upon as little better than a more reputable mode of begging" [Spiro p. 290, n.]), Spiro highlights the intense dichotomy between the status of monk and that of nun [*silavin* ?]. We are of the opinion that *silavin* is much more highly respected by the Burmese population than Spiro suggests. The simple fact that the "monasteries" that they live in are entirely supported by lay donations is revealing. Further, some, although very few, have received the highly honorific academic title of *dhammacariya*.

References

Aubin, F. (1975) Le Statut de l'enfant dans la société mongole, in J. Brodin (Ed.) *L'Enfant. Recueils de la Société*, pp. 459--599 (Bruxelles, Éditions de la Librairie encyclopédique).

Aung San Suu Kyi.(1995 [1991]) *Freedom from Fear* (New York, Penguin Books).

Bagshawe, L.E. (1998) The 'Moral and intellectual improvement of the people'; Western education in Burma to 1880, in P. Pichard and F. Robinne (Eds) *Études birmanes en hommage à Denise Bernot*, pp. 269--286 (Paris, École Française d'Extrême-Orient).

Bartholomeusz, T.. (1992) The Female mendicant in Buddhist Sri Lanka, in J.I. Cabezon (Ed.), *Buddhism, Sexuality and Gender*, pp. 37--61 (Albany, SUNY).

Bernard-Thierry, S. (1997) Enfances khmères d'hier et d'aujourd'hui, in F. Blanchon (Ed.) *Enfances, Asie IV*, C.R.E.O.P.S., pp.337--344 (Paris, Presses de l'Université de Paris-Sorbonne).

Bernot, D. & Pasquet, S. (1991) Les bonzillons: deux petits Birmans au monastère, *Cahiers de l'Asie du Sud-Est 29*, (Paris: INALCO) pp. 111--132.

Boisvert, M. (2000) "Early forms of Buddhist and Christian Monasticism", in W. Johnston (Ed.), *Encyclopedia of Monasticism* (Chicago, Fitzroy Dearborn Publishers).

Boisvert, M. (June 1996) *Maranasati*: Textutal Interpretation and Contemporary Practice, *Buddhist Studies Review*, Vol.13/1, London, pp. 37--54.

Bopearachchi, E. (1994) *L'Éducation bouddhique dans la société traditionnelle du Sri Lanka*, (Paris, L'Harmattan).

Buddhist Legends. (1979 [1921]) Translated from the original Pali text of the Dhammapada commentary by E.W. Burlingame, 3 Vols, (London: Pali Text Society).

Cardinaud, M.-H..(1998) Femmes et contes en Birmanie, in *Études birmanes en hommage à Denise Bernot*, P. Pichard and F. Robinne (Eds), pp. 385–391 (Paris, École Française d'Extrême-Orient).

Hla Maung (No publication date) *My Early Monastic Education* (Yangon: International Institute of Advanced Buddhistic Studies).

Htun Hmat Win, S. (1986) *The Initiation of Novicehood and the Ordination of Monkhood in the Burmese Buddhist Culture* (Yangon, Department of Religious Affairs).

The Jataka or The Stories of the Buddha's Former Births (1981) E.B. Cowel (Ed.), Vol. I-VI, (London, Pali Text Society).

Jord, I. (1988) Bhikkhuni, Thilashin, Mae-chii: Women who renounce the world in Burma, Thailand and the Classical Pali Buddhist Text, in *Crossroads 4--1, Special Burma Studies Issue*, pp. 31--39.(De Kalb: Northern Illinois University).

Kaung, U. (December 1963) A Survey of the History of Education in Burma before the British Conquest and After, *Journal of the Burma Research Society* (Yangon), Vol. XLVI/2.

Khaing, M. (1996 [1946]) *Burmese Family* (Bangkok, Ava House).

Khaing, M. (1984) *The World of Burmese Women* (London: Zed Books).

Lévy-Ward, A.. (1997) 'Trois jours, l'enfant des esprits, quatre jours, un être humain'; les rituels de naissance et d'enfance en Thaïlande, in F. Blanchon (Ed.) *Enfances, Asie IV*, C.R.E.O.P.S., pp. 217–233 (Paris: Presses de l'Université de Paris-Sorbonne).

Martin, M-A. (1997) *Les Enfants au Cambodge: de la tradition à la modernité*, in F. Blanchon (Ed.), Enfances, Asie IV, C.R.E.O.P.S., pp. 310--335 (Paris: Presses de l'Université de Paris-Sorbonne).

Maung, M. (1991) *The Burma Road to Poverty* (New York: Prawger).

Maung, M. (1998) *The Burma Road to Capitalism* (New York: Prawger).

Ménard, G. (1999) *Le Petit traité de la vraie religion* (Montréal: Liber).

Mendelson, E.M. (1965) Initiation and the paradox of power; a sociological approach, in C.J. Bleeker (Ed.), *Initiation: Contributions to the Theme of the Study-Conference of the International Association for the History of Religions Held at Strasburg*, September 17th to 22nd 1964, pp. 214–221 (Leiden, E.J. Brill).

Parlier-Renault, É. (1997) L'image de l'enfant dans l'art bouddhique de l'Inde, in F. Blanchon (Ed.) *Enfances, Asie* IV, C.R.E.O.P.S., pp. 311–336 (Paris, Presses de l'Université de Paris-Sorbonne).

Ray, N. R. (1946) *An Introduction to the Study of Theravada Buddhism in Burma*, (Calcutta, Calcutta University Press).

Spiro, M. E. (1970) *Buddhism and Society; A Great Tradition and its Burmese Vicissitudes* (New York: Harper & Row).

Tambiah, S. J. (1976) *World Conqueror and World Renouncer; A Study of Buddhism and Polity in Thailand against a Historical Background*, (Cambridge, Cambridge University Press).

Wijayaratna, M. (1991) *Les Moniales bouddhistes; naissance et développement du monachisme féminin* (Paris, Cerf).

6

Hinduism and Tribal Religion: An Anthropological Perspective on Interaction*

K.S. Singh

This paper intends to explore the relationship of Hinduism and tribal religion. It critically examines the view of the orientalists and anthropologists who described tribal religion in terms of a set of primitive values surviving in Hindu religion, the inevitability of tribal religion being swallowed up by Brahmanism, etc. Nothing of the kind has happened. Tribal religion retains a great deal of internal autonomy in spite of tribals having embraced Hinduism or Christianity. There are many aspects of the relationship of tribes with the Hindu shrines, with Jagannath or Danteshwari cults, of various modes of worship and perceptions, shamanism, and interaction of male and female spirits. Tribal religion is no longer identified with animism, but is seen as part of the wider culture and society of the tribal people which is rich, positive, harmonious and autonomous, with a very healthy set of relationships with natural environment. Finally, the paper discusses the process of revivalism in tribal societies, a strong urge on the part of tribespeople to return to the roots. Recent trends in some parts of the country suggest the resurgence of pristine elements of tribal religion by those who have gone

* This is the revised version of a paper presented at a seminar on "Historical and Contemporary Character of Hinduism" at the Nehru Memorial Museum and Library, New Delhi, May 19–23, 1986.

out of its field. At the same time, we also witness that both Hinduism and Christianity have endeavoured to tribalize themselves.

I

Many years ago, I had visited a little-known village Diuri, tucked away in a remote part of Ranchi (Jharkhand) to see a temple that housed a Hindu deity, Mahishasura Mardini, but was worshipped by a tribal. The temple looked old enough to have belonged to the later medieval period, constructed in the Shikhar style, and the village looked like a relic of an ashram with thatched roofs all around, even though it was entirely populated by tribals. A tribal acting as a priest to an evidently Hindu deity is a fact that continues to surprise anthropologists even today. For me it appeared to be part of the process of penetration of classical forms of Hinduism such as Vaishnavism and Shaktism, along the two rivers Suvarna Rekha and Shankha—the names are suggestive indeed! Later I was to discover many such temples along the banks of the two rivers which formed the subject of a paper written in 1961.[1] Place names such as Gopivallabhpur and Nandanagaon lent support to the theory of Vaishnava influence in the area, which weakened but did not disappear altogether. Twenty-one years later, I visited the village again[2]. By this time it had turned into a bustling centre of pilgrimage connected by a national highway, and the shrine attracted hordes of politicians, businessmen and bureaucrats, all eager to propitiate Shakti. On the face of it, all of this looked like part of the revival of Shakti worship centreing around the Tantra Peethas located and rediscovered at places as far apart as Rajarappa, Danteshwari and so on. Revival of Shakti worship again appears to be part of the larger process of the scramble for power, of the commercialization of values and the search for Lakshmi, which marks the post-Independence phase of our national life. But what was important in this case was the fact that the tribal who acted as priest to a deity which was Hindu did not raise any eyebrows at all. In fact, his status as a priest was accepted by all concerned. Over the past few years, a mass of material has been collected on similar phenomena, noticed by me[3] as early as in the 1960s, which have now been encountered all over middle India, in the south, part of the north-east, etc., a critical analysis of which will help us understand various facets of the relationship of the Hindu and tribal religions.

In this paper, we start with the definition of the two religions as given in the census and other official literature although it is not free from difficulties. We further propose to examine their relationships in terms of the existing hypotheses of the orientalists and anthropologists, its various facets, the current trends highlighted by anthropological researches and so on.

II

Though it might look a little odd we would like to begin with Nirad C. Choudhuri's observation on the non-existence of any relationship between Hinduism and aboriginal religion. In his book on Hinduism, which is widely read, he says:

> There has grown up a definite school of historians of Hinduism, especially at the popular level, which regards the full-grown religion as the product of an interaction between the Indo-European religion of the coming Aryans and the religion of the aboriginals of the country...I am convinced no such interaction ever took place...no scrap of evidence exists to prove the existence of any kind of developed religion among the aboriginals of India... Yet, the myth of aboriginal influences still dogs the history of Hinduism[4].

Nirad Babu then goes on to describe human sacrifice and phallicism as the features of the religion of Indo-European peoples. The cults of Shiva and Durga were, according to him, not borrowings in some of their aspects from aborigines but imported from outside. Nirad Babu is obviously not aware of the mass of ethnographical and anthropological evidence on the interaction at the grass-roots level of what we call tribal and Hindu religions, which has been generated by researches in recent years. This goes to show how the communities known as tribals today have contributed a great deal to what is known as the local forms of Hinduism. The ethnographers identified their contributions in terms of the primitive concept of taboo, *mana* and soul substance, ancestor worship, and the corpus of rituals and customs *(Lokachara* and *deshachara)* shared by the tribals and non-tribals.

However, it should be noted that what orientalists and anthropologists described as tribal religion in their works or as survival of primitive elements in Hindu religion as they discovered it in the 19th and early 20th century, has many ingredients which do not belong to the religion of the present-day tribals. They seem to have probably belonged to the communities which have ceased to be tribals today. Many of the elements described as tribal or aboriginal, particularly those belonging to the Tantra traditions had already been absorbed into the great traditions, both Buddhist and Brahmanical. Not only had the Tantra works been written down in Sanskrit language but the Tantra deities, icons, symbols and rituals had become part of the great traditions. This process was probably complete by the early medieval period. The ferocious tribal deities had been tamed[5]. However, the echo of the orientalists' perception of the aboriginal religion still survives. In a study of Hinduism of tribal deities of Orissa, there is a mention of Durga, etc., as being of tribal origin[6]. However, the evidence of present-day gods and goddesses of the contemporary tribal people being Hinduized is not very strong. The Mundas' Sing-Bonga or the Oraons' Dharmesh or the Gonds' Burha Deo remain as tribal as ever, in spite of valiant attempts being made to link them to sun worship or some gods of Hindu pantheon. The question arises, has the process of Hinduization stopped and if so what are the reasons thereof or whether the process was itself not adequately understood?

Probably the most influential formulation on the relationship of Hindu and tribal religion came from Sir Alfred Lyall, which held the ground for well over eighty years. According to his views, spelt out in a series of papers which may be described as torrents of eloquence, he argued that Brahmanism was in full tide and that it was only a matter of time before it swallowed up primitive religion. Brahmanism, according to him, was a proselytizing religion particularly in relation to the tribal people.

"...If by Brahmanism we understand that religion of the Hindus which refers for its orthodoxy to Brahmanic scriptures and traditions, which adores the Brahmanic gods and their incarnations, venerates the cow, observes certain rules of intermarriage and the sharing of food, and which regards the Brahman's presence as necessary to all essential rites, then this religion can hardly be called non-missionary in the sense of stagnation and exclusive immobility, because it still proselytizes in two very effective modes.

"The first of these modes is the gradual Brahmanising of the aboriginal, non-Aryan, or casteless tribes. The clans and races which inhabit the hill tracts, the outlying uplands and the uncleared jungle districts of India, are melting into Hinduism all over India by a process much more rapid and effective than individual conversions. Among all these aboriginal or non-Aryan communities, a continued social change is going on; they alter their modes of life to suit improved conditions of existence; their languages decay and they gradually go over to the dominant Aryan rituals. They pass into Brahmanists by a natural upward transition, which leads them to adopt the religion of the castes immediately above them in the social scale of the composite population among which they settle down. And we may reasonably guess that this process has been working for centuries though it is likely to have been much more rapid than ever under British rule. The 'ethical frontier' described in the *Annals of Rural Bengal* is an everbreaking shore of primitive beliefs which tumble constantly into the ocean of Brahmanism".[7]

From this point Lyall proceeds to construct a typology of assimilation of tribes into the great Hindu community as caste or sub-caste through the mediation of Brahmanism.

"Thus Brahmanism is all over India a necessary first stage for the outlying tribes towards Indian civilization, or admission to the citizenship of the great Hindu community; it very rarely implies any ethical change, or even a formal abandonment of one ritual for another, it is usually a rapid sliding into Hindu customs and an attempt at social assimilation. But the complete process does necessitate a considerable change of worship and ways of life, for perhaps the surest sign of a family's reception into Brahmanism is that whereas the Brahman formerly was never called in, he is latterly found officiating at domestic epochs and ceremonies, of birth, marriage, or death. This implies conformity to Brahmanic rules of eating, intermarriages, and the like, and the evolution of a caste or subcaste"[8].

It should be noted that Sir Alfred's polemics against Brahmanism was part of a debate on whether or not Brahmanism was a proselytizing religion which in turn would justify a similar role for Christianity in India. It also represented a typical 19th century view of the processes of assimilation then described as Brahmanization or Hinduization which by present-day researches seemed rather simplistic. In fact, the process of social mobility described as sanskritization has been found out to be a more complex process today in its cultural and structural aspects. There are also non and anti-Brahmanical aspects of it. Nevertheless, Sir Alfred's ideas were seminal and were picked up and explored in regional situations by ethnographers. For example while the Kadars' religion was described as a form of rude animism, their assimilation into the Hindu system of belief was noted. "For all this, the Kadars, if questioned about their religion will reply that they are Hindus and will talk vaguely about their Hindu gods (Parameswar-Vishnu) as if they live in the very odour of orthodoxy, instead of being in fact wholly outside the sphere of the Brahmanical system. To talk about Hindu gods is usually the first step towards that insensible adoption of the externals of Hinduism which takes the place of formal and open conversion which sterner and less adoptive creeds demand."[9]

Within the framework of the ideas enunciated by Lyall, J. H. Hutton, a professional anthropologist, was probably the first to have reconstructed tribal religion as an integrated whole. He is credited rightly with having rescued tribal religion from the waste paper basket of animism, and identified the parameters of its autonomy and the range of its linkages with Hinduism. However, like other census officials he too was prone to describing tribal religion as the "surplus material not yet built into the temple of Hinduism"[10] and to highlighting the process of the tribes being swallowed up by this religion. In 1931, of the total number of tribes estimated at 24.6 million, 8.28 million, i.e., only about one-third, was returned as adhering to tribal religions. The majority of the tribals was Hindu; there were also Christians; a growing number was made up of Buddhists and Muslims. This Hinduization of tribes was ascribed to three factors, namely, (a) the energetic propaganda by the Hindu Mahasabha to return as Hindu every person whose religion could not be found to have originated outside India, that is, practically everyone except Muslim, Christians, Parsis and Jews, (b) agitations by such tribes as Gonds and Oraons to be returned as Hindu and (c) action of the overzealous enumerators mostly Hindus, particularly in the north-east at work among Khasis, Kachari and Miris. While this process of returning tribals as Hindus or Hinduized, which continued to be reported over subsequent censuses could be related to some of the above mentioned factors, the Hindu Mahasabha was given an importance by Hutton that it did not deserve. W. G. Archer also blamed the Hindu enumerators for returning tribals as Hindus and pointed out that the census questionnaire was even skewed to achieve this. The arms of the colonial administration were long enough to have contained these biases, but why was this not done? Was this because the census enumerators were only recording a process?

There were other factors behind this process of Hinduization too, of which the census authorities were only dimly aware, namely, the transformation of the tribe into the peasant as a result of the transfer of technology and the acceptance of *jati* mores. Hutton mentions a Korwa telling the census superintendent of the Central Provinces, "If we had plough cattle, we would be Hindus".[11] Hutton did not elaborate on the economic dimension of the process, and instead chose to attribute it to the difficulty of defining Hinduism with its great latitude of religious beliefs and practices, which "makes it possible for a Hindu socially to have a religious belief shared with others who do not regard themselves as members of the same society." It was really not wholly so. The economic dimensions which did not fall within the ambit of the census authorities to explore was as important, if not more, than the social. These trends have persisted since then. Even though the census data on tribal religion have never been exactly comparable, the number of tribals following their religion declined by 33 per cent between 1921 and 1931. It declined from roughly one-third (8.2 million) of the tribal people in 1931 to about 6 per cent in 1981, with Hinduism claiming 87 per cent and Christianity 7 per cent of adherents among these tribals.

Even so, Hutton and those who have written about this subject seem to have underestimated the autonomy of tribal society and particularly of its religion. In spite of the tribal returning themselves overwhelmingly as Hindus or Christians, tribal religions have not disappeared, as feared, even though the censuses continue to return most of the tribes as Hindus or Christians. Many elements of tribal religion are as alive, even vibrant, as ever. As studies have recently shown, tribal religion has not lost its distinct identity in spite of its long years of interaction with Hinduism and Christianity.[12] It has maintained its system of beliefs and practices including propitiation of spirits, and reliance on magic and witchcraft, its priesthood and its calendar of fairs and festivals which reinforce the tribals' sense of solidarity. Recent trends even suggest the revival of many of pristine elements of tribal religion by those who have gone out of its fold. Therefore, the assumption that the survival of tribal religion is at stake needs to be reconsidered.

III

As I mentioned above, more evidence has come in on the relationship of the tribes with Hindu shrines. Lord Venkateshwar of Tirupati, the richest of the Hindu shrines in the world is associated with the Kuruba and Lambadi tribes. The earliest texts refer to the Kuruba as hunters and food-gatherers who guided pilgrims, beating drums to scare animals, to the shrine situated across the seven hills. One of them refers to the deity standing on the deforested plot of land, tall and visible from all sides. The Kurubas also participated in many a ritual. The Lambadis, a nomadic tribal group are mentioned as worshipping Balaji as their family deity as early as the 13th century.[13]

Yet another form of relationship is suggested by the delightful stories current among many communities in the South, of gods making love to rural belles and taking them as consorts. The Soliga living in the Biligiri Rangana mountain range of Karnataka regard the local Vaishnav deity

Rangaswamy as a brother-in-law. Was this a Brahmanical device of converting the Soliga tribe to Shri Venkateshwara faith? Was it one of the ways of involving the Soliga in the non-priestly roles performed at the shrine? The story is too sweet to be ignored.

"Long ago there lived one Bomme Gouda, a headman of the Soliga who had seven daughters. The youngest was Kusumale with very beautiful long curly hair [tresses like these could still be seen among these people]. Vaishnava god Rangaswamy, who is the presiding deity of the area, while wandering about in the forest saw the Soliga girl, fell in love with her and desired her to be his consort. The Soligas collect roots and tubers in the forest. So one day, the god created an illusion *(maya)* making night look like daybreak which was the time for Kusumale to go out for collection of roots. That day Kusumale collected heaps of roots, which was not usually available in such large quantities. She was happy to collect them but could not carry them on her head. She looked for help and found a very old man with an emaciated body and decided to seek his help. The old man, none other than the god Rangaswamy himself, said he would help her on the condition that she married him. Kusumale asked how she could marry him when he looked like her grandfather with his age and condition of the body. The god persisted and she finally yielded. She was happy to carry the roots to her house even though she had to accept unwillingly the old man as her husband. When she reached home, her father scolded her for having accepted an old man that too from outside the community as a husband. He told both of them to go away. The god then took her away. When followed by the girl's father the god paid him a winnowful of gold coins and disappeared."[14]

There are many elements in this story which fit into the Soliga social structure. They have a system of marriage by elopement or marriage without performing rituals. The Soliga say that when the god himself did not observe any ritual for marriage, why should they? They also perform some roles in the temple of Biligiri Rangana mountain. They pull the car *(rathotsava)* and float *(teppa)*. The Soliga have to offer 'free' *(bitti)* service and though they are given articles of food like ragi, salt, oil, pulses, etc. The duties they perform cover carrying the deputies *(utsava murthi)* of Rangaswamy and his consorts, arranging for decoration at thoroughfares where the car (*rath*) is taken out in procession and performing all works outside the temple. They are treated with much respect by the Brahman priest and are allowed to enter the shrine at all times. After all who can prevent them from visiting their brother-in-law ? A seal of the god with his consort (who is not the tribal woman, Kussumale) is given to the Soliga who settle all disputes in their community in the presence of this seal (*mundre*). Some Soliga observe fast on Saturday as this day is sacred to the god. Rangaswamy is also the family god of many castes and communities living in the adjoining plains who throng in large number to the shrine during festivals.

The Chenchus, also a tribe , living in the northern part of the Nallamalai hills adopted Shaivism in the middle ages and regarded Shiva (Srisaila Mallikarjuna) of Srisailam temple, as their brother-in-law (Chenchu Mallanna). Shiva is described differently as moody, a maverick, "a god of the mountains, of hunters, forest people, robbers and those whose dwelling place is the cremation (or burial) ground." They were assigned special duties in service of Srisailam temple and endowments were made to them, which surprised even an anthropologist. When Vaishnavism came to their land, they adopted it and made Narasimha their brother-in-law. A delightful Chenchu myth is also worth mentioning here. According to this myth, sung by bards, "Narasimha, a stranger wanders into the Nallamalai forest around Ahobilam which was the domain of a Chenchu chieftain. Here he encounters a Chenchu belle, the daughter of the Chenchu chieftain,while she was hunting. They fall in love and the Chenchu girl seeks the consent of her father for their marriage. As Narasimha was a stranger to them and to their land the chieftain wants to first ascertain whether or not Narasimha would be a suitable husband to his daughter. Narasimha was made to demonstrate his abilities in collecting honey by climbing precipices and trees, in gathering queen termites (*putta junnu*) by digging up termite mounds and his prowess as a hunter. Narasimha accomplishes these tasks to the satisfaction of the chieftain and wins the hand of his daughter. There are beautiful sculptural representations at Ahobilam, Srisailam and several other temples in Andhra depicting this myth. In one panel, the Chenchu girl, wearing a leaf skirt with a bow and an arrow is shown as a huntress. In another, she leans on her bow as if a thorn was in her foot and Narasimha, a tiny figure, is shown removing the thorn. Chenchus of Ahobilam region consider Narasimha as their brother-in-law and they have a special right to enter the Ahobilam temple which has become purely Brahmanical now. We are further told about a Chenchu myth , a puranic version of the Laxmi-Narasimha myth. "God Vishnu takes the man-lion incarnation (Narasimha Avtar) to exterminate Hiranyakasipu, a demon (*rakshasa*). After killing the demon, and still in a fit of rage, he wanders into the forest. He comes across a Chenchu belle (the daughter of the chieftain) in the forest and his anger cools down and he follows her, thinking that she is his consort Laxmi, into the Chenchu's garden. He soon realizes that she is a Chenchu girl, but still marries her with the consent of her father and takes her to his heavenly abode." The root paradigm of the folk and puranic myths is the same, but what is important is that Narasimha in the folk tradition not only exists in the human plane but is also subjected to a series of tests to be accepted as a worthy husband to the Chenchu girl.[15]

Contemporary studies on the relationship of tribals with Hinduism have highlighted yet another form of association. The masterly study of Jagannath cult raises more issues than it answers.[16] Jagannath is crafted in wood. Wood as a medium is widely used by the Mundari groups of tribal people. The Mundas have their god, Marang Buru, in wood. Some of them also call Jagannath their Marang Buru. Wooden memorial pillars are a common site in the Munda and Savara countries. Jagannath was discovered by the Savara community and is described as a Savara deity. The Savara have a role in his worship. But there is still a more important question. Jagannath as an unusual deity Krishna and Balaram are on best of terms. Subhadra was a dear sister but had been given away in marriage to Arjun and no longer belonged to their lineage. Evidence has it that Jagannath was not a trinity in the beginning. There are historical references to only one god. What does the trinity represent then? Balaram has actually been associated with Nagas. The Nagas existed and Naga cult prevailed in coastal regions of Orissa and beyond. Subhadra could represent the mother goddess widely prevalent in Orissa (Bhubaneshwari, Sambaleshwari, etc.). The trinity could as well represent the amalgam of the three cults in Orissa.

Much has been written on how Jagannath cult was used to consolidating the political authority of a particular lineage and identified with the rise of Oriya nationalism. Danteshwari in Bastar performed a similar role. The Kakatiya chief came to Bastar in response to the prayer of the people, with the goddess Danteshwari, and went from village to village and was identified with the local deity 'Mauli' and emerged as the apex deity for Bastar. Later Danteshwari was installed at Jagdalpur where she is worshipped by the Oriya priests. There are two perceptions of Danteshwari: one, Danteshwari as Mauli and, second, Danteshwari as the apex deity at Dantewara with Bastar Raja as her representative. This explains the close ties between ruler and tribes. At another level, Danteshwari is also Kali and Mahadurga, twin faces of Maheshaki, worshipped by an Oriya and a Bhatra tribal priest Dantewara is a typical tantra peetha located at the confluence of the two rivers, Sankani and Dankini, one falling into the other. One thing that emerges clearly from the analysis of Danteshwari worship is that different perceptions of the deity coexist[17]. Chamundeshwari at Mysore is yet another example.[18]

In a study of village cults of western Bengal we are told how the village deities have evolved through history, from ordinary, isolated folk deities to the deities of Hindu pantheon, from belonging to a particular caste to belonging to all, and from recipients of simple offerings to objects of complex, modernized celebrations.[19] Dharamraj is a case in point. Originally, the deity of Dom caste, he has emerged as a village, even a regional deity, performing a role and function in relation to larger communities. Again, the interesting point is that perception and worship of these deities among various communities are different, which reflect hierarchy, differentiation and contradictions that exist in rural society. For example, the so-called low and high castes perform rituals differently and look at the deities differently. There are both *shastric* and *lokachara* rituals performed during the worship of the same deity, at different points of time, by different people. Then again, Kali at one point is a folk deity worshipped like any other folk deity by the 'lower caste people'; at another level she is a sanskritized deity worshipped by high castes. Yet another important point is that in spite of the growing influence of Brahmanism or Hinduism or sanskritization of folk deities mediated by the local Brahmans, a great deal of non-Brahmanical rituals and perceptions continue to survive. Both milk and rice beer are offered to deities. *Yajna* and shamanism coexist. Indigenous traditions have not been wiped out. There is a clear recognition of distinct roles of Brahmanical and non-Brahmanical rituals. Both traditions coexist without any apparent conflict and are accepted by all concerned. This significant information should act as a corrective to the largely-held view that there are strong, dominant, centralizing influences swallowing up local forms of religious beliefs.

Anthropological studies of Hinduism have served as a corrective to its idealistic somewhat overblown version, and have highlighted its materialistic aspects, the structure and function of its components and its regional bases. Textual material has been used to explore its relevance to the understanding of anthropological processes at work. Hinduism has now been studied in its organizational and institutional aspect, and in terms of its network of sacred complexes and pilgrimage centres.

The relationship of Hinduism and tribal religion has thus been explored in many other ways. Tribal religion is seen in relation to the local forms of Hinduism as far as shamanistic practices, rituals and propitiation of local deities are concerned. It has also been seen in the regional context. Dominant centres of Hinduism have emerged in Tirupati in Andhra Pradesh, Guruvayur in Kerala, Kamakshya in Assam and Jagannath Puri in Orissa, as symbols of cultural identity at the regional and national level in which local communities including tribes are involved.

The relationship between tribal religion and Hinduism can also be seen in terms of the influence of Bhakti movements upon the tribal people. The spread of Vaishnav ideas started in the later middle age and penetrated deeper during the colonial period with the opening up of tribal areas and with the influx of Hinduized peasant communities, traders and moneylenders. The tribal revivalist movements reflected the impact of the Bhakti cults. It was not only through the contact with the Hindu peasant communities that the tenets of Vaishnavism spread, the artisan groups also played their role in transmitting religious concepts and forms. In western India, among the Bhils and other communities the carpenters gave an anthropomorphic form and content to the disembodied tribal spirits and gods. Terracotta horses and ancestors as deified heroes became popular and are still so.

Closely related to this process has been the attempt by scholars to describe the tribal people as the people at the receiving end and their religion as little tradition. This view has to be re-examined. While the dominant religion whether it is Hinduism, Christianity or Islam has influenced the tribal people, it will not be entirely correct to represent them as subservient to dominant religions. The great and little traditions are conceptual categories set up by scholars. They are based on the intellectual perception from above. They do not reflect the people's perception from the bottom upwards. For a tribal, worshipping at the sacred grove is a tradition, which is all important for him. It is neither great nor little. It is his own, which gives him his identity and shapes his survival and continuity. It is not that he is not aware of the dominant forms of culture around him, but it is equally true that he is soulfully attached to his own life and culture-supporting systems.

We may now turn to a few more aspects of the relationship of Hinduism and tribal religion. One relates to the vast underworld of black magic and witchcraft in which both peasant and tribal communities are steeped. It was noted earlier that this was an area where much acculturation had taken place. The names of Shiva and Chandi had travelled far and wide and been accepted by the practitioners of black magic. The entire corpus of Sabar tribal *mantra* or incantations was in a local dialect of Hindi, not in tribal language. Even those tribal people who could not utter a word of Hindi knew the *mantra* by heart and could recite them. For long, the missionary anthropologists believed that all this was alien to the tribal ethos, but witchcraft is recognized as part of tribal way of life. The incidence of witch killing is the highest in tribal areas. What lends significance to this form of crime is that it is perpetrated against women who have been the custodians of power and influence arising out of their possession of the knowledge of witchcraft. Again shamanism, among peasants and tribes, has attracted much notice in the recent years and it is again an area where they have interacted in the rural setting in order to cure disease, ward off evil and restore harmony disturbed by malevolent spirits.

The other area, closely related to the first, is the widespread cult of female spirits or mother goddesses among the peasants, artisans and tribal people. This is an area which needs to be explored. Researches in recent years have touched only the fringe of this important aspect of relationship among those communities. The cult of female deities is ancient and widespread but not so well-known in the context of its spread among the tribal people and in the tribal areas. The mini-epic of the Mundas, *Soso Bonga* or Asur story , tells us of the emergence of the Munda god, the Sing Bonga, and of origin and influence of innumerable Asur female spirits which still plague the Munda's existence. Enormous material has been generated from central , western and southern India on the survival and functioning of the vibrant tradition of the worship of female deities, which require analysis and understanding. A couple of hypotheses may be offered at this stage. First, the survival cults all over the country of female deities, which represent sexuality and fertility is truly amazing. They are feared and respected. They are both malevolent and benevolent, to be kept away or propitiated. The second hypothesis is that they have a world of their own and are autonomous in their roles and functions. Often, male and female spirits are sought to be integrated through marriage. A theory of spousification has been put forward to suggest integration of the male and female based cults, or the dominance of the male over the female in the patriarchal society. Sometimes the union is not complete. For instance, it is said that Ganesh and Kartikeya were born of Shiva's seed but not out of Parvati's womb. In her incarnation as Sati she remained fiercely independent. She even assumed the form of Sita to test Rama, when Shiva and she went to offer their sympathy to him after Sita was taken away by Ravana, which embarrassed Shiva no end. It was in her second incarnation as Parvati that she became the perfect wife, but she was not the mother of Shiva's children. However in a number of cases the theory of spousification worked, such as Vishnu-Lakshmi and so on. Union through marriage was considered inevitable. This author took the marriage of Sing Bonga and mother goddess at Diuri for granted but it has not happened. Probably, I underestimated the strength of the two separate traditions. In the tribal areas, the male and female spirits have remained separate and have not met, in spite of the Shiva-Shakti traditions and attempts under Hindu influence to bring them together.

We will now discuss the emerging trends in the perception of tribal religion. First, tribal religion is no longer identified with animism, as the religion of the 'savage' based on human sacrifice, blood letting and mumbo-jumbo of all kinds, though such a stereotype continues to persist in the movies. Tribal religion is now seen as part of the culture and society of the tribal people which is rich, positive, harmonious and autonomous, with a very healthy relationship with natural environment which should be an environmentalist's delight today. This area is being increasingly explored now with such formulations as nature-man-spirit complex and so on. The sacred groves of the tribals where tall, stately Sal trees still look down upon you, like *Deokull* elsewhere, are probably the only instances of the survival of the primeval forest which has disappeared everywhere. The spirits still inhabit trees, streams and valleys of the tribal world and weave an intricate but fascinating web of relationship between man and environment, which is in such striking contrast to the alienation that has occurred elsewhere.

Secondly, the tribal world today particularly in middle India has become the battleground for control over the tribal's abundant resources and over their ways of life and religion. Both Christians and 'Sanatani' Hindus are locked in conflict which goes back to the colonial times when aided by the resources of traders and merchants from Hindu heartland, efforts were made to check the spread of Christianity supported by superior resources. Tribals are Hindus, they said, even as they tried to impose the Sanatani form of Hinduism on the tribal people, whose religion, though close to the local forms of Hinduism, still had distinctive features going back to their separate, isolated and distant existence. In post-Independence years, as Christianity spread, the Hindu backlash intensified. Hanuman cult has become more visible with his image installed at the most unlikely places. The Oraons are being represented as the devotees of Ram (O, Ram). Hanuman's birth place has been 'discovered' at a place called Anjan, a historical site of some value, a few miles from Ranchi where a temple has come up. Political and commercial interests have continued with this form of penetration.

The tribals have reacted to these developments in two ways. First, they have been influenced by the resurgent forms of both Hinduism and Christianity in their area. They have joined the swelling ranks of the followers of the two religions and adopted their norms and symbols. Second, there has been a going back to the roots, a revival of tribals' own way of life, and of the tribals' own traditional religion which centred on the sacred grove *(Sarna).* While the censuses have occasionally reported on the local forms of tribals' traditional religion, its influence is more widespread than suggested by the number of their adherents. In a way this return to the roots was a feature of tribal millenarian movements in the colonial period. In recent years, this trend has been strengthened by two factors. One, Christianity in tribal areas has indigenized itself by liberally borrowing from local traditions. Second, in spite of efforts to impose the 'Sanatani' form of Hinduism, there has been a greater appreciation of the need to preserve the similarities with local forms of Hindus.

The tribals have also responded by institutionalizing their religious observances, even making them look 'militant' in tune with their rising aspirations. Today in and around Ranchi, all major tribal festivals are celebrated in a big demonstrative way, processions are taken out, cultural events are organized and high-flown speeches are delivered. Tribal identity is emphasized. There is a lot of flexing of muscles, shouting of slogans, display of weapons and beating of drums. These processions are modelled on the militant forms of Ramanavami and Muharram.

IV

The 19th century perception of Hinduism may again be described in the words of Sir Alfred Lyall who attempted a definition of the Hindu and Hinduism as follows:

> "Now just as the word Hindu is no national or even geographical denomination but signifies vaguely a fortuitous conglomeration of sects, tribes, races, hereditary professions, and pure castes, so the religion of this population of Hindu is at first sight a heterogeneous confusion"[20].

Such a view cannot be accepted anthropologically a hundred years later. Hinduism appears to be neither a heterogeneous confusion nor a fortuitous conglomeration but a historical process that has articulated the pluralities of all types, structural, ideological and processual. It has been an ongoing, an ever-growing process reaching out and subsuming traditions, structures and substratums at different historical levels without destroying their identity. These various components have been in a stage of vibrant interaction with one another within an ever-widening framework of a deeply felt cultural identity over the historical period. Thus Hinduism does not have any of the elements of a structured religion; in fact it is loosely structured which explains why it has been resilient and tenacious enough to survive and expand.

This brings us to the question of ideology and transcendence. Many an attempt was made within the idealistic and non-idealistic systems of philosophy to explain the heterogeneity of Hinduism. The concept of *moksha* or *nirvana* and of *advaita* sometimes provided the framework that could accommodate diversities and explain unity in diversities or diversities in unity. Some even tried to explain the undifferentiated state of human consciousness in terms of the undifferentiated societal state that might have existed at the beginning of social evolution, the state of primitive commune. Yoga has even been represented by some as a way of going back to the roots of human consciousness, at which lurked the folk memory of this state. What is of social significance for us is that the ideal of transcendence was sought to be used as a unifying principle that cut across social barriers. Many within the fold of Hinduism tried to grapple with the problem of inequality. The reformers belonging to some sections including the lowly placed ones made valiant efforts to project equality in the name of equality before god. In contemporary Hinduism the concept of *advaita* was used again and again to unify, consolidate and reform. If Brahma was himself undifferentiated why would society remain so differentiated, unequal and iniquitous, asked these reformers. This dilemma dogged every thinker and activist from Adi Shankara who shrank from the very touch of a Chandal until he was reminded of his philosophy of *advaita* to Vivekananda. Shankara explained it away by representing the Chandal as Shiva, composed a hymn in his honour, put him on a pedestal and all was forgotten.

In the vastly transformed social scenario today, there can be no shying away from the ugly reality of inequality and division. The tribals' and Dalits' perception of Hinduism, too, has a point even though it is not easily recognized that some of the most powerful movements for equality have emerged from the ranks of the oppressed who while remaining within the Hindu fold have invoked and questioned some aspects of the religion called Hinduism as their leaders have understood and interpreted them.

V

Syncretism as a theoretical issue has been intermittently under attack. It has been dismissed as a medieval relic. It is regarded as a consequence of conflicts and divisions, which are highlighted repeatedly by those who are opposed to it. Those who disapprove of syncretism ask what is the value of syncretistic culture when the house is on fire. Then there are those who believe that it is not syncretism, but concentration of forces or cultural homogenization which holds key to power relations in society. Sikhism, from the perspective of such a view, for example, is not valued for its basic syncretistic form but for its contribution to consolidation of the Sikh identity, which is necessary to give a sense of power to the community. Syncretism, no matter however witty, is a reality today. It cannot be ignored or abandoned. It starts right from the period two cultures meet, and people start interacting as they settle down after conflict. Syncretism is visible in all societies, all civilizations and all cultures, in day-to-day life and it survives all conflicts and catastrophes.

Notes

1. K.S. Singh, "Temples in Ranchi District", *Dr. Satkari Mookherjee Felicitation Volume.* Chowkhamba Publication, 1969.
2. "A Temple in a Tribal Village", Paper presented at the Seminar on Village India. Festival of India, London, 1982; Later published in *Human Science, Journal of Anthropological Survey of India,* Vol. 37, No.2 (1988).
3. K.S. Singh, "Tribalization", *Tribal Society in India,* Manohar, 1985.
4. Nirad C. Chaudhuri, *Hinduism: A Religion to Live,* New Delhi: B. I. Publications, 1979 pp. 96–98.
5. Rai Bahadur L.K. Anantha Krishna Iyer, *Lectures on Ethnography,* University of Calcutta, 1925, pp. 262–263.
6. Eschmann Annacharlotte, "Hinduisation of Tribal Deities in Orissa: The Shakti and Shiva Typology". *The Cult of Jagannath and Regional Traditions of Orissa,* edited by A. Eschmann, Herman Kulke, and Gaya Charan Tripathi, Manohar, 1986.
7. Sir Alfred Lyall, *Asiatic Studies, Religion and Society,* Vol. 1, Cosmo Publisher, New Delhi, p.135.
8. Sir Alfred Lyall, *Asiatic Studies, Religion and Society,* Vol. 1, Cosmo Publisher, New Delhi, p.135.
9. Sir Alfred Lyall, *Asiatic Studies, Religion and Society,* Vol. 1, Cosmo Publisher, New Delhi, p.135.

10. J.H. Hutton, *Census of India*, 1931, Vol. I, p. 399 (also see K.S. Singh. Foreword, Census of India, 1931), Vol. I, Gian Publication (reprint), 1986.
11. J.H. Hutton, *Census of India*, 1931, Vol. I, p. 399 (also see K.S. Singh. Foreword Census of India, 1931), Vol. I, Gian Publication (reprint), 1986.
12. J. Troisi, *Tribal Religious Beliefs and Practices among the Santals*, Manohar, 1979, pp. 272–274.
13. T.S. Naidu, A Communication,
14. S.G. Morab, A Communication.
15. M.L.K. Moorthy, "Traditional Fishers, Hunters and Foragers and Shifting Cultivators in Andhra Pradesh: An approach to the study of lifestyle" a paper presented at the UNESCO Workshop on Cross-cultural Lifestyle Studies with Multimedia Computerisable Documentation, Indira Gandhi National Centre for Arts. New Delhi, 9–13 January 1989.
16. *The Cult of Jagannath and Regional Traditions of Orissa,* edited by A. Eschmann, Herman Kulke, and Gaya Charan Tripathi, Manohar, 1986.
17. Field notes, K.S. Singh.
18. B.B. Goswami and S.G. Morab, *Chamundeshwari Temple in Mysore,* Anthropological Survey of India, 1975.
19. R.M. Sarkar, *Regional Cults and Rural Traditions: An Interacting Pattern of Divinity and Humanity in Rural Bengal,* Inter-India Publication, 1986.
20. Sir Alfred Lyall, *Asiatic Studies: Religion and Society,* Vol. 1, Cosmo Publisher, New Delhi, p.135.

7

Tribal Religion and Hindu Cults: Case Studies from South India

T. Madhava Menon

Some European writers (Dumont 1970, Walker 1986) have sought to argue that tribal communities are an integral part and parcel of the 'universal' Hindu ambience of India, that their beliefs and customs are 'nothing but' special forms of the 'wider Hindu system', and that, far from being 'isolated, non-Hindu, rigidly bounded communities', they are different from the Hindu types only in degree and not in kind. This kind of prejudice noticed in the perception of these authors is 'pre-programmed' to seek and find in 'Hinduism' a key to all the tribes who are in India. Their premise is replete with an implicit 'definition', viz., any community anywhere in India as now politically constituted is 'Hindu', if it is marked by hierarchy and the acknowledgement of the privileged positions of Brahmins, and the implied observance of 'purity and pollution'. These authors are not overly concerned with the belief systems regarding cosmology, nature of deities or notion of life after death; even communities that do not believe in the reincarnation of souls are considered 'Hindu' on the basis of social structure exclusively.

'Hinduism' is an undefined and probably indefinable term. Any person in India who does not declare any notable religion is returned legally as a 'Hindu'. Amoebic in its structure, ingesting what it cannot assimilate, formless and flexible, 'Hinduism' perpetuates itself by the proliferation of varying configurations. It is an accretion of beliefs and observances, mostly temporal and variable, but some primordial, surviving in a matrix of coexisting rites and practices, and is not bound to any defining text, though the Vedas are generally unquestioned as authority. As is well known, the "Vedas" were reduced to writing quite late, and are better known as the *sruti* 'what has been heard'. Its sociological purpose has been defined by factors of dominance and advantage, driven by a continuous urge to adopt certain sanctified practices of Brahmins as 'sanskritizing' or ennobling symbols of refinement. This has put a premium on the Brahmins, self-imposed at the top rung of the hierarchy, who (or others imitating them) claim an exclusive right to specialize as religious practitioners, and whose employment confers prestige to the individual or institution so employing them.

In this article, it is argued that religions of several tribal communities in south India indeed had several features that were not integrally part of the 'Hindu' faith as practised by the majority of the non-tribal communities of the region. On the other hand, many deities and forms of worship of tribals and ritual acts practised from time immemorial by tribal people, have actually influenced the religion and practices of the 'Hindu' majority of the region. The 'Great Tradition' did not always influence the 'Little Traditions'; at least in one case, that of the Kurichiya (see discussion below), the latter threw the former upside down! It will be shown that tribal religions have been and continue to be under pressure to accept the 'superiority' of Brahmins; the pressure increases in proportion to the prosperity of the tribal community concerned. Conversely, there is 'tribalization' of Hinduism by the adoption of deities and forms of worship from the folk forms. 'Hinduism' is not just one mainstream; it has several streams that ultimately inundate islands of differences within their catchments. It is a syncretistic accumulation of several layers of faith and observance, and often merely the result of 'official' or 'census' classifications.

I

The tribal communities in Kerala and Tamil Nadu, long before they came into contact with 'Hindu' castes and creeds of the region, had developed religious faiths and practices of their own without reference to those of the latter. The tribal people were aware of the significance of religion both as praxis leading to immediate relief from distress and conferment of short-term tangible benefits, as well as of a transcendental relationship between themselves and forces controlling the universe. These religions took many forms, and they generally tended to be centred on the dominant physical features of their own environs, to which they attributed divinity, or on deified heroes, ancestors, spirits, and icons of beasts and birds. Hence, they and tribespeople elsewhere were conventionally termed 'animistic'. As the pressure of non-tribal populations increased, and mountains and forests into which the tribal communities had retreated became accessible to non-tribals, contacts between them became greater. Historically, such contacts varied in intensity from place to place and period to period. In south India, classical Tamil literature (Chilappadikaram) describes that Chera war-lords used to make periodic forays into tribal territory to terrorize them, and confiscate their treasures of forest produce, including ivory and pepper, which the Chera used to export to the West in return for horses, gold and wines. Such raids were, of course, sporadic, and did not have a permanent impact. Hoysala monarchs claimed from the 12th century AD titular supremacy over the Nilgiris, home of Toda, Kota and Kurumba tribes, but this was nominal. The Vijayanagar empire included this territory in its jurisdiction, but there is no evidence to show that it administered it. The Mysore Sultans (Hyder Ali and Tippoo Sultan) over-ran it, as it was in the path of their military campaigns. It was only after the British became masters in 1799 that the external presence became permanent. Along with the British came a horde of plainsmen in various capacities, as labourers in plantations owned by Europeans, as traders, petty officers, contractors and moneylenders.

The Wayanad and Attappady areas, home to Adiya, Kattunaikka, Kurichiya, Paniya, etc., and Kurumba, Muduga and Irula respectively, were endemically malaria-ridden, and inhospitable to plainspeople. But Wayanad was part of the scene of wars between the British and the Mysore Sultans, and later of what is probably the first revolt against the British in India, viz., the Pazhassi and Kurichiya revolt of 1802–1812 (Menon, 2000:179). This led to ingress of plainspeopie into Wayanad and into Attappady, where malaria was eradicated only after Independence. Until then, the tribal people had been terrorized by local chieftains, whom the former always kept away, by prompt submission of various items of forest produce as annual tributes.

II

We will examine below the historical and anthropological issues involved in the occurrence of tribal religion, process of culture contact, substance of syncretism and culture change by citing cases drawn from south Indian states of Kerala and Tamil Nadu.

The Religion of the Toda

The Todas have fascinated Western anthropologists ever since the appearance of Rivers' classic description (1906, reprint 1986). In practice, Toda religion is a highly ritualized buffalo-cult, represented by the holy places where their dairies are located. The dairies were thought of in anthropomorphic terms (Emeneau, 1971), but they have no anthropomorphic representations of deities. The first of the gods, Pithi, was born in a cave. His son, Ön, married Prarkurs and was dairyman-priest of Nö:rs clan; his son, Puv was the priest at Kür; other gods also served as dairy priests. Ön and his wife Teikerzi went to the hills near Kundah; he produced 1,600 buffaloes, but she did better with 1,800. Clinging to the tail of the last of his buffaloes came the first Toda man.Teikerzi, associated with Nö:r's hamlet, is the most dominant of their deities; she divided the buffaloes into grades of sanctity, and is credited with the origin of most of the Toda institutions. Rivers (1906:I, 186) and Walker (1986:121) were told that she lives in England and America, as much as in the Nilgiris. An indefinite number of gods arose out of her. After her, the cult hero Kwoten laid down most of the rules and procedures for their customs, ways of life, and worship. The dairies are arranged in a hierarchy of sanctity, and with each is associated a herd of holy buffaloes. The conservatism of the Toda is evidenced by the fact that descriptions of Rivers have been largely confirmed as being the practice, with minor changes, half a century later by Walker. So strict are the requirements of ritual purity and abstinence from contact with others that at the highest level of the hierarchy of dairies, there have been no volunteers to take up the job of priest for more than a generation now, despite the high prestige and perquisites of the job.

The Toda life-cycle rituals were unique because of traditional systems of polyandry, social acceptance of paternity, and performance of a second 'funeral' for the dead. These had nothing whatsoever to do with corresponding Hindu observances; in the northern homelands of 'Vedic' Hinduism, the Brahmin-dominated 'Agamic' variety of popular Hinduism in south India, or the folk varieties of worship of mother goddesses and village deities throughout India. They did not believe in reincarnation of the soul, a cardinal diagnostic of Hinduism. Instead, they had a localized sacred geography, including a 'world of the dead', to which souls proceeded after the 'second funeral'. Perhaps as a late addition, a myth was introduced that life in the 'world of the dead', though pleasant, entailed walking on its very hard floor; so, after untold years, the legs of the deceased got worn down to the knees, and Ön sent them back to the verdant Nilgiris to be reborn as Toda babies.

In spite of a century and a half of contact with Brahmins, after the British opened the Nilgiris, the Toda do not hold them in high regard, nor do they believe in the Brahmins' 'sanctity'. The ritual purity on which the Brahmin based so much of their greatness was insignificant in comparison with the much stricter specifications in this regard that Toda dairy priests observed. The Toda are vegetarians, except that they eat ritual offerings of buffalo-meat at the 'second funeral'; thus, Brahmins could not claim superiority in this regard either. Nevertheless, where Brahminical Hinduism failed, the ambient Tamil folk religion succeeded. They worship at the Mariamman (Tamil Mother Goddess) temple in Ooty, and perform some ritual services like pulling her chariot at the annual festival. They also make it the venue of the ear lobe piercing ceremony of their children. Traditionally, this used to be in the settlement in the vicinity of the dairy temple. The modern Toda accepts the efficacy of his own system, as well as that of those of the popular south Indian variety, but not those of the ambitious local Brahmins. But the narrow end of the Brahminical wedge has found a way as several Toda men have become devotees of Ayyappan, the syncretistic deity of south India, whose hill-top temple at Sabarimala attracts increasing number of pilgrims every year, when it is open for about two months annually (please see below for more details on the Ayyappan cult).

Walker (1986:157) argues that the Todas are located "within, rather than outside the Hindu world of south India" because he sees in their social organization existence of hierarchy in the form of a 'superior' section, the Torthoral, and an 'inferior', the Teivaliol. The main characteristic of the Toda religion is the concept of purity and pollution, in respect of the buffalo-cult observances, to which there is no parallel in 'Vedic' or 'popular' Hinduism. Hierarchical social organization is not unique to Hindu systems, but generally true of all human society. In the Toda case, the inferior sub-division supplies the 'professional' priestly practitioners; members of the Torthoral function as priests only in their own temples. This is the reverse of 'Brahminical Hinduism'. Within the sub-divisions, there is no regime of endogamous hierarchy parallel to a caste structure, though those belonging to certain specified settlements of hoary antiquity possess the more prestigious dairy-temples. Thus the Toda cannot be emphatically branded as another special case of the Hindu 'generality' merely on the basis of hierarchical grading of two moieties, and observance of pollution and purity in regard to worship.

A 'congregation of gods'

The Paniya used to be agrestic slaves in Wayanad, Kerala, 'bought and sold' along with the master's lands. The bonding used to take place in the shrine of regional mother goddess, Valliyoor Bhagavathi, at the annual festival. Aiyyappan (1992:87) recorded that they "only borrowed and adopted from their master's scraps of religious rites and had a very superficial knowledge of the gods and goddesses of folk Hinduism". The Brahmins had no concern for them, because they were the poorest of the poor. "The Paniyas seem to have been only borrowing the gods and goddesses of their employees. In eastern Wayanad, (where there is a sizeable population of Tamil estate labour), the Paniyas have ... the smallpox goddess, ... Mari Amma, whose shaman is expected to speak in Kannada. Some Paniya families have borrowed Malakkari from the Kurichiyas, and the Paniya shaman of Malakkari uses the typical Kurichiya idioms and slang terms" (Aiyyappan, 1992). The Paniyas also worship a Muslim saint, whose shaman pretends to smoke bidis and eat non-vegetarian food, after going through motions of performing namaz and speaking with Muslim intonation. The strangest deity among them is Sayippu Teyyam ('Sahib' God), dressed in pants, shirt, sola topi (hat), smoking a cigar, and demanding distilled country liquor and biscuits in propitiation of his irresistible wrath! This exotic god is also known as Kumpani or Bombay Teyyam, the former signifying the British East India Company, and the second referring to the time when Malabar used to be administered from its Bombay (Mumbai) offices. The Paniya had a chance to come across this curious but vicious being at the beginning of 19th century, when the British grabbed the area.

However, regenerating the grand theses of philosophico-religious evolutionism, they also re-affirm belief in a single great Creator-God, who is formless and omnipresent, and to whom no formal worship need be offered. The Paniya are totally unaffected by Hindu belief-systems; they in fact consider that 'life' consists of atomistic units, each about one-seventh of the size of a mustard seed; while in the body, these particles are powerless, but when the body dies, they fly off at terrific velocity to their places in the Sun and the Moon, and if interrupted, they can do serious harm. In their universe, there are thousands of gods and millions of demons, inhabiting 17 worlds above and 7 below.

The Paniyas too are now being drawn into the torrent of Ayyappan adoration, and thereby resultant subservience to Brahminical Agamic forms of worship to a very little extent.

Tribal Matriliny and Cultural Sovereignty

The Kurichiya of Wayanad are a land-owning tribe, who did not enslave the Paniya. They observed the highest levels of ritual purity, considering the touch of even a Nambudiri Brahmin as polluting. In fact, they would not allow Brahmins beyond their front veranda. Perumal, their supreme god, is passionless and beyond the ken of humans. Perhaps finding such an abstract form 'inadequate' to meet the needs of a dynamic human community, Kurichiya in ancient period appealed to Him that he should be immanent. Therefore, he became Malakkari, the dark god of the mountains. Armed with bows and arrows (the characteristic weapons of the Kurichiya), He subdued the myriad gods and godling who infested the area, and assigned specific jobs and responsibilities to each of them The fierce and fearsome Kali opposed Him; He threw Her into the sea, and then She was rescued, greatly reduced in size, by some fisherfolk. She is still around, inducing people to commit incest! Another mother goddess Karimpilli Bhagavathi challenged Him to attend to the difficult delivery case of a Kurichiya woman. He could not, and appcaled to Her to help the suffering human. She demanded that He marry Her; He agreed, and She has been, ever since, helping Kurichiya women through their delivery pangs. He also deputed gods, one each, specifically; as guardian deity of each Kurichiya family; they are the Munnaman (third or mediator) gods. Another god's sole responsibility is to look after students' welfare, especially of acolytes training for office as sacerdotal performers. In each household, a deified ancestress presides in the kitchen and guards the women; even the mediator gods cannot impose punishments on the women without her consent. She usually makes the culprit fall ill. Nevertheless, many gods of the local Hindu folk have intruded into Kurichiya reverence: Muthappan of north Kerala, who had taught humans to tap the toddy palm, and several deified hero-humans, including Kurichiya women. They found for Pillyaran, somewhat similar to the ubiquitous Ganapathi, an innocuous job, viz., being the bodyguard of the deified Kurichiya heroine Velinilam. The Kurichiya do not engage Brahmin priests; members of the tribe who feel a strong calling train themselves as religious performers under respected gurus. Their own guardian deity protects them during the period as acolytes, as they graduate from the lesser to the greater deities, until they can perform for Malakkari Himself.

The Kurichiya represent a tribal group who hold on to a matrilineal culture, with uxorilocal residence and are self-confident about their own right and might. They were self-sufficient materially and culturally, and were not overwhelmed by ambient Hindu institutions. For example, the 12th century Tirunelli Vishnu temple, Wayanad, has been an important sacred centre where the Hindus regularly hold several celebrations. The rituals and musical traditions of the temple are popular not only among the local Hindus of Kerala but also of Tamil Nadu and Karnataka. *Skanda Purana* and *Padma Purana* assert that the temple was established by Brahma, the Creator, and hallowed by the presence of Vishnu and Siva. However, Kurichiyas do not attach any special significance to it. Not over-awed by the 'Great Tradition', they 'reduced' even the dreaded Kali to being merely the patroness of incest! Neither do they adore Brahmins, nor do they engage them as sacerdotal agents. "The Kurichiya ... are at one end of the Sanskritization continuum representing the lowest degree of involvement in Puranic Hinduism, which has been present without break but only to a minor degree in Wayanad" (Aiyyappan and Mahadevan 1990:79).

Though the Kurichiya faith in their own gods and religious form is unshaken, they nowadays worship some local Hindu deities too. Many of their men undertake the pilgrimage to worship Ayyappan of Sabarimala, thus notionally entailing their subordination to Brahmin sacred specialists and their establishment, particularly the statutory Devaswam Board, that prides itself in the ardour of orthodoxy.

Glorification of Tribal Deity

The Attappady valley is the home of Palu Kurumba, Muduga and Irula tribes. It is the southward extension of the Gudalur plateau of the Nilgiris, east of the watershed line of Western Ghats, and is at an average elevation of 800 to 1,000 meters above mean sea level. The dominant physical features are a 2,000-metre needle-shaped peak, Malleeswaran Mala, and the Bhavani river that flows around it. The peak represents their tribal god, Malleeswaran. According to their legends, he was a Muduga chieftain, who left on a pilgrimage long ago. The tribe practises polygyny, and a man usually entrusts his first wife to recruit the subsequent ones. Malleeswaran had entrusted this task to his first wife before he left, without knowing that she was then pregnant. She delivered a girl who grew up to be a stunning beauty by the time he returned. He assumed that she was the girl recruited by his first wife, and wanted to espouse her, disbelieving her assertion that she was indeed his daughter. Rather than commit incest, the brave girl jumped to her death, and Malleeswaran in remorse turned himself into the peak. The people of the valley have so located their (traditional) hamlets that they all command a view of this towering deity, to whom they offer obeisance every morning. On Sivaratri day, worshippers climb the peak and light a fire there, which is the signal for the people to break their fast. Incidentally, Sivaratri coincides with the end of the tribal cultivation and the commencement of the season for the collection of non-timber forest produce in the region. At the foot of the peak, near the Bhavani, they had established a small place of worship, where an Irula pujari used to light a lamp and offer prayers. The devout offered surplus agricultural produce as offerings, which they scattered, for the needy to collect.

After malaria was eradicated, plainspeople from Tamil Nadu and from Kerala 'invaded' the place. The settler hordes alienated the tribal lands and exploited the tribal labour. In the course of their prosperity, the Hindu settlers also started worshipping at the humble temple of Malleeswaran. About 30 years back, the Hindu Tamilian settlers wanted to grab control of this temple, dedicated to a tribal deity, but alert local officers intervened and ensured that the Irula tribe retained it. The Irula used surplus income from the temple to build a structure in the Dravidian architectural style. The Irula pujari imitated the camphor waving and other techniques of worship usually practised by non-Brahmin Tamilian priests.

The settlers invented a new mythology, according to which Siva and Parvathi, incurably peripatetic, had landed on the peak. Parvathi wanted a temple to be built there and daily worship offered. Siva, more realistic, ordained that it would suffice to light a fire on top on Sivaratri night; people should break their fast after seeing it. After all, Malleeswaran is only a 'form' of Siva! It is now understood that the statutory Hindu Religious Endowments Board has notified a 'scheme' of management of the temple, envisaging a 'suddhi kalasam' to remove pollution of the installation, and the appointment of Brahmin priests.

Regional Tribal Worldview

The Kurumba, a sub-tribe with a large population, and the Alu Kurumba of Nilgiris, exhibit a case of strange adoption of 'Hindu' deities. They worship Baruma Raja (Brahma Raja/Brahma), a deity rarely worshipped in south Indian popular Hinduism. Emme Daruma Raja (Yama Dharma Raja) is the Hindu God of Death, whom also the Alu Kurumba worship. These deities have been integrated with the tribal worldviews and the regional belief systems. The Nilgiri tribes show regional similarities in belief systems. The Kurumba and the Soliga believe that every human has two souls, one bigger than the other one. The former, according to the

Kurumba, is associated with a Visible Shadow, and the other, with an Invisible one. During lifetime, the two are conjoined and their shadows united, but at the time of death, Emme Daruma Raja forcibly draws them out of the body. The Visible Shadow wanders about, but the little soul lingers around until the 'second burial', a megalithic custom of depositing the clavicle in an *ossuary*. Thereafter, it undertakes a hazardous journey to rejoin the bigger soul, to live happily ever after with the spirits of their ancestors.

These tribes seem to have developed the notion of sacred geography and the adventures of the soul, from the Toda. Essentially, the high points are the passage of the soul over a 'string-bridge'; and here those who had led unblemished lives have no difficulty, but others fall down, to be festered by leeches until the sympathetic souls of their ancestors, already in heaven, come to their rescue. Another is a celestial dog, who forces those who had committed incest to a 'canine ravishment' before letting them proceed. "What is expressly to be noted ... is the fact that the concept of reincarnation has not gained ground in the religion of the Alu Kurumbas so far" (Kapp 1985:243).

III

Course of Syncretism

Dumont (1970) and Walker (1986) tend to generalize on the supposed 'Hindu' character of the tribal population simply on the premise of the structural similarities of social organization with a rudimentary hierarchical grading, and the observance of certain notions of 'pollution' and 'purification'. Dumont has found caste-like organization among non-Hindus also (1970: Chapter X), but considers it as the result of the social structure of those who had been converted to other religions, being resistant to change in an egalitarian direction inherent in these religions (Islam and Christianity), in other words, a relic of the 'Hinduism' from which they had been converted. The implication is that any social structure in which hierarchy and observance of pollution and purity are determinants of behaviour is 'Hindu'. 'Hinduization' involves sharing of a belief system, of which belief in the reincarnation of the soul, the sanctity of the Veda, however unknown and unapproachable they be to the believer, and the acceptance of the pre-eminence of the Brahmin as the agency between god and man, have been essential features. Just because a social structure exhibits some form of stratification, or because some observances distinguish between 'purity' and 'pollution', it cannot be concluded that such a social structure is 'Hindu'. The people may become Hindu by a process of adoption of belief systems, and the social structures and behaviour that may be entailed by such belief. Whether the tribal society concerned is hierarchical or egalitarian can be discerned by a diachronic study of the polarization of statuses as it has developed by economic and political processes, rather than caused by its having been 'Hindu'.

'Syncretism' has been defined as the "attempted reconciliation or union of different or opposing principles, practices, or parties, as in philosophy or religion" (*Webster's Unabridged Dictionary*). Syncretistic adoption of belief systems and the associated structural and behavioural features has been the driving force in the Hinduization course of tribal communities. The illustrative cases narrated above, a very small cross section, limited for reasons of space, show that the adoption of belief systems is a slow process. The more 'different' the beliefs are from those of 'popular Hinduism', the less Hinduized in structure and behaviour is the tribal community.

In an insightful passage written about a century ago, L.K. Ananthakrishna Iyer recorded:

> Special interest attaches to the religion of the Kadars (a "primitive ST community of Kerala) as representing a comparatively early stage in the process of conversion to Brahminism which the aboriginal races of Bengal are undergoing. The real working religion of the tribe is pure animism of the type which still survives comparatively untouched by Hindu influence among the Santals, Mundas and Orans of Chota Nagpur. Like these, Kadar believe themselves to be encompassed about by a host of invisible powers some of which are thought to be their ancestors, while others seem to embody nothing more definite than the vague sense of the mysterious, uncanny, with which the hills, streams and the lonely forests inspire the savage imagination. Of these shadowy forms, no images are made nor are they conceived of as wearing any bodily shape. A roughly moulded lump of clay in an open glade, a queer shaped stone bedaubed with vermilion---this is all the visible presentiment that does duty for all. Their names are legion, their attributes are barely known. But so much is certain that to neglect their worship brings disaster to the offender, death or disorder to the household, murrain upon the cattle and blight on his crops. In order to avert these ills, but, so far as I can gather, without the hope of any benefit from the gods, who are active only to do evil, the Kadar sacrifices pigs, fowls, goats and pigeons and offers ghee, molasses and the heads of Indian

> corn in the sacred groves in which deities are supposed to dwell. The priest is a man of the tribe who combines the sacred functions with those of the barber to the Kadars of the villages of the neighbourhood. For all this, the Kadar, if questioned about their religion, will reply that they are Hindus and will talk vaguely about their Hindu gods (Parameswar, Vishnu) as if they live in the very odour of orthodoxy, instead of being in fact wholly outside the sphere of the Brahminical system. To talk about the Hindu gods is usually the first step towards that insensible adoption of the externals of Hinduism... The next step is to set up Brahmins, whose influence, furthered by a variety of social forces, gradually disposes of the tribal gods and transforms them into orthodox shapes, and gives them places in the regular pantheon, as local manifestations of this or that well-known principle, and relegates them to a decent and inoffensive obscurity as household or village deities. Last of all, if the tribe is an influential one, it gives itself brevet rank like the Rajputs (Iyer, 1909, reprint 1981:11--12).

History indicates that local chieftains were granted lateral entry into Kshatriya Varna, and there are several instances of such a process all over India in the distant past; thus the ancient Chera, Chola and Pandya kings became 'instant Kshatriyas'. Sponsored by the secular power, so legitimized and acclaimed by the Brahmins, propaganda was mounted from the places of worship to 'convert' the local population to acceptance of the essence of Hinduism, viz., belief in the theory of reincarnation of souls, eternal damnation by repeated rebirth in low life forms if Brahmins are offended, subservience to the caste hierarchy, acceptance of the superiority of the Brahmins, and the exclusive right of Brahmins to mediate between man and god. Later, the Bhakti cult helped the spread of these influences to a wider mass of the population through the harnessing of music and dance and eroticism in the cult practices. In these cult practices, deities, elements, cultural forms, myths and tribal ceremonies are integrated, or syncretized into the local brand of Hinduism.

A strange case of syncretic adoption of Hindu deities is observed among the Mala Ullada, an impoverished forest-dwelling tribe of south Kerala. Their traditional deity is Thalaparamalaswamy, represented by the dominant peak in their territory. Kappiri, Thokutty, etc. are other deities, representing and represented by natural objects. In the early 1930s, anthropologist L.A. Krishna Iyer who was also a forest officer used to camp and conduct fieldwork among them. As a devout Brahmin, he had installed a stone as a Siva Lingam and worshipped it daily. Mala Ullada also continued to worship it, a Velichappad (holy performer) discharging priestly as well as shamanistic functions (Nandi et al, 1971:90). In the south, the annual festival at the local temple is the occasion where vestigial rights of the original tribal communities to whom the place of worship belonged are given symbolic recognition. In some temples of Tamil Nadu, a member of a scheduled caste ties *tali*, in token of marriage, around the neck of the village goddess. In Kerala, a Velichappad, necessarily a non-Brahmin, takes up the symbolic sword of the deity, who possesses his body and utters commands through him. In Attappady, it may be the continuing right of Muduga and Kurumba headmen to make the arduous annual climb to the top of the Malleeswaran peak to light the fire, however, when the threatened 'scheme' of the Hindu Religious Endowment Board succeeds, a Brahmin and the Devaswam Board will garner the gifts of the devotees at the more accessible 'temple'. The 'low' caste and the tribal indeed could never cross the threshold of sanctified boundary, fixed by the Brahmins.

Ayyappan—A Quintessential Syncretistic Deity

The evolution of the syncretistic cult in south India is best illustrated by the Ayyappan cult, which has rapidly become an all-India phenomenon. Ayyappan or Ayyanar is a village deity in Tamil Nadu and Kodagu area, functioning as a protective agency (Srinivas, 2002:349). He has several 'equations'—with *Dharma Sastra*, from Kerala's Buddhist past, *Amara Kosha* having 'Sastha' as a synonym of the Buddha, and with Vishnu because of a verse in *Vishnusahasranama*. *Bhagavata Purana*, circa 4th to 6th century, relates that when nectar was obtained after churning the milky ocean, the Devas defrauded the Asuras of their rightful share by interposing Vishnu disguised as Mohini, a bewitching damsel who charmed the latter into fighting among themselves, while the Devas finished off the precious fluid! Siva, not available at the time because of his diet of Vasuki's vomited poison, later insisted on seeing the Mohini form of his colleague; he was bewitched, and instantly incontinent, embraced 'her' and begot Ayyappan, delivered by incising Vishnu's thigh.

Obviously so strangely begotten a baby, however divine, could not be accommodated either in Kailasha or in Vaikuntha, and was abandoned in the forest. Millennia later, a Pandyan prince of Madurai, while hunting in these forests, came upon him and adopted him. Outstandingly quick in learning all the skills of princely accomplishments, he was to become the heir apparent, but the jealous queen pretended illness for which her co-conspirator, the physician, prescribed tiger's milk, hoping that

Ayyappan would be sent on this errand, and would be certainly killed. Ayyappan set forth and had a fracas with a Muslim trader Vaver, who was his equal and settled a treaty of friendship with him. Then, a transformation came over him; he befriended the tigers with love and brought a whole herd of lactating tigresses to the palace, seeing which the queen and her conspirators instantly died of fright. Nevertheless, Ayyappan was disgusted; he renounced the world and retreated forever into the forests of Sabarimala. Due to the earnest prayers of his devotees, he conceded to them the right to travel on pilgrimage to his seat during a period of about six weeks every year, after observing strict vegetarianism, abstinence from sex, etc.

The story indicates the Buddhist influence in Ayyappan's conversion. The vows of abstinence are similar to the sila of right conduct. The devotees take saranam in Ayyappan, like the three refuges in Buddhism. The friendship and tolerance with Islam is also significant; some Muslims who claim descent from Vaver present themselves at the temple during the annual pilgrimage season, open a stall and dispense prasadam, which consists of dried pepper, indicating that Vaver was a trader in that commodity long ago. Significantly, the observances that devotees have to undergo at present are virtually unchanged from those days when L.A. Krishna Iyer described as having been practised by Mala Arayar, a Schedule Tribe, of the area.

"His worship at Sabarimala betrays many animistic features... Sasta is very frigid in his tastes and expects a high standard of purity in his votaries for fourteen days. They should abstain from meat and sexual intercourse. The Malayarayans go in batches led by Periaswamy, who is the head of the fraternity. During the period of abstinence, they propitiate Sasta, Karuppuswamy, Kochukadutha, Ganapathi and other crests of hills. The day before their march to Sabarimala, all votaries put their kit together ... After taking part in Pettathullal, which is an interesting ceremony ... they begin their march... and reach Azhutha in the evening ... they reach the banks of the Pamba. The Pambavilakku forms one of the most enchanting scenes at night on account of the illuminations and is considered to be in honour of Sasta, who is said to be cooking his food and dining among the Ayyappans (all pilgrims to Sabarimala are called by the name Ayyappan if male, and Malikappuram, if female - T.M. Menon) that night in disguise ... The next morning the votaries reach the Sabarimala pagoda, break a coconut ... and worship the deity. They make offerings to Kochukadutha and Karuppuswami. At night comes Makaravilakku, when there is a procession from the shrine of Malikappurathamma (Mother Goddess) to Ayyappan's shrine ... Next morning they bathe ... and enjoy a feast. Then they return home. Sasta's boons to votaries are phenomenal and enlarge the circle of his votaries" (1937:190–193).

Another tribal community, the Kochuvelans, have a tradition that one of their ancestors defeated Ayyappan in a trial of archery; a truce was struck whereby Ayyappan would withdraw to the point reached by the Kochuvelan's arrow and vice versa; the Kochuvelan's arrow landed at Sabarimala, and Ayyappan's much nearer at Thalapala Mala. All the pilgrims now adopt the Malayaraya rituals, described by Iyer, though with minor variations. Most importantly, the pilgrimage has always been open to all without discrimination of caste or religion, and all 'Ayyappans", as the worshippers are equal—no caste pollution is observed. The essential rites continue to be: taking the vow of pilgrimage by wearing a chain round the neck, observance of abstinence for 41 days, taking refuge in Ayyappan, filling of a peculiar head load pack in which the sacrificial coconut filled with ghee and sealed with wax is kept in one compartment, and provisions for the pilgrim in the other compartment, chanting "Ayyappan Saranam" as many times as possible every day, setting out on the pilgrimage under the leadership of a veteran, and also paying homage to Vaver at the mosque in Erumeli (Pettathullal). For first time pilgrims, they climb with stops for worship at various points, the Pamba river worship, the homage at the sacred 18 steps leading to the temple, and the breaking open of the sacrificial coconut and extraction of the ghee in it, which is then handed over to the Brahmin priest at the sanctum sanctorum for *abhishekam* on the deity, and then return home are observed. The involvement of the Brahmin priest is essentially only for the performance of the *abhishekam*; the pilgrim's preceptor, who may belong to any caste, can perform every other rite.

At present, the entire pilgrimage is organized as a commercial operation, vehicles proceeding to the banks of the Pamba. The crowds are considerable, and the Travancore Devaswam Board makes crores of rupees auctioning several categories of rights. Officials of the police and a miscellany of government departments are on duty round the clock. Donkeys overloaded and overworked as transports of every requirement die of ill treatment. One of the most fascinating examples of mass credulity is a mysterious light that appears at dusk believed to be lit by the gods themselves in honour of Ayyappan; it is actually lit by the employees of the Devaswam Board and the Forest Department, a well-known fact.

The worship at the temple is totally Brahminical. *Tantrasamuccayam*, the 13th century authoritative text on the techniques of worship in Kerala temples, does not contain instructions on the rituals for worship of Ayyappan. They are prescribed for the first time in *Sésasamuccayam*, an addendum compiled about two centuries later. The 'Technical Auditor' is the hereditary Tantri, who likes to portray himself as steeped in the odour of orthodoxy. The priests are appointed from among Nambudiri Brahmins, who have had considerable experience in similar capacities at lesser temples, and are selected by draw of lots from a short list prepared from among the thousands of applicants by the Tantri. In several decisions, the High Court of Kerala has held that the Tantri's decision on sacerdotal matters is final. However, that does not prevent the Devaswam Board from milking all sources of income to maximize its revenues from the pilgrimage. The rights once enjoyed exclusively by tribal communities, especially at the temple of the Mother Goddess, are now subject to auction and control by the Board, though they retain token entitlements.

IV

Conclusion

The tribal communities, intimidated by the overwhelming presence of 'Hindus' around them, are sequentially indoctrinated to adopt 'Hindu' belief systems, at times on account of the fabricated myths which have no doctrinal rationale or sometimes due to the fear of rebirth in undesirable life forms for transgression of Brahminical codes of conduct. The major objective behind the indoctrination is often the maximization of benefaction to Brahmins and to their organizational institutes who wield secular power (for e.g., 'instant Kshatriyas' in the past, and now, statutory 'Devaswam Board') through obtaining fees and privileges. In order to make such basic principles operational the priestly class can stoop to any level. So much so that any belief, custom or observance may be adopted either way, from Hindu fold to the tribal fold and vice versa. What we see in the 'Hinduization' of tribal religions is actually the syncretistic adoption of certain elements from varied forms of worship on part of the tribes who thereby are brought under the institutional umbrella of 'Hinduism'.

It is not the social structure, as theorized by the Western anthropologists, that drives the trend, but belief. It is seen that tribal religions have been and continue to be under pressure to accept the 'superiority' of Brahmins; the pressure increases in proportion to the prosperity of the tribal community concerned. As we discussed, the religions of several tribes in south India indeed had several features that were not integrally part of the 'Hindu' faith as practised by the majority of the non-tribal communities of the region. On the other hand, many deities, forms of worship and ritual acts practised since time immemorial by tribal people, have actually influenced the religion and practices of the 'Hindu'" majority of the region. The 'Great Tradition' did not always influence the 'Little traditions'. Antithetically, there is 'tribalization' of Hinduism by the adoption of deities and forms of worship from the folk forms. 'Hinduism' is not just one 'mainstream'; it has several 'streams' that ultimately inundate islands of difference within their catchments. Both tribal religion and Hinduism thus ultimately emerge as syncretistic agglomerations of several layers of faiths and observances.

References

Aiyyappan, A. 1992. *The Paniyas.* Calcutta: Institute of Social Research and Applied Anthropology.

Aiyyappan, A. and T.M. Mahadevan 1990. *Ecology, Economy, Matriliny and Fertility of Kurichias*, Delhi: BR Publishing Corporation,

Dumont, L. 1970. *Homo Hierarchicus: The Caste System and its Implications*; English Trans., George Weidenfeld & Nicholson Ltd.Indian Edition, New Delhi: Vikas Publications.

Emeneau, M.B. 1971. *Toda Songs*; Oxford: Clarendon Press.

Iyer, Ananthakrishna L.K. 1909 (1981). *The Cochin Tribes and Castes of Cochin,* Vol. I; Reprint 1981, New Delhi: Cosmo Publications.

Iyer, L.A. Krishna. 1937. *The Travancore Tribes and Castes*, Vol. I, Thiruvananthapuram: Supdt., Govt., Press.

Kapp, D.B. 1985. The Kurumbas' relationship to the megalithic cult of the Nilgiris Hills (South India), *Anthropos* 80–1985:493–534.

Menon, T.M. (Ed) 2000. *A Handbook of Kerala*, Vol. I; Thiruvananthapuram: International School of Dravidian Linguistics.

Nandi, S., C.R. Rajlakhmi and I.Verghese. 1971. *Life and Culture of Mala Ulladan*. Calcutta: Anthropological Survey of India.

Rivers, W.H.R. 1906. *The Todas*. New York: MacMillan.

Srinivas, M.N. 2002. *Collected Essays*. New Delhi: Oxford University Press.

Walker, A.R. 1986. *The Toda of South India: A New Look.* New Delhi: Hindustan Publishing Corporation.

8

Synthesis of Buddhism and Hinduism in Western Himalayas: A Study of the Kinnauras of Himachal Pradesh

Manis Kumar Raha

In every society, whether it is a caste or a tribe, religion plays a very important role. The manners and beliefs of all people are guided by the religion they have embraced. In every possible way, they always obey the dictum of their religion. Even the very social formation of their society has a strong support of the religion. For all their activities—economic, social and political—religion is the guiding factor. An intimate relation and interaction between socio-economic life and religion is seen in small communities with low level of technology and who live in inaccessible areas with inhospitable or extreme environmental conditions. It is truer for a tiny community like Kinnaura who have lived in isolation for centuries in the high altitudes of the western Himalayas. At the high altitude of the western Himalayas in an extremely inhospitable atmosphere, the Kinnaura with features of agrarian-transhumance and an affiliated way of life, have accepted the fatalistic theory of life, which is also true for many other communities with agrarian-pastoral economy, accompanied by low level of technology in a harsh and severe climate.

The Kinnaura or Kinnara, a scheduled tribe of Himachal Pradesh, inhabit the Himalayan district of Kinnaur, which is situated in the north-easternmost part of Himachal Pradesh bordering Tibet. This tiny district is not very old; it started functioning as a district only since 1960. Just after Independence, it was a part of the erstwhile Mahasu district and thereafter, a part of Shimla district. During pre-Independence period it was included in the kingdom of the erstwhile princely state of Bashaha. The district is connected with the state capital Shimla by the new Hindustan-Tibet Road (National Highway 22). The district is divided into three administrative units or Community Development Blocks, namely, Poo, Kalpa and Nichar. Of these three blocks, Poo is situated in Upper Kinnaur bordering Lahaul and Spiti district and Tibet. The Nichar block is included in the western part of the district and its borders touch Shimla district. The Kalpa block is situated in the south-eastern part of the district and is sandwiched by Poo and Tibet at one end and Tehri and Uttar Kashi districts of UP on the other. The Kinnauras live in a large number of villages spread over these three blocks. The district of Kinnaur has a total population of 71,270 according to the 1991 census, of which 38,394 are males and 32,876 females. This population covers 39,609 belonging to the scheduled tribes and 19,153 belonging to the scheduled castes.

This Himalayan district has three distinct culture zones. Zone one includes the whole of Poo Tehsil and Hangrang sub-Tehsil of Poo block, and is dominated by the adherents of Mahayana Buddhism (Lamaism). In zone-two which includes Nichar block, the dominance of local Hinduism is seen. Zone-three shows the presence of both the religious traditions, i.e., both Buddhism and Hinduism are embraced by the inhabitants of this zone. Here we notice an extraordinary intermingling of dual religious traditions. The main cause of this phenomenon is the continuation and presence of these two religions in different parts of this district, which has had a noticeable impact on the people. The culture and structure of the society have thus been patterned accordingly. However, some differences are also observed in the lifestyle of the people of different areas of this district. Differences are lesser compared to similarities. The people agree that there is a smooth undercurrent of cultural similarities in the quandary of cultural diversities (Raha, 2000).

The people of Kinnaur are popularly known as the Kannaura, Kinnara or Kinnaurese (Raha and Mahato, 1985). They have been mentioned in different ancient Indian classical texts and are considered as divine humankind along with the Gandharvas, Yaksas, Kiratas, Apsaras, Khasas, Guhakas, Siddhas and others. While they have been considered as the Gandharvas in the *Mahabharata*, they are associated with the Kiratas and Yakshas in *Matsya Purana.* They have also been described, like the Gandharvas, as Gitamodirah, i.e., delighting in songs, Devagayakah or Svaragagayakah, i.e., celestial singers; *sahasrasogandharvakim purushakinnarajob* (Das, 1954). Many of the mythologies establish their divine origin. According to the *Bhagavata Purana* Brahma has created both the Kinnaras and the Kimpurushas. They have also been regarded as the sons of Kashyapa. However, the *Vayu Purana* has accepted them as the sons of Asvamukhas. The *Vishnu Purana* has also considered them as Asvamukhah and found them as the inmates of Kailasa. Many other mythologies and ancient Indian literature have described them in different ways and have traced their divine connection.

The present-day economy of the Kinnaura is based mainly on agriculture. Their involvement is also found in other services, construction, livestock, forestry, orchard and also as agricultural labourers according to the 1991 census. But in the past, particularly prior to 1962 (the Indo-Chinese conflict compelled the government to close the border), the Kinnaura were engaged in three major economic pursuits, namely, agriculture, animal husbandry particularly rearing of sheep and goats, and trade with Tibet (Raha and Mahato 1985, Raha 1992a, 992b, Raha 2000). They were forced to take up these three major sources of livelihood because of the severe geo-environmental conditions which remained rocky, infertile mountainous land which failed to ensure sufficient agricultural production, and as there was heavy demand for the cattle, in this inhospitable geo-environmental condition, the Kinnauras had to supplement their economy with animal husbandry, particularly by the rearing of sheep and goat, and trade with Tibet mainly for wool and some other life saving and essential items like rock salt, butter, pasmina, borax, ponies, brick-tea, etc,. (Raha, 2000). The trade with Tibet and grazing of animals like sheep, goat, dzo, dzomo and yak in the alpine pastures of Tibet by the Kinnauras had continued in the past for centuries. But during 1962, when the border between India and Tibet was closed, the Kinnauras had to leave trade and take up some other economic pursuits. Besides terrace cultivation, they had to take up service and they stopped giving importance to animal husbandry and horticulture. A large number of constructional and development works were initiated after 1962 which have given them enough opportunity for employment and earning livelihood. The improved network of roads, market economy and higher education have added new dimensions to their economy.

The Kinnaura society is based on internal social and cultural hierarchy (Raha 1978, 1987, 1995; Raha and Mahato 1985). The Kinnauras are socially divided into two distinct categories, namely, the Khosia or Khas who are also known as the Rajputs or Kanet and the Beru. The Beru are further subdivided into the Domang which includes the Lohar (blacksmith) and the Badhi or Ores (carpenter and mason), Chamag which covers the Koli (agriculturists, spinner, weavers, leather workers) and Chanalas which include the Nangalus (basket makers). The Khosia group is, on the other hand, subdivided into three status groups (Khel) such as Orang, Maorang or Orang-Mech and Waza, each of these being further subdivided into a number of Khandans (lineages). While these social formations are well developed and clearly visible in zone-two and zone three, these are somewhat rudimentary in zone one (Raha 1978, 1987, 2000; Raha and Mahato 1985). Thus, in the Kinnaura society the Khosia enjoy a much higher social status than the Beru. The former is numerically the most dominant group. Again among the Beru, the Lohar and the Badhi consider themselves superior to the other two Beru groups (Raha, 2000).

Both khel and Khandan are patrilineal groupings but while the former is endogamous, the latter is strictly exogamous. Again both the Khel and the Khandan are further stratified on the basis of hierarchy. The Orang Khel is the most superior one while the Waza stand at the bottom of the hierarchy. In between comes the Maorang Khel. Similarly, the Khandans of the Orang enjoy the highest social status, while those of Waza get the lowest position. The Khandan of the Maorang khel occupies the intermediate position. Because of their highest social status, the Khandan of the Orang Khel always occupies important positions in different social-religious and social-political contexts. The prime religious and political functionaries come from Khandans only (Raha, 1987).

The interesting feature of the Kinnaura society is the presence of two religious faiths---Hinduism and Mahayana Buddhism (Lamaism). As already said, Buddhism is dominant in zone one, whereas Hinduism (local) prevails in zone two, but interestingly both these religious faiths are simultaneously pursued by the the people of zone three. The people here practise both religions and perform rituals of both religions. They go to the Hindu temple as well as the Buddhist monasteries. They invite Brahmin priests from Sarahan and also the Buddhist monks for performing rituals.

The coexistence of these two religious faiths is not a new phenomenon. It has been there for several centuries in the Kinnaura area. Consequently, their synthesis is not unanticipated. Hence, about one hundred and eighty years ago, Frazer (1820) observed that, "Although the Kinnaurese are recognized as Hindoos by descent and general profession, they most generally follow Lama religion." Further, according to Thornton (1854), "The religion of Koonawar in the south is Brahmanism, in the north Lamaic Buddhism, and in the middle a mixture of the two systems". Similar synthesis of the two religious faiths has also been noticed by Atkinson (1882) who found that, "The people of upper Kunaore are of Tibet origin and Buddhist in religion. Buddhism extends down the valley of the Sutlej as far as Sarahan between which and Pangi is a debatable ground common to Hindus and Buddhists." Rose (1911), Joshi (1911) and Haden (1913) also witnessed the same synthesis. An official publication of the Government of Himachal Pradesh in 1971 also confirmed this synthetic pattern. It stated, "Broadly speaking, the people in the southern part of the district follow Hinduism, in the north Buddhism and in the middle a mixture of the two religious systems is being followed," Though both Hinduism and Buddhism are found to be practised by the Kinnaura at present, it is difficult to say which one is the oldest one. Some impression in this regard may be drawn from the *Punjab States Gazetteer*, Vol.VIII, Simla Hill States (1910) which revealed that:

> "Before the spread of Buddhism, the people of these hills worshipped according to the Vedas, and afterwards returned to true Hinduism. But the view usually taken by the independent authorities is that the popular religion of these hills is a primitive form of animism or demon worship which has been overlaid with a thin veneer of Hinduism" (also see Mumgain, 1971).

As far as the distribution of population of Kinnaur based on their religious faiths is concerned, the 1971 census clearly indicates that the overwhelming majority of the population of this Himalayan district (85.25 per cent) had embraced Hinduism. The percentage of that population which has accepted Buddhism was only 14.22 per cent of the total population. But according to the 1961 census, the strength of Hinduism was 91 per cent and that of Buddhism only 9 per cent (Chib, 1984). While Hinduism had a negative growth at 13.65 per cent from 1961 to 1971, growth rate for the Buddhism in this tiny Himalayan society was as high as 63.21 per cent. Of course, the growth of the people who have embraced Sikhism during this period was also found to be high at 64.81 per cent (Chib, 1984). The 1971 census indicates that majority of the Buddhists (93.41 per cent) live in Poo sub-division (zone one). On the other hand, in Nichar sub-division (zone two) 0.32 census of the total Buddhists of the district and 33.25 per cent of the total Hindus of the district live. While only 6.27 per cent of the total Buddhists of the district live in Kalpa sub-division, here the strength of those who had embraced Hinduism is 43.49 per cent of the total Hindus of the district.

Again, as we see the strength of different religions in different sub-divisions or culture zones from the 1971 census, it is seen that out of the total population of Poo sub-division (zone one) a majority (59.17 per cent) had embraced Hinduism while the Buddhists are only 40.32 per cent. But in Nichar sub-division (zone two) almost all people (99.46 per cent) are Hindus. Almost the same picture emerges in Kalpa sub-division (zone three) where Hinduism had an overwhelming majority (97.03 per cent) whereas the Buddhists were in a small minority (2.31 per cent).

The Buddhists

The Kinnaura particularly of upper and middle regions, have strong faith in Buddhism, particularly Mahayana Buddhism (The Great Vehicle), and are further divided into three sects, Nyingma-pa, Duk-pa and Gelug-pa. The people belonging to the first two sects are more numerous than those of the third one (Raha and Mahato 1985, Raha 1995, Chandra 1992). A survey conducted in 1970–72 by the author in the Buddhist dominated areas of Kinnaur revealed that people belonging to Nyingma-pa and Duk-pa are numerically more dominant than their brethren belonging to the Gelug-pa sect. Chandra (1992) also confirms this distribution. Sen (1970) found the adherents of the Duk-pa sect in 22 out of 32 villages and the Gelug-pa sect in the remaining 10 villages. Over 150 years ago, Gerard (1841) found almost the same distribution. Chib (1984) after surveying Kinnaur villages found that in 57 out of 77 villages the inhabitants in one form or another practise the Lamaistic faith. Thus we are told that in many cases in different hamlets of the same village, different sects are followed. In these 57 villages, 75 groups emerge as belonging to different sects. Out of these 75 groups, 20 follow Dukpa sect, 21 follow Nyingma-pa, 4 follow Chodpa, 3 follow Thoma, 23 follow Gelug-pa, 2 follow Gningthi and one each follows Chhogle and Zagchhen sects. It is observed that Gelug-pa, Nyingma-pa and Duk-pa are the dominant sects. The Gelug-pa followers are found to reside in the "Sangla and Bhaba valleys and in the villages lying near the southern border of Kinnaur" (Chib, 1984). The Nyingma-pa and Duk-pa are found to reside in Pooh and Moorang Tehsils (Chib, 1984).

The Buddhists in Kinnaur propitiate a number of deities and spirits of Mahayana Buddhism and perform different rituals. The place of such worship and the training schools for the Lamas (monks) are the monasteries. The nuns (Zomo) have their own monasteries. Both Nyingma-pa and Duk-pa wear red robes and red hats. Yellow garments and hats on the other hand distinguish the Gelug-pa. While the members of the former two sects have freedom to marry, the members of the last sect are prohibited from marriage. Chandra (1992) has also found that the

Nyingma-pa and Duk-pa are more commonly known by their red robes or hats while the latter, the Gelug-pa by their yellow robes. The yellow hats, i.e., Gelug-pa Lamas are specially independent; they rear no families. The red hats, i.e., Nyingma-pa and Duk-pa sometimes do have families (Chandra, 1992).

In Kinnaur some of the Lamas are found to be married, and lead married life simultaneously along with their lamahood. The male members who opt to become Lamas do not consider marriage as conflicting with the life of a Lama. About 150 years ago, Gerard (1841) gave an account of the Lamas of Kinnaur. This gives us some idea about these functionaries of Buddhism in Kinnaur:

> "The Lamas in Koonawar belong to three sects Geloopa, Dookpa and Neeng ma. The Geloopas or Gelookpas are reckoned the highest since the head of their religion at Teshoo Loomboo and Lhasa are of the same sect. They wear yellow cloth garments and the cap of the same of various shapes. The Dookpas are dressed indifferently, but have red caps and the Neengmas wear the same or go bare headed, the two former do not marry but there is no restriction on the Neengmas..."

The Hindus and the Regional Cults

In Kinnaur, an autochthonous or native form of Hinduism is prevalent. The Hinduism of Kinnaur cannot be treated at par with the classical Hinduism of the immediate Himalayan Plains or the rest of India. Rather it is Hinduism which is impregnated with animism. It is observed that the popular religion of these hills is a primitive form of animism or demon worship, which has been overlaid with a thin veneer of Hinduism (Mumgain, 1971). While it enjoys a commanding position in Nichar block, it is found to be practised by many in Poo block also, which was once a stronghold of Buddhism. In Kalpa block, it is practised side by side with Buddhism. Raha and Mahato (1985) reported that the local Hinduism of Kinnaur is characterized by its numerous gods (Devta) and goddesses (Devi). These Devi and Devta may be divided into two categories—the principle deities and the subordinate deities. Each deity has its demarcated area over which it exerts authority and control. Each of these areas runs parallel to the traditional politico-administrative divisions of the erstwhile Bushahar state. These administrative units are Riyasat, Khunt, Ghori, Kim, etc. The Riyasat, i.e., the erstwhile Bushahar State has the supreme deity Bhima Kali, whose temple is situated at Sarahan, the summer capital of Bushahar state. Under this deity there are a number of Khunt deities. Each Khunt deity has control over a number of Ghori deities. Each Kim or household has its own deity and a number of Kim deities grouped under a Ghori deity and so on. Each of these deities is the social, religious and administrative head of all the people living in the area under its control; no one undertakes any work, social or otherwise, without the approval of the deity concerned (Raha and Mahato, 1985). Besides, there are a large number of cults present within the Hinduism of this area. Each of these cults is associated with a particular deity of a particular locality. The people of the locality are the followers of this cult. Some of the important cults are Shakti cult or Kali cult, Shiva cult, Vishnu cult, Dabla cult, Nag cult, Deodum cult, Gyalbo cult, Kuldeo cult, etc. There are a number of fairs and festivals in which one or the other of these deities presides. In many of these festivals, the worship is performed by the villagers. In special cases, they bring Brahmins from Sarahan (the seat of Bhima Kali, the presiding deity of Bushahar state) as there are no Brahmins in Kinnaur district.

Religious Functionaries

Both Buddhism and Hinduism as prevalent in Kinnaur are associated with a number of functionaries who perform a number of religious rites and rituals. Among the Buddhists of Kinnaur, there are Lama (monk) and Zomo (nun), and among the Hindus, a large number of functionaries execute the rituals and ritual related services.

Lama: The Monk

Each monastery of Kinnaur is run by a number of Lamas. There is a procedure of adopting the local children to become Lamas, under which the youngest male child from the Rajput or Khosia family becomes a Lama after taking the necessary training of Lamahood in the monastery. A Lama is required to pass through a period of celibacy. In Kinnaur, the Lamas do not wander from place to place living on alms and gifts from their devotees, instead they remain in monasteries in the village or in their neighbourhood or even in their own houses (Chandra, 1992). In addition to his routine responsibility of undertaking religious activities in the monastery, a Lama sometimes performs rituals in the house of the laity as a priest. In Kinnaur all the villages do not have monasteries. Consequently, Lamas visit different villages serving the adherents. While the Lamas of Tibet and Ladakh live in the monastery, wherever present, the Lamas of Kinnaur are allowed to live in their own houses in the village, though ideally they are supposed to stay in the monastery of their village. Chandra (1992) found that out of seventeen Lamas of a village, thirteen did not live in their village monastery, but in their houses. In another village (which does not have a monastery of its own, though there is one in the neighbourhood) also, all Lamas stayed in their own houses. Thus, we find two categories of Kinnaur Lamas, one preferring to stay in their own houses, and the other Lamas who never left the monasteries. The local informants report that the Lamas, who stay in their houses, are generally not very conversant with the Buddhist doctrines of their respective sects. They do not devote sufficient time to be trained properly in the monasteries. Many of the Lamas who live in the monasteries (though most of such Lamas hail from outside Kinnaur, not all of them hailed necessarily from Ladakh and Tibet) are better trained and well-versed with monastic life and the Buddhist doctrines of their respective sects. In the monastery, a Lama is required to go through different courses in a sequence. On completion of these courses, the Lama attains Lamahood. In Kinnaur, those Lamas who live in the monastery are highly esteemed. "The more one can have control over spirits, demons, ghosts and corpses, the higher and better Lama he is. This remains the general expression of the Kinners about the Kinnaur Lamas" (Chandra, 1992). In Kinnaur, there are two types of Lamas, Gyalong (celibate) and Dugpu. The former are strict followers of Lamahood. They do not marry, or shave their head and they essentially live in the monasteries. On the other hand, the Dugpu may live in their houses and may marry but they do not shave their head (Raha and Mahato, 1985).

Zomo: The Nun

In Kinnaur society, the Zomo are found in almost all villages where residents practise Buddhism. Those women in the Kinnaura society who do not marry and renounce the world and like to lead an ascetic life become Zomo (Raha and Mahato, 1985). Crooke (1896) found that the Kanet girls who did not marry but wanted to devote their time to the study of the Buddhist scriptures became Zomo or Jomo. Many women who want to end their rebirth, and are desirous of getting salvation and entering into heaven accept Zomoship. The Zomo normally live in monasteries (nunneries). There are also other reasons, more social, for accepting Zomoship. Polyandry is said to be partially responsible for Zomoship in Kinnaur society. Due to the practice of polyandry many young girls remain unmarried. In fact, these girls prefer the monastic life to the agony of such polyandrous married life. Andrew Wilson also found this a valid reason. Physical appearance is another factor. Normally beautiful girls get married easily but the uglier ones remain unmarried. So some of them become Zomo. Gerard (1841) did not find a single beautiful

Zomo in the nunnery, though he found handsome Lamas in the monastery.

In Kinnaur society, only the women belonging to Rajput or Khosia segment can become Zomo. The scheduled caste women have no right to become Zomo. Those young girls who are in their early teens and keen to become Zomo, enter the nunneries where they get necessary religious training as prescribed by different Buddhist sects. The initiation ceremony starts after obtaining the consent of their parents. During initiation, their heads are shaved and they are given gowns of different colours to put on, as prescribed for different sects. In the past, they used to wear headgear, yellow in colour, trimmed in red (Gerard, 1841). However, nowadays they are not seen wearing such hats. The Zomos remain unmarried throughout their life and never indulge in sexual intercourse with anybody, not even with a Lama or a laity (Raha and Mahato, 1985).

The Hindu Religious Functionaries

Several religious functionaries are attached to the Hindu temples in Kinnaur. Most prominent among them are the Kardar. They remain attached to the temple (santhang) of a deity. They are Rajput or Khosia by caste and not Brahman as the Brahmans remain attached only to the temple of Bhima Kali at Sarahan. In Kinnaur, there is no Brahman family and so the Brahmans are not found to function as the Kardar. For the temples belonging to the Koli, the second numerically dominant caste of this Himalayan district, the functionaries are Koli by caste. Some Kolis also act as musicians in the Rajput temples. The Kardars actually serve the deity and control the socio-religious administration of the social-political units like the Gaon, the Ghori, the Khunt, etc. (Raha, 1978). These functionaries do all sorts of work related not only to the deity and the temple but they also stand between the deity and the public as a mediator or intermediary. A villager cannot directly approach the deity and tell his or her problem. He or she will have to take help of the Koli functionaries as some of these functionaries only have the right and ability to customarily approach the deity.

The Pujaras: The Ritual Performers

The Pujara is one of the three very important temple functionaries, the other two being the Grokch and the Mathas. The duty of the Pujara is to perform rituals regularly. He goes to the temple either in the morning or in the evening or both times to worship the deities. Besides the regular worships, he also performs worships on special occasions. He even goes to individual houses if any worship is to be conducted there. For this he is paid either in cash or in kind or both. But for regular worship in the temple and also for his position, he gets some portion of land which he cultivates. As his post is hereditary, after his death his next brother occupies his position; in absence of the brother, his eldest son becomes the Pujara and then he occupies the land.

The Grokch: The Shaman

The Grokch is another important functionary. The villagers regard him as the most important functionary as he is the person who narrates the problems of the villagers to the deity on behalf of those who want to approach the deity for solutions or take the deity's advice on certain issues. No other functionary can speak to the deity directly. It is impossible for the common people to talk to the deity directly. The Grokch invokes the deity periodically when the villagers approach him with problems of the village. As a special case even when an individual with a serious problem approaches the Grokch, the latter invokes the deity. On the day of invocation, normally during day time, the Chalias take out the deity in a palanquin. They lift the palanquin on their shoulders and then start rhythmic swings or movements, up and down and side to side. The Grokch while touching the moving palanquin starts chanting hymns. Then he gradually narrates the problems to the deity. The office of the Grokch is also hereditary and like the Pujaras, he is entitled to a piece of land for his service.

The Mathas: The Oracle

The Mathas is also another very important functionary. He acts as the oracle and informs the public about the will, advice, order or decision of the deity. He is the only functionary who can understand the mind of the deity. The method, by which he understands the mind of the deity, is very exciting. After the Grokch completes his chanting and narration, the Mathas comes in; he touches the palanquin and starts chanting a hymn. Then he requests the deity to speak and give his/her decision, advice, etc. He may have to make such a request more than once. All along, the Chalias swing the palanquin. All of a sudden, the palanquin tilts a little more on one side. This tilting indicates the will, advice, order or decision of the deity, positive or negative. The Mathas only can understand the real meaning of the tilt. He divulges the meaning to the public. The public will have to obey the will of the deity. There is indeed a complex system of propitiation of the Hindu deities in Kinnaur society, which is very different from the standard form of Hindu worship observed elsewhere.

The Mathas also gets an area of land for his service and his office is also hereditary. He is considered as the mediator between the deity and the public. The Khajanchi, Chalia, Krosia (Deotu), Halmandi and Baijayantri are other religious functionaries. The Khajanchi, who is also known as the Kaithas, is the accountant or the treasurer of the temple. He keeps accounts of all income and expenditure of the temple. He also keeps account of donations given to the temple or the deity, payment and of loans, interest on loans, income from temple repayment land and so on. He also keeps account of the expenditure incurred during some festivity or puja. He also keeps the temple records. There are at least four Chalias in a temple. Their duty is to lift and carry the palanquin on which the deity is kept. At a time four Chalias lift the palanquin, two on each side. They hold the horizontal rod of the palanquin on their shoulders, and when required swing the palanquin. The Krosia or Deotu guards the temple. There may be one or more Krosia in a temple depending upon the size and importance of the temple or the deity. They are provided with spears to protect the temple property. The Halmandi acts as the messenger of the temple. When there is any festival or puja or during the time of the visit of some deity, he informs the villagers. The Baijayantris or the musicians play musical instruments when there is some puja, festival or visit of the deity. But they do not belong to the Rajput or Khosia group. They are normally Koli, the scheduled caste.

In Kinnaur, as already mentioned, a common villager or the laity has no right to approach the deity and narrate his or her problem. Even a group of villagers cannot do this. Similarly he or she or a group of villagers cannot directly receive the verdict of the deity in the form of advice, order, decision or the will of the deity. They at the same time cannot propitiate or worship a Gaon, Ghori, Khunt or Riyasat deity directly. For all these, they have to depend on a few functionaries who only have the auspicious religious rights. They stand in between the deity and the villagers. If a villager or a group of villagers have some problem such as marriage of their children, serious illness of some relation, outbreak of disease, agricultural failure and trade problem, they first consult with the Pujaras. Considering the importance of the issue, the Pujaras conduct worship on an appointed day by arranging lifting of the palanquin of the deity. On the appointed day the Chalias, after puja conducted by the Pujaras, lift the palanquin and start swinging it. The Grokch on behalf of the devotees narrates the problem to the deity and the latter gives the verdict through the Mathas. The villagers have no option but to obey the verdict of the deity delivered by the Mathas. The important religious functionaries of the Kinnaur society are from not only the Rajput (Khosia) caste; they also belong to the superior Khel (Orang) and superior Khandan of the Rajput segment. Unless one is a Rajput belonging to Orang Khel, one cannot become an important functionary of the Hindu temple or the Chief Lama of the Buddhist monastery.

In the past, in order to have control over the subjects and to keep solidarity during external invasion and internal feuds, the king of Bushahar exerted his power over his subjects through the Wazirs (head of the Khunt) and more importantly through the above mentioned Hindu religious functionaries or the Buddhist Lamas of the monasteries who were very loyal to him. Even in case of the election of the office bearers and members of the Charbhai, the traditional panchayat, the verdict of the deity used to be sought as to who will contest as a candidate. Here also, only the Rajput of highest Khels and Khandans used to emerge as contestants. So the common people of Kinnaur remained perpetually subservient and at the mercy of the deity. They could not disobey, disregard or disrespect the sacred will of the deity.

We have observed that a number of functionaries, both Hindu and Buddhist, play crucial roles in the cultural life of Kinnara people. There are two types of Lamas, Gyalong and Dugpu and a category of nun called Zoma. It is mostly the people of the Rajput or Khosia caste who can become Buddhist functionaries. The Hindu religious functionaries, Kardar, Pujara, Grokch and Mathas also belong to Rajput or Khosia caste. Thus we see a virtual monopoly of a higher caste over positions of sacred specialists. We notice only a negligible role of Brahmans in the ritual sphere of the Hindu segment of the Kinnars. The predominant religious roles performed by the Rajput clans in both the religious domains of Hinduism and the Buddhism provides a unique character to the cultural landscape of this western Himalayan region of India. Notwithstanding this parochial sort of theocratic arrangement, we also notice a strong undercurrent of religious homogenization and cultural syncretism witnessed in concurrent pursuance of two local variants of Hinduism and Buddhism by people who employ both Hindu and Buddhist sacred specialists for performing local rituals.

References

Chandra, R., 1992, *Highlanders of Northwestern Himalayas* New Delhi, Inter-India Publications.

Chib, S.S., 1984, *Kanauras of Trans Himalayas,* New Delhi, ESS Publications.

Crooke, W., 1896, *Tribes and Castes of North Western Provinces and Oudh,* Vol-III, Calcutta, Superintendent, Government Press.

Das, S.R., 1954, A Note on the Kinnaras, *Man in India* Vol., 34 No. 1.

Frazer, J.B., 1820, *Journal of a Tour through part of the Snowy Ranges of the Himalayan Mountains*, London: Administrative Publications.

Gerard, A., 1841, *Account on the Koonawar in the Himalayas etc.*, London. M. Millan.

Government of Himachal Pradesh, 1971, *Statistical Abstract, Kinnaur*, Simla: Government of Himachal Pradesh.

Haden, Sven, 1913, *Trans Himalayas.* Vol.III, 1910. London: Macmillan and Co.

Joshi, T.R., 1911, *Notes on the Ethnography of Bushahr State, Simla Hills, Punjab* (Ed) H.A. Rose, *Journal of Asiatic Society of Bengal,* September, Vol.VII No. 9 (N.S.)

Mumgain, M.D., 1971, *Himachal Pradesh District Gazetteer, Kinnaur,* Simla: Government of Himachal Pradesh.

Raha, M.K., 1978, Stratification and Religion in a Himalayan Society. In *Himalayan Anthropology* (Ed) James P. Fisher. The Hague: Mouton and Co.

—, 1987, The Khandan System among the Kinnauras of the Western Himalayas. In *The Himalayan Heritage* (Ed) M.K. Raha, Delhi: Gian Publishing House.

—, 1992a, Economic Strategy, Religious Dualism and Change in Diverse Cultural and Ecological Settings: A Case from Western Himalayas. In *The Himalayas and the Himalayans* (Ed) M.K. Raha, Calcutta: Anthropological Survey of India.

—, 1992b, The Changing Economy of the Kinnaura. In *Tribal Transformation in India* (Ed) Buddhadeb Choudhary, New Delhi: Inter-India Publications.

—, 1993, Politics, Political Organization and Religion in the Himalayas: A Emerging Pattern. In *Polity, Political Process and Social Control in South Asia* (Ed) M.K. Raha and I.A. Khan. New Delhi: Gyan Publishing House.

—, 1995, Society and Religion in Kinnaur. In *People of the Himalayas* (Ed) M.K. Raha, Calcutta: Anthropological Survey of India.

----, 2000, Structure and Culture in a Himalayan Society. In *Science and Culture* Special issue on the Himalayans, Vol.65 No. 11 & 12.

Raha, M.K. and S.N. Mahato, 1985, *The Kinnaurese of the Himalayas*, Calcutta, Anthropological Survey of India.

Rose, H.A., 1911, *A Glossary of the Tribes and Castes of Punjab and N.W.F.P.* Vol-II Lahore: Government Press.

Sen, B., 1970, *Social Changes in the Himalayan Villages: A Case Study of Three Villages in Kinnaur District* (Unpublished Ph.D. dissertation).

Thornton, E., 1854, *A Gazetteer of the Territories under the Government of the East India Company and the Native States in the Continent of India*, London: Administrative Publication.

9

Monotheistic Islam and Pluralistic Islamic Traditions of India

Shibani Roy and S.H.M. Rizvi

Review of the existing literature on Islam and its global spread indicates that the earliest contact between Indian people and Islamic world may have been first established in the southern parts of India. Indeed the age-old trade relations between Arabia and India not only initiated the exchange of goods and commodities but also the religious and philosophical dialogue involving moral values and ethics. It was the interest of the trade which led to the Arab conquest of the Sind during early eighth century. The exposure of India to Islamic influence continued unabated till the establishment of Delhi Sultanate in 1206 AD. Thereafter, for over five hundred years, the Muslims remained politically dominant till the advent of the British in India. At the outset, it may be mentioned that the number of Muslims who came from outside India was very small. Among these migrant Muslims, only a few came with their families, and thus, the vast majority of the Muslim population of India have actually been converts from various segments of Indian population. The historical accounts of enforced and large-scale conversion of individual families do not explain the existence of a sizeable number of Indian Muslims in northern India as early as 13th century AD. There must have been other forces, besides the political impetus, of which we do not have adequate knowledge. Further, while conversion from Hinduism to Islamic way of life took centuries, during the long process numerous communities continued to retain Hindu influence in their social life.

A cursory glance at the customs and ideas reveals that Hindu customs and rites have far greater hold on the Muslims than Islamic customs and practices. Certain customs have been so internalized that their origin remains debatable. For example, there does exist a controversy about the origin of *purdah* system, yet, there can be no doubt that Muslims have directly or indirectly enforced this practice. On the other hand, the Muslim women lost the status accorded to them in the Islamic laws by the absorption of Hindu ideas. The daughter lost her rights of inheritance as found amongst the Pangal (the Manipuri Muslims). The interplay of these two major social forces resulted in the emergence of a Muslim population of India, which presents a complete and sometimes partial conglomeration of Hindu and Islamic rites and customs. The main difference between Hindu and Islamic approach is that Hinduism was mainly a religion of a specified class, with, only the Brahmans being entitled to rites, duties and privileges, acting as a mediator between common men and God, whereas, Islam was a religion of masses, where every follower was treated equally with the same law. This egalitarian essence of Islam was greatly influenced after reaching India, where the religion was confined within the ruling circle or the aristocracy who in their turn were patronized by the religious clergies like mullah and Kazi. Sufism was greatly responsible for bringing closer Islam and Hinduism, since, most of the Sufis believed in the doctrine of unity of existence being a manifestation of God. They did not distinguish between Hindus and Muslims and opened their shrines (dargah) for both to commemorate ceremonies such as Urs. Thus Sufism could demolish the barriers of language and religion and Islam learnt the language of the people. An outstanding example of this change is *Padmavat* of Mallik Mohammad Jais, which was written in Avadhi dialect. This served as a model for the *Ramacharit Manasa* of Goswami Tulsidas which attained the status of a scripture (Mujeeb, 1972).

Thus the Indian Muslims represent a culturally and ethnically diversified group bound together only by their common belief in Islam. Even in the religious domain, Muslims are classified into different sects and have diversified schools of legal jurisprudence. These groups form a firm basis of differentiation amongst the Indian Muslims. However, the divisions and sects among Muslims appear to be too simplistic to outsiders, more so due to the ideological overtone of egalitarianism; the actual situation reveals a most complex setup representing neither the Hindu varna order nor the Western class pattern, yet drawing clear boundaries through diversified ethnicity and differing religious ideologies.

A Muslim may marry any woman outside the prohibited degree, by social sanction, but in practice it is found that some Muslim groups manifest various social and cultural differentiation which have been enhanced by restricted or almost closed marriage circles (Rizvi and Roy, 1984). The Chhipa community of Rajasthan which is predominantly found in Barmer, Jaisalmer, Pali and Kota districts, practise the age-old traditional method of dyeing by vegetable colours. Till date, the non-Muslim population of the surrounding areas utilize the services of the village Chhipa and thus, they have confined themselves and are restricted within a limited area. On the other hand, the Arab community of Junagadh district of Gujarat stand out as a proof to the history when Arabs formed a part of the invading army. These families still cherish and maintain the banners which their ancestors had carried with them. These banners carry the names of the family, village and ancestors, written in Arabic. The Singis are another fast disappearing Muslim community still found in pockets in and around the districts of Rajasthan bordering Pakistan. They derive their name from their medical apparatus made from a bull's horn *seeng*. The Koya of Lakshadweep islands have various customs to alienate them from the neighbouring Muslim population by practising matriliny. The Bora is a trading community confined mostly to rural areas of Assam. The Ruhela or Rohilla of Uttar Pradesh are of Rajput parentage. They are confined to Bulandshahar, Saharanpur, Meerut and Muzaffarnagar districts of western Uttar Pradesh bordering Haryana and Delhi. Though numerically small, they exhibit definite customs and rites which speak of their Rajput ancestry. One of these is the avoidance of first cousin (father's brother's daughter) marriage keeping with the Hindu traditions. The neighbouring Meo and Muslim Mina (Padihar) are examples of the Muslim rural elites who gave the converts freedom to practise and continue their pre-change religious customs.

Let us first view the diversity of beliefs and synthesized customs of some Muslim communities, selected randomly from north to west and south to east.

Northern India

In Haryana, a large number of Muslim agriculturists were worshipping their ancestral village deities till the late part of the 19th century. In Rajasthan and bordering Haryana, the Mina and Meos have purely Hindu names with the suffix of Khan. They celebrate not only Diwali and Dussera but also Janmashtami. The Padihar Mina in Bharatpur, Agra and neighbouring Dhaulpur areas of Uttar Pradesh eat beef unlike the Hindu Minas living in Sawaimadhopur and Jaipur districts of Rajasthan. The presence of shrines such as Panchpira, Bhaiya or Bhairoji in the villages dominated by Meos and Minas is an example of continuance of the original faith even after conversion to Islam. The heroic and semi-divine personality Shiekh Moinuddin Chishti is venerated today by all the Indian communities. But Meo being in close proximity of Ajmer show greater reverence for the said Pir. Yet, Meos do not marry within the gotra. In Ratlam and other districts of Madhya Pradesh, Kunjra, Behna and Kaji Muslim cultivators follow Hindu customs in their marriage, worship the goddess of smallpox (Shitala-mata) and give a lot of importance to *toran,* the decorative paper-cloth hanging on the door, during marriage rites which is a pan-middle India phenomenon. The Mahdawi of Ahmedabad (Gujarat) are organized in *daira* (circle) and the society does not permit any marriage beyond Mahdawi. This has resulted in the formation of a highly inbred group having minimal social interaction with other neighbouring Muslim communities such as Dawoodi Bohra, Sulemani Bohra, Khoja and Kutchi.

The Mahdawi movement during the 16th century had an impact on other tribes of Gujarat also such as Koli, Bhil and Siddi. Some sections of these tribes, though converted to Islam, yet, could not be weaned away from their indigenous religious practices. Likewise, a section of the Siddis of Gujarat embraced Islam. However, the survival of worship of trees and rivers among them speaks of the emergence of a new form of religious cult based on two principles, one belonging to a male fertilizing element in the form of the river and other a female producing element in the nature of vegetation. The presence of the shrine of Udorelal who is considered an incarnation of a river god reinforces their indigenous form of nature worship. The Ismaili Khoja community regarded *zaqat* to Agha Khan who is considered the unrevealed Imam. The manual prepared by one of the Pirs of this community, Saaduddin, is read by each Khoja and accorded the same amount of sanctity as accorded to the *Quran* by other Muslim communities. Besides Muslim Rajputs and Jats, we come across numerous smaller Muslim rural families in Indo-Gangetic plains who believe in the miraculous powers of saints, living or dead. Even for regular daily work, they depend on miracles and magic to a great extent. This is in total contravention of Islamic tenets, which believes in an omnipotent Allah. In the district of Purnea (Bihar) the dividing line between the religious beliefs and practices between lower caste Hindus and Muslims is very faint. In every village, one can find a *Kalisthan*---shrine dedicated to the worship of goddess Kali, and the presence of *Khudaighar*---God's house attached to almost every Muslim house. In these shrines, the prayers are offered in which the names of Allah and Kali are used. The Bengali Muslims of Kishangunj district (Bihar) build little shrines for *Baisahari* (the snake goddess) which is a Hindu deity of that area. In the central districts of Madhya Pradesh such as Damoh, Saugar, Jabalpur and Mandla we find a community known as Mirdha or Patel who have Hindu names and dress exactly like the neighbouring Hindus in *dhoti* and *kurta* and revere Bhawani and other Hindu deities.

As stated elsewhere (Roy, 1984, Rizvi and Roy 1984), Gujarat has been a melting pot of diverse ethnic groups and beliefs. In this region, we find a diversified Islam in the form of beliefs practised by Khoja, Bohra, Mahdawi, Siddi, Aliya, Arab, Baluch, Barot, Bora, Bhatti and others. The socio-religious practices of these communities could not be ascribed to the Islamic pattern. The presence of Hussaini Brahmans in Allahabad, Ganchi, and Madari and various offshoots of Sufi sects add to the kaleidoscopic pattern of Indian Muslims.

Western India

The Dawoodi Bohras are original residents of Gujarat and Maharashtra. They do not have a second opinion about their conversion from Anavil Brahmans and Lohana Rajputs. Moreover, this fact gains repeated confirmation from the various rites and customs practised by this group which are alien to the general pattern of Islam. The first is the concept of *pakeezgi* as found amongst the Bohras which is unique to them and has a regional character. *Hammam* (bathroom) is considered *napak* (ritually unclean) by them, hence separate set of slippers are assigned for offering the *namaz* (prayer) and practice of taking off the slippers on entering a room give a legitimacy to their conversion from a Brahman caste. The Dawoodi Bohras of Rajasthan abstain from eating beef. Likewise, the average consumption of goat's meat is far below the average quantity consumed by other neighbouring Muslim communities. It may be noted here that Bohra is one of the richest Muslim communities of India. They are so strict about *zabah* (ritual slaughter of animal) that even fish is eaten only after performing *zabah* which is a very cumbersome and tedious activity. Among other Muslim communities, fish can be eaten without performing *zabah.* During ceremonial occasions, distribution of jaggery and coconut forms the main item, whereas in Islamic traditions dates are considered to be auspicious fruit for ceremonial distribution rather than coconut. The *artiutarna* and *ghudchadi* are the two pan-Hinduistic rites practised by the Bohras. Thus the groom rides on a decorated horse and proceeds to the bride's place where the ceremony of *artiutarna* is performed by the female relatives who welcome him by offering flowers, fruits and sweets. Instead of Islamic lunar calendar, the Bohra follow a luni-solar calendar in which the number and dates are fixed. Thus the Bohra calendar is always a few days ahead of the Islamic calendar which sets them apart from the other Muslims. In keeping with the egalitarian attitude of Islam, the Bohras do not display any form of hierarchy in their social system. The named social categories (Roy, 1979) are mainly determined by the ware they deal within business. In Rajasthan duolocal pattern of residence is adopted. After marriage the women being mostly 'visiting wives' whose priorities lie with the natal home. This might be attributed as the vestiges of matriliny as practised by the Brahmans on the western coast of India. On the other hand, in keeping with ancient Islamic traditions this is probably the only Muslim community today which practises clitoridectomy. Their dialect Bohri is a mixture of Mewari, Urdu and Gujarati. Thus, among the Muslim groups of India so far recorded, the Bohra exhibit firm coexistence of traditional Islam along with Hinducentric mores and values.

Southern India

Kalpeni is one of the ten islands which constitute the Lakshadweep islands in the south-west coast of India. The actual date and historical situations leading to entry of Islam in these islands are not known. However, from the accounts of Abdulla Ibn-e-Mohammad the tentative date fixed is AH 41. It is believed that Abu Baqar's (the first Khalifa) grandson Ubaidullah sailed and reached these islands, married a local woman who was the first convert. Gradually the residents of all other islands embraced Islam. Today people of Kalpeni belong to the Shafi school of Sunni division of Islam. Three distinct social divisions are found amongst them, which is contrary to the preachings of Islam. The three divisions are Koya, Mali and Melachari. All these divisions are strictly endogamous in nature. The islanders are matrilineal, the descent being traced through the mother. The traditional pattern of residence is duolocal, the husband visiting the wife every night. Thus a majority of husbands are 'visiting husbands'. They have adopted the Malayali word *taravad* which signifies lineage. Paternity right of the father is established by the custom of offering gifts to the wife during childbirth. The solar calendar followed by the mainland Malayali determines all the rites of intensification for the islanders, while the Islamic lunar calendar regulates their religious rites and festivals. Coconut is considered to be an auspicious fruit and is offered in the mosques. The women are in no way segregated or put behind veils. They contribute to the family and spend a considerable part of their time in rope and coir making. Blood-letting (practised by the Singis of Rajasthan) is an accepted norm of ethno-medicine amongst them and mostly people subscribe to it to keep their blood 'pure'. The rites of *nikah* (marriage) and circumcision have been adopted by the islanders which form the essential elements of Islam. However, the puberty rites similar to that of Nairs are gradually being discarded. Thus this island society presents an amalgamation of the patriarchal stance of Islam and the traditional matrilineal social structure of the mainland Malayalis of Kerala.

North-East India

North-eastern India being a tribal dominated area, is inhabited by a multitude of various ethnic-linguistic groups, who live in the hills and the plains, including foothill areas and thereby giving rise to different cultural zones. Except for the systematic penetration and spread of Christianity no other religious missionaries had significantly contributed to the social system of these tribal groups. The colonial rule finally put its stamp on the area and people by creating a service class, the forest areas which were ruled for centuries by independent tribal groups were brutally subjugated, to a considerable extent. This was followed by exploitation of land and people by the administrative machinery. It is surprising to note that the local populace except in few localized instances offered no resistance. The people were not mobilized by either political or religious personalities. It is surprising to note that no Muslim dervish or godman had ever visited these areas. The entry of Muslims in North-East India was limited to Assam valley mainly as prisoners of war.

The contact of Islam with the Khasi, Jaintia and Garo tribes of Meghalaya dates back to 17th century when Muslims initiated the visits to these hills for establishing trade links and other related activities. During and after the colonial rule, a number of Muslims from as far as Afghanistan, Kashmir, Punjab, Rajasthan, Uttar Pradesh, Bihar, Madras, Hyderabad, Cachar and Dacca migrated to this region. A close study of this hybrid section of community reveals that there was no organized or systematic process of Islamization. The impact of Muslim culture had been relatively negligible since the converts were mostly women belonging to a highly organized matrilineal Khasi society wherein the women reigned supreme in household and trade. This was the reason that despite the prolonged contact with Islamic traditions, the Muslim Khasis retained their tribal identities except in few families which are considered to be the exceptions. The Khasi Muslims observe all the Khasi customary ceremonies and festivals and follow matrilineal lineage pattern. In contemporary era, the Muslims of Meghalaya play significant roles in the socio-political arena. The main reason for this being the retention of their tribal identity by which they derive several benefits from the administration, which are denied to the other Muslims groups. Some of the evolving social segments are Kharpuri, Kharchana, Kharbuli, etc. The most striking feature amongst the Muslims of Meghalaya is their linguistic divisions. Two distinct groups are discernible amongst them, the Urdu speaking and non-Urdu-speaking people. Though both the groups have taken up spouses from the indigenous tribal population, yet, at the home front they distinctly characterize their differential cultural background. Amongst the Urdu speaking come men from Punjab, Uttar Pradesh, Bihar and Rajasthan while the non-Urdu-speaking constitute the Assamese, Silchari-Bengali (Sylheti) and Manipuri Muslims. The distinctive bio-cultural features characterize each of these groups, prime amongst them being the dialect.

Another exemplification of the coming of Muslim populace from the plains to Meghalaya may be traced in early 19th century during the establishment of British government offices at Cherrapunji. Along with the British officers came a retinue of menial staff who were Muslims. Later, the opening of the Survey of India office at Shillong inducted many Muslims. These people were sent to Quetta for training. Most of them returned from there with the honorific title of Khan affixed to their names. This group started claiming their descent from Pathan ancestors. However, at Shillong they were referred to as 'survey khan' by the local Muslims. In the meantime, the men who had accompanied the British espoused the local Khasi tribal women by converting them into Islam. However, the Khasi being matrilineal, these women could never totally alienate themselves from their natal homes since a woman had a lot of familial obligations and duties. Further, they were never totally incorporated within the Muslim populace who treated them poorly for being 'half Muslim'. Independence of the country and later the formation of Meghalaya as a state brought in significant changes. For the first time the children of mixed parentage realized that concealing their tribal identity does not lead them anywhere. Instead, adopting their mother's clan name brings a lot of privileges and opportunities through governmental measures for social welfare of tribal communities. Thus amidst the multitude of ethnic groups another group emerged which asserted its tribal bearings. A cultural milieu evolved where the mother's matrilineal relatives had as much importance as the father's relatives. The language, behaviour and custom was a blend of at least two distinct cultures, one strictly patriarchal, while the other comprised of matrilineal Khasis. The conglomeration of these opposite traits gave rise to unique familial-jural situations pertaining to distribution of property, residence pattern after marriage, authority pattern of man/woman in a predominantly matrilineal realm, etc. This group presents contrasting features. During 1985, this group had organized a movement (Seng Samla Muslim) which had distinct and defined objectives.

In the first ever Muslim invasion of Assam (by the Turkish army) in AD 1532, the Muslims were defeated and taken as prisoners of war by the Ahom kings and kept in different parts of Assam. The Muslim prisoners of war were known as Maria. Their traditional occupation was brass making. These men took Assamese women as their spouses and adapted themselves to the indigenous culture of the land with the exception of their Islamic names. The final strengthening of Muslim population took place in the 17th century by the coming of Azan Fakir or Shah Milan. He had been instrumental in revitalizing Islam in Assam. This was followed by the coming of other Muslim missionaries whereby a large section of the indigenous population was converted to Islam. The total number of Muslims enumerated in Brahmaputra valley reached 21,99,330 during 1961. Sayyad, Garia and Maria are the three main categories of Muslims of Assam. Sayyad claim their descent from Arab immigrants, the Garia claim their origin to Gaur (the ancient Muslim capital of Bengal) region, while the Maria are brass makers. Thus in hierarchy, the Sayyads are at the top of the social ladder followed by Garia and Maria. All these three categories maintain considerable distance in social and marital spheres though education is gradually eroding these social barriers.

The recorded history of Manipur state indicates the coming of Islam in the early 17th century (1606 AD) but according to legends and oral traditions prevailing among Pangal (Manipuri Muslims), Islam came into Manipur even earlier. The Manipuri Muslims, locally referred to as Pangan or Pangal, can be divided into two major sub-divisions—Khunja (agriculturist) and Ingkhol (artisan). According to the 1991 census, there were 1,33,535 Muslims in Manipur spread over 69 villages in the valley. According to the palace records *(puiya)* Manipuri Muslims are further divided into 30 lineages *(sagei)* but this number varies between 31 and 46 according to local knowledgeable informants. These lineages are based on occupation. For example, Maibam connotes physician while Chesam lineage is assigned the occupation of paper making. These lineages are exogamous and regulate the institution of marriage. In the prescribed mating system we come across the avoidance of marriage with one's father's brother's daughter in total contrast to Asna Ashariya of Uttar Pradesh and Delhi among whom this type of consanguineous marriage is considered to be an obligatory duty.

The Pangal cannot be identified with any of the prevalent Muslim sects present in India, mainly due to the late arrival of Islam in this region wherein the Islamic traditions are yet to penetrate the existing cultural milieu which is mainly dominated by Meiteis. The resurgence of Vaishanavite and Sanamahi movements amongst the Meitei has greatly affected the Muslim sections and we come across instances of initial sparks of Islamic revivalism borrowed from neighbouring Cachar and Bangladesh. It has been observed that the emergence of *purdah*, segregation of females, adherence to *nikah* (marriage) and formation of *madarsa* (traditional Islamic school) coupled with adoption of 'named categories' (such as Sayyad, Mir, Pathan and Shiekh) are the Islamic traits gradually being adopted by Pangals. In the process of formation of Manipuri Muslims it has been presumed that a handful of soldiers captured as prisoners of war were allowed to marry with Meitei women by the king. This was a gesture to integrate these soldiers in the Meitei society in order to gain knowledge and expertise in making guns, gunpowder, paper, woodwork and pottery. However, the influence of Islamic traits on such unions was minimal to the extent of observance of certain tenets of Islam only in the privacy of home. For instance, circumcision which features as one of the integral rites for believers of Islam and by which they are incorporated as a member of the religious community, is observed with a lot of festivity and the young boy attired as a bridegroom is taken around the neighbourhood before the actual rite. However, among the Pangal this important rite (*sunnatauba*) is performed with a sense of secrecy with the only witnesses being the parents and the Muslim barber (Napit) who is actually the migrant expert from neighbouring Cachar hills. Besides, another significant Islamic rite of *aqiqa* (shaving of head) which is an important passage rite amongst other Indian Muslims is absent among the Pangals. Also the significant Islamic rite of *bismillah* (the ritual of inception of religious education through reading *Quran* and writing of alphabet of Arabic language by a child) has not been prevalent among the Pangals with the result that the majority of Pangal men and women are deprived of learning the holy book which is an important prerequisite for the followers of Islam. Consequently till date the mullahs (religious preachers) are brought to Manipur from neighbouring areas of Assam and Bangladesh to lead the people in their religious observances and to attend to the working of the local mosques. Besides, their religious ignorance is constantly being gainfully utilized by the office bearers of religious institutions for deriving monetary benefits. Regular cash donations are taken from the villagers in the name of charity. Further, the absence of a Haji (a Muslim who has been to Macca and Madina) amongst the Pangals confirms their naivete about their religion. The visit to Macca and Madina does not form an important feature of a Pangal's life. Further, Sufism, one of the significant Islamic religious movements, had never reached these people. This fact is further strengthened by the conspicuous absence of any mausoleum, shrine or dargah in Manipur state. The native pattern of union of man and woman could not be changed by the democratic style of Islamic marriage rite observed elsewhere, whereby a woman had full right to refuse a man. The custom of payment of bride price has taken such an enormous shape that the parents sanction their children to elope rather than go through the expensive marriage rituals where exchange of presentations weigh heavily on the respective parents' shoulders. It is interesting to note that the Pangal youth have fruitfully utilized the pre-Islamic trait of marriage by elopement (*chenba*) in today's world.

An important aspect of Meitei marriage negotiations is consultation with the Meitei astrologer who matches the stars of prospective spouses and finalizes the auspicious day of marriage. The Pangals still have faith in these Meitei astrologers. The Pangals being rural settled agriculturists strictly observe the rites of intensification by the solar calendar followed by the Meitei, except for Id and other major Islamic festivals for which they fall back upon the Islamic lunar calendar. The Pangals also celebrate *Thabalchongba* (analogous to Holi festival) with the same fervour as celebrated by the Vaishnavite Meiteis. Finally the Pangals exhibit their Manipuri leanings through their language. The script of the Meitei language (Meiteilon) is common to them except for inclusion of a few words of Arabic, Persian and Bengali origin which had to be included in their dialect due to their Islamic bearing. Thus, words such as *sunnat, ijjat, haq, hukum, kanungo, darker* are used in common parlance amongst the Pangals.

Recapitulation

The preceding account of spread of Islam (see spread of Muslim population in India in Annexure-I) and its distinctive acceptance in various ecological zones of India, clearly manifests the strong pull of original religious-cultural beliefs which survived in all historical phases. We thus witnessed the coexistence of pre-change religious beliefs with the adopted religious beliefs of the people. The prevalence of the concept of 'ritual purity' (bathroom being considered 'ritually impure') amongst the Bohras is an example of perfect assimilation of two counter-forces in the Indian religious scenario. The liberality that was one of the salient features of Indian culture had been mainly instrumental for the gradual diffusion and acceptance of this alien religion in a land where Hindu philosophy and teaching reigned supreme for centuries.

In the spread of Islam, contributions of various Islamic missionaries who by their sheer charisma made innumerable followers were no less important. Thus, Islam with a worldview of non-hierarchy, monotheism and 'messianic historical ethos' was unlike the great Hindu tradition. Its socio-democratic attitude and non-ritualistic approach towards the common man attracted people from various segments of Indian society. Further, history reveals that abstract monotheism as preached by the Sufi saints and philosophers not only came to be accepted by the Hindu masses but also formed a bridge between the Hindu traditions and Islam. Akbar's *Dine-e-Ilahi*, Dara Shikoh's synthesis of Upanishadic monotheism with Islam and Amir Khusro's linkage of Hinduism to the Islamic sphere gave rise to many a distinctive literary works. The decline of Islamic traditions came with the advent of the British colonialists and the final substitution of Persian by English in 1932 acted as a dwindling force. The foregoing ethnographic account of the Muslim populations in various geographical zones of India clearly exhibits the retention of regional cultural characteristics and its congruence with Islamic traditions.

Annexure I

Spread of Islam in India (Based on 1991 census)

State/Union Territory	*Muslim Population*	*Per cent to Total*	*Per cent*
India	101596057	12.12	32.76
Andhra Pradesh	5923954	8.91	30.66
Arunachal Pradesh	11922	1.38	135.01
Assam	6373204	20.43	-
Bihar	12787985	14.81	29.50
Goa	61455	5.25	48.74
Gujarat	3606920	8.73	24.05
Haryana	763775	4.64	45.89
Himachal Pradesh	89134	1.72	28.04
Jammu & Kashmir	3843451	64.19	-
Karnataka	5234023	11.64	25.71
Kerala	6788364	23.33	25.49
Madhya Pradesh	3282800	4.96	31.21
Maharashtra	7628755	9.67	31.40
Manipur	133535	7.27	34.44
Meghalaya	61462	3.46	48.34
Mizoram	4538	0.66	105.80
Nagaland	20642	1.71	74.84
Orissa	577775	1.83	36.83
Punjab	239401	1.18	42.42
Rajasthan	3525339	8.01	41.46
Sikkim	3849	0.95	18.76
Tamilnadu	3052717	5.47	21.14
Tripura	196495	7.13	41.84
Uttar Pradesh	24109684	17.33	36.54
West Bengal	16075836	23.61	36.89
Andaman & Nicobar	21354	7.61	31.91
Chandigarh	17477	2.72	91.74
Dadra Nagar Haveli	3341	2.41	72.93
Daman and Diu	9048	8.91	26.65
Delhi	889641	9.44	84.65
Lakshadweep	48765	94.31	27.75
Pondichery	52867	6.54	44.20

References

Mujeeb, M. 1972. *Islamic Influence on Indian Society*. Meerut: Meenakshi.

Rizvi, S.H.M and Shibani Roy. 1984. *Muslims: Bio-cultural Perspective,* New Delhi: B.R. Publishing Corporation.

Rizvi, S.H.M., Shibani Roy and B.B. Dutta. 2000. *Muslims,* Delhi: B.R. Publishing Corporation.

Roy, Shibani. 1979. *Status of Muslim Women in Northern India: A Study in Dynamics of Change*, New Delhi: B.R. Publishing Corporation.

Roy, Shibani. 1984. Concept of Zar, Zan and Zamin: A Cultural Analysis of Indian Islamic Tradition of Inheritance and Kinship, *Man in India*. Volume 64: 32–39.

Roy, Shibani. 1984. *Dawoodi Bohras of Rajasthan*, New Delhi: B.R. Publishing Corporation.

10

Assimilation, Adoption and Blending of Religious Traits and Cultural Revivalism: The Rajbansis of North Bengal

Rajatsubhra Mukhopadhyay

The Rajbansis constitute one of the largest scheduled castes of West Bengal. They are widespread throughout northern parts of Bengal (commonly known as north Bengal), and in Purnea (Bihar), and Goalpara, Kamrup and Nowgaon districts of Assam and West Garo Hill district of Meghalaya. Among the neighbouring countries, the Rajbansis have a sizeable population in Rangpur, Dinajpur, Bogura, Rajsahi and Mymensingh districts of Bangladesh, in Jhapa and Morong districts of Nepal and in some pockets of Bhutan plains.

The social origin and background of the Rajbansis has been a matter of great controversy. On the question of their ethnic affinity with the Bodo-speaking tribal communities and particularly those of Koch, there are diverse views which ultimately instead of simplifying the problem, have made the issue more complicated. Bewildering hypotheses regarding the origin of the Rajbansis as a distinct community have been put forward by the colonial ethnographers and Indian anthropologists as well. The most commonly used conceptual frame in which that has been examined is the 'transformation of tribes into Hindu castes' through several processes of social assimilation since pre-colonial time (Risley 1915, Bose 1941, Srinivas 1956, Sinha 1965). Such explanations continue to overemphasize the 'tribe-caste dichotomy' and 'continuum' in the context of Hinduization process in India. However, in reality, the absorption of the tribals into the Hindu religion was rarely a complete one. In the case of Rajbansis too, their integration into the Hindu society remains ambiguous and the status of its social identity is becoming a political issue. This paper probes into that particular problem from the religious premise of the Rajbansis taking 'syncretism' in perspective.

I

It is commonly believed that the Koch tribe itself, as and when completed Hinduization, took the more honorific and dignified appellation of 'Rajbansi' to denote their 'royal lineage' and to validate their claim of 'Hindu status'. Or, to put it in another way, the Koches had adopted for themselves the designation 'Rajbansi' after their conversion to Hinduism. The adoption of the designation was, surprisingly, so complete, that in the census of 1881, not a single person was returned as Koch in Cooch Behar, the cradle of the community itself (Risley, 1891: 491).

History reveals that in the early part of the 16th century, the great Koch king Biswa Singha of Cooch Behar kingdom, with its capital at Kamatapur, was most honourably accepted into the Hindu fold. Not only the king, many members of his community also gave up their tribal designation and opted for Hindu epithets. Biswa Singha became a great patron of Brahminism and for whom the Brahmins manufactured a divine ancestry. He brought Brahmin priests from Kanauj, Mithila, Navadwip and Benaras. He was a great devotee of Siva and Durga.

Contesting the view of the British ethnographers that 'the Koch and Rajbansi came out from the same stock', about a century ago Monmohan Roy, a deputy magistrate of Rangpur, advocated that they really include two communities of different origin and faith. The original Rajbansis were of Dravidian origin and Vaisnavas by faith, while the Mongoloid Koches worship Siva and Sakti (1902: 79–80). These differences ultimately got blurred owing to considerable intermingling between these two communities and the term 'Rajbansi' became a common appellation to all alike. Thus there was always some difficulty in distinguishing Rajbansis from Koches and Paliyas. In 1939, Cartier in his *Report on the Survey and Settlement Operation* noted, "The Deshis and Koches, isolated local castes of Malda, were backed with the all-Bengal Rajbanshi caste in the census" (cited as footnote by Ray, 1984:69).

Even in later periods, several lower castes and tribes scattered over north and south Bengal such as Jalia Kaibarta, Tiyars, Namasudra Pods, Rabhas, Garos, etc., and even many Koches were recorded as under Rajbansi. Hence the census figures revealed a wide variation in the number of the Rajbansis, since 1911, in different districts of Bengal (Kumar, 1973: 5). Sanyal (1965) also said that Jelia Kaibarta, Namasudra, Bagdi, Malo, Koch, Mog, Dhimal, Pod, Rabha, Mech and Kantai broke away from their original caste or tribal fold and recorded themselves as Rajbansi. From the view of 'syncretism', the emergence of such a broad-based social formation under the generic name 'Rajbansi' has had some special significance.

It is said that in the wake of Hinduization of the royal families, the lower grade Koches who were refused a decent status in the Hindu fold adopted the faith of Islam in preference to zealot Hinduism. Thus a large section of Koches became Muslims (Nasya Sheik), and the higher grade Hinduized Koches; both styled themselves Rajbansis (Hunter,1974: 80). They had many similar social and religious customs and practices. The Nasyas continued to worship Satya-Narayan Deo as Statya Pir and Bisa Hari Debi as Bisa Hari Bibi. They thus internalized and reinterpreted many religious elements and traits drawn from their pre-Islamic tradition.

In another context, it has been observed by Bhadra: "There was a strong tradition of *pirism* among peasants in Dinajpur, mostly Rajbanshis and Muslims. Many Rajbanshis had been converted to the *pir* variant of Islam and were called *nasyas* ... Along with this, Vaishnavism had spread among the Rajbanshis and survived the onslaught of a Kshatriya movement led by Rai Bahadur Panchanan Barma. These two religious movements---Vaishnavism and *pirism*---have always overlapped, producing shifting and intermediate boundaries" (1989: 60). The worship of Pagla Pir by the Rajbansis of Duars and Cooch Behar in the month of *Paus* (December-January) is the best example of fusion of Rajbansi religious traits with Islamic ones.

It is a fact that a major section of the Koch Rajbansis of north-eastern region embraced Hinduism following the preaching of Vaishnava cult by Srimanta Sankardev, a well-known Vaishnava reformer and preacher of the 16th century. The Koch kings were profoundly influenced by Sankardev. However, Vaishnavism in an articulated form first spread among the Rajbansis of greater parts of rural Cooch Behar during 1891--1900. Around that time, as noted by Mukherjee (1963: 80), the Rajbansis were not wearing sacred thread but worshipping a few Hindu deities. However, Vaishnavism could not thrive due to subsequent spread of Brahminical usages and organized social mobility movement within their society. It was revived again on a limited scale during 1956--60 due to contact of indigenous Rajbansis with the Vishnavite Hindu refugees and their preachers. The influence of Vaishnava cult on the local populace can be very well surmised through the existence of a few petty *satras*, *sakha-satras* and *samuhas* in the bhakat dominated villages of this region.

It has been curiously observed by Vas (1992:44) that the the religious practices of the Rajbansis of Rangpur, who professed to be Vaishnavas, were not all that free from some aboriginal rites. Thus the Koch godling like Buri (the presiding deity of rivers and *hats*) was also worshipped as Burichandi by the Rajbansis without the ministration of a Brahmin priest. The very nature of this *puja* had many aboriginal traits of its own. Further, Das Gupta while writing about the Rajbansis of eastern India made some interesting observations. He says, "Their (Rajbansis) allegiance to *namgan*, in the face of their obedience to Sakta deities is quite interesting. It is, therefore, no wonder that a non-bhakat Rajbansi who habitually takes part in *namgan*, every evening, next morning attends a temple with a pigeon to be sacrificed to a deity. This testifies to the dual nature of their ritual life and their concordance for everything they feel religious" (1969:28).

On the question of Hinduization of the Koches and their transformation into Rajbansi, Grierson wrote: "The name Koch infact connotes a Hinduized Bodo who has abandoned his ancestral religion for Hinduism and ancestral Bodo language for Bengali or Assamese. Rajbansis are the Hinduized Koch of Rangpur and Goalpara" (1967:95). It is suggested that with the spread of Hinduism in its Shakta and Vaishnava forms, and introduction of Brahminism, the impetus for social transformation from the Koch---Rajbansi rulers were also accompanied by the slow, gradual sanskritization from below where the whole tribe or some lineages among them transformed their way of life (Nandy and Raman, 1997: 450). In this process of social transformation and elevation, the 'Koch-Rajbansi' ultimately turned as a principal group or generic category into which many other indigenous communities were absorbed or accommodated. Those assimilated communities, in addition to some Hindu deities, were allowed by the alien Brahmin pundits to continue and retain their old religious rites and practices in order to avoid any clash with the native priests. Such a duplex religious formation had obviously hastened the process of syncretism in a big way. The author has described some other aspects of the process of Hinduization among the Rajbansis elsewhere (1999, 2000).

II

Since long, the whole Rajbansi tract of the north-eastern Bengal and Assam has been under the domination of diverse faiths, dogmas and beliefs. Nandy and Raman in this regard categorically maintain that "their (Rajbansi) religion is a curious blend of nature worship, Shaktism, Vaisnavism, Tantricism, Siddha and even Sufism" (1997: 454). Commenting on the faith of the Rajbansis, Risely writes, "The precise form of Hinduism followed by the Rajbansis seems to vary in different parts of the country according to the influences to which they are subjected. In Rangpur they profess to be Vaishnavas, while in Darjiling, where Tantric ideas are perhaps more prevalent, their favourite goddess is alleged to be Kali" (1891: 491–500).

There are two great sects among the Rajbansis—the Vaishnava and Shakta. Siva is also generally worshipped by them with diverse names like Bura Thakur, Mahakal, Jakha, Maharaj, Dhumbaba, etc. In Rangpur, the worship of Dharma holds a prominent place in the religious observances of the Rajbansis. Dharma is the omnipresent and omniscient god of justice and the sun is regarded as his emblem, and Sunday is considered as god's day (*deobar*). However, in north Bengal, from the folk songs particularly sung to appraise Dharma Thakur, one may assume this god is nothing but another form of Siva, which is worshipped exclusively by the Rajbansi women without taking any service from Brahmin priests.

With reference to north Bengal, adoption of the deities, rituals and practices of the upper caste Hindus (mostly Bengali immigrants) has broadened the traditional religious organization of the Rajbansi, and the local Brahminical and Vishnavite traditions are being followed by their community men. Put it another way, the Rajbansi's contact with the Hindu and other faiths led to the gradual adoption of popular Hindu deities, festivals and religious beliefs. That, however, did not involve any significant break with the past. The Rajbansis adopted those without giving up their own traditional deities and traits. They have also retained a large portion of their old religious beliefs and usages.

In addition to the Hindu gods and goddesses like Vishnu, Siva, Kali, Durga and Saraswati, the Rajbansis worship many pre-sanskritic folk deities of their own. Chief among them are Bisahari (snake goddess), Hudum-Deo (rain god), Madankam (god of generation), Sonarai (god of wild animals), Goraknath (god of cowherds), Bhandani/Dangdhorimao (protector of crops), Tista Buri (saviour from floods and illness), Masan (protector from evil spirits), Saleswari (forest god) and Gram Thakur (god of prosperity). These apart, there are many other minor deities. For more details about the deities, rituals and festivals of the Rajbansis, the reader may refer to Sanyal (1965) and Ray (1999).

Some curious manifestations of syncretism, as have been observed in the case of Rajbansi cults and deities deserve mention here. A few of their deities interestingly embodied elements from Hindu religious tradition and established new relations with the Hindu pantheon. Thus Horibola is equated with Vishnu, Saital Bishari with Lakhindar and Behula, and Madan with Krishna. In certain cases, they reinterpret pre-existing rites, ideas, symbols and divinities in terms of new cultural reorientation. Here the case of three particular deities may be cited as illustrations.

Bhandani/Dangdhorimao

The four-armed goddess with a golden complexion is worshipped by the Rajbansis for three days after Bijaya-Dashami ceremony. Bhandani rides on a tiger and is supposed to protect her devotees from the attack of ferocious animals. In Rajbansi belief she is the custodian of all the belongings of goddess Durga. On some considerations, Bhandani is regarded as one of the diverse manifestations of Devi Durga. So in some places, Lakshmi, Saraswati, Kartik and Ganesh were later added to the image; and the appearance of the tiger is being transformed into a lion. The worship of Bhandani is thus integrally related to that of goddess Durga.

Mahakal

Worshipped by the Rajbansis at any time of the year, usually in a thatched hut, Mahakal is a form of Lord Siva riding on an elephant. Women assume the leading role in the worship of this god with the assistance of Brahmin priests. It is believed Mahakal protects the people and their crops from the attacks of elephants.

Masan

Masan is worshipped as a form of Shiva in some places and as one of his attendants in some others. There are fourteen types of Masan. He has a revolting appearance. With his large eyes and massive moustache, he looks terrible. However, the image of this god differs from place to place.

Maharaj

Traditionally, Maharaj is a fertility god associated with agriculture. He is said to facilitate the abundance of agricultural produce and has now turned into one of the forms of Lord Siva. Maharaj is still widely worshipped as a public deity after harvesting of autumn paddy by the

Rajbansis of Malda and Dinajpur. In this worship no Brahmin priest is required. It is officiated by their community priests called *gosains*, and goats and pigeons are offered as sacrifices.

The above referred cases perhaps succinctly justify the presumption that when the Rajbansis of this region took to the worship of Durga and Siva, they saw in it a continuity with their own indigenous pre-Hindu worship. Thus, as has been aptly observed by Nandy and Raman (1997: 452--53), the acceptance of Hinduism on the part of the Rajbansis was possible precisely because of this perceived continuity between their own ancestral religion and the one they were adopting and adapting. The Rajbansi's religious organization is therefore a synthesis of their traditional deities, rituals and beliefs and those of caste Hindus.

III

The Rajbansis are traditionally nature worshippers. So they have many river and forest deities, and worships associated with agricultural operations and prosperity. They believe in ghosts and evil spirits like *bhut*, *petteni*, *surs*, etc., who cause peculiar uncurable diseases, mishaps and sufferings in case they get displeased; and make offerings to them for their propitiation. Different types of witchcraft namely *lagani charani*, *jokha*, *jukhini* are very much in vogue particularly among the Rajbansis of rural areas. Among the religious functionaries, the important are Adhikari, Pad-Dhari, Deosi and Deori. Socially, all belong to the Rajbansi community. The Bengali and Asamiya Brahmins serve as priests when they are called in on special occasions. On a further glimpse of their rituals, it is seen that there are certain rituals of the Rajbansis in which Brahmins are not called in to officiate. Most of their household deities are worshipped without the help of Brahmins and involving the aid of community priests like Deori or Deosi. There are also certain *pujas* which are performed only by the Rajbansi women. The concepts (though confused) of the Rajbansis on sin and virtue, doctrine of *karma*, purity and pollution, re-birth and salvation are being greatly influenced by the prevalent Hindu beliefs and observances. Their certain ceremonies, rites and rituals connected to rites of passage have been influenced considerably in course of their prolonged association with the immigrant Bengalis.

In an acculturated state of condition, even the Rajbansis themselves fail to provide any clarity as to whether a particular religious trait is their own or is borrowed. Here, one may face the difficulty of exactly guaging the nature and extent of syncretism. On this score, what classical

Hinduism proposes and what the Rajbansi insiders put forth as their views do not, in many cases, go hand in hand. And unless this situation provides sufficient or proper clarity, there is a possibility that an empirical enquiry into 'syncretism' may suffer in the circumstances when the insiders (here the Rajbansis) themselves are unable to define the clearcut boundaries of what is their own original trait and what is not. Moreover, when an indepth search is made on syncretism, the variables are not defined well by the Rajbansis with clarity, especially those pertaining to deities, worships and celebrations. Their explanations often suffer from some kind of vagueness.

IV

N.K. Bose was perhaps the first scholar to delve deep into the process of Hinduization of tribes in India. In his paper, "The Hindu method of Tribal Absorption" (1941), he points out that the Hindus generally exercised a policy of laissez faire with regard to the social and religious practices of tribal peoples even when they came within Hinduism, and this cultural autonomy may partly have been responsible for keeping the subjected tribes satisfied and also taking the edge off their discontent to a certain extent. In the light of said observations, we can look into the question of syncretism in the case of Koch-Rajbansis, who unlike other tribes have taken theoretically to Hinduism as a whole.

According to Bose, as perceived by Munshi (1979:294), the Hindu 'catholicity' had three distinct features: (i) Although the policy was not to displace the original social and religious culture of the tribes, but rather to preserve it, yet, something had to be done to bring the tribal cultures in line with Brahminism; (ii) Once a tribe came under the influence of the Brahminical people, a strong tendency was set up within it to remodel its culture more and more closely in conformity with the Brahminical way of life; (iii) The tribes, however, could not be allowed to come very close to their superiors and towards higher standards of culture. As an interplay of those factors, many 'forms of culture' came into existence where Hinduism ultimately turned into a 'federation of faiths', and Hindu civilization tended to cherish all adventures towards 'cultural federalism'. Thus Bose goes further than merely identifying the basic outline and features of tribal acculturation in Hindu society.

In the case of Rajbansis, the process of sanskritization started with their simple claim of getting recognized as members of the greater Hindu society. To validate that claim, the first step was the gradual adoption of some deities of Hindu pantheon and the ritual services of the Brahmins.

However, there was no compulsion on the part of the Rajbansis to totally abandon or discard their old (so-called non-Hindu) deities and traits. Rather, they were allowed by the Brahmins to continue worship of their indigenous deities with the assistance of their community priest (Adhikari). That dualism perhaps put the Rajbansis in an ambiguous social position in the structure of Hindu society. It is not known what caste status they actually assumed after adopting Hinduism, even when they are said to have accepted the ethos of Varna system and have been absorbed into it. As a case in point, the reader may refer to a recent anthropological study by Banerjee (1993).

The interaction between the indigenous Rajbansis and immigrant Varna Hindus in the north-eastern parts of Bengal and Assam had produced an 'accommodative' social adjustment which has shown a tendency to become relatively stable and mutually acceptable. The two groups have participated in an exchange of cultural forms and rituals for a long time. In this process, a Rajbansi godling often got a new interpretation, and with time many of their old deities came to be merged with the major Hindu deities. One can also explain this particular process of syncretism in the theoretical frame of reference of 'Great-Little tradition'.

With regard to the manner in which transformation has taken place in the religious life of the Rajbansis (and other tribes as well) along with their cultural contact and absorption into the Hindu society, there exists some controversy. Xaxa, for example, in a recent paper observes: "The integration of the Koch-Rajbanshi who have embraced Hinduism as well as Bengali/Assamese with the dominant regional community had been far from complete" (1999:1521). Quite a similar view has been expressed by Nandy and Raman in their statement: "The Koch Rajbanshis are not by any means fully integrated into caste society inspite of centuries of sanskritization" (1974: 454). Mukhopadhyay also holds the same view and writes: "Their (Rajbansis) nature of assimilation with the Hindu society was perhaps somewhat partial. In terms of cultural approximation, such an assimilation may be equated with the particular form what Elwin has called 'Hinduized without being Hindus' or 'imperfectly integrated classes of Hindu society' as perceived by Ghurye" (Mukhopadhyay, 2000: 114).

On the issue of absorption of the Rajbansis into the Hindu fold, one vexing question that needs thorough probing is----To what extent was it possible for the Rajbansis to embrace the Hindu pantheon, deities and practices without becoming a part of Hindu society, and maintain some continuity with their traditional faiths? The anthropologists may possibly come out with some valid answers if they carefully examine the syncretic aspects of Rajbansi religion not only in the context of the past but also of the present. And that has been an urgent task in the wake of Kamtapur movement launched by the Rajbansis of north Bengal and their assorted move for cultural revivalism.

References

Banerjee, Gopa, 1993. Basilardanga: A Village in North Bengal, in Surajit Chandra Sinha (ed.), *Anthropology of Weaker Sections*. New Delhi: Concept Publishing Company, pp.61–84.

Bhadra, Gautam, 1989. The Mentality of Subalternity: Kantanama and Rajdharma, in Ranajit Guha (ed.), *Subaltern Studies: Writings on South Asian History and Society*, Vol.VI. Delhi: Oxford University Press, pp.54–91.

Bose, Nirmal Kumar, 1941. The Hindu Method of Tribal Absorption, *Science and Culture* (7), pp.188--94.

Das Gupta, Biman Kumar, 1969. A Note on the Rajbanshi (Rajbansi) of Eastern India with Special Reference to Social Movements. *Bulletin of the Anthropological Survey of India* 18(1), pp.1--44.

Elwin, Verrier 1942. *Loss of Nerves*. Bombey: Privately printed. p. 1.

Ghurye, G. S. 1943. *The Aboriginies So Called and their Future*. Puna: Gokhale Institute of Politics and Economics. p. 21.

Grierson, G.A.(ed.), 1967. *Linguistic Survey of India* (Reprint), Vol.III, Part II, Delhi: Motilal Banarsidass.

Hunter, W.W. 1974. *A Statistical Account of Bengal* (Reprint). Vol.X, Delhi: D.K.Publishing House.

Kumar, G.D. 1973. *Ethnic Affinities of the Rajbansis of North Bengal*. Florida: Miami.

Mukherjee, Bhabananda, 1963. Socio-Economic and Religious Organisation of the Rajbansi. *Bulletin of the Anthropological Survey of India* 12(1 & 2), pp.65--80.

Mukhopadhyay, Rajatsubhra, 1999. Khatriyaization among the Rajbansi: An Apprisal. *Man in India*, 79(3 & 4), pp.347--358.

Mukhopadhyay, Rajatsubhra, 2000. Hinduisation of the Tribes in India: The Case of Rajbansis, in Pranab Kumar Bhattacharyya (ed.), *The Kingdom of*

Kamata-Koch Behar in Historical Perspective, Calcutta: Ratna Prakashan, pp.103--21.

Munshi, Surendra, 1979. Tribal Absorption and Sanskritisation in Hindu Society. *Contributions to Indian Sociology* 13(2), pp.293--317.

Nandy, Vaskar and Vasanthi Raman, 1997. The Long Transition: The Koch-Rajbanshis of North-Eastern India, in Dev Nathan (ed.), *From Tribe to Caste*. Simla: Indian Institute of Advance Study, pp. 446--460.

Ray, Girijasankar, 1999. Uttarbange Rajbanshi Kshatriya Jatir Puja-Parvan (in Bengali), Dibrugarh: N.L. Publishers.

Ray, Rajat Kanta, 1984. *Social Conflict and Political Unrest in Bengal 1875--1927*. Delhi: Oxford University Press.

Risley, H.H. 1891. *The Tribes and Castes of Bengal*. Calcutta: Bengal Secretariat Press.

Risley, H.H. 1915. *The Peoples of India* (2nd Ed.). London: W. Thacker and Co.

Roy, Monmohan, 1902. Some Notes on the Rajvamci Caste. *Journal of the Asiatic Society of Bengal* 71(2), Part III, pp.79--80.

Sanyal, Charu Chandra, 1965. *The Rajbansis of North Bengal: A Study of a Hindu Social Group*, Calcutta: The Asiatic Society.

Sinha, Surajit, 1965. Tribe-Caste and Tribe-Peasant Continua in Central India. *Man in India*, 45(1), pp.57–83.

Srinivas, M.N. 1956. A Note on Sanskritization and Westernization. *Far Eastern Quarterly* 15(4), pp.481–496.

Vas, J.A. 1992. *Eastern Bengal and Assam District Gazetteers: Rangpur* (Reprint). Delhi: Indian Publishers Distributors.

Xaxa, Virginius, 1999. Transformation of Tribes in India: Terms of Discourse. *Economic and Political Weekly* 34(24), pp. 1519–1524.

11

The Ollek Cult in a Tribal Area of Andhra Pradesh

P. Venkata Rao

Colonial rule and penetration of Hinduism and Christianity prompted the tribes to launch movements in different states of India. Imposition of new religious orders were meant to pull the tribal people away from 'animism' and to implant a new moral order (Mahapatra, 1972; Singh, 1982; Shah, 1990). Contact with non-tribal societies and various related influences resulted in culture change in tribal societies. The Hindu influence had introduced features like hierarchy and other caste values in the tribal communities (Mandelbaum, 1970:595). A movement with cultural undertones generally undergoes changes in the process of establishing itself in different locations. This paper focusses on such a process while trying to understand the nature and concerns of an adopted religious reform movement in Visakhapatnam Agency of Andhra Pradesh. The aim of this paper is to look into the historical background of growth, spread and linkages of Mahimadharma which originated in Orissa and nature of inter-religious blending which characterizes this sect, which has a strong following among several tribes of the Visakhapatnam Agency of Andhra Pradesh[1].

Several tribes like Bagatha, Konda Dora, Valmiki, Kotiya, Gadaba, Jatapu, Mannedora and Mukadora inhabit the Visakhapatnam Agency region. Large-scale immigration of non-tribals into this region in the early nineteenth century had influenced the social patterns of the tribals. In this area, a system of social hierarchy based on food habits and occupational practices came into being which got expressed in the commensal relations and marital practices. The features of Hindu caste society like purity, pollution and social hierarchy appeared in the tribal communities of this area (Reddy, 1973). In fact, in this region a long association of the tribal communities with non-tribals can be seen. The Bagatha are said to have served under local zamindars with *bhakti* (devotion), hence they came to be known as Bagatha (Thurston, 1909: 128; Aiyappan, 1948: 71).

The Bagatha claimed a status similar to that of Kshatriyas. To retain this status they stopped eating beef. Among other major tribes, Konda Doras trace their origin from Pandava kings of the *Mahabharata*, whereas Valmikis trace their descent from the sage Valmiki, composer of the *Ramayana*. Both Konda Doras and Valmikis eat beef but the former have a higher status in relation to the latter as they avoid dealing with hides and skins which are handled by the Valmikis. Gadabas are said to be palanquin bearers to the rulers. According to Thurston (1909: 243), this tribe owes its name to the fact that its ancestors emigrated from the banks of Godavari and settled at Nandapur, the former capital of the Rajah of Jeypore. About the Jatapu, the *Vizagapattam Manual of 1891* observed that, "These are a civilized section of the Khonds who speak Khond on hills and Telugu on plains and are now a distinct caste. They consider themselves superior to Khonds who still eat beef and snakes. They have taken some of the customs of the plainspeople".

The religious practices of the tribes in this region exhibit a mixture of animism and Hinduism. Animistic practices are clearly visible in the festivals celebrated by the tribal groups. The major festival of the tribes in this region is Vittu or Vittingi also known as Chaitra panduga which is a festival connected with communal hunting. A number of first-eating ceremonies known as kottalu are connected to various agricultural and minor forest produce. Hindu festivals like Mahasivaratri are popular and non-tribal shrines like Simhachalam (near Visakhapatnam city) are familiar to the tribals in the Visakhapatnam Agency.

The presence of Ollek[2] faith among the tribal people is another instance of blending of a Hinducentric cult with tribal culture through contact between tribals and non-tribals. The devotees of Mahima cult belonging to different tribes of the region are called Ollek; thus the new religious order is sometimes called Ollek cult.

The term 'Alekhism' is also used for the distinctive religious faith of Mahimadharma[3]. Followers of this faith are from different tribes, inhabiting about one hundred villages in erstwhile Araku and Paderu tehsils of the Visakhapatnam district of Andhra Pradesh. The Ollek are conspicuous by their dress as all males and females wear ochre clothes. Sonya Maha Sonamandir, the place of worship at Karaiguda near Araku acts as a pilgrimage centre for the followers of the faith. The Ollek gather here for their annual worship on the full moon day falling in the month of Fagun (February). The Gurugaddi (seat of the teacher) located at Dhenkanal district in Orissa, where the founder of the Mahimadharma was buried after his death, is the main divine centre towards which all Ollek look for guidance and direction.

The Olleks maintain a distinctive life style in contrast to the fellow tribals in the neighbourhood with their emphasis on purity, cleanliness, vegetarianism, rigid marital and sexual observances, and adoption of Sanskritic practices and deities. In multi-tribal villages, the houses of Olleks are generally clustered. Men do not cut their hair. Cleanliness is given importance. Members of the faith clean their teeth with female calfs' dung[4]. The Olleks take bath regularly and are strict vegetarians and teetotallers. Spices and chillies are avoided in food. Salt is used in small quantities. They take cow's milk, the consumption of which is avoided by other tribals in the region under the belief that it is a sin to consume food meant for young calves. Supper is taken invariably before sunset. Members of the faith do not take cooked food from outsiders. Whenever they visit other villages, they cook their own food. The Olleks greet all Olleks and non-Olleks with folded hands.

The Olleks in the region collectively worship Trinadha, Surya, Agni and Buddha. Fruits, coconuts, sweets and flowers are offered to them. Breaking of coconuts is observed at Karaiguda temple. *Surya namaskaram* (sun worship) is offered regularly in the morning and evening. Among the Olleks *Sanyasis* who have renounced family life have a respectful place while *Gruhis* lead a family life. Such *Sanyasis* are referred to as *Gurus*. The *Gurus* worship fire, putting ghee in it while praying. The *Gurus* preach *go seva*, *bhu seva* and *guru seva* (to serve the cow, land and teacher).

Though the Olleks belonging to the Bagatha, Kotiya, Konda Dora and Valmiki tribes maintain strong solidarity, no inter-community marriage between Olleks belonging to these groups is allowed. The fission among tribals into Olleks and non-Olleks, and mainly as the population of the Olleks is small, had its own implications for the purpose of marriage. It is said that initially the Olleks married among themselves. But since the size of the Olleks was not large enough for procuring suitable mates the Ollek followers were compelled to seek brides from non-Olleks, whom they consider as of lower rank. But brides from non-Olleks could not always abandon non-vegetarianism.

Consanguineous marriages have been a dominant and prevalent trend among the tribes of the region and following the principle of cross-cousin marriage, the Ollek girls were getting into non-Ollek families and were forced to give up vegetarianism (Reddy, 1979:41). When non-Ollek girls are married and incorporated by Olleks, the girls undergo *suddi* (purification) by drinking uncrossed cow's urine. Such women are not allowed to visit their natal homes as they may be tempted to eat non-vegetarian food in their own houses. The *Sanyasis* or *Gurus* follow a strict life of celibacy whereas for common Olleks strict self-control in sexual life is required. Marriage by capture, an acceptable norm in other tribes, is denounced by the Olleks. Premarital sex and polygyny are prohibited. The Olleks refrain from sex on Mondays, Thursdays, Saturdays, new moondays and full moondays.

The Ollek women follow menstrual seclusion for seven days and eat food cooked by women from other Ollek households. Purification of the house involves not only use of *gamaya pavitram* (cow dung) but also sprinkling cow urine[5]. The duration of birth pollution (*sottak*) differs according to the sex of the child. *Sottak* period lasts for 12 days in the case of male child and 21 days in the case of female child. The purification rite is conducted by the *poojari* (priest) or *Guru*, who sprinkles the urine of a newly born calf. The house is cleaned with *gamaya pavitram*. Naming of the child takes place on the 13th day or 23rd day. The *poojari* collects *amanya* (fee) at that time. It is claimed that *amanya* will be sent to Gurugaddi at Dhenkanal. As part of purification all old earthen vessels are broken and food is cooked in new vessels. The *poojari* of the Karaiguda temple plays an important role in birth and death purification and marriages. He performs the main ritual in the form of fire worship on Phalguna Purnima day (full moon day in February) at the temple. Except the *poojari*, nobody enters the sanctorum of the temple. The *poojari* crawls on hands and knees inside the sanctorum so that his feet do not touch the floor. While worshipping, a conch is blown and a *thudum* (local version of a drum) is sounded. Sandalwood is sprinkled in the sanctorum where only a *jyothi* (lighted wick) is placed and no idol is kept. The poojari goes round the temple carrying a light which has a wick made of camphor, ghee and cotton. He prostrates at the temple entrance five times before offering prayers. Places of worship located at Kamyyapeta and Paderu are regarded as sacred centres of the Olleks in the Paderu area. The temple at Paderu was constructed by Swami Dayanidhi.

The Olleks have rigid religious and social customs which enforce social control in society. These cultural practices are the chief cultural markers which differentiate the Olleks from the non-Olleks. The members are expected to strictly adhere to the norms of the faith. The person who locally checks violations and provides guidance at village level is termed as *bodobhai* (elder brother). Violators are initially persuaded to change their attitude. If they persist, fines are imposed on them. For example, if an Ollek is found to have illicit sexual relations he has to pay a fine to the *bodobhai* or to the *poojari* of the Sonya Maha Mandir at Karaiguda. In addition an expiation ceremony called Bhogam involving putting ghee into the fire is undertaken. In extreme cases, the wrongdoers are expelled from the cult.

The existence of the adopted faith in the less accessible, hilly and forest region inhabited by tribal groups indicates definite level of contact of tribal faith with non-tribal faiths of different regions. Observance of menstrual pollution and birth pollution periods can be regarded as a sign of adoption of certain elements from Hinduism. The importance given to pollution and purification, cow worship, ghee, cow's urine and dung also represent the incorporation of elements from Hinduism among the Olleks, though theoretically they place themselves outside the ambit of Hinduism, being staunch adherents of Mahimadharma. The emphasis on rigid self-control as can be seen from the food taboos and sexual prescriptions is unique to Alekhism.

Different philosophies are associated with the Ollek cult (Mahima philosophy and Alekhism). Alekhism has close links with Hinduism. According to a study in Orissa, the birthplace of Mahimadharma, it is based on the philosophy of Brahma worship and preaching of monotheism. It recognizes five cardinal virtues from Vedas, Upanishads and Gita, viz. harmlessness, truthfulness, non-stealing, chastity, non-acceptance and Brahmacharya. It is a movement against animal sacrifices and caste prejudices. The ways followed by Mahimadharma to appeal to God are prayer, performance of *homa* and distribution of offerings among children. It is said that the founder of Mahimadharma, Mahima Goswami came to the world to revive Hindu religion from the age of degradation (T.R.B., 1968: 45--47). In another work, Alekhism has been traced from Kapila's Sankhya system of philosophy, which requires rigid discipline in the mode of living and meditation. The adherents are not supposed to observe caste system and are refrained from taking of *prasada* or food offered to god, cooked or uncooked. Alekhists are expected to take food on the road (while begging), but not inside the house or verandah. Alekhists should not take food after sunset. Alekhists admit only Alekha as a supreme being, which is absent in Buddhism but is similar to Brahman or supreme soul of Hinduism (Mishra, 1986: 179–184).

According to Eschmann (1986), Mahimadharma is an autochthonous reformist movement of Orissa that turned against Jagannath worship. It received wider attention when followers of Mahimadharma tried to burn the idol of lord Jagannath at Puri. Behera (1997) argued that at a theoretical level it is not logical to pose Mahimadharma in contradiction to Jagannath cult, when both draw legitimacy from the same sources. It is not an alternative or counter-movement to Jagannath worship and can be considered as a successor movement. The attempt to burn the idols of lord Jagannath was a move against the rituals of Jagannath cult. It is said that Mahima Goswami (the founder of Mahimadharma) also known as Mukundadas, initially believed in the existence of Hindu gods and goddesses who were supposed to be under his command. In early twentieth century, the disciple Biswanatha Baba systematized the teachings by way of sanskritization and remodelled them vis-à-vis Hindu texts. In tune with the traditions of Jagannath temple, Mahimadharma welcomes all castes and encourages eating together. In Mahimadharma, Jagannath has been frequently invoked but he occupies a subsidiary position. Jagannath was the first to know of the advent of Mahima Goswami, left Puri and came to him to become the first disciple. Lord Jagannath was also associated with the story of Bhima Bhoi, a blind Khond tribal, regarded as the most famous exponent and intellectual preceptor of Mahimadharma. Thus, Mahimadharma which originated as a reform movement castigating the Jagannath tradition had relied on it for gaining popular acceptance thus standing in almost paradoxical relation to the tradition which it accepts on the one hand and rejects on the other hand (Mishra, 1986; Eschmann, 1986).

Mahimadharma: Combination of Buddhism, Hinduism and Jainism

Several published documents are available which trace the origin and growth of Mahimadharma in Orissa (Eschmann, 1986: 376–379). But historical sources are not available for spread of Mahimadharma in Visakhapatnam Agency. The followers of the faith are a minority group set in remote tribal areas, contiguous with tribal areas of Orissa. Different versions are available about the diffusion of Alekhism into Visakhapatnam Agency. According to one version, around 1920, several households of Raj Bagathas had embraced Jainism, which was regarded as superior to Vaishnavism or Saivism. In fact, it is the Jain faith of

Holeyaka variety which came to be known as Ollek. The Bagatha converts called themselves Maha Jain Bagathas (Reddy, 1979:41). This view implies that Saivite and Vaishnavite influence had been there in the area. The problem with this argument is that though Jainism has spread into Andhra region, many of the practices of the present-day Olleks go against the preachings of Jainism. Jain writers like Soma Deva strongly condemn the Hindus for following stupid practices such as sun worship, morning and evening ablutions, fire worship, bowing to the tail of cow, taking cow's urine, etc. (Hanumantha Rao, 1993:187).

A popular local version from Araku region links up Ollek cult to Buddhism[6]. Some Olleks trace their origin to the period of Ashoka. After the bloody Kalinga war, Ashoka took to Buddhism and renounced worldly life. During the reign of Ashoka, Andhra region became a stronghold of Buddhism. Some of his soldiers settled down in the hilly tracts of Visakhapatnam Agency and followed Buddhism as preached by Upagupta and other monks. Eschmann also mentions that Mahimadharma can be viewed as neo-Buddhism and is linked to Digambara Jainism. According to her, it takes up the Buddhist concept of emptiness (*Sunya)* and identifies it with Hindu conceptions of Parama-Brahma and Iswara-Purusha (1986:378–389). It is observed that the Olleks in Visakhapatnam Agency strictly follow the four holy truths of Buddhism.[7]

The Mahimadharma, which has originated in Orissa, does not possess a unified sectarian system though its local version and individual groups are equally important vis-à-vis the original version. Due to split at the level of the principle group in Orissa, two divisions, viz., the Balkaladhari (who wear bark clothes) and the Koupinadhari (those who wear other clothes) has come into existence. Of these two, Balkaladharis are mostly from caste groups whereas the Koupinadharis are mostly tribals. Balakaladharis are also known as Kumbhipatias (who wear bark of the khumbhi tree). Koupinadharis are known as Kanapatias (who wear ochre dyed cloth). It is said that the faith spread outside Orissa since 1881 (Eschmann, 1986:376, 387). It is the Koupinadhari influence which has penetrated into Andhra Pradesh where they are called Olleks.

The Olleks in Visakhapatnam Agency are in possession of a Telugu booklet issued by the Andhra Koupinadhari Mahima Samiti (year of publication not mentioned). It consists of the rules to be followed by the members, and also a list of devotees and the villages they belong to. The suffix Bhakto or Bhaktulu is added to all the names. According to the booklet, Yogeswara Mahima Prabhu was said to have first introduced the

Mahimadharma at Puri in 1826. It mentioned that he travelled for twelve years without eating food (taking only water). After arriving at Khandagiri at Kapilasam near Dhenkanal in 1839, he performed *tapas* for 34 years in Atmayoga Samadhi. While travelling, he propagated Eka Brahma Upasan and Satya Mahima Dharma. Yogeswara Mahima Prabhu initiated ninety-two of his disciples into Brahma Avadhuta order. They propagated Alekha Mahima Sarana and converted people to Koupinadhari Mahima Samaj. Guru Dhaman also known as Mahima Gaddi in Dhenkanal district of Orissa formed the base. This place is the burial site of Yogeswara Mahima Prabhu also known as Yogeswara Swami, who died on 1876 on Phalgun Sukla Pakshhca Chaturdhi. The booklet has the photos of Sant Srimat Ganeswara Baba who is said to be Mukhya Sabhapati. Names of Srimat Madana Baba and three Upa-Sabhapatis are also mentioned. Sriman Tygai Mohan Chana Das is the Sampadakulu[8]. The prescriptions for the members are as follows:

1. Members should adhere to *ahimsa*. Only *satvik* food should be consumed. *Tamas* food, i.e., spicy food, meat and alcohol are to be shunned.
2. Members should take bath in the early morning. Sun worship in the morning and evening has to be carried out. Alekhya Ekakhsara Nama Japam and wearing ochre cloth are necessary. No food is to be taken during night by Olleks. Intercourse during menstruation period is prohibited and menstrual restrictions are to be followed by purification after eleven days. Looking after guests according to one's ability is prescribed.
3. Members (Olleks) should not steal. They should not indulge in adultery.
   Killing animals for food or sacrifice is prohibited.
4. Food offered to Alekha Brahma only should be eaten by Olleks. Food offered to any other deity is not permitted to be eaten by members.
5. *Sanyasis* should avoid touching women and gold. They should not stay for more than one night in a village. They can take *bhiksha* from one house only.
6. Satya Mahima devotees should read the *bhajans* written by Bhima-Bhoi.
7. Eka Brahma Upasan, Ekakhsara Mantra Deeksha and Anasakta Jeeva are prescribed for the Olleks.

Thus, we notice that these prescriptions emphasize *ahimsa* (non-violence), vegetarianism and high levels of morality. They indeed represent a combination of elements from Hinduism, Buddhism and Jainism. In Orissa, adherents of Mahimadharma can take dry fish and meat of wild animals. Nevertheless, they do not catch fish but obtain it from others. Eating meat of domestic animals is prohibited (T.R.B., 1968: 68). In divergence to the Orissa precept, however, the tribal adherents of Mahimadharma in Andhra Pradesh (Visakhapatnam Agency), both *Gruhis* and *Sanyasis*, are said to be avoiding all non-vegetarian food. The morality, food prescriptions and prohibitions appear to be more elaborate here when compared to the norms mentioned in Orissa[9]. But, being illiterate, the Olleks are unable to properly spell out concepts like *Sunya*, Brahman, and practices like initiation, Sarana, Darsana, confession, Gurupurnima observance and Satsang-goshthi which are important for followers of Mahimadharma in Orissa (Eschmann, 1986:395).

Despite its emphasis on egalitarianism, however, the tribal members of this sect in this region of Andhra Pradesh could not change their age-old practice of prohibition related to dining and marriage with fellow Olleks of other tribes. Social mixing is confined to pilgrimage and occasional communal eating at the place of worship. Dance and music which are close to the hearts of the tribals in this region are avoided by Alekhists as they are supposed to divert the mind from god. Many tribesmen found the rigid practices difficult to follow especially the rigid food regulations, as also marital and sexual prescriptions. Vegetarianism and other rigid customs[10] are not appealing in this area where annual traditional hunting festival is an important occasion for all tribes. Animal sacrifices remain an integral part of tribal life in this area as these are undertaken to appease various spirits and deities for their protection and curing various diseases. Those who turned towards Mahimadharma are left with herbal remedies only. Further there is no material benefit involved in taking up Mahimadharma. On the other hand, tribals who converted to Christianity in the Araku area, were allowed to retain non-vegetarianism and alcoholic drinks apart from getting education and other material benefits provided by the missionaries. Some of the Olleks from 'lower ranking tribes' are found to be relaxing the rule of not taking food and water from non-Olleks in their interaction with 'higher ranking' tribes like Bagatha, Kotiya and Nooka Dora. The Ollek did not enjoy the patronage of the Muttadar (tribal chiefs) and zamindar who wield political authority in this region whereas in Orissa, the birth place of Mahimadharma, where it has better following, it enjoys close connections with royalty[11]. Though Mahimadharma is not attracting new members, their strength is being maintained because of internal growth and incorporation process through marriages. Women coming from non-Ollek families add to the growth and perpetuation of the community.

Conclusion

The persistence of Mahimadharma for more than half a century has not only elevated the status of the followers of the faith, the members have acquired a distinctive identity which they are maintaining. The Mahimadharmaites denounce many tribal practices but no antagonism or tension seems to exist between members of the different faiths. The Olleks being a minority in the tribal villages do not pose a threat to the traditional tribal practices. On the other hand, Olleks are found to be participating in local annual festivals which are linked to the agricultural cycle, and they pursue several other local cultural practices. They are also found to be attending the worship and festivals of village deities, particularly when organized for protection from evil forces and seasonal diseases. Calendars and pictures of Hindu deities are found in the houses of Olleks who are expected to be monotheistic and avoid idol worship. The tradition of living together in multi-tribal villages and the conventional interdependent relations between the tribal communities in this area facilitate these adaptations towards peaceful coexistence.

It seems likely that the Ollek movement must have spread either along with or after the emergence of caste-like hierarchy among the tribes.[12] What is significant is the spread of a reform movement which aimed to denounce the casteist practices in the tribal area. In this context, one opinion is that features of caste-like hierarchy amongst tribes found in this area are purely an indigenous growth. In this area, the society has developed all the essential characteristics of caste system, which has neither been imposed nor maintained by any external agency (Reddy, 1973:167). The penetration of ideas and practices of Hinduism and other religious cults, such as Mahimadharma, with evidence of non-tribal contacts since pre-colonial era, seem to have inspired the growth of synthesized traditions in this area. In the course of such interface between non-tribal and tribal cultures and traditions in the Visakhapatnam Agency, a strong blending of the elements of Buddhism and Jainism got submerged within this reformist religious movement.

Notes

1. Data for this paper were collected during the course of fieldwork in Araku and Paderu areas in the Visakhapatnam Agency (This nomenclature was introduced by the British to place tribal areas under a special administrative system). Original fieldwork was conducted during 1978--80, when author was involved in a study of tribal development programmes (see Rao, 1988), but subsequent visits were made in 1992, to update the material.
2. Padmavati and Sreedhar (1994) have explored the intricate beauty of the religious practices of the Ollek 'cult'.
3. The Mahimadharmaites believe in one Supreme Being called Alekha. The real Guru is Alekha Parabrahma or Sunyabrahma. The Supreme Being as in the panchasakha conception is identified with sunya (emptiness) which is beyond all existence and non-existence (Eschmann, 1986:389--390). Mahima means glory/radiance. Alekha refers to an indescribable entity.
4. Other tribals in the area use small twigs of trees like *kanuga* for brushing their teeth. However, Olleks consider it sin to pluck young branches of trees (Padmavati and Sridhar, 1994: 355).
5. Purification for the non-Ollek tribals involves sprinkling of turmeric water and applying turmeric paste (Padmavati and Sridhar, 1994: 354).
6. Saffron-Clad Sons of the Soil. *Indian Express*. March 9, 1994.
7. Padmavati and Sridhar 1994: 352.
8. Even illiterate Ollek members are in possession of the book for the sake of photographs.
9. Eschmann mentions that the following taboos are to be observed by the members: worshipping of idols, killing animals and eating meat, stealing, telling lies, committing adultery, accepting food from others, using chairs or elevated seats, and taking food after sunset. Members should perform Sarana (shelter) and Darsana (view) at prescribed times after taking bath which involves Sastanga pranama and offering prayer facing sun-rise in the morning and sun-set in the evening. Worshipping fire is important. The members are to observe the prescribed directions for sexual consummation after marriage. They are to exercise propriety, good will and kindness towards all creatures. They have to put on ocher clothes in a strictly laid down manner in which cow dung must be used. The monks or Sanyasis are to work for the welfare of the Gaddi, welfare of the community and the entire world (Eschmann, 1986: 394--295).

10. According to Eschmann, by way of rejecting idolatry and caste system, the faith gave certain ideology to the illiterate masses to elevate their status without any material benefits. The rigid rules however prevented the practice of many professions. A sense of isolation had grown among some members, which resulted in their leaving the Mahimadharma (Eschmann, 1986: 394, 405).
11. Tribal Research Bureau (T.R.B., 1968:48), and Eschmann (Eschmann, 1986:388) describe the association of the rulers of Dhenkanal (Orissa) with Mahima Goswami, the founder of Mahimadharma.
12. It is observed that the converts to Mahimadharma in Orissa are generally from Hinduised tribes and not from primitive tribal groups (T.R.B., 1968: 52).

References

Aiyappan, A., 1948, *Report on the Socio-economic Conditions of the Aboriginal Tribes of Province of Madras.* Madras: Government Printing Press.

Bharadhwaj, Gopal, 1977, "Socio-political Movements among Tribes of India". In S.C. Dube (ed.) *Tribal Heritage in India: Ethnicity, Identity, and Interaction.* New Delhi: Vikas.

Behera, Subhakanta, 1997, "Jagannath and Alekh: A Study in Juxtaposition", *Economic and Political Weekly,* 2096–97.

Eschmann, Annecharlott, 1986, "Mahimadharma: An Autochthonous Hindu Reform Movement". In Eschmann, A., Herman Kuke, and G.C. Tripathi (Eds), The *Cult of Jagannath and the Regional Tradition in Orissa.* New Delhi: Manohar, pp 375–410.

Hanumantha Rao, B.S.L., 1993, *Religion in Andhra Pradesh.* Hyderabad: Directorate of Archaeology and Museums. Government of A.P.

Indian Express, 1994, "Saffron-Clad Sons of the Soil", March 9.

Mahapatra, L.K., 1972, "Social Movements among Tribes of India". In K.S. Singh, (ed.) *Tribal Situation in India.* Simla: IIAS.

Mandelbaum, David, G., 1970 (1972), *Society in India.* Bombay: Popular Prakashan.

Mishra, Binayaka, 1986, *Indian Culture and the Cult of Jagannath.* Calcutta: Punthi Pustak.

Padmavati, A. and Sridhar, J., 1994, "The Ollek Cult", *Man in India,* 94(4); 349–357.

Rao. P.V., 1988, *Institutional Framework for Tribal Development*. New Delhi: Inter India Publications.

Reddy, A.M., 1979, "On the Dynamics of Tribes and Sub-tribes in Visakhapatnam Agency", *Man and Life* 7: 1 & 2, pp. 33–50.

Reddy, N.S., 1973, "Caste in a Tribal Society: The Formative Process", *Contributions to Indian Sociology*, (NS.), 7, 159–167.

Shah, Ghanshyam, 1990, *Social Movements in India: A Review of Literature*. New Delhi: Sage.

Singh K.S. (ed.), 1982 (1983), *Tribal Movements in India* Vol. I and II, New Delhi: Manohar Publishers.

Thurston, Edgar, 1909, *Castes and Tribes of South India*. New Delhi: Cosmo Publishing House, Vol. I & II (Reprinted in 1987).

T.R.B., 1968, Impact of Satya Mahimadharma on Scheduled Castes and Scheduled Tribes in Orissa. *Adibasi*. (The Journal of the Tribal Research Bureau, Bhubaneswar) X, 1: 44–65.

12

The Lingayat Sect: Cultural Synthesis and Politics of Coalition in South India

Suresh Patil

The Lingayats are a religious community consisting of various castes held together by the bond of their collective religion. They are also known as Lingawants, Lingangis, Lingadharis, Sivabhaktas and Virasaivas. The members of the community prefer to be called Virasaivas. They derive their name from the Sanskrit *linga,* the phallic emblem, with the affix *ayta*. In fact, the name literally describes them, for the true Lingayat wears on his body a silver box containing a stone phallus which is the symbol of his faith, and the loss of it is tantamount to the absence of spiritual faith. This emblem is worn by both the sexes. The origin of Saivism is lost in obscurity, but it may be said that the Saivism is a blend of two lines of the pre-Aryan and the Aryan-Vedic elements. The characteristics of Saivism are the exaltation of Siva above all other gods, and the intensely personal nature of the relation between him and his devotees. In south India, Saivism is traceable from very early times and its influence grew, by its conflict with Buddhism and Jainism in the age of the great Pallavas.

The Lingayats, of late, have been claiming that their religion is distinct from the Hindu religion. However, the fact remains that their religious beliefs are syncretistic and it includes many elements of Hinduism, though its founding father, prophet Basavanna preached opposing Hinduism and the Hindu caste system. As in the case of Christianity in some parts of India, the social barriers of caste have proved too strong for the orthodox (Lingayat) religion (*Encyclopaedia of Religion and Ethics*, Siribner's Sons, New York, 1909). Jackie (1983), Bradford (1976), Ishwaran (1983), McCormack (1963), Umapathi (1980) and Parvathamma (1972) have published important anthropological works on Lingayats. However, in other disciplines like folklore and Kannada literature, important studies on Lingayats exist.

The Lingayats who form a religious community arose in rebellion against Hinduism, particularly against the Brahmanical ideologies and its practices of social discrimination. When it was born, Lingayatism was an inspiring sect with the aim of eradicating social evils associated with the Brahman-centred Hinduism. Basava, the founder of the Lingayat sect, was a great visionary, a religious reformer, teacher, theologian and administrator of the royal treasury of the Chalukya king Bijjala I (dominion 1156–67). Basava, from the very beginning of the movement, attracted various middle-and-low ranked communities with his radical ideologies. According to the south Indian oral tradition, he is the actual founder of the Lingayat sect, but the study of Chalukya inscriptions indicates that rather than founding a new sect, he in fact revived a pre-existing sect. His propositions and beliefs are contained in several works such as the *Basava-Purana*, one of the revered holy books of the Lingayat sect, written in the 14th century by Bhima Kavi, in Kannada language, which is partly based on an earlier Telugu rendition of *Palkuriki Samantha*. Through this new creed of Lingayatism, Basava tried to bring about social equality among various castes that were earlier hierarchically placed and were antagonistic to each other.

Basava helped to spread the Lingayat sect by teaching and through sacrificing his material possessions. Historical records suggest that he used to disperse funds to Lingayat guilds. His early life was unstable. It was his uncle, a prime minister, who first used his influence in the king's court to secure an appointment for his erudite relative. Basava was appointed chief of the treasury, and for several years, he and his faction enjoyed a great deal of popularity. The Buddhists and Jains were apparently resentful of his power, and his enemies pointed out that he had depleted the treasury by excessive patronage of Lingayat mendicants. Because of these accusations, which took the shape of revolution, he fled the kingdom (For detailed accounts refer to *Encyclopaedia Britannica*).

The followers of the Lingayat sect also call their sect Virasaivism and hence regard themselves as Virasaivas. The orthodox Virasaivas claim that Virasaivism is as old as Brahmanical Hinduism if not older. Several myths are associated with this sect. Accordingly, they believe in the myth of the existence of five spiritual teachers (panchacharyas) in all the *yugas*, the Hindu aeons, cosmic time cycles, *krita*, *treta*, *dwapara* and *kali.* The parable further says how they established five centres at different places in the country to perpetuate the Virasiava faith. In Kaliyuga Revanasidda is said to have established a centre at Balehalli, Marulasidda at Ujjayini, Panditaradhya at Srisaila, Ekorama at Himavatkedara, and Viswaradhya at Kashi (Murthy, 1956). These places are spiritual centres headed by members of the Jangam order, the priestly caste among the Virasaivas. A network of Virasaiva monasteries are spread over the whole of Karnataka and each monastery (mutt) traces its descent from one of the five centres. The myth seeks to gain authenticity, not only by tracing Virasaivism's origin but by trying to establish that the sect is as ancient and widespread as Brahmanical Hinduism. The antiquity and the places referred to in the myth are a reflection of such an effort (Parvathamma, 1977: 244).

The new faith was established with the honest goal of bringing about social equality and homogeneity among highly stratified communities and it succeeded largely in achieving this goal during its initial days. Nevertheless, later course of history shows that this homogeneity could not live up to the declared ambitions of the founder of the sect. However, the distinct identity and principal anti-Hindu ideology of Virasaivism survived in all ages. It is not easy to abandon the fundamental caste-based framework of rural India, which places communities in various segments. Thus, many groups that were drawn into the Lingayat fold slowly revived the age-old practices. Parvathamma and several other scholars have discussed the issues of inter-caste amalgamation and constraints involved in the homogenization process within the Lingayat sect. Parvathamma (1977:248) has discussed the occupation-related features of Virasaivism including the phenomenon of occupational heterogeneity among Virasaiva sub-castes. Thus, she says, priests, potters, traders, oilmen, etc., are all recognized within the Virasaiva sect as distinct sub-castes. Moreover, ironically, these occupational groups form a hierarchy. Those who are barbers are regarded as the lowest and subjected to discrimination at the hands of both Virasaivas and others. No one including an 'untouchable' accepts cooked food from a barber. Parvathamma observed that, "Though Virasaivism tried to carve out a new path for itself, it fell in line with traditional Hinduism. Over a period of time it equated ritual status with social status, and conformed to the traditional ranking of castes based on birth, and occupational differences" (1977:249). Notwithstanding these drawbacks, Lingayatism is a notable example of a synthetic movement, which introduced many revolutionary changes, and an ideology based on anti-Brahamanism.

The Lingayats are distributed in many parts of south India, but they are more numerous in several northern districts of Karnataka and are distributed in some districts of Maharashtra and Andhra Pradesh, adjoining the state of Karnataka. In some coastal districts of Karnataka such as Uttara Kannada and Dakshina Kannada, the Lingayats are relatively insignificant in terms of their population size. Having been drawn traditionally from the erstwhile occupational castes, most of the Lingayat groups belong to occupational groups, and the bulk of them comprises peasants. It is therefore a customary practice in north Karnataka to refer to rural Lingayats as 'Vakkaligaru' which literally means cultivators.

District	*Population in 1921*	*Population in 1931*	*District*	*Population in 1921*	*Population in 1931*
Bangalore	46472	52282	Dharwad	354481	380854
Belgaum	248484	303851	Bijapur	263529	361764
Bidar	51739	54393	Belgaum	248484	303851
Bijapur	263529	361764	Gulbarga	192836	203300
Chikmagalur	62754	65238	Mysore	159820	168618
Chitradurga	122171	140987	Chitradurga	122171	140987
Bellary	84837	—	Raichur	109232	117814
Dharwad	354481	380854	Shimoga	104538	106504
Gulbarga	192836	203300	Tumkur	91019	103519
Hassan	84528	85600	Bellary	84837	—
Kodagu	0	5068	Hassan	84528	85600
Kolar	11345	12366	Chikmagalur	62754	65238
Mandya	33382	35688	Bidar	51739	54393
Mysore	159820	168618	Bangalore	46472	52282
Raichur	109232	117814	Mandya	33382	35688
Shimoga	104538	106504	Kolar	11345	12366
Tumkur	91019	103519	Kodagu	0	5068
Uttara Kannada	6039	4721	Uttara Kannada	6039	4721
	20,29,127	22,02,567		20,29,127	22,02,567

No population of the Lingayats was returned in the South Canara district, which is a southern coastal district of Karnataka. From the above table it may be seen that the Lingayats are highest in number in Dharwad district (3,80,854), followed by Bijapur (3,61,764), Belgaum (3,03,851), Gulbarga (2,03,300) and so on. Uttara Kannada (4,721) and Kodagu (5,068) are the districts where Lingayats are distributed in less number. The total population of the Lingayats as per the 1921 census was 19,42,369, and 22,02,567 in the 1931 census. These population figures are derived from the census of the erstwhile Princely State of Mysore, the Bombay Presidency and the census of the Dominion of Nizam. The figures are further adjusted as per the changes in district boundaries. In case of Bellary and Dakshina Kannada district, the figures were drawn from the census of Madras Presidency, as these were part of that Presidency.

The results of the general elections of 1957, 1962 and 1967 turned the Lingayats into the most powerful and dominant political force in Mysore State, later renamed as Karnataka. Manor (1977:169) writes, "Even a casual reader of the Indian press at election time will frequently come across references to the Lingayats and the Okkaligas in the commentary on the State of Mysore. It is said that these two numerically majority communities, with their enormous land support dominate the political life of the state. The historians of old Mysore, India's second-largest and most progressive princely state then, and roughly the southern half of the post-1956 State of Mysore or Karnataka, must also come to terms with these castes." The following table by Manor (1977) show that Lingayats are as powerful, or at time more powerful than the Okkaligas:

	Per cent of village headman		*Per cent of village headman*	
	Okkaligas	*Lingayats*	*Okkaligas*	*Lingayats*
Bangalore	27.1	4.7	64.2	13.8
Kolar	22.4	1.5	62.6	0.9
Mandya	49.6	6.3		
Mysore	11.1	18.2	60.5	26.9
Hassan	31.6	14.3	50.1	39.1
Tumkur	16.9	12.0	40.8	24.8
Chikmagalur	12.0	19.1	24.9	46.1
Chitradurga	2.3	21.5	16.7	56.6
Shimoga	6.7	20.6	16.0	62.5
Mysore State	20.4	11.9	47.3	30.6

Source: Data of 1935. From Manor (1977).

Manor (1977:175) also confirms heterogeneity among the Lingayats. He says, "The Lingayat movement preached a casteless society and thus drew converts from a wide range of occupations. Consequently the Lingayats of princely Mysore included washermen, barbers, weavers, oil-pressers, tailors, carpenters, goldsmiths, potters and others... But such groups constituted less than 20 per cent of the sect's population. Most Mysore Lingayats fell into the following classifications (percentages approximate):

Priests (three sections)	9%
Merchants (Banajiga section)	14%
Agriculturists (three sections) over	50%

The Lingayats were regarded as a caste in pre-Independence censuses (Hutton, 1946:118). In Mysore, as in British India (McCormack, 1963), the treatment of Lingayats as a single caste in the courts of law operated as a stimulus to achieve solidarity within the sect. As with the Okkaligas, the Mysore censuses in the 20th century listed no sub-divisions of Lingayats and the princely government recognized only the coalition of all Lingayats, as a single category. From the early 19th century, Lingayats of several sections had served on the staff in the Mysore palace and made common cause against Brahman rivals for themselves and for the sect as a whole. This factor of coalition as a historical actuality has recently re-emerged as a purely political phenomenon to maximize their status and gains, particularly by means of further unveiling their sectarian unity which has helped them to stand up as a numerically strong single community in the field of electoral politics.

The Lingayat sect had been so successful in the past that almost all castes in certain areas came under its sway. Such Lingayat groupings established almost a parallel caste system in some areas. Thus, all the castes that are found in northern Karnataka have a Lingayat sub-group amongst them. It looks as if the caste structure found anywhere else in India is replicated among the Lingayats. The most numerous communities among the Lingayats are the Panchamsalis, Kudu Vokkaliga, Sadaru, Linga Reddi, Jangamas or the priests, followed by artisan groups like Madivala (washermen), Kumbara (blacksmith), Badiga (carpenter), Balegara (bangle seller), Kumbara (potter) and so on.

The continuity and survival of the Lingayat sect is solely dependent on symbiotic relations that exist amongst its many member-groups, who often identify themselves and function according to principles of their former jati professions and prejudices. Some of them even continue to observe old Brahmanical rituals, which are generally forbidden under Lingayatism. Some of these issues are discussed below in the context of brief ethnographic descriptions of such *jatis* (sub-castes) within the Lingayat sect:

Lingayat Jangama: In Mysore district, the Jangamas and Aradhya Brahmans are regarded as closely related. In these districts, life cycle rituals of Lingayats may be performed by either caste, while in northern Karnataka the Jangamas are the priests for most of the castes except the Brahmans. The other major functions of Jangamas pertain to only the Lingayats and are not open to Aradhya Brahmans. This is to provide most of the recruits for the Lingayat ascetic orders, especially for the order of the red robed Virakta monks. The Lingayat monasteries are of two types, celibates (Virakta) and non-celibates. The Lingayat Viraktas are celibate, and they preside over their own monasteries. Viraktas are not necessarily always recruited from the Jangam sub-caste. The main occasions when Jangam or Aradhya priests need to be present are childbirth, naming ritual, the puberty (maturation of a girl), marriage and death.

Lingayat Telis: The Lingayat Telis are converts to Lingayatism from the Teli caste. They are known as Gandlas in Telangana region of Andhra Pradesh, Telis in Maharashtra, and Ganigaru or Kari Ganigaru in Karnataka. They have hypergamous divisions, Silwant, Dikshawant and Rawat, modelled on the type prevalent among the Lingayats proper, with whom, however, they are allowed neither to eat nor to intermarry. Their intermarriages are regulated by the same rule of exogamy as practised by the Lingayats proper. Occasionally they show respect to Brahmans. They were also identified under the Gandla caste.

Lingayat Simpis: The Lingayat Simpis (tailors) comprise of descendents of two followers of Kinnuri Brahmayya, the first goldsmith disciple of Basava. Their rites and ceremonies closely correspond with those of the Jangams. There are also Lingayat Panchals including the five artisan classes (Badiga, Kumbara, Akkasali, Gejjigar etc.).

Lingayat Nagleek/Siva Simpis: The Lingayat Simpis (tailors) comprise two endogamous divisions: Nagleek Simpi, and Siva Simpi. The Nagleek Simpis are mostly found in the Talukas of Shorapur, Shahapur, Pargi, Andol and Gulbarga, and they claim descent from Godand Bhat, a

Brahman, and his wife Domava, who were among the disciples of Basava. It may be that the adoption of tailoring, as their occupation, has separated them from the main Lingayat community. The Siva Simpis are all Dikshawants. Most of them are cloth merchants, and have the title 'Chetti' attached to their names. Both Nagleek and Siva Simpis are staunch followers of the Virasaiva Lingayat sect, and are administered, in their religious and ceremonial observances, by the laws laid down by Jangams.

Phularis: The Phularis are Lingayats who are recruited from among the Gurava caste of Maharashtra and the Tamad caste of Telangana (Andhra). They are not dogmatic Lingayats as other proselytes are and they still cling to some of the old cultural customs and religious practices of their parent caste. They wear both the sacred thread and the *lingam*. They indeed tend to maintain dual religious identities.

Lingayat Koshtis: The Lingayat Koshtis (weavers) are called Hatkars, who, before their conversion, are said to have belonged to the Devanga caste; but they continue to worship Chaudamma as their tutelary goddess. Their ceremonies are a mixture of Brahmanic and Lingayat rituals and rites, in which the latter preponderate.

Lingayat Kumbhars: The Lingayat Kumbhars, who claim to profess Lingayat religion and are thus called Lingyata Gowlis, employ both Brahmans and Jangams as their religious specialists during marriage and mourning of the dead. They regard their women as being ceremonially impure during childbirth and during the menstrual period, though these notions are not sanctioned by their adopted sect. These Brahmanical notions are repelled in Lingayat sect. They have such divisions as Dikshawant and Silwant, but intermarriages between them and the other Lingayat groups are not allowed. They are very numerous in Karnataka, but are also found in small numbers in Marathawada (Maharashtra) and Andhra Pradesh.

Lingayat Hajams: The Lingayat Hajams are divided into two hypergamous groups, Silwant Hajams and ordinary Hajams. They adhere strictly to their creed and conduct all their ceremonies under the guidance of a Jangam (Lingayat priest).

Lingayat Dhobis: The Lingayat Dhobis claim to have descended from the followers of Madiwal Machayya, the washerman disciple of Basava.

Karikuldawaru: The Karikuldawaru are an agricultural caste found in Karnataka. Very little is known regarding their origin and the etymology of the name they bear. They conform closely to the beliefs and rituals of the Lingayat sect.

Kursalis: They follow the Jangam creed. They marry their daughters by performing meagre rites and pay a bride-price to the father of the girl. The Kursalis have no definite system of selection of a mate, and they regulate their marriages simply by old rules of kinship. They are very lax in observance of strict rules and ceremonies attributed to the Lingayatas.

Jyandras: The Jyandras, Jadras or Jarads ('great man' in Canarese) are like the Hatkars, recruited from the Devanga weavers. They have three endogamous divisions: Padsalgiri, Lingada Keri and Kurwale, the last one being regarded the lowest of the three. The first two divisions ate together in the past, but did not intermarry.

Discussion

Basava's philosophy was based on egalitarian principles. The new faith, which he founded, was opened to one and all, both low and high in hierarchy. The initiation of such a sect in such a rigid cultural environment was a revolutionary step. Through his charisma and his sacrifices in life, he could attract people hailing from the highest as well as lowest castes in hierarchy. Madigara Haraliah who belonged to the 'untouchable' cobbler caste (Madiga) and Dhor Kakkiah who belonged to another 'untouchable' leather tanning caste (Dhor) were his most admired disciples. Basava was able to synthesize most of the cultural differences between such disarray of castes and their individual ritualistic traditions and mould them into one single faith by introducing many uncomplicated principles, which aimed at anti- Brahamanism.

However, in course of time, the Lingayat adherents succumbed to the age-old principles of pollution and prohibitions based on old Hindu ideologies, though all major rituals of Lingayatism survived among them in a syncretistic style. Lingayatism, during that period, existed in different communities without any centralized command. This was the case at least till the early decades of 20th century, as revealed by the return of various sub-groups among the Lingayats in the census of 1881, 1891, 1901 and 1911. By the 1920 census, however, the process of fission was reversed and a period of consolidation began. The 1921 and 1931 censuses did not give sub-groupwise figures of the Lingayats. In both these censuses, all the sub-groups (castes) of Lingayats were returned under the term 'Lingayat

Veerasaiva'. The concerns and demands of the emerging social and political situations prompted this process. The elite among the Lingayats launched a massive movement to reorganize the scattered Lingayat community as one solid block vis-à-vis non-Lingayats. They formed various associations like Karnataka Lingayat and Education Society and Mysore Lingayat Education Fund Association. It was realized by the leaders that only by instilling a strong sense of oneness among all the castes under Lingayat sect, and by invoking the egalitarian principles propagated by Basava, will it be possible to achieve greater solidarity. It was felt that only by ensuring internal unity would they be able to capture the political power for the people that was introduced by the British Government.

In the recent period, this process of bringing about unity among the Lingayats has gained further momentum. The heads of the mutts of Lingayats have declared that there should not be any more discrimination between the sub-groups. With the blessing of religious heads, this move has succeeded and inter-caste discrimination has receded. It has also helped to bring about solidarity at the economic and political levels. In these circumstances, the Lingayat leaders and heads of the religious monasteries decided not to return Lingayats as Hindus in the census of 2001. Enthusiastic efforts were made to canvass this among the people by declarations and putting banners on the roads. The Lingayats were advised through these banners to state their religion as 'Lingayat/ Veerasaiva', when the census enumerators ask "What is your religion?". This is a major stand taken by the Lingayats to re-establish their distinct religious identity outside the purview of Hinduism. The sect leaders argued that if the Lingayats were branded as Hindus, then the concept of ritual purity, pollution and accompanying low-high statuses for the sub-groups would automatically follow which is antithetical to the fundamental doctrines of Basava. Ironical as it may seem, what was achieved and lost by Basava is now being regained perhaps not because of the force of the doctrines of Lingayatism but due to the politics of coalition in order to consolidate political power.

References

Assayag, Jackie, 1983, *Religion et societe chezles Lingayat - Virasaiva de L'lede du sud*, Ph.D. thesis, Nanterre University.

Bhat, H.K., 1975, A Formal Analysis of Lingayat Kinship Terminology, *Bulletin of the Anthropological Survey of India,* Vol.24, Nos.1–2, pp.24–29.

Bradford, N.J., (N.D.), The Indian Renouncer: Structure and Transformation in the Lingayat Community, In: *Indian Religion,* R. Burghart and A. Cantlie (eds.) London: Curzon Press.

Bradford, N.J., 1985, From Bride Wealth to Groom Fee: Transformed Marriage Customs and Socio-economic Polarization Amongst Lingayats, *Contributions to Indian Sociology,* Vol.19 No.(2) NS. 269–302.

Bradford, N.J., 1976, *Affine and Devotee: A Study of the Lingayat Sect of North Karnataka,* Ph.D. Thesis, University of Sussex.

Chekki, D.A., 1968, Some Aspects of Marriage Among the Lingayats, *Man in India,* Vol.48.

Chekki, D.A., 1968, Mate Selection, Age at Marriage and Propinquity Among the Lingayats of India, *Journal of Marriage and family,* 30(4) 707–711.

Hutton, J.H., 1946, *Caste in India: Its Nature, Function and Origin,* London: Oxford University Press.

Ishwaran, K.A., 1983, *Religion and Society Among the Lingayats of South India,* New Delhi: Vikas.

Kittel, F., 1875, Seven Lingayat Legends, *Indian Antiquary,* 4, 211–18.

McCormack, 1963, Lingayat as a Sect, *The Journal of Royal Anthropological Institute,* 93(1) pp.59–71.

Manor, James (1977) "The Evolution of Political Arenas and Units of Social Organisation; The Lingayats and Vokkaligas of Princely Mysore in Srinivas M.N., S. Sheshaiah, N.S. Parthasarathy (eds.) *Dimensions of Social Change in India,* Bombay: Allied Publications (169–187).

Pandyarajan, M.C.K., 1939, *Veerasaiva Prabalavan Veerasaiva Lingayat Podunala Sangam,* Trichy: Imperial Press.

Parvathamma, C. 1972, *Sociological Essays on Veerasaivism,* Bombay: Popular Prakashan.

Parvathamma, C. 1977, "Religion and Social Change": A Study of Tradition and Change in Veerasaivism" in Srinivas M.N., S. Sheshaiah, N.S. Parthasarthy (edited) -- *Dimensions of Social Change in India,* Bombay: Allied Publications (243–252).

Pillai, S.A., 1973, Renaissance of Veerasaivas in Kerala, A paper presented in the 19th Session of All India Veerasaiva Mahasabha, Bangalore.

Sadashivaiah, H.M. 1967, *A Comparative Study of Two Veerasaiva Monasteries: A Study in Sociology of Religion,* Mysore: Prasaranga, pp.64–66.

Sargant, Norman Carr, 1963, *The Lingayats: The Vira-Saiva Religion,* Bangalore: Christian Institute.

Tipperudraswamy, H., 1990, Virasaivism, In: *South Indian Studies*, Nayak, H.M. and B.R. Gopal (ed.). Mysore: Geetha Book House.

Umapathi, B.U., 1980 *Serological Basis of Caste Distinction among the Lingayats of Dharwad District*, Ph.D. Thesis, Karnataka University, Dharwad.

Venugopal, C.N., 1980, Some Aspects of Lingayat Ideology and Monastic Organisation, *The Eastern Anthropologist*, 33(4).

13

Jewish Heritage, Hindu Tradition and Syncretistic Amalgam among the Syrian Christians of Kerala

B. Francis Kulirani

This paper discusses the Jewish heritage, Hindu tradition and the syncretistic amalgam that is visible among the Syrian Christians of Kerala on account of perpetual cultural symbiosis that has been in operation between these historical traditions over centuries in Kerala. In the historic origin of the Syrian Christians, one may trace an element of Jewish tradition to start with, right from the first century. The visible sign of syncretistic sway on this count in the Syrian Christian community is evident in that they continue with the traditional vocation of trade and commerce. In the traditional society of Kerala, there was an absence of the Vaisya Varna category. The Jews followed by the Christians and the latter by the Arab traders initially filled this void. Then there was advent of the caste Hindus who too made their presence felt in Kerala. Because of these factors, several elements of Jewish customs and Hindu cultural-religious notions and traditions prevailed which had a great impact upon the Syrian Christians. In this paper, syncretism is understood as a blending of ideas and practices, synthesis of customs and traditions, and similarities in rituals. Since the syncretistic influences in the life of the Syrian Christians has a long tradition, this paper first deals with the historical contexts and then examines the anthropological issues.

I

The most populous and prominent among the Christians of Kerala are the Syrian Christians. They claim that they are the descendants of those converted to Christianity by St. Thomas the Apostle in 52 AD. The Kerala Christians would accept it as having historical validity because it is based on a strong and persistent tradition. A long and vigorous debate has been raging on the subject (K.J. John, 1981:3). However, it cannot be denied that there may be some truth in the tradition, for it is an accepted fact that there was heavy traffic between the Red Sea coast and the west coast of Malabar from ancient times (Charleworth, 1928). It is very likely that Thomas, one of the twelve disciples, came to Kerala carrying the Gospel and that at least some of the Jews who heard him became Nazarenes, the followers of the Nazarane. Therefore, the earliest Christian community in Kerala could have been drawn from the Jews. But unfortunately the tradition has been vitiated by the accretions of palpably anachronistic elements. A few Jews might have converted but not Nambudiri Brahmins as the Aryan inroads into Kerala began only after eighth century AD. Likewise, it is said that St. Thomas built seven and a half churches (sic) and erected stone crosses in many places during his tour of Kerala. This also cannot be true because the practice of building churches and venerating the cross came into vogue only after the third century. How then did the story originate? Obviously, it was the product of a particular thought-process and particularly of the caste-ridden society that was formed after the arrival of the Nambudiri Brahmins. The provocation for it seems to have been the coming of a large group of Judaic Christians from Syria under the leadership of a wealthy merchant Thomas of Cana or K'nai Thomman as he is generally known. According to the tradition they reached Cranganore in 348 AD and settled down on the southern side of the palace of Cheraman Perumal. Among the newcomers there was a bishop, Mar Joseph of Edessa, and besides him, other priests, clergymen and women numbering about 400. The early Christians were in all probability like a flock of sheep without a shepherd and hence were indeed happy at the arrival of these new co-religionists from Syria and they were only too willing to accept Mar Joseph as their pastor.

The Syrians being a large group continued to use Syriac among themselves as the language of communication and worship. Thus, it became the liturgical language for the whole congregation, which composed of the old Nazarenes and the new Judeo-Christians. This congregational connection paved the way for the Church of Kerala being brought under the jurisdiction of the Church of Persia. Although the two groups joined together for the purposes of worship, they remained separate and were known among themselves as Vadakkumbhagom or Northists and Thekkumbhagom or Southists, according to the places of their residence on either side of the palace of the Perumal. In course of time the Northists grew wealthy and powerful and hence became bold and demanded marital union with the fairer daughters of the Southists. This might have happened after the century when the society had become entrenched in caste system. The Southists being an endogamous group and claiming caste superiority contemptuously rejected the demand of the Northists. This provoked the latter to invent in retaliation the story of St. Thomas and the Nambudiri Brahmins, never realizing that it is absurd to connect the Apostle of the first century with the Nambudiri of the eight century. Significantly enough, the term Thomas Christians denoting the Northists and so assiduously used by them first, came to be used during this period.

Documentary evidences about the presence of Christians in Kerala in the sixth century, ninth century and thirteenth century are available (cf. Hambye 1952, Mudadan 1984). In 1502 when Vasco de Gama was at Cochin, a delegation of Christians visited him. They had brought with them a letter from their feudal lord requesting the king of Portugal that they be governed and ruled by him (*Govarnados e reqidos per ellee*) so that the Moors would protect them from oppression and harassment. The cordial relations thus began turning sour in course of time with the result that the Christian community was split into two, one supporting the Portuguese and the other opposing them. The Portuguese were looking for some justification for closing the contact and cutting off the Kerala Christians from the Persian prelates. Soon they found that the Kerala Church was Nestorian in character. (Nestorins, a fifth century bishop of Persia contended that Christ had in him two distinct natures, the divine and the human nature. In his human nature, he was Jesus of Nazareth the son of Mary. The Catholic doctrine is that Christ was at once God and man.) This was sufficient reason for the Portuguese to prevent Persian prelates from coming to Kerala. One is tempted to conclude that the fight against Nestorianism was a fight for promoting their commercial interests. Latinization gained momentum with the holding of Seynod in 1599 at Diampar (Udayamperur). Thus, whole parishes were latinized. The Portuguese could do this without difficulty in the coastal areas like Cranganore, Cochin, Alleppey and Quilon, which were under their direct control. Thus large numbers of the early Christians of these areas were latinized (Mudadan, 1984: 298). Of course new converts from the highest to the lowest were added on to them and that was how these areas became predominantly Latin Christian, and are so even today. But most of the Syrian Christian writers are assiduous in contending that the Chruch of Kerala was never Nestorian and hence the latinization programme so vigorously persued by the Portuguese was unnecessary. This however, is against the overwhelming evidence provided by a long array of eminent Western writers like Cardinal Tisserant (1957), Medly Cott (1905), Brown (1950) and Howard (1864).

The Portuguese wanted to create a Christian province in Kerala, which would be a bastion of strength and support. They began to recruit the latinized Christians to form Christian militia. The authorities also encouraged the Portuguese soldiers to enter into marital union with local women. The children born of this union were known as Mesticos or those of mixed origin. They had also recruited a number of interpreters to help them in their commercial transactions. They were called Topases, from the Tamil word *Topassi* meaning one who speaks two languages. Thus the Anglo-Indian community of Kerala originated. All these groups were being cultivated to enlarge the numbers of those who would be loyal to them. They could win over only a section of Christians while the rest clung doggedly to their ancient traditions. This was because the real motive of the Christians in submitting to being governed and ruled by the king of Portugal was more temporal than spiritual. The ancient rulers had granted certain privileges and property rights. These in course of time had been taken away, so they wanted them to be restored. Moreover, they also wanted the Portuguese to take effective steps to protect their trade interest. But the Portuguese were tardy in taking action to redress their grievances, so they felt disillusioned (Mudadan, 1984: 301). The last straw was when Mar Ahathalla, a Persian prelate reached Mylapore, on his way to Kerala. He claimed that he was sent under the authority of the Pope in reply to the insistent demand of Syrian Christians. However, the Portuguese detained him at Mylapore. This was the signal for revolt. The people all over the interior gathered in churches to voice their protest at this high handedness of the Portuguese. When they heard that the Portuguese ship carrying Ahathalla was coming to Cochin, they gathered in large numbers to offer him an enthusiastic welcome. Though the ship called at the port, the Portuguese did not allow him to disembark and it left for Goa. With this the pent up emotions of people burst into an angry revolt. They gathered in front of the church at Mattanchery, Cochin and holding on to a rope tied to the cross, vowed that they would never again submit themselves to Garcia or his Jesuits. This is known as the Oath at the Coonan (bent) Cross, which took place in the year 1653. Later they proclaimed the Archadeacon (the administrator of Malabar Church) as their prelate. Most of the Churches of the Archdiocese of Cranganore followed him, loyal to the Pope of Rome leaving only a few, which remained. But soon, as a result of the labours of Carmelite missionaries who were deputed by Rome, many churches were brought back into the Catholic fold. This reunification process was gathering momentum when a new prelate from Persia, Mar Gregarious, appeared on the scene. Immediately the Archadeacon and his followers joined him and they became the new party of the *Puthan Kootukar*, while those remained loyal to Church of Rome were known as the old party or the *Pazhaya Kootukar*. Thus the ancient Syrian Church of Kerala was spilt into two. For a long time the *Puthen Kootukar* drifted riderless in the cross currents of shifting loyalties to prelates of different denominations until at last they came under the West Asian Church of Antioch and are known as the Jacobites or the Malankara Orthodox Syrian Church, while the *Pazhya Kootukar* followed the east Persian liturgy and they are known as the Syro-Malabar Church. Before long, new hierarchies were formed separately for the Syrians and the Latins, thus completing the division between the two Catholic groups. A third group of Catholics came into being, when in 1930 Mar Ivanios and his followers broke away from the Malankara Orthodox Church (Jacobite) and were united with the Church of Rome. They however, remained a separate entity known as the Syro-Malankara Church. Thus at present there are three distinct groups among the Catholics of Kerala—the Syro-Malabar, the Syro-Malankara and the Latin Church.

Meanwhile, in the wake of the British conquest of India, Protestant missionaries began proselytization work in many parts of Kerala. Under their influence, a splinter group called the Reformed Jacobites was formed and they are today known as the Marthoma Syrian Church. From this, yet another radical group was formed known as the St. Thomas Evangelical Church of India. A century earlier, in 1772, a small group had broken away from the Puthan Kootukar to form Thozhiyur Independent Syrian Church. Fragmentation took place also among the Pazhya Kootukar, though on a minor scale. Some years later, Elias Melus, another Catholic prelate was sent to Kerala as the bishop of Syrian Christians, and many churches accepted him as their bishop. They felt that he was too old as not to have the authority from the Pope. He went about ordaining priests and even got from Persia a prelate to assist him. He too was excommunicated and was forced to return to Persia. Nevertheless, his followers came together and formed the independent Syro-Chalden Church of Malabar. Later they placed themselves under the authority of the Nestorian Church of Mesopotamia. In the meantime, many protestant missionary societies were doing proselytization work in different parts of Kerala with considerable success. In 1947, they all came together to form the Church of South India. Besides this, there are a number of other Protestant churches active in different parts of the state, like the Pentecostal Churches, Assemblies of God, Church of God, the Salvation Army, Seventh Day Adventists, Jehovah's witnesses, etc. Thus, the Christians of Kerala can truly be likened to various kinds of fish caught in St. Peter's net.

II

The syncretistic influences in the traditions of the Syrian Christians will have to be understood in the above historical context. Here syncretism is understood "as a blending of ideas and practices, by means of which either one set adopts more or less thoroughly the principles of another or both are amalgamated in a more cosmopolitan and less polytheistic shape. An outcome of the process is the borrowing or assimilation of deities, synthesis of customs and traditions, similarities in rituals, new political alliances and so on" (Moffat, 1921).

The historic origins of the Syrian Christians have an element of Jewish tradition to start with, right from the first century. The visible sign of syncretistic influence on this count that is evident in the Syrian Christian community is that they still continue with the traditional vocation of trade and commerce. In the traditional society of Kerala, there was an absence of the Vaisya Varna category. The Jews followed by the Christians and the latter by the Arab traders initially filled this void. The elders of these communities were addressed by suffixing honorific terms like Manpila (noble son) with the names in case of men and Pemppila (noble daughter) for women, indicative of the high social status enjoyed by them in the society. This was in practice even until the middle of last century. Some elements of Jewish customs associated with the celebration of marriage prevailed among the Syrian Christians. On the eve of the marriage, the bridegroom had to undergo the *anthamcharthal* (first shave by the Ambittan, (barber), ceremonial bath by the brother-in-law and feeding of milk and sweets by close relatives). In the case of the bride, the ceremony was known as *chanthamcharthal* or *mylanchidal* (literally beautification and application of mehandi on the palm). The Southists or the Thekkumbhagom sub-group of the Syrians even today has a large collection of marriage eve songs. A similar custom exists among the Cochin Jews also. The custom of *kuravaidal* (ululation) as the newly married couple enters the house, by the women folk also existed in the past. The coming of the Knanaya Christians in the fourth century paved the way for the renaming of the St. Thomas Christians or the Nazrani Mappillas to Syrian Christian due to the adoption of Syriac in the liturgical services. The status rivalry between the native Christians and the migrant Judeo-Christians on account of the denial by the latter to give their daughters in marriage to the native Christians led to increasing 'Brahmanisation' of the customs and practices by the former subsequently. This process might have gained momentum because of conversion, carried out by the Nambudiris.

A whole lot of customs and practices of the high caste Hindus were followed by the Syrian Christians, some of which are still in vogue. Some of the customs that have survived are described here. *Ponnum-vayambum* (a mixture of gold and a herb) after being ground in honey is given to a newborn baby, *annadhanam* (first feeding of cereal) and *ezhuthinirithal* (learning of alphabet) are some of the pre-conversion ceremonies performed in childhood. Child marriage was a custom in the past. There we notice the prevalence of the practice of dowry which also has its origin in the local high caste Hindu custom, like the customs of *tali* tying, *manthrakodi* (bridal veil), ceremonial receiving of the bridal couple with lighted lamp, etc. Until 16th century, the men kept their hair long and tied it in a tuft and the bridegroom had the privilege of wearing a gold crown. Observance of old death rites like *pulvili*, *chatham* or *ande* are still common practices. The women of the community also have the privilege of carrying a palm-leaf umbrella (an exclusive privilege of the Nambudiris women) to hide them while walking in the street. Until the arrival of Portuguese, eating meat was a rare practice and so was use of alcohol. They also enjoyed the privilege of *panthy fojanam* (to eat on plantain leaves folded into two during social feasts squatting on long grass mats). Many delicacies are also common to both. The architecture of the early churches were similar to Hindu temples, the only exception being the huge stone carved cross in the front courtyard, which was decorated with oil lamps during feasts. The church processions still resemble the Hindu temple processions in all their paraphernalia. Under the influence of colonial rule and European Christianity, both Roman Catholic and Protestant, the modes of religious observances and particularly their mode of worship and lifestyle became westernized increasingly, and at the same time the community further got fragmented into many denominations.

As mentioned earlier, besides various denominations, the succeeding Christians of Kerala remained divided according to the castes to which they belonged and hence followed their caste traditions and customs (Kulirani, 1999). The denomination division among the early Christians had certain unique features. However, in all spheres of the inter-community interactions, it was essentially the caste considerations which coloured their attitude towards each other. Consequently even the stratification element, which shaped old caste-order, though now devoid of ritual factors to considerable extent, survives and regulates the life of the Christians. Thus, the ideal Christian egalitarian objective remains a distant dream even among the adherents of the Catholic sect of Kerala. Only one major change distinctly observed among all sections of Christians is that they consider no article of food or drink as taboo.

The Kerala Christians continue to observe pollution after birth and death. Although disapproved by the Church, the belief in astrology and in calculation of and determination of the auspicious days and time, is fairly widespread. Except among those Christians who follow their old Hindu caste traditions rigidly, women are not considered polluted during menstruation periods. The age of marriage is generally above 18 for girls and 20 for boys. No consanguineous marriage is allowed except where it is permitted by the caste tradition. Dowry practice is very much prevalent. Strict monogamy is practised. Widow remarriage is allowed. In certain churches, especially among the Protestant, divorce is permitted. But it is strictly prohibited among the Catholics. Among most of the Christian groups tying of *tali*, a Hindu practice of Kerala, is the essential symbol of marriage.

The Christian communities not only maintain their old caste-like identities, but also zealously guard them. Thus, we witness the survival of the custom of caste endogamy among the Kerala Christians. The early Christian groups have certain art forms peculiar to themselves like the Margomkali and Paricha Muttukali among the Syrians and Chavittu Nataka among the Latins. These traditions not only survive they also help them to draw boundaries amongst themselves within a single Christian fraternity. Marriage within the endogamous group is more strictly observed among the K'nanite community, which is strictly endogamous.

III

This paper has discussed the syncretistic religious and cultural traditions among the Syrian Christians of Kerala in the context of their historical Jewish heritage (which had resulted on account of adoption of an alien religious order), survival and continuity of Hindu-centric beliefs and customs, and perpetual cultural symbiosis which operated between these historical traditions over centuries in Kerala. We traced the element of Jewish tradition in the very historic origin of the Syrian Christians, right from the first century. The visible sign of such tradition among the Syrian Christian community is evident in the continuation of the traditional vocation of trade and commerce. We observed that many elements of Jewish customs have survived among the Syrian Christians.

The advent of the caste Hindus and close interaction between the Hindus and the Christians resulted in a long process of sharing and adoption of each other's cultural-religious beliefs, customs and traditions. As mentioned earlier, despite existence of various Christian denominations, the successive Christians of Kerala remained divided according to the castes to which they belonged earlier and hence they continued to follow and even zealously guard many of their caste traditions and customs. The Kerala Christians continue to observe the notion of pollution after birth and death. The belief in astrology and in calculation and determination of the auspicious day and time is widespread. Consanguineous marriage dowry system, strict monogamy and widow remarriage are all very much prevalent among all Christian sections. It is in the celebration of marriage that we witness the ultimate manifestation of syncretism. Tying of tali, a Hindu practice of Kerala, is the essential symbol of marriage. The Southist or the Thekkumbhagom subgroup of the Syrians even today conducts performance of old marriage eve songs. A similar custom exists among the Cochin Jews also. Indeed the coming of the Knanaya Christians in the fourth century had paved the way for the renaming of the St. Thomas Christians or the Nazrani Mappillas to Syrian Christian due to the adoption of Syriac in the liturgical services. Besides, several marriage related rituals, many rituals of life cycle such as feeding a certain herb preparation, after grinding in honey, to a newborn baby, ritual of annadhanam (first formal feeding of cereal) and ezhuthinirithal (first formal learning of alphabet) are some of the prevalent pre-conversion ceremonies. Then, observances of old death rites like pulvili, chatham or ande are still common practices. The women of the community also always enjoyed the privilege of carrying a palm-leaf umbrella (an exclusive privilege of the Nambudiri women) to hide them while walking in the street. The architecture of the early churches have been similar to Hindu temples, the only exception being the huge stone carved cross in the front courtyards which are decorated with oil lamps during feasts. The Church processions in Kerala, as we discussed, still resemble the Hindu temple processions in all their paraphernalia. Thus, we see that a whole lot of customs and practices of the high caste Hindus are followed by the Syrian Christians, which, as we discussed, are still in vogue.

References

Brown L.W. 1950. *The Indian Christians of St. Thomas*. Cambridge: Cambridge University Press.

Charlesworth, M.P. 1928. *Trades Routes and Commerce of the Roman Empire*. London, Oxford University Press.

Hambye, E.R. 1952. 'The Syrian Church in India till the advent of Portuguese', in *The Clergy (Monthly)* 16 pp.376--89.

Howard, G.B. 1864. *Christians of St. Thomas and the Liturgies*. London, Oxford University Press.

John, K.J. 1981. *Christian Heritage of Kerala*. Cochin, Diocesan Press.

Jussay, P.M. 1990. 'Christians of Kerala', A Communication received by the Anthropological Survey of India.

Kulirani, B. Francis. 1999. 'The Dalit Christian Dilemma.' in *The Journal of Anthropological Survey of India* Vol. 48. No. 2 p.117--126.

Medly Cott, H.E. 1905. *India and the Apostle Thomas*. London, Oxford University Press.

Moffat, James.1921. 'Sycretism' in *Encyclopedia of Religion and Ethics*. Ed by James Hastings, Vol. XII p 155--157. Edinburgh, T&T Clark.

Mudadan, A.M. 1984. *History of Christianity in India*. Vol.I, Bangalore: Theological Publications.

Narayan, M.G.S. 1972. *Cultural Symbiosis in Kerala*. Trivandrum: Kerala Historical Society.

Pylee, L.M. 1969. St. *Thomas Christians and the Archdiocese of Verapoly*. Cochin, Diocesan Press.

Tisserant, Cardinal. 1957. *Eastern Christianity in India*. (Translation by E.R. Hambye) London, Green Publication.

14

A Bhagat Movement among the Patelia of Gujarat

R.K. Sinha and William Ekka

The Patelia are a scheduled tribe of Gujarat. A considerable number of the Patelia, after migrating from the original home state of Gujarat, live in Madhya Pradesh (MP). The various census reports of MP mention that they have sprung from the alliances of Bhil tribe and Rajput caste. But, several knowledgeable informants of the Jhabua and Dhar districts (MP) observed that the Patelia originated from the alliance of Bhils and Sirvis, the latter being a caste of Gujarat. This assumption corresponds with the observed similarity between the Patelia and the Sirvis, as regards their dress, decoration, habits and nature, and certain other features.

The Patelia are found in large number mostly in those villages which lie along Dohad road, which runs into Gujarat. In the Jhabua district, they are concentrated largely in the Kali Devi and Rama block. In the Dhar district, they are found in some villages of the Nalcha block. According to the census of 1961, there were 1,217 Patelia also in the Nimar district of MP. In Jhabua and Dhar districts, they have been grouped together with the Bhils and their sub-groups. In fact they have been treated as a sub-group of the Bhil. According to the census of 1961, there are reported to be 37,455 Patelia in the whole of Gujarat.

The Bhagat Movement

In recent times, the Patelia have come under the influence of a Krishna cult among them. This cult is locally known as Parnami Dharam and its followers are called Parnami-Panthi or Bhagat-Panthi. This cult has a temple at Jamnagar, Gujarat, which is called Khijara-Mandir. The temple of Dhakorjee in Gujarat is said to belong to this cult. Ordinarily, the term Bhagat refers to such an individual who vows to lead a simple and pious life and who strictly abstains from drinking liquor and taking non-vegetarian food. Among the Patelia, the opposite term of Bhagat is Nagad, which refers to the traditional Patelias, who follow the tribal religion.

The Krishna cult was introduced to the Patelia about three decades ago. Those who have accepted it have started worshipping Lord Krishna in the form of a child of 11 years and 52 days. Jhabua district was the first where a few Patelia of Rajalla village were initiated into this cult through the efforts of one Jamabhai of Dohad (Gujarat). He was a Bhagat-Panthi. He persuaded his brother-in-law, Somalla of Rajalla village to adopt the new religion. In turn, Somalla got about ten more people whom he coaxed to become Bhagat. Then Jamabhai invited the area-priest of Parnami Dharam, known as the Gurujee Maharaj to Rajalla village to initiate willing persons into this cult. After some time, more persons became Bhagat-Panthi and their number grew to 20 in Rajalla. Some more Patelia from the neighbouring villages also accepted the cult. The influence of the new cult however remained localized among the Patelia of the area, particularly because in the neighbouring Dhar district, the Patelias have not accepted the cult.

It is important to note that the above mentioned areas are tribal dominated areas and many tribes live in these areas, but this cult has some footing only among the Patelia. This has encouraged the preachers of the cult to work and to intensify their activity only among the Patelia. Two persons who have actively worked for the spread of this cult among the Patelia are Chunnilal Byas of Ratlam who is a Brahman by caste and Natwarlal of Harkundi, Jamnagar (Gujarat), who belongs to the Bhat caste. Both of them are directly attached to the Parnami-Panthi Dharam, whose headquarters is located at Jamnagar (Gujarat).

Through the efforts of these two persons, the cult has taken the form of a movement among the Patelia. While Chunnilal has concentrated his efforts among the Patelia of Kokawad, Petawad, Kalyanpura and Narsingpura of Rama block, Natwarlal has set his eyes on people of the Matasula, Ranapur, Jamua, etc., for doing his bit for the cult. The rationale for the acceptance of this cult among the Patelia is said to be their desire to upgrade their social position from the rest of the Patelia.

It is important to mention that this Bhagat-Panthi cult has been affirmed by only some of the literate and affluent sections of Patelia and it has lesser popularity among the rest of the Patelia. Again, it may be mentioned that the emergence of this cult and its acceptance among the affluent sections of tribes has worked as a vehicle for securing a higher social position in the area. Since the followers of the new sect are mostly literate, knowledgeable persons, who have also sound economic position, they are quick to establish rapport with the preachers and at the same time they have been quick to shun their traditional habits, practices and old elements of religion which clash with the aims and scopes of the new Bhagat-Panthi cult. On the other hand, the traditionalists, the adherents of tribal religion, who are referred to as Nagad-Patelia, as opposed to the Bhagat-Patelia, are not paying much heed to the new religious movement.

The Bhagat Cult: Objectives and Organization

The principal aims and objectives of the Bhagat cult are:

(a) To turn the Patelia into a Bhagat, devotee and worshiper of Lord Krishna.

(b) To work for the salvation of the people.

(c) To reform the Patelia by inducing them to give up non-vegetarian food and alcohol.

(d) To teach them the lessons of the *Gita*.

(e) To help them learn and adopt devotional songs in the praise of Lord Krishna through their active participation in the Bhajan-Mandalis.

The Parnami-Dharam, with its headquarters at Jamnagar, Gujarat, has a small organization in Patelia area for expanding the Bhagat cult. Different areas, which are associated with the Parnami-Dharam organization, have their area-priests. The prime task of the area-priest is to initiate the willing persons into the cult. It is achieved by inviting some of them into their *Bhajan-Mandali* as guest members. Again, some of them are invited to attend the *prarvachan* (preaching in the form of lecture) delivered by their renowned Gurus, when they visit the area. Through all these activities, the Bhagat cult organizers have been able to popularize the cult in Patelia areas. There are also instances when the Bhagat Gurus go around visiting the Patelia villages from time to time to renew contacts with the followers and to enthuse others to accept the teachings of the cult. Such visits help the cult to increase the number of its followers. The expenditure involved in the visits of the Gurus is borne by the Bhagats of each village collectively. In case of their inability to bear the expenditure, the local priest incurs it. Sometimes additional funds are raised collectively to give a memento or a gift to the preachers.

Under an area-priest, there are local priests. A local priest is generally an influential person and is well-known for his zeal to work for the propagation of the movement. He is the head of the local organization of the Bhagat movement. Several villages fall under the jurisdiction of the local priest. He is entrusted with the task of convincing the people of his village about the sanctity of the cult and of ensuring that the followers (Bhagats) strictly follow all rules and prescriptions of the cult. Sometimes he also narrates the ill-effects of native customs and practices.

The local priests lead a simple and pious life. In the morning and evening, the Bhagat priest worships Lord Krishna and Radha whose idols are kept in one corner of his hut. He regularly conducts *Arti* (ceremonial adoration with lighted lamps), burning incense and clarified butter and offering some sweets. A mounted picture of Radha and Krishna is kept on a table alongwith a few books of the cult written in Hindi and in Gujarati, at the hut of the local priest.

Bhajan-Mandali

The Bhajan-Mandalis help in achieving the objectives of the Bhagat movement. It is a gathering of Bhagat Patelias in which devotional songs are sung in congregation in praise of Lord Krishna. It serves other purposes also. It attracts the attention of other Patelia who are not the followers of the cult. Besides, it indirectly helps the participants to become confirmed Bhagat. It also strengthens the solidarity and cohesion among the Bhagat Patelia.

Bhajan-Mandali is headed by and held under the supervision of the local priest. It is necessary to hold the religious meeting of Bhajan-Mandali twice a month in each village where the Bhagat Patelia reside. The Bhagat Patelias from neighbouring villages also come to participate in it. Hence, it is held on different days in different villages. Generally, it is held in the house of one of the Bhagat Patelias. Before it concludes, the venue of the next meeting for Bhajan-Mandali is decided. One of the devotees volunteers to hold it in his house and bears the expenditure involved in it. The host has to buy such articles as incense, clarified butter, coconut and the things for making *prasad—halwa* or *laddu*. Jaggery and sugar may also be offered as Prasad. Also, the participants are to be provided with *biri*, tea and some light refreshment, since it is a night-long programme, which commences after the evening meal.

Method of Initiation

After a person makes up his mind to become a Bhagat, he requests the local priest to make the necessary arrangement for his initiation into the cult. A person willing to adopt the cult generally declares his intention in the gathering of the Bhajan-Mandali. Then the local priest communicates it to the area-priest, or to religious heads at Ratlam or Jamnagar, and with the consent of the latter a date is fixed for initiation. On the fixed date, the priest comes and the Bhajan-Mandali is held in the house of the new entrant. At the time of initiation, the new cult seeker offers the priest a coconut and Rs.1.25 in cash as *dakshina*. Then, the area-priest administers a vow to the entrant not to take non-vegetarian food or drink liquor. He also asks him to bathe daily. This is followed by the singing of *bhajan* in which he participates, after uttering the name of Lord-Krishna. At the end, the area-priest blesses the entrant with the *mantra* of Radhe-Krishna. It is reported that sometimes the area-priest also gives a *kanthi* (a string of beads) to the entrants.

Acceptance of Bhagat cult is an individual affair. Only an initiated person or one who has received the *mantra* from the area-priest becomes a Bhagat. The other members of his family remain Nagad until they also individually undergo the initiation ceremony. However, usually after the head of the family becomes a Bhagat the other members of his family also follow suit. Thus, there are twenty Bhagat Patelia families in Jamnia, five in Nawapara, one hundred persons in Going Para, twenty in Narsingpura, three in Para and twenty in Rajalla, whose informants were interviewed during the fieldwork.

Influence of the Bhagat Movement

Before the effect of the Bhagat movement on the Patelia is examined, it is necessary to give a brief picture of their traditional way of life. Traditionally, the Patelia are non-vegetarian and they drink liquor. Those Patelia who adhere to tribal religion sacrifice goat and chicken and offer liquor to their deities such as Khataria, Bhario, Jog-Mata and observe Pipal-Puja. They believe that their deities and evil spirits can cause death and sickness. Hence, when they fall ill they approach their traditional priest and sorcerer/medicine-man called Badwa, to get cured. They solicit the assistance of a child during magical practices. They observe Gal, and a number of vow fulfilment rituals of the Malwa area, for being cured from diseases. Again, the Nagad section claims a high bride price. There is also the tribal practice of acquiring their life partner by elopement and intrusion. After a death, they perform the purificatory ceremony, called

Nukta or Dahara, on the twelfth day of death. However, they are not strict in observing this rite on that particular date. Sometimes, it is not performed even for a year or two after a death. They also do not care for cleanliness and remain without bath for several days.

The Bhagat Patelia do not eat non-vegetarian food or drink liquor as per the vow they took at the time of initiation. Hence their marriages and other ceremonial feasts are held without meat and liquor. Instead, they entertain the people with jaggery and tea on such occasions. They no longer appease and worship their traditional deities and do not depend on the Badwa for the diagnosis and treatment of diseases. Instead, they now celebrate Hindu festivals, especially those associated with Lord Krishna. Thus, they treat Janmasthami as their most important festival. Also, on the eve of Sharad Purnima of Ashwin (October-November), they organize Bhajan-Mandali on a large scale. On that occasion, they also perform Raslila of Lord Krishna in which both men and women participate wholeheartedly.

The Bhagat movement has influenced the whole life of the tribal Patelias. Its impact on the cultural sphere has also been great. They look upon the reformation of several old tribal customs as revolutionary. They were looked down upon because of the practice of acquiring life partners by elopement and intrusion, which used to be resorted to by many because of high bride price among them. In fact, the eagerness to avoid such annoying customs has also prompted many a Patelia to adopt the Bhagat cult. Among several changes introduced in tribal society after adoption of the cult is reduction of the heavy amount of the bride price and fixing the same at Rs. 5.00. It is resolved that even an amount of Rs.1.25 should be sufficient as a token bride price, in order to enable them to acquire life partners through negotiation. Like the Hindus, the Bhagat Patelias now immerse the ashes of the dead in the river, and perform the purificatory death rites strictly on the twelfth day of death. They have also developed a habit of taking bath everyday after becoming Bhagat.

Discussion

The Bhagat movement or the Krishna cult has not yet taken deep root in the Patelia tribal society of Gujarat and Madhya Pradesh, and there are several instances where the Patelias who once enthusiastically adopted the cult have reverted to their old unrestrained way of life because they found the new religion and its rules too difficult to emulate. There is little possibility of the whole Patelia society becoming Bhagat. Besides, in every culture there is a factor of conservatism which restrains it from changing absolutely and suddenly. Furthermore, those who revert to old religious faith do introduce some ethics and social values learnt from the Bhagat preachers among the non-Bhagats.

However, the impact of this Bhagat movement on the Patelia is quite clearly visible. In the first instance, it has divided the Patelia society into Bhagat and Nagad segments impairing the social solidarity and cohesion among members. The Bhagat Patelias claim a higher social status than their Nagad brethren. Besides, the Bhagat prefer to marry among themselves. However, being small in number they are often forced unwillingly to establish marriage relationships with the Nagad. It is only the brides who are accepted from the Nagad segment. Nevertheless, while accepting the Nagad girl the Bhagat impose the condition that the girl will become Bhagat after the marriage. In execution of Bhagat-tribal marriages, the religious customs of both segments are often mixed which is acceptable to both the segments. A large number of such Nagad girls who become Bhagat after marriage, often continue to adhere to many of the old tribal customs. Even food habits are never completely abandoned by them. The Bhagat Patelias ensure that their girls are not given to the Nagad in marriage. This kind of social hiatus and absence of reciprocity among the members of the same tribe appears to be untenable. This, however, remains only a transitory phase as the Patelias agree that many old tribal practices do survive even in the Bhagat segment of the Patelias, and such blending of dual religious and cultural elements among them is never seen as an aberration by the rest of the Patelias. Such religious movements bring the tribal people closer to Hindu society but the process of syncretism allows dual religious traditions to flourish and coexist.

15

The Donyi-Polo Faith and the Process of Homogenization among the Tribes of Arunachal Pradesh

Tamo Mibang

The name Adi is a generic-composite term. It includes various tribes such as Minyongs, Padams, Gallongs, Pasis, Paggis, Karkos, Shimongs, Komkars, Ashings, Thangams, Milangs, Boris, Bokars, Ramos and Pailibos. This paper will discuss in brief the old and distinct belief systems of these diverse people and installment of a new indigenous religion among them. The new religion introduced, called Donyi-Polo faith, is continuation of an old belief which has been evolved so as to incorporate within it several allied tribes. The paper also discusses the multifarious roles of Miri, the tribal priest, in social and religious life.[1] Through the ages, man has evolved a spiritual world of his own from which he derives inspiration and guidance for his everyday life. The Adi tribes of Arunachal Pradesh have also developed such a supernatural world which comprises benevolent and malevolent spirits, whose abodes are the air, the cloud, the sky, the jungle, snow-clad mountains, rivers, the agricultural field, the village council hall, the granary, the house and all other places under the earth. All these places are given specific names. The Adis are pragmatic people and their attitude to religion might originally have been influenced by the sense of mystique and reverence. On certain ceremonial occasions, they offer sacrifices to propitiate those unseen potent powers, followed by community feast and they drink in the name of the creator. Sacrifices during agricultural ceremonies are performed with a hope to ensure good crops, prevent damage to them, to keep away pests and evil spirits and to bring prosperity to the village.

It is pertinent to refer to Verrier Elwin, who denounced the general attitude of the European writers that the tribes did not have any religion at all and that it was a mixture of various idolatries and superstitions (Elwin, 1955: xviii-xix). Indeed, the views of Western commentators on the tribal people does not seem to hold good. The Western scholars explored the religion of the people of the central zone of Arunachal only, and they did not study the Monpas, the Sherdukpens, the Khambas, the Membas who profess the Mahayana form of Buddhism, the Khamtis who follow Hinayana Buddhism and the Noctes who follow the Mahapurushia form of Vaishnavism. All these people as per social requirements, contacts and environment adopted different religions. On the so-called animism which is considered a characteristic of primitive religion, E.O. James observes that the doctrine of animism represents the material and spiritual aspects of the phenomenal world by resolving the universe into a fundamental dualism of Body and Soul. This indeed is the spirit of religion in the tribal world. Nevertheless, it is not proper to brand some people as animists or to state that their religion is inferior to others. It is not right to think that one's own religion is the right one. In this context, one can cite a mother's attitude to her child. If someone says anything about the physical features or colour of her child, she naturally feels bad and tries to defend the child. She normally says, "*Siisang nade Siibang siyeku*", which means "In course of growth, the child will become healthy and handsome". In the present situation, due to emergence of competitive forces, the indigenous religions of the tribal people are facing a situation similar to that of the child, though it is beautiful, full of life and hope. The reason is that the tribal people do not have their religious scripture, system of regular prayer and so on. However, some of the tribal groups have recently developed new religious systems as is evident from the activities of Donyi-Polo movement in the Adi-speaking areas of Arunachal Pradesh. The Adis while highlighting the greatness of their new religion say that there is nothing sweeter than one's own home, nothing more loveable than one's mother, and nothing more beautiful than their flora and fauna. As an individual, one is nothing more than a particle of dust in this world. Even if one dies, day and night will continue to take their turns as usual, the trees and plants will flower in season, the wind will continue to blow, and the sun, the moon and the stars will continue to appear in the sky. This is considered a kind of message to human beings that amidst silent dust, our society will continue with rich traditional heritage.

The Donyi-Polo religion is not confined just to the Adi tribes; it has also influenced such dissimilar tribal communities of Arunachal Pradesh such as the Tagins, the Hill Miris, the Nishings, the Sulungs, the Apa Tanis, as well as the Mishings of the Brahmaputra valley of Assam.[2] While examining the Donyi-Polo faith of these vast people, an outsider will feel perplexed with regard to the concept of Donyi-Polo, whether the tribal term 'Donyi-Polo' refers to God or the sun and the moon or the religion of the tribal people. In fact the term has a wider connotation. It has three different meanings. It is used to refer to the Almighty God. It is also used to denote the sun and the moon. Further, it is the name given to the traditional belief system of the people. Therefore, in the present context Donyi-Polo is neither God nor the two celestial objects nor an object of worship but the spiritual, ideological and philosophical idea, which inspires people to lead meaningful life on this earth. In other words, the faith of the people on the supreme power, God, as manifested in the form of the sun and the moon and the associated practices of worship of this absolute power is called Donyi-Polo. According to Talom Rukbo, Donyi-Polo, in the spiritual sense, means the synthetic form of the sun and the moon, that is, the power which is absolute and that governs the universe scientifically and eternally through heat, light, air, water, life and death. The virtues derived therefore are social discipline, devotion to work, hospitality, kindness and truth (Rukbo, 1992).

According to Adi belief, God rewards those who are guided by pious sense and those who deviate are punished. He is neither a generous-hearted being nor a sea of compassion but an impartial body. He is addressed as:

Donyi mikmi serine
Polo migo serone.

It means, "O Almighty God!, you are powerful, you are omnipresent and you are ever vigilant." Donyi-Polo is regarded as supreme. He reigns unchallenged and is the eye of the world. He watches everything; he is the witness. He shows the right way. He protects and also punishes. He shows mercy. He is the lord of truth and oath is taken in his name. Nobody can escape from his eyes. He is remembered at all times, not only at the hour of distress but also during the time of happiness. He is always in their hearts.

It is difficult to trace the evolution of faith in God, but it is interesting to explore how our forefathers developed the concept of God, i.e., Donyi-Polo. They might have felt the presence of a potent power in their surroundings and at the same time a sense of fear and security due to which they submitted themselves to God to propitiate the omnipresent and to understand the mysteries of the universe beyond their grasp. Appeasing the unseen power proved to be working and thus began rites and rituals. This is one of the first experiments of mankind with his surrounding. To carry on the experiment, a gifted one was born in the society. That was the beginning of the religious functionary, the Miri. He gradually also became the physician/medicine-man/sorcerer. He sings, dances and performs rituals for God. When involved in divination to trace the cause of a disease, he falls in trance and travels to an unseen world to establish communication with spirits by invoking hymns. The style of his song is classical which is not intelligible to the commoners. His songs are sometimes slow and, melodious, and sudden and harsh, and are imitated by the members present, in chorus. The hymns are supported by the music of a sword or sometimes a bunch of Kering Ripum (*ghunghru*). It is amazing to note how our forefathers composed these hymns with their fertile imagination. Here are a few lines:

He nane, naane kuwai
Abe naane, naane kuwai
Yaa...(in chorus by the members)
Ngo mibo taabe
Ebe gemangkom
Uyu yaaso e
Gonjonge gemangkom
Taabe dulem
Dukkange yeku bong.

(I do not possess any extraordinary power. I am a simple human being, but then I shall try my best to trace the footprint of the dearest one.)

He loolo, loolo kiwai
Alo loolo, loolo kuwai,
Ao regonge kuwai
Kaaling ao e
Regonge kuwai.
Yaa ...(in chorus).

(Oh, where are you wandering about? I am looking all around for you. My heart is burning. Dearest one, come back with me.)

When the invocation song is in full swing, the patient on the bed silently enjoys the melody; the sudden and harsh tune of chorus agitates the patient and again the melodic tune soothes him. When the Miri is in trance, all the members sitting around the fireplace ask him the whereabouts of the soul of the sick man and the evil spirits responsible for the ailment. He then tells about the soul and the spirits. He appeals to the evil spirits to return the soul in exchange for offering of *mithun* (bison), pigs, chicken, food, drinks, etc. It is believed that the spirits answer the questions of the members through the the Miri. The sick man is made to sleep. The sacrifices of mithun, fowl and so on which the Miri prescribes are a costly affair. However, to our conviction it is not the sacrifice, which cures the patient but the invocation songs that produce miracle. The Miri occupies an indispensable position in tribal society. On all occasions, at the time of birth, death or sickness, he is called for. In return, he is presented with the special parts of the animals sacrificed and valuable beads.

Some renowned Miris like Rumdong, a legendary figure among the Adi Minyongs, had sometimes transfigured himself as beautiful deer during community hunting being chased by the hounds; in the process many of the hunter shot their sharpened arrows into its body and chased it the whole day but failed to catch it. The deer ran with such a speed as if it was not pierced at all. What a wonderful animal? By the evening, when all of them returned to their village, Rumdong Miri gave back their arrows, which they shot at him on that day in the jungle. Nothing could poison the priest par excellence who played with sharpened poisonous arrows of the people. As a matter of fact often when he was in trance, he used to turn hysteric and he used to pierce sword into his chest without causing bleeding or wound. There are witnesses who saw him to swallow eggs which came out from the toes, and transforming dead fish into a living one and also making valuable beads from charcoal.

One of the important aspects of the ritual performed by the Miri is the oral prescription to the patient, which has its scientific value. He advises the patient to take light food, to abstain from eating fish, meat, chilies, etc., for at least two or three days and also other food items like red pumpkin, yam, ginger, mushroom, certain green leafy vegetables and some wild fruits. In some cases, meat of boar, bear, squirrels, etc., are restricted for up to one year. However, it depends on the nature of the disease of the patient. The movement of the patient is also restricted for one or two weeks. He is advised not to expose himself to the sun or rain. He is forbidden from going towards the river or streams, from moving in the northern or eastern direction and so on. Thus the Miri heals the patient with different methods. A modern physician also advises his patient in a similar way according to the gravity of disease. However, the faith of the patient on the person curing is also an important part of the treatment and healing process.

The Miri is the repository of all traditional knowledge inherited through oral traditions. He uses several methods of medication upon his patients and he does not fully depend on divine acts. One more custom noticed is the treatment of fractures in the body by the Miri using honey wax (Ngutkion). Here is an example. In the month of August, 1974, in a village near Along, one young man's right arm was severely fractured by a rolling boulder. He was hospitalized at Along General Hospital; his arm was x-rayed and found that it was totally fractured. Immediately he was advised to go to Assam Medical College, Dibrugarh. The patient and his wife expressed their unwillingness to go to Dibrugarh and preferred the treatment of a local Miri and so they requested the doctor to discharge him. He was discharged at his own risk. He then left for Yemsing village for treatment. To every body's utter surprise, within one month's time he was completely cured by the application of honey wax. There was no trace of fracture in the arm. This is not surprising, as honey has healing properties. It is said that in ancient times, it was used for dressing up wounds. It dries the wound, induces tissue growth and kills the bacteria that cause infection. Nevertheless, the medicine man is important since only he knows how to apply honey wax and keeps the technique a secret.

There is another peculiar method of prophecy performed by Miri, the tribal diviner. While in trance, he robs the body of the patient by using bamboo shavings and water. Then he collects the dirty water in an *Etkam* leaf and then drinks it without any hesitation. After this, he waits for some time to experience a reaction. If he vomits, it indicates that the patient is not likely to be cured. If he does not vomit, it is considered good and the patient is expected to recover within a few days. Sometimes, the Miri simply touches the body of the ailing person or reads his pulse to diagnose the problem and prescribes ritual treatment to heal the sick, and that works.

When a young mother is having a difficult delivery, the priest is called to look into the problem. He sacrifices a fowl or hen to appease the concerned spirit and then the fowl is thrown at the outskirts of the village. If this exercise fails, then he sacrifices a dog and the bleeding dog is also immediately thrown away. He chants:

Menape lenla, Menape lenla;
Arang delo duumapeka, ome lai ao elai;
Nok legape kampo kampona ati em ngolu si mebi tung.

(Come out, come out immediately, do not stay inside any longer. Whether you are a daughter or son, beautiful things are ready for you, come out, come out.)

Every human being faces death. No one can evade it. When all attempts to cure an ailing person fail death is finally accepted. He dies slowly in agony but his last desires remain, so he asks for a little beer or water to support himself during his journey towards the unknown world where his grandparents are waiting to receive him. His pulse stops and his body losses warmth. Close relatives sitting around start weeping and mourning. Then an expert or a priest sings *penge* (dirge) narrating his life-cycle and achievements, then describing the route he is to follow while going to the new land, and also warns him against the obstacles on the way. The song becomes so poignant that everyone's eyes sitting around become red and tears roll down their cheeks. The priest-singer further sings how the deceased's lifespan was designed and fixed by the creator in the womb of his mother:

Ane ke togie ruubum below
Konno ke takare duubar lendagem
Mi kope takare duubar lendagem
Kingki Baabu etponem ponrung bido
Siisang etponem ponrung bigo
Koomang naane beyingem yiirung bido
Giisang beyingem yiirung bido.

(While you were in the womb of your mother, Kongki Baabu, the designer fixed the span of your life with *etpon*, i.e., the rope with which you were to be carried on the back of the mother. Also by Koomang Naane, the goddess of designer, you were tied with *beying*, i.e., a rope made of yarn which is tied around the waist of the child.)

The singer continues:

Kongki Baabu ke etpone pondage delo
Koomang Naane ke beyinge yidage deme
Kingki etponem pontenge bito nape.

(The rope and the string of your waist were probably shortened by Kongki Baabu and Koomang Naane so you are leaving this world ultimately).

The priest further narrates the effects of dream on human life. The dream-lands of the rich and poor, singers, priests, hunters, etc., are vividly mentioned. Finally, he asks the deceased to go on and live in peace, not to return to this land or to the family and not to give any sort of trouble to any member. This song signifies that the people believe in a life after death and that living and dead continue to be united in one family.

The Adis bury the dead in the Ago-golung, i.e., the burial ground in the outskirts of the village, in a very systematic manner. A bamboo rack is erected near the graveyard. All belongings of the deceased such as clothes, *mithun* horns, hunting trophies, etc., are displayed on it. However, for children and poor men such decoration/structure is of little significance. The Adis believe that the *aith,* i.e., the soul becomes a *urom* (spirit) after death, but it lingers in the corpse until the burial. At night, when the world sleeps, a sound of someone walking is heard inside the house, searching and touching belongings. Then the members shout: *"Urom e adungku, urom e adungku"* (spirit is coming back, spirit is coming back). Then they get up and light the fire. For a rich man or woman, *mithun* and pigs are sacrificed after the burial with a belief that the animals would accompany the soul in his journey and he would continue to enjoy the same status. This sacrifice is called Dotgang, which means sacrifice and feasting of the mourners. With this, they propitiate the spirit and separate themselves from the departed soul psychologically.

The popular belief among the Adis is that simple, clean and generous-hearted men attain eternal peace after death, but notorious, cruel men do not reach the land of eternal peace, and continue to struggle and hover around the earth. Persons who meet an accidental death go to the land of the evil spirits responsible for his death. The soul of one who dies of drowning goes to the abode of the water god; the soul of one killed by a wild animal remains with the animal and that of one who dies by falling from a tree goes to Taleng Among, i.e., the sky and remains in the clouds.

Thus, we see that the indigenous religion of the people of Arunachal is well-developed and cannot be regarded as animistic or inferior to any other religion. It brings inspiration, hope and courage in the tribal life. It is associated with social ethics that unite and discipline the tribal people. Their virtues are discipline, devotion to work, generosity, hospitality, truth and kindness. Their sun and moon religion and their tribal medicine man/diviner help them to achieve these virtues.

What is unique about this Donyi-Polo religion is that it has spread into several tribal communities in recent years, such as Minyongs,

Padams, Gallongs, Pasis, Paggis, Karkos, Shimong, Komkars, Ashings, Thangams, Milangs, Boris, Bokars, Pailibos and Ramos, who profess this new religion enthusiastically and in the process continue to adhere to respective customary tribal religions. There is no doubt that Donyi-Poloism has had an integrative effect on the diverse tribes in the recent years and has helped in homogenizing divergent cultural traits in this high mountain region of the eastern Himalayas by shaping inter-ethnic harmony.

Notes

1. The paper is based on data collected from the Minyong -Padam tribe by the author, who belongs to the indigenous tribal community of Arunachal Pradesh.
2. Arunachal Pradesh, formerly North-East-Frontier-Agency (NEFA), emerged as a state in 1987. The Adi tribes are concentrated in the East and West Siang districts of Arunachal Pradesh. Anthropological Survey of India has identified 15 Adi sub-tribes most of whom have distinct cultural religious traditions. They are Ashing, Bokar Bori, Gallong, Karko, Komkar. Milang, Minyona, Pailibo, Pangi, Pasi, Ramo, Shimog and Tangam. Linguistically the Adis are closely linked with the Hill Miris, Tagins, and Apa Tanis (Singh, 1995:53). Despite homogenizing effect of Donyi-Polo religion, different sub-tribes have their religious specialists who perform different kinds of rituals to propitiate tribal deities, and benevolent and malevolent spirits. Thus the Adi --Ashing regard the evil spirits as responsible for all human sufferings, illnesses and natural calamities. The tribal religion of the Adi-Bokars is sobopanam (Datta Choudhury, 1995) which is practiced side by side with Donyi-Polo religion. Similarly the Adi-Bori people profess Dony-Polo but also believe in a number of spirits. They have shamans too who are called as Nybu, who is an intermediary between the spirits and the human beings (A.R. Das, 1995). The Adi-Gallong have an exorcist (Nyigre), who exists in society side by side with Dony-Polo religious specialists. The Adi-Milang also venerate Donyi-Polo, the supreme --being, but at the same time they believe in several supernatural powers. They have two types of sacred specialists, one conducting folk ritual dances and another curing diseases (Husain, 1995). Among the Adi-Minyong also traditional tribal religion has been succeeded by Donyi-Poloism. However, three

types of sacred specialists among them keep traditional religion alive (Husain, 1995). The Adi-Padams also, according to Dhar (1995) believe in several spirits and deities and at the same time have faith in Donyi-Polo, Sun-Moon God. Even Christian Padams continue to adhere to the old tribal rituals and rites. The tribal religion of the Adi Pailibo is called yoyo. They have now started worshipping Dony-Polo but their religious specialists survive in society (Datta Chowdhury, 1995). The Adi --Pangi profess Dony-Polo at community level, but at home they worship tribal spirits who cause disease to human beings and cattles. An association called Kine-Name-Doibote (Earth-Mother-Sky) has come up. It mobilizes people to worship the Mother Earth and the Sky, and not to convert to Christianity (A.R. Das, 1995). Among the Adi Pasi old tribal religion, Dony-Polo religion and Christianity (in plains areas) exists. Christian Pasis observes all tribal religious festivals and rituals (Husain, 1995). The Adi Shimongs believe in several spirits and deities. The Miri (priest) performs most of the rites. They also revere the supreme deity Dony-Polo. The recently converted Shimongs continue to observe rituals and rites associated with old tribal religion, and participate in tribal Solung and Dree festivals (Dhar, 1995). These additional materials drawn from ethnographic works dealing with other Adi tribes, drawn from secondary source, are helpful to ascertain the high level of cultural homogenization and religious syncretism which have occurred in vast areas of Arunachal Pradesh.

[The Editor of this volume has added the above material here only to provide an extended perspective].

References

Bose, M.L. 1997. *History of Arunchal Pradesh*, New Delhi. Concept Publishing Company.

Datta Choudhury, S. 1995. Adi-Bokars and Adi – Ashings in *Arunachal Pradesh. People of India.* General Editor K.S. Singh. editors: P. Dutta and S. I. Ahmad. Calcutta: A S I.

Dhar, B. 1995. Adi Padams, Adi Shimong in *Arunachal Pradesh. People of India*. General-Editor K.S. Singh. Editors: P. Dutta and S. I. Ahmad. Calcutta S I.

Das, A. R. 1995. Adi Pangi and Adi–Bori in *Arunachal Pradesh. People of India.* General Editor K.S. Singh. editors: P. Dutta and S.I. Ahmad. Calcutta: A S I.

Elwin, V. 1955. *India's North-East in the Nineteenth Century*, NEFA, Shillong.

Elwin, V. 1959. *A Philosophy of NEFA*, NEFA, Shillong.

Husain, Zahid. 1995. The Adi Galong,The Minyong, Adi Pasi in *Arunachal Pradesh. People of India*. General Editor K.S. Singh. Editors: P. Dutta and S.I. Ahmad. Calcutta: A S I.

Rukbo, T. 1992. *Donyipoloism Through Questions and Answers*, D.P.Y.K., Pasighat.

Singh, K.S. 1995. *Arunachal Pradesh. People of India*. General Editor K.S. Singh. Editors: P. Dutta and S.I. Ahmad. Calcutta: A S I.

16

Matriliny, Tribal Religion and Christianity: Syncretism in Khasi Society

Deimaphishisha Sun

The homeland of the Khasis is in the Khasi and Jaintia Hills of Meghalaya. Assam bounds it on the east, north, north-west, and Bangladesh on the south and south-west. The northern part of the Khasi territory is known as Ri Bhoi, which is formed of hillocks and flat lands. The central portion is known as Ri Lum, which is dominated by ranges of hills and the southern region constitutes the Ri War region marked by steep slopes descending towards Sylhet area, now in Bangladesh. We can divide the Khasis into the four territorial groups, such as the Khynriams of the central plateau of the Khasi Hills, the Wars who inhabit the War area in the south, the Bhois who occupy the Bhoi area in the north and the Pnars of the Jaintia Hills, who are also known as the Syntengs. The Khasi/Jaintia are identified with the Mon-Khmer people of the Far East mainly on the basis of similarities of language, megalithic culture and iron smelting. Modern linguistic studies have shown that there exists some important relations between the Khasi language and the Mon-Khmer groups of languages. The conformity of Khasi to Mon-Khmer is shown also in respect of gender, syntax, monosyllabic and morphological construction (Bareh, 1964: 4--5).

In this paper, we will discuss the pattern and process of syncretism in the wider context of matriliny as pursued by the Khasi-Jaintias, status of tribal religion which is very complex in nature and which has strong bearing in continuation of matriliny, the trend of religious revivalism and the impact of Christianity, which in the ultimate analysis seems to have minimal effect in the life of a highly conservative people.

I

The uniqueness of the Khasi culture finds expression in its matrilineal social structure which has survived with time, despite the impact of many exterior cultural forces. The Khasi tribe is composed of matri-clans, sub-clans and family groups. The matri-clan traces its origin to the ancient mother known as 'Ka Iambu Tynrai' who is the mother of the whole of 'Shi Kur' or the matri-clan. Next in order is 'Ka Iawbu Jymmen', the descendants of one great grandmother of a sub-clan or 'Kpoh'. 'Ka Iawbu Khynraw' is the ancestress, young grandmother of the family or 'Iing'. The grandmother, her daughters and the daughter's children live together under one roof and the grandmother remains the head of the family. As the Khasis have the matrilineal social system, the children identify themselves as members of the mother's matri-clan and adopt the name of the mother's clan. The traditional house of the mother or residential house is referred to as 'Ka Jung Kmii'. Special importance is given to this house where all social-economic and ritual activities are performed. Unlike other societies of the world, by law of inheritance, the property descends from the mother to the youngest daughter and again from the latter to her youngest daughter. The house is also known as 'Ka Iing Seng', as ritual performances take place there. Ancestral landed property always transfers through the unilineal matri-clan channel, making women the sole custodian of main source of the economy. Not only the youngest daughter, but all her female siblings are fully protected economically in the tradition-bound Khasi society. Even though the mother's residential house 'Iing Kmil' is inherited by the youngest daughter, and she also essentially becomes its keeper and organizer of family rites and rituals, the house may not be recognized strictly as her private or personal property; rather she lives in the house more in the capacity of a keeper since it is an ancestral property. For the same reason, she cannot dispose the property or articles belonging to the family at her own will. For doing so if the need arises she will have to depend on the advice of her maternal uncles, failing them her elder brothers, who act as her counsellors. This inherited ancestral property by the youngest daughter is known as the 'Ka nong tymmen', and property and earning which she may accumulate in her lifetime is known as 'Ka nong khynraw' (self-acquired property). The latter is solely hers and she can dispose, give or present the same to anyone she pleases in her lifetime.

The youngest daughter, Ka Khadduh, who takes the place of the mother, has a specific duty in organizing important religious rites and on such occasions, her house forms a meeting place of her kith and kin. She also has responsibility towards her unmarried brothers and sisters. She acts as a guardian to the parents and homeless members of her family and when in need she grants shelter to them (Bareh, 1964:9–10). In earlier times, if the youngest daughter had embraced Christianity, she was prohibited from participating in Khasi ritual rites and was deprived of her rightful inheritance, but in contemporary times this is not the case anymore. Even if a Khadduh has embraced Christianity she can claim all her rights (Miri in Mawrie, 1981: 16–17). The Khasi system of kinship is based on clan exogamy and clanspeople, with common ancestry, and could not inter-marry. Intra-clan sexual relationship is regarded as a sin (ka-sang) and the persons who commit such a crime are excommunicated from the society. The society places the demands of kinship above the rule of the state and at par with religious precepts (Bareh, 1964:18).

II

The Khasis believe that God exists and there is only one God who is omnipresent, omnipotent and eternal. The Khasi term for religion is *Ka -niam tip briew tip blei* (religion of knowing man and god). Theology is a Greek word (*theo* means god and *logy* means wisdom). It may be stated that the Khasis too have their theological reasoning as any other people of the world. For a Khasi the knowledge of man and knowledge of God go together. What is important for the Khasi is not commitment to a doctrine or dogma but his behaviour and conduct with fellow human beings. Knowledge of man consists fundamentally of the basic truth that he must have in his life, within a framework of rules and duties. The Khasi religion *(Ka Niam)* however, also includes the rules (*Ka rukom*), hence, the phrase *Ka Niam ka Rukom*. Indicated in *ka rukom* is the ceremonial aspect of religious observance, which must be in accordance with the norms laid down in *Ka niam* (Mawrie, 1981:33). All religions are based on faith. Faiths, with their many dimensions, are conveyed by parables passed down from one generation to another. Among the Khasis it was said that in olden times when God was walking hand in hand with man, there was a mountain serving as a ladder of communication between heaven and earth. The ancestors of the Khasis belonged to the *Hynniew Trep* (Seven clans) who came down to settle on earth but they continued to have regular contacts with their kith and kin of the khyndai trep (Nine clans) who were associated with God. The story goes that both the Hynniew Trep and the Khyndai Trep were related to one another by the comings and goings through the mountain, known as the Navel peak of Heaven-*U lum Sohpetbreng*. But later the members of the Hynniew Trep sinned against God and thus broke their ties with Him.

Another parable of the Khasis is that of '*Ka krem lanet, Ka Krem latang*'. According to this parable, at one time when everyone was innocent, a thanksgiving dance was arranged and everyone was invited including the sun and the moon, who were sister and brother. But when they danced, everybody started to laugh at them. This is because sin had entered man's heart and thus everybody could see evil. Out of shame, the sun fled to '*Ka Krem Lamet Ka Krem Latang*' and the earth was enveloped by total darkness. At this stage, the people looked up to god for mercy. A mediator U Syiar (the cock) came forward and volunteered to go to the sun and beg her to light up the world again. The sun agreed and told him that she will come out after he has crowed three times. From that time onwards, the cock is known as 'the liberator of mankind'. He became the principal consecrated animal, and ultimately stood as the symbol of the Khasi religious faith (Bareh, 1964: 21). For the Khasis, religion is a relationship between man and God and this relationship is governed by two factors such as *Ka Nia* and *Ka Jutang* (reason and covenant). Man is a creature of God and he belongs to God during and after his lifetime. There is a covenant between God and man from the beginning of time. The covenant is that as long as man is alive he should abide by the command of God and in return God will take care of him (Mawrie, 1981: 35). The basic tenets of Khasi religion are *Kamai in Ka Hok* (Earning righteousness), *Tip briew tip Blil* (Knowing man and God) and *Tip run tip kha* (Knowing maternal and paternal relations).

The religion enjoins an urge for knowledge, viz., (i) the knowledge of God (*Ka Niam tip Brew*), the knowledge of men (*Ka Niam tip-kur*) and (iii) knowledge of one's fellow people *(Ka Niam tip-kur tip-kha*) (Bhattacharji, 1984: 327). It is on the basis of reason and covenant that the Khasi establish and uplift their religion. As long as man keeps and follows the covenant and abides by them, no one can put him down. Thus one can say that for a Khasi, the covenants are the commandments or laws. U Rabon Singh states that, "The Khasi religion is usually known as the 'religion of divinations' or 'that which primarily involves calculations and judgments, because in it consists of man's urge to achieve what is good and righteous through the means of correct calculation and judgment', a calculation which cannot be wrong" (This citation is taken from the Khasi book *Ka Kitab Niam-Khein Ki Khasi* by U Rabon Singh and quoted in Sujata Miri's "Introduction" to H.O. Mawrie's *The Khasi Milieu*, 1981). The Khasi believe that their religion is a God given one. It teaches the man how to restore the broken relationship between God-and Man. They have a strong belief in God, Creator (U Blei Nongthaw). Thus, the divination and the cremation of dead are attempts to find that way back to God.

Medicine and religion are interlinked in the religious system of the Khasi society. A diviner is consulted on important occasions by all, Christians and non-Christians. The Khasi believe that the diviner receives his supernatural powers by communion with the spirit of one of his ancestors. His advice is sought in the event of misfortune, illness and premature death. Divination by breaking eggs on a wooden plank (*diengshat*) is the common method. The diviner makes auguries by breaking eggs and predicts good and bad omens by examining the relative portion of the broken egg shells on the wooden plank which may be either concave or convex. Another device for finding out the good and bad omen and the causes of misfortune and untimely death is the examination of the entrails of chickens and goats. The diviner is credited with the power of finding out the source and nature of sorcery which caused illness and death (Mathur, 1979:63–64). A Khasi believes that if God is angry with him something bad will befall him, like an illness. For this purpose, one ceremony known as Ka shat ka khein has to be performed in order to find out the cause of the same so as to make amends. Amendments are made in another ceremony known as Ka Loit ka law, followed with a prayer of thanksgiving to God.

The Khasi religion is an integral part of the clan system. Man, while coming to earth, or in other words when he was born, had been placed in a family and in a clan. He was under the protection of the godhead of the clan, the ancestress (*ka Iawbei*), the defied father (*U Thawlang*) and maternal uncle (*U Suidnia*). They together constituted the family cause (*ka Dawing*). This may be the reason why the Khasis glorify the dead. Certain rites are performed so as to summon their assistance for the living. The ancestress (*ka Iawbei),* the deified father and the maternal uncle are considered to be the founders of a particular clan. Stone monuments are erected in their memories and thanksgiving are periodically offered to them. When all these founders of a clan are happy and satisfied with their living successors, neither a devil nor any evil can cause harm to them as the family cause (*ka Dawing)* is fulfilled. However, this paying of respect to the departed soul should not be mistaken as worshipping, as some scholars have suggested (Natarajan 1977, Mathur 1979, Chattopadhyay 1978). Thanksgiving ceremonies to the departed ancestors are instituted so as to win their favour and blessings. Funeral rites are always performed accurately so that the spirit of the dead may go straight to the house of God and join with his predecessors in peace. Great care is usually taken to preserve the corpse before cremation. Religious rites such as sacrifice, offerings of food to the dead, prayers and addresses are strictly performed in conformity with old religion as a token of purification of the deceased before crossing over to eternity, for the Khasis do not believe in reincarnation of the spirit after death, but they believe that the deceased is already in God's midst. Thus, the reference '*bam kwai ha iing U Blii*' which means 'partaking betel nut in the house of God', (which is) an ultimate bliss for a Khasi. After the cremation, the bones of the deceased are collected and kept in a piece of white cloth which is then laid in a small cairns (*mawshyieng*). This is a temporary resting place. Since bygone days, a ceremony is performed for the collection of bones, from the cairns, to be carried to a permanent place known as cromlech (*mawbah),* where bones of the entire clan are kept. The Khasis also believed that souls which have lived a righteous life go to become one with the predecessors, whereas bad souls go to an underground abode of evil spirits (*Khyndai pateng niamra*) (Bareh, 1964: 23) It is God as *ka Nongshynshar* (the ruler) who will reward and punish man according to his deeds. Since the Khasis pursue a matrilineal social structure, all religious rites and ceremonies are always performed in the residence of the youngest woman in the lineage of each clan. Her house is known as 'Iingseng-Iingkhadduh'. All brothers and sisters belonging to the family or the clan assemble together in her house. For the completion of all these religious rites a cash subscription known as 'U Synniang U Bynhil' is collected from all adult members of the family or clan.

The word 'God' to a Khasi does not fall under the conventional gender, for 'God' is considered as the alpha and omega. As all things emerged from and end on Him, therefore whether we call Him 'U Blei' which is the masculine form or 'Ka Blei', the feminine form, it does not make a difference, for He is all powerful and a formless being. According to Chowdhury (1984) it is quite probable that this could be due to the recognition of male and female principles in creation. The Khasis address God by many names based on the need of the situation. This justifies the relationship of God with man in every sphere of life, but this does not mean that Khasis have more than one God. They are monotheists and believe in only one God who is omnipresent, omnipotent and eternal. Some other names by which God is addressed are U Nongbuh, U Nongttthaw—the planner and creator, U Nongsi, U Nongpynlongg—the giver and dispenser of life, Ka Nonglynshar—the ruler, Ka lulogkur---God of the clan, U Blii longopah—God of wealth and others. This shows that the Khasis believe that God is the supreme being and is present in one and all. The Khasis believe that God's unique gift to man is intelligence which animals are devoid of. Because of this gift man has the power to develop his personality according to his potentiality, but as the world is full of evil, man needs the presence and strength of God so that he can fight against the world. He believes that so long as he keeps the covenant, God shall never desert him.

III

Christianity was sown in the Khasi Hills as early as 1813, with the advent of Krishna Chandra Pal, a Bengali Christian convert of William Carey, the founder of Serampore Baptist Mission. Pal was succeeded by Alexander B Lish who opened three schools at Cherrapunji, Mawmluh and Mawsmai. He also translated the Gospel of St Matthew into Khasi. William Carey himself took the initiative to get the New Testament translated into Khasi (Marak and Das, 1973) but failed to arouse much interest. This mission ran for a period of five years from 1833 to 1838, but came to an end due to vehement protest from the natives. Thomas Jones, a missionary of the Welsh Calvinistic Church Organization arrived at Cherrapunji on 22nd June, 1841 along with his wife. He took over the mission activities from the Serampore Baptist Mission. He started the first school at Mawsmai, then Mawmluh. He translated the Bible into the Khasi language by using the Roman script. For this reason, he is known as the father of Khasi literature. His first two books in the Khasi language were *Khasi Primer (Ka Kitab ba nyngkong)* and Christian Catechism (*Ka Kot Tikir)* (Rana, 1989). Besides the mission schools, Jones erected two missionary houses at Nongsawlia. Apart from schools, hospitals and dispensaries were also opened. Both Jones and his wife worked with great zeal along with a few Khasi converts, though diehard elements among the Khasi adopted a hostile approach to the activities of the missionaries. Rev. and Mrs. William Lewis and Dr. Owen Roberts later joined the Joneses in 1843.

During 1878–88, the number of converts in the Khasi Hills increased. In 1907, nine per cent of the Khasis were Christian, three per cent were Hindus and the remaining were orthodox Khasis. After 20 years of the arrival of the Welsh Calvinistic mission, another denomination, the Roman Catholic Mission, came to the Khasi Hills around 1890. Among the Catholic denominations, it was the Catholic of Salesian Mission Society which first laid its foundation in these hills and then the others followed suit, such as the Catholic Holy Cross Mission, the Little Flower Society, etc. (Marak and Das, 1973). A number of convents, schools, technical institutions and colleges were established by the Roman Catholics---Loreto Convent in 1909, St. Mary's in 1913, St. Edmund's in 1905 and the Don Bosco technical school in 1923. The Roman Catholics controlled the institutions for higher studies while the former concentrated mainly on primary education (Mathur, 1979). After the arrival and establishment of these two denominations, missionaries from other denominations started flowing in. Among these are the All Saints Church, Seventh Day Adventists, All in One Christ, Church of God, etc. Christianity has spread in the vast rural and urban areas of the Khasi Hills. The foreign missionaries have departed years ago, but Christianity has established itself in vast areas. The local missionaries are taking the responsibility of conducting the activities connected with the church. This is solely true in the case of the Protestants belonging to the Welsh Calvinistic Mission and All Saints Church associated with the Church of England. According to the 1991 census, population of Christian Khasis of different denominations in the Khasi and Jaintia Hills are as follows: East Khasi Hills (4,01,852), West Khasi Hills (1,98,880), Jaintia Hills (1,38,280).

IV

With the coming of Christianity and Western education, transformation in social life became inevitable. The Christian converts abandoned their former religious rites and beliefs to a great extent and accepted Christian teachings gradually, but they continued to revere and preserve their rules of inheritance, household usages and observance of the age-old Khasi cultural and political customs (Natarajan, 1977). So large was the spread of Christianity that some orthodox Khasis saw it as a threat which will erode the social structure. With this view in mind, sixteen non-Christian Khasi formed an association on 23rd November, 1899, known as Khasi Youngmen's Association with an aim to caution the Khasi people and to rejuvenate the moral teachings and tenets passed on from generation to generation. In 1901, the association was renamed 'Seng Khasi' and prominent persons like Babu Jeebon Roy and Radhon Singh Berry joined this association. In 1905, when the Christian movement was in full fury, the Seng Khasi took upon itself the responsibility of defending the Khasi religion. According to them, the main purpose of the organization was "to defend the faith of the forefathers, to understand the true meaning of conscience and truth as handed down by them which have been misled by the foreigners." Seng Khasi declared itself as an association of those Khasis who adhered to the traditional Khasi religious faith. The members of the association were called Khasi-Khasis so as to distinguish themselves from those Khasis who had adopted Christianity (Sen, 1994). It should be noted here that when the sixteen persons had formed the association, their aim was only to create awareness among the Khasis, concerning the onslaught of the missionaries, but when the name was changed to Seng Khasi, the stress was on religion. The leaders of the Seng Khasi tried to revive and to reform the original version of the Khasi religion. Having initiated the process of revivalism and reformation of the Khasi religion, the Seng Khasi propagated through this organization the following principles: to abide by the matrilineal system of descent founded by the ancestors, to love and respect one's kith and kin, both on the maternal and paternal side, to believe in God, and to serve God through service of people. Besides above principles, the leaders of the Seng Khasi movement announced the following aims and objectives: to uphold and strengthen the belief of the Khasi Pnar descendants of Ki Hynniew Trep (The Seven Families) in their ancestral religion, rooted in the womb of time, to hold gatherings of the Khasi Pnars who follow their matrilineal system and those who are faithful to the spiritual and moral laws of their society, to be conscious about the need for progress, to make an endeavour towards that end, by keeping the body healthy and sound, by improving the mind in the pursuit of knowledge, by involving oneself in an effort to do good and by cultivating a spirit of love for justice and goodwill towards all men, to be courteous, self-respecting and self-disciplined in all matters and to propagate the principles of the Seng Khasi (Das, 1989).

The Seng Khasi adopted the Red flag and a crowing cock as particular symbols. The design proposed by U Hipshon Roy was accepted in 1961. Thus, the Seng Khasi flag depicts a crowing cock in a white circle with a red background. The red background signifies courage and the circle in white represents the world. White stands for the fundamental belief of the Khasis and his faith that he comes to this world to learn truth. The crowing cock symbolizes the ancient culture, rites and traditions of the Khasis. It is believed that when sin darkened the world, it was the cock who went and requested the sun to light the world again. From that time onwards, the cock is known as the 'liberator of mankind' (Rana, 1989: 124--125). The Seng Khasi started organizing archery competitions and traditional dance performances such as Ka shud mynsiem and the Nongkrem dance. The Christian Khasis initially were advised not to take part in these events. In the next phase of the cultural history of the Khasis, however, it was found that the Christians too gave their support in the form of participation in the festivities and contributions of articles in newspapers and development of literature. The Catholics were found to be more tolerant than the Presbyterians (Natarajan, 1982). Some individuals worked effortlessly for cultural revivalism. They were the enlightened youth who received their higher education at Calcutta and other centres. They felt that branching Khasis into two, i.e., one under the umbrella of Seng Khasi and another under the umbrella of Christianity was not an important agenda, and that the main issue is the survival of their identity, being a minor group in a huge country, India, with all its cultural complexes. The traditions and usages of the Khasis have also received appreciation of other noted scholars such as Jr. G. Costa, Victor G. Bareh, Hamlet Bareh to name a few (Bhattacharjee, 1984: 334). U Saso Tham, a Christian Khasi, composed a brilliant poem entitled, '*Ki Hynniew Trep*' that depicts the divine origin of the Khasi people (Natarajan, 1977: 168–169). Rabon Singh, another Christian wrote "*Ka Niam Khasi, Ka Kitab Jingphawar* and *Ka Jingiathuhkhana Purisram*" that dealt with Khasi religion, rites and sacrifices, divinations, etc. Attempts to break away from the mainstream of Khasi culture were abandoned by the Christians under the impact of changed situations. A sense of tribal heritage developed and was cultivated among the Christian and non-Christian Khasi. The ancient customs and manners no longer remained a taboo to the Christians. The trend is evident from acceptance by the Christian Khasi of the tribal norms like dances and observance of state religious ceremonies. Christian Khasis have now started taking pride in their cultural heritage (Mathur, 1979: 148).

V

The contact of the Khasi people with Islam was of a different nature in comparison to Christianity. Islam has not developed through any systematic process of proselytization. Historical records show that the Khasis first came into contact with the Muslims around the 17th century AD when the Muslims began paying occasional visits to the Khasi Hills as wanderers, traders, fortune-hunters, etc., Many of them settled in the hills and adopted Khasi customs. Some Muslims seem to have been honoured with chieftainship in certain Khasi states. For example, the Syims (Chiefs) of Mawiany are believed to have descended from four migrant families (Bareh, 1967, quoted in Mathur, 1979: 42). During and after the British rule, a number of Muslims from Kabul, Kashmir, Punjab and other places migrated to Assam and settled down for trade and employment. A good number of them married Khasi women and are mostly concentrated in Laban area of Shillong. Initially, such marriages did not receive the approval of the Khasi society but subsequently it was approved and accepted. The Muslim ritual for wedlock 'Nikah' sanctified such marriage. Mathur's (1979) survey of 50 Muslim Khasi families of Shillong shows that the children born out of a marriage between a Muslim father and a Khasi mother were regarded as adherents of Islam, but for all other purposes they were treated just as any other Khasi. The Muslim Khasi women, almost as a rule marry within Muslim families. A survey conducted by Mathur (1979) reveals that out of 64 married women, 36 Muslim Khasi women established marital relations with non-Khasi Muslims, whereas out of twenty-two married men, only six were married to Muslim women. This has helped to strengthen and expand the span of the Muslim group among the Khasi and also maintain the group boundary. While among the general Khasis, the inheritance goes to the daughters and the youngest daughter 'Khadduh' gets the lion's share of the property, but this is not the case among the Muslim Khasis. The youngest Muslim daughter does not get any preferential treatment regarding the ancestral property and cannot be the sole heiress of the ancestral house. In a majority of the Muslim Khasi households, the youngest daughter has been challenged as she no longer has to perform the traditional Khasi religious rites. But this is not the case with all the Muslim Khasis. The Muslim law of inheritance has been enforced in only a few cases, whereas in many cases, they follow the traditional Khasi way of inheritance (1979:42–54).

Here, we can see a difference. Here no individual helps to create a section of people. This is unlike the Christian missionaries whose main aim is to convert the Khasis into the new religion. Islam has developed mainly on the strength of the Muslim immigrants and their wedlock with the Khasi women, who may or may not embrace Islam. A very limited number of Christian Khasi have entered into marital relations either with Muslims or Muslim-Khasis, and if they had embraced Islam at an early period of their marriage, majority of them have now reconverted themselves to Christianity.

Unlike the Christian Khasis who were more in number and were automatically being accepted by the society, the children born of the union of Khasi women and non-Khasi Muslims find themselves being pulled by the two contrasting traditions of their parents, the Khasi tradition and Muslim tradition. They have no place in non-Khasi Muslim society. They find themselves uprooted from their tribal moorings and deserted by the non-tribal Muslims. In many such cases there was reconversion either to Khasi religion or Christianity. Despite long contact with the Islam, the Muslim Khasis have tried to preserve their tribal heritage. Some of the Khasis who have married Khasi or non-Khasi Muslims have not changed their Khasi tradition. They observe all the customary Khasi ceremonies and festivals and also reckon their descent through the female line. Some of them adopted Muslim titles along with maternal clan titles and some have simply adopted only the maternal clan title as any other Khasi would. A Muslim Khasi generally retains his maternal clan title as any other Khasi would. Thus, we see that, on one hand the Khasis are tolerant enough to accommodate a foreign ideology, namely Islam, and on the other, Islam has made quite a large measure of compromise and adjusted itself to Khasi culture.

VI

The Pnar Khasis, also known as the Jaintias were influenced by Hinduism as early as the fifteenth century, when the Jaintia king shifted his capital from Sutanga to Jaintiapur, a place in Sylhet area of Bangladesh. Nartiang, which has the stronghold of Hindu culture was the summer capital of the Syiem. Although he lived at Nartiang, the family members stayed back at Sutanga. The Jaintia Syiem constructed two temples at Nartiang and Brahmans were appointed as priests. The Sutanga Syiems had even adopted the Hindu names, Hindu rites and ceremonies for which they were known as Hindu kings. Though the Syiems encouraged the performance of Hindu rites and sacrifices, including the custom of sacrifice to the goddess Kali, the family members and majority of subjects were excluded from taking part in them, except for the villagers of Nartiang as they were under considerable influence of Hinduism, though they continued to propitiate the tribal Khasi deities. This contact with Hinduism did not affect the ritualistic observance of Khasi tribal religion, including life-cycle rituals such as elaborate funeral rites and election to the Syiemship.

Many eminent Khasi scholars, specially the non-Christian Khasis have been influenced to a certain degree by the Hindu literary tradition. The works of Babu Jeebon Roy, Sib Charan Roy, Maham Singh and Khongphai may be mentioned in this connection. Babu Jeebon Roy wrote many books such as *Ka Niam Jongki Khasi: The Religion of the Khasis* (1897), *Hitopadesha* (1898), *Ramayana* (1900), *Buddha Dev* (1901). Sib Charan Roy wrote the famous book *Ka Bhagawad Gita* in 1903. It was his earnest desire that the Khasis should be liberated from fear whether of Khasi demons or Christian hell. Every Khasi home should have the *Gita* and also be proud that this great treasure is accessible to them in their mother-tongue. Some of the Khasi elites like Maham Singh and Khongphai tried to compare Khasi religion with the Hinduism. According to Maham Singh, the forms of religious ceremonies performed by the Khasis are very similar to those of the Hindus. The Khasis, like the

Hindus, cremate the dead and offerings are made to them. The Khasis also worship ancestral spirits, believe in the efficacy and holiness of animal sacrifices, performances of religious dances and festivals (Mathur, 1979: 25; Das, 1989).

VII

In course of time, Christianity and the traditional Khasi religion, as revived by the Seng Khasi movement, flourished and developed cooperatively. In the process, many indigenous cultural elements and fragments of traditional belief were grafted within the Christian beliefs of the Khasis. It may therefore be surmised that the Christian Khasis continue to pursue tribal religious beliefs obliviously. We can also say that the Khasis who have adopted Christianity have not embraced Christianity in its purest form, since they continue to remain under the clutches of their tribal superstitious beliefs and religious convictions. This ongoing trend whereby the Khasis have embraced a new religion but have still not totally abandoned their old religious-cultural beliefs may be described as syncretism. In varied domains of day-to-day life, the Khasis, whether Christians or not, adhere to tribal customs, beliefs and practices of their ancestors, which have religious overtones. A few important examples may be cited here in order to depict the syncretistic value-system of the Khasi people. For example, in the case of a newborn baby, the stool passing out of its bowels is believed by the Khasis to be ancestress stool (ka eit iawbei). When the infant parts the lips smilingly before attaining self-consciousness, the Khasis believe that the child is in conversation with the ancestress (Rkhei iawbei). The scratch marks appearing on the belly of the mother after delivering the baby is known as ancestress scratch (trud iaw bei) and the original hair of an infant, not yet one year old, is called ancestress hair (*niuh iawbei*) and no knife, scissors or blade should touch the infant's head until it has crossed one year (Mawrie, 1981:78). It is also believed that no food item should be denied to a pregnant woman. For during that particular period, it is the body in her womb who wants the food, and not the mother. If for some reason, the desired food item is not given, then it is believed that the baby will be born with extra saliva (*jaw duid)* coming out from its mouth. Such beliefs are recurrent among the Christian and non-Christian Khasis alike. On the first birthday of the baby, the eldest maternal uncle of the baby is to cut the baby's hair. Christian Khasis continue to observe such customs without fail.

There is also an old practice among the Khasis of applying a black *tikka* on a baby's forehead or typing a matchstick to the baby's cap to ward off 'the evil eye'. And if ill-luck still strikes and the baby is supposedly attacked by the 'evil eye' known as *sabut* then a woman specialist is called to find the solution. The old lady will take some lime on her fingers or on a betel leaf *tympew*, start chanting to the evil eye by spitting on the lime and rubbing it on her fingers or the betel leaf, and then order the evil eye to leave the child alone and go to its own place or else it will be embarrassed in front of the world. When this is done, the lime is applied to the baby's stomach and feet as a sign of condemning the evil eye. Then the remaining lime is thrown in the direction where the sun sets by saying, "*Phet shaba sep ka sngi, sep u bani*" (Run to the place where the sun and the moon set). To free an individual from the evil eye is not the only duty of this lady specialist. When called upon, she massages women during pregnancy and also after delivery. She advises pregnant women about precautions to be taken and also gives a bath to newborn children. She also prepares a concoction from different herbs along with rice-beer which works as a medicine *(dawai niang sohpet)* particularly in destroying the germs present in the navel of the newborn baby. This Khasi tribal woman, as a repository of traditional knowledge, emerges as a shaman and medicine woman simultaneously. Coming to the wedding ceremony, the Christian Khasis get married in the church, following Christian precepts and wear Western dress during marriage, a white gown with a veil which is distinct from the Khasi tribal dress. As a matter of fact, except the marriage vows in the church, almost all other rituals concerning marriage are observed even today in the customary tribal way. Thus the food items, such as rice, pork, etc., have to be carried in pots known as *khiew phiang* from the bride's house to the groom's house in the morning of the wedding day. Only the family members of the groom are allowed to take this special food. On the wedding day, the groom leaves his house accompanied by his maternal and paternal uncles along with other relatives and friends, with blessings from all concerned. The only change seen in observance of these customs among the Christians is that the journey is made first to the church and then directly to the bride's house. The groom on leaving his mother's house and on the way to church is not supposed to look back. This is indeed an old Khasi religious custom which is followed by all Christians. A group of men from the bride's family meets the groom's party half way and they stop to exchange greetings and betel nuts and they jointly march to the church, awaiting the arrival of the bride. After the wedding and on reaching the bride's house, the mother of the bride blesses the couple on the doorstep and anoints the groom's head with oil, welcoming him to the family.

A few days after the wedding, a day is fixed for the bride and her family members to visit the groom's mother's house. This is a very important customary visit known as *leit kai ung kiaw*. The mother of the groom anoints her daughter-in-law's head with oil and blesses her on the doorstep wishing goodness and joy. The bride takes gifts in the form of food known as *ki kpu* to her mother-in-law's house. She stays in the latter's house for a few days and then returns back with her husband to her mother's house. These are universal tribal customs followed by all sections of the Khasis.

With the spread of Christianity, many tribal practices such as cremation rites and preservation of the dead body for several days have been abandoned, but the belief regarding the soul, *Myniem*, has not been totally given up. In this regard, the two faiths intertwine. Both the religions (tribal Khasi and Christianity) do not believe in reincarnation, after death. The Christians believe that good souls will go to heaven and bad ones will go to hell, whereas for traditional Khasis, souls which have lived a righteous life go to be one with the predecessors in the God's mist, whereas bad souls go to an underground abode of evil spirits known as *khyndai pateng niamra*. The belief that the soul of the deceased comes for the last time to the house on the third day is not repudiated by the Christian sections of the Khasis. It is for this reason that the house of the deceased is kept open until the third day in view of his supposed visit and hence all elders generally remain awake during this period. The custom of collection of funeral subscription, *u synniang u bynhei* for the completion of the religious rites (though in Christian way) is still being carried out and whenever anyone talks about a person who is dead, the people will touch the *shangkwai* (basket for keeping betel-nut, betel-leaf and lime) and repeat the words *bam kwai ha iing u Blei*, meaning "partaking betel nut in the house of god". This old religious-cultural Khasi custom of paying respect to the dead ancestors has survived among the Christian and non-Christian Khasis uniformly.

Another important feature that still prevails among the Khasis (Khasi-Khasis and Christian Khasis alike) is their superstition concerning the timing for starting any important work. The month of April or Jaisong, as per Khasi calendar, is regarded as a bad month for beginning any new work such as a new business, construction of a new house, or a marriage. Jaisong is related to a storm (*'eriong)* and it is believed that all the good will of the occasion will be blown away by the storm; hence no new work should be started during this month. Thus till date all Khasis, Christians and non-Christians alike, adhere to this age-old belief and they do not take up new work or fix a marriage date during this month. Here again we notice survival of the old spiritual order.

VIII

According to Khasi belief, there are different kinds of deities. Different authors have differently named and identified the deities as spirits, deities, gods and demons such as Gordon (1907), Natarajan (1977) and Mawrie (1981). Some family members keep the devils as their household deities and worship them so that in return the devils will give the keepers wealth and earthly prosperity. These devils are of different types and have different powers. Some of the well-known ones and which are strongly affirmed by the Khasis today are Ka Taro, Ka Shwar, Ka Bili and U Jhlen (Mawrie, 1981: 42). Just mere mention of any of their names sends shivers to one's spine, for if a person is afflicted by anyone of them, it is a known fact that his sufferings will be of a very serious nature. Ka Taro is well-known amongst the Pnar of Meghalaya. Ka Taro brings suffering to those persons who have stolen something from its keeper. The thing taken may be as small a thing as a safety pin or betel nut or may even be money. It may even visit the close friends and relations of its keeper. The sufferings brought by it are unbearable and unless the thing taken is given back, the patient will not be cured. It is necessary to offer a prayer to the concerned deity by engaging an expert medicine man. The author has witnessed several cases in the recent past in which people are reported to have suffered due to the influence of Ka Taro. Ka Shwar is yet another ferocious devil known to the Khasis. It torments its victim by strangling or twisting the neck. It attacks those people who make trouble for its keeper, and only persons who are well versed in the ways of this deity can cast off its evil spell. Ka Bili (poison deity) is a common and well-known devil among the Khasis. It is of various types and works in different ways. Some poisons act very slowly, with chronic pain resulting in death, whereas others act so fast that death takes place almost immediately (Mawrie, 1981:45). It is also said that when this deity attacks a person there is no cure. It occurs yearly, i.e., it occurs at a particular time of the year for a person who is afflicted by it. It cannot be totally cured and efforts of specialists in the field of medicinal herbs almost frequently fail. But the most dangerous deity well-known all over Meghalaya is U Jhlen. This deity demands human blood and in return it will shower immense wealth on its keeper, but if the keeper cannot satisfy the deity, it will put him to shame before the world by taking the shape of a fish, cat or snake and sets him on to the roof top. The traditional belief in the power of U Jhlen is strong and it persists in the minds of Christian Khasis, even those residing in the urban areas of Shillong. The fear of such a devil is so strong that the Khasis hesitate to take Kwai (betel nut) and tea from the hands of an unknown person or unfamiliar neighbours and friends. Their Christian faith still cannot lead them to do away with their fear and belief in what is locally known as 'U Nongshohnoh' (a person who works for the jhlen-keeper). In case of illness suspected to be due to U Jhlen, even the Christian Khasis in the urban areas resort to the traditional way of curing the patient or victim of his/her diseases, with the help of a member from the Syiem's family (Marak and Das, 1973).The Khasi and the Pnar are indeed highly superstitious people in their mental outlook and this we may say because of their dependence on divination, despite high level of literacy and Christianity.

The Khasis' adherence to their tribal food items is also great. The Khasi people have various food items derived from their surrounding area which are traditionally consumed in a variety of ways. Their contact with the Christian missionaries however introduced them to new food items. But this introduction did not deter or stop them from relishing their traditional food items also. Different types of cakes known as *Putharo, Pumaloi, Pudoh, Pusyep* are prepared from rice after grounding the rice and turning it into powder, with a mortar and pestle (*U thlon*g and *Synrei*) and are relished by the Khasis. Leafy vegetables such as 'U jarain' (Faqopyrum esculentum), 'U jajew' (Oxalis martiana), 'Shirkait', the banana flower (Musa paradisiaca) and the soft portion of bamboo shoot 'lungsief' (Dendrocalamus hamiltonli) are some of the food items which are taken by the Khasis mostly in rural areas (Bhowmick, Das and Ganguly, 1984). 'Ktung' (dried fish) and Jungrymbai (condiment prepared from the seeds of beans) are other special food items common among the Khasis (Christian Khasis and Khasi-Khasis alike). A special dish known as 'Jadoh' is served on many occasions. It is prepared by mixing the rice with pig, cow or chicken blood; hence, the name 'Jadoh'—'Ja' stands for rice and 'doh' for meat. Another delicious dish is 'Dohkhlich' which is prepared from a pig's or cow's head, mixed with onion, ginger and salt to taste. Hence, despite the coming of Christianity into the hills, and even after the introduction of changes in the lifestyle and consumption pattern, the Khasis have not altogether abandoned their traditional food items. Coming to the traditional Khasi dresses, it appears that for the mens folk, old dresses have totally disappeared. Only on festive occasions, such as annual dance celebrations, revived by the Seng Khasi, the men folk put on old dresses of dhoti, pagri and waistcoat. But for everyday wear, the present trend is to wear Western garments like suit, necktie, trouser and shirt. But the women folk are still very much attached to their traditional dresses; especially on ceremonial occasions, a Khasi girl takes pride in wearing her traditional dress known as 'Jainsam'. This is being followed by both the Christian and non-Christian Khasis. Thus in food and dress codes also we notice continuity of tribal patterns.

IX

According to Khasi tribal belief, God is manifested in different places—in groves, forests, hillocks, peaks and rivers. For this reason, these places are regarded as sacred and they are therefore the places of worship. This philosophy of pantheism shapes and dominates the tribal world view of the Khasi-Jaintia people even today. The Khasi and Jaintia Hills have a large number of 'groves'. The sacred groves (*law kyntang*) are restricted to older settlement areas and can be found in Raliang, Nartiang, Shangpung, Sutnga and Jowai in the Jaintia Hills, whereas in the Khasi Hills, the groves are found in Mawsmai, Mawphlang, Nongkhlaw and Shillong peak. It is even today considered an anathema *(sang)* to cut live wood from these forests or to remove anything from the groves, for it is held that God would be offended if any part of such forest is cut, trees lopped, flowers plucked, cattle grazed or fires lit. However, there is no harm if any villager removed dead wood from the sacred groves for domestic use. The village councils and religious leaders usually regulate management of the groves. Groves are meant for village deities -- 'U ryngkew U basa'. The groves are however the property of the village. Hunter (1879) records the Viceroy making village and Syiem officials responsible for conserving such groves in 1874. Rules allow occasional dead firewood collection by an individual but it should not be for sale. Rules also permit felling of trees for ceremonies such as Behdiengkhlam, ancestor worship and certain other cremations. The sacred groves among the Khasis can be classified as Ki Law Lyngdoh (Forests under the control of traditional religious leader; Mawphlang is included in this class), Ki Law Kyntang (Forests of great value for sacrificial and religious ceremonies), Ki Law Niam (Religious forest; these may not be distinct as the above two), Ki Law Adong (Forests protected for non-material use, for example, water) and Ki Law Shmong) forest resources for village use, (Rodgers, 1994).

This consecration of the groves among the Khasis since olden times is ritualistically being followed till date. The 'Law Lyngdoh' at Mawphlang is one of the well-known sacred groves and the members of the Lyngdoh clan are maintaining it. Whether rural or urban, Christian or non-Christian, all the Khasis recognize and respect the sacred identities of these groves. This is indeed yet another example of the syncretistic value-system of the tradition-bound Khasi people. Some of the other beliefs among the Khasis that persist are related to agriculture. Thus, one who has an unlucky hand (sniew kti) should not sow seeds and raise the plants. Seeds should be sown or trees planted when the moon is waxing and not when it is in wane. A red sky in the evening is a sign of fine weather tomorrow (Gordon, 1907: 43).

X

The prominent domains of Khasi society where traditional faith still holds its foundation are the matrilineal social structure and the mode of deriving descent through the female line and recognition of and respect for associated ritual-jural privileges. All these jural-ritual norms and customs still endure as vigorously as ever before. Another norm of the ancient faith that is strictly adhered to is the rule of clan exogamy. Even today, a Khasi, whether a Christian Khasi or a Khasi-Khasi, will not dare to think of offending the rules of clan sanctity, rules prohibiting marriage within the same Kur (clan). Hence, we can conclude that though many Khasis have accepted Christianity, but they are largely under the garb of their old religious beliefs. We can say with authenticity that the adoption of the new religion on part of the Khasis is only a part adoption. Our analysis has revealed that there are many similarities between the Christian teachings and the teachings of the Khasi religion. According to Christian teachings, there is only one God who is the supreme being. The Khasis also believe that there is only one God who is omnipresent, omnipotent and eternal. The Khasi religion is based on reason and covenant and if a person abides by them, then in the next life he will be joined with his predecessors in the house of God and will have betel nut there which is the ultimate bliss for a Khasi. It is almost true with the Christians.

Many scholars have called the Khasi religion an ancestor-worshipping religion. Traditional Khasi religion pays a lot of respect to the dead predecessors and especially to the ancestress (Ka Iawbei), the deified father (U Jhawlang) and the maternal uncle (U Suidnia). Stone monuments are erected in their memory and thanksgivings are periodically offered to them. This respect and reverence for the dead ancestors, despite adoption of Christianity is an important syncretistic element, which remains in force. A distinguishing feature of paying respect to the ancestors in an adjusted form is observed in the Christian Khasi families belonging to the Roman Catholic denomination. Once a year, the Catholic Khasis used to place wreaths of flowers and burn candles on the graves of their beloved ones. This tradition gets fused in a syncretic manner in the still prevalent functional ceremony called '*Ban kynmaw uit ia kiba la uit noh*' (to remember those beloved ones who were gone). Though there would be no such flower-giving ceremony among the members of the Protestant Church, yet the Khasi Presbyterians place floral wreaths on the graves of their loved ones. In the case of the Presbyterians, it is done based on an individual family basis, unlike the Catholics who observe it as a whole through the church. Hence, we can infer that the attachment and respect shown by the Christian Khasis for their ancestors is basically the same as those Khasis who continue to follow their traditional faith, but it is asserted in a moderate capacity among the former, as we discussed above. In multiple domains of day-to-day life, the Khasis, whether Christians or not, adhere to tribal customs, beliefs and practices of their ancestors, which have religious overtones. The Khasis have embraced a new religion, Christianity, nevertheless they have not totally abandoned their old religious and cultural beliefs. This coexistence of dual religious beliefs may be characterized as syncretism.

Acknowledgement

Without the strong persuasion and guidance of Dr. N.K.Das, who has intimate familiarity with the Khasi culture through his long stay in Shillong, this paper could not have been written. The author is indebted to Dr.Das for his warm preferential treatment and encouragement and for giving the opportunity to participate in this pioneering endeavour. The views expressed in this paper are however those of the author alone, who is a physical anthropologist belonging to the Khasi community.

References

Bareh, H: 1964. *Khasi Democracy* Shillong: Ri Khasi Press.

Bhattacharji, J.B.: 1984. Changing Khasis: A Historical Account. In *Tribes of North East India,* Sebastian Karotemprel (Ed.) Calcutta: Farma KLM Private Ltd.

Bhowmick, D.C., Das, M.M. and Ganguly, P.: 1984. Food Habits of the Khasi People: A Study of Tradition and Change. *Human Science* 33(4): 263--269.

Chowdhury, J.N.: 1984. The Khasi: Connections about their Origin. In *Tribes of NorthEast India,* Sebastian Karotemprel (Ed.) Calcutta: Farma KLM Private Ltd.

Chattopadhyay, K. 1978. *Tribalism in India.* New Delhi: Vikas.

Das, N.K. 1989. *Ethnic Identity, Ethnicity and Social Stratification in North East India.* New Delhi: Inter-India Publications.

Gordon, P.R.T.: 1907[1975]. *The Khasis.* Delhi: Cosmo Publications (First Published 1907).

Hunter, W.W. 1879. *A Statistical Account of Assam.* London:Trubner and Co.

Mawrie, H.O. 1981. *The Khasi Milieu (with introduction by Sujata Miri)* New Delhi: Concept Publishing Company.

Marak, S.A. and Das, M.M. 1973. A Few Aspects of the Khasis of Shillong. *Bulletin of the Anthropological Survey of India.* XXII (1--2): 86--175.

Mathur, P.R.G. 1979. *The Khasi of Meghalaya.* New Delhi: Cosmo Publications.

Natarajan, Nalini. 1977. *The Missionary among the Khasis.* New Delhi: Sterling Publishers.

Natarajan, Nalini. 1982. Impact of Missionary in Khasi Society. In *Tribal Movements in India.* Volume-I. K.S. Singh (Ed.) New Delhi: Manohar.

Rana, B.S. 1989. *The People of Meghalaya* Calcutta: Punthi Pustak.

Rodgers, W.A. 1994. The Sacred Groves of Meghalaya. *Man in India* 74 (4): 339--348.

Sen, Sipra. 1994. *Meghalaya: A Bibliography.* New Delhi: BRU Publications.

17

The Coexistence of Christianity and Tribal Faith: The Nicobarese of Little Andaman Islands

Anstice Justin

The Nicobarese are spread out in twelve islands of the Nicobars. On account of varying historical influences, the Nicobarese show differences from each other in cultural and linguistic terms. They are broadly divided into the northern, central and southern groups. Car Nicobar, is the northern-most island. Chowra is the island of potters and witch doctors (Pandit, 1970). The Nicobarese are traditionally dependent on canoes as an important item of trade. The ceremonial travel by such canoes to Chowra is part of the initiation into adulthood. The other items of trade are pigs, coconuts, tools such as *dah*, and cloth. Another source of leisure is fishing (Whitehead, 1924:89, *In the Nicobar Islands*. London). Although Christianity has spread throughout the Nicobar archipelago quite a few Nicobarese still follow the traditional tribal beliefs. The fact remains that in the dense forest environment, they continue to live in the constant fear of spirits of many kinds, under the spell of witch doctors and consequently they adhere to observing the traditional practices of propitiation of these spirits. They also constantly indulge in driving away these spirits during year long festivals of *kio'lo's*, with blood-sacrifice of fowls (hayom) and pigs (ha-un or noote, as referred to in these islands), with much pomp and show of majestic dancing and singing. Even today, the traditional 'animistic' practices have not been completely given up by the Nicobarese even after prolonged contact with Christianity, especially in central and southern groups of Nicobar islands. The old tribal religious practices survive in many areas including Dring or Daring village in the coast of Kamorta island, Jhoola village of Kotchal island, and in some villages of Bompuka, Teressa and some islands in the southern groups. Education, Christianity and incessant contact with the outsiders has now resulted in change of outlook, often leading to conflict with the traditional animistic beliefs. For instance, young educated people have become increasingly skeptical about the performances of the witch doctors and the spirits, which they claim to invoke. It is observed that the witch doctors and sorcerers have theologically been rejected and the Nicobarese generally always agree that the significance of sorcery is now shaken. Interestingly, however, there are witch doctors, medicine-men/women and shamans who are very much around and it has not been possible for the Nicobarese to abandon them completely. In fact the witch doctors, medicine-men/women and shamans continue to enjoy their traditional statuses and they have even found a niche in the theological lap of Christianity, and thus their services are fully acknowledged.

A suitable case study of syncretism is worth mentioning here. Mercy is a local Nicobarese girl of Chuchucha village of Car Nicobar. As a child of about seven-eight years she used to be literally the stick-bearer of her grand father, Martin of Pitko lineage of Chuchucha, whose eye sight was faulty. Her grandfather was a shaman, a medicine-man. So, Mercy would pluck herbal leaves while Martin would specifically explain to her the kinds of leaves, bark of trees, roots, seeds flowers and fruits that are important. Thus, she was acquainted with the herbal leaves, which are plucked for various ailments.

In the early 1970s, under the rehabilitation programme of the Andaman and Nicobar administration, Mercy's name cropped up as one of the settlers from Chuchucha village, Car Nicobar to be settled permanently in Little Andaman. She saw this as a new chapter in her life. While settling in Harminder Bay village of Little Andaman island, Fabian, a Nicobarese settler, hailing from Kinuvo village of Car Nicobar came in contact with Mercy and they finally got married. After a few years of settling down in Harminder Bay village, she fell ill for about six months. According to her, the cause of sickness was attributed to a sorcerer who used his sorcery powers to eliminate her. Fortunately, her grandfather prepared some ointment of herbal leaves mixed with coconut oil, which helped her recover. She claims that one day, when she and her husband Fabian were sleeping the door of her house opened suddenly and a strange creature with a human head and a horse's body entered and began instructing her to render services as a medicine-woman on the island. Surprisingly she found herself fit as a fiddle the next morning. On that day she received a letter from her grandfather, from Car Nicobar, who told her to dig out human bones buried by her enemy, near the first two pillars of her house near a bamboo ladder. She did so and found the bones. According to her, soon after seeing that strange creature she found herself a different person altogether. She began to heal various patients brought from Car Nicobar including non-Nicobarese patients. She even cured the wife of a highly qualified medical practitioner.

Mercy's healing ritual begins with a prayer and by receiving the blessings of the elder presbyter (Christian) which are regarded as the essential part of her healing ceremony. After the prayer and blessing, the patient is asked to take off his shirt. A pig is then brought and its blood is taken out then Mercy and her assistants would smear the patient with the blood. As a rule, the blood is allowed to take its own course of healing the patient, while she and her assistants keep heating coconut oil mixed with herbal medicine in a vessel, which is then applied all over the body of the patient. After an hour, she with her assistants bathes the patient. After this, she rubs and anoints the patient with the herbal oil prepared for the purpose. She also revealed that toddy, a prized drink in Nicobar, is also mixed with certain leaves and is then taken as a kind of tonic by some patients with specific ailments. Besides this, a herbal juice is given to the patient every morning and evening. Mercy would pay a visit everyday to inspect her patient. As a rule, she would impose certain food restrictions on the patient. This is a disease-based kind of taboo. The healing effect of her medicine cannot work if a patient violates the food taboo. Eating meat, smoking *yong pop* (cigars made of tobacco rolled in pandanus leaves), and drinking alcohol are strictly prohibited.

Summing up the above case study of Mercy Fabian it could be stated that she insists too much on the simple functional role of the Christian presbyter to bless the healing rituals and the herbal medicines. This may be analyzed as a symbolic act only which amounts to nothing in comparison to the complex healing operation this woman shaman conducts so meticulously using traditional knowledge based on the medicinal leaves and the knowledge of healing. Here we witness the blending of traditional magical-religious practices of the Nicobarese, transmitted through generations as oral tradition, with contemporary justification through induction of the Christian religious authority.

There are many areas of Nicobarese life where we see continuity of old religious-cultural practices generally unhampered or slightly modified and adjusted to suit the Christian spirit. There are certain complicated feasts associated with the dead people, particularly those who had acquired special statuses during their lifetime. In the continuation of traditional feasting of the Nicobarese, we witness a sort of localisation process at work within Christianity. Such feasts are held even today after the mourning period. There are many animistic tribal beliefs, which exist even today. Despite adoption of Christianity, the Nicobarese conventionally observe the following tribal ritualistic practices:

(a) *Haka ap*: Offerings made to the canoe.

(b) *Haka pati*: Offerings displayed when a newly-built house is to be blessed ritually by (the Christian) presbyter. In a non-Christian situation, the tribal priesthood occupies the leading place.

(c) Prayer and blessings offered by the presbyter while the foundation structure of house is laid. Here some tribal practices find a place too. Coins are put at the base of the pillar/foundation to ward off evil influences of malevolent spirits, and also to ward off the sorcery of witch doctors who secretly desire to harm the residents of the house.

(d) Display of *kareava*, *intekui* and *viniil kui*, fetishes and devil frighteners which are kept at the entrance of houses especially in central and southern Nicobar islands. In these islands, the prayers and elaborate rituals are still observed which are meant to invoke the spirits of the ancestors to fetch prosperity for them and to ward off unexpected obstructions which may be faced by them.

(e) Display of offerings and associated rituals during the kiolo known as *kane-enjta-anug* (literally to expel the foreigner). Actually, it also means to expel all kinds of diseases (which are brought by outsiders to the islands). Charms are also put up on the beach and settlement area.

Coexistence of Christianity and Tribal Faith

With the advent of the Christianity, many of the old superstitious beliefs were wiped out. With Christianity grew admiration for education. With suppression of inter-ethnic blood feuds and wars, the population steadily grew. In the whole process, however, the Nicobarese only selectively adopted certain useful elements of the new faith and never completely discarded their old tribal values, beliefs including their old magical-healing practices and cultural traits. There has been no direct confrontation between two dogmatic traditions. Rather, there have been several instances of localization of implanted Christian religion, by blending it with tribal customs and rituals, as per conveniences and crises of the indigenous Nicobarese people.

References

Pandit, T.N. 1970. Andaman and Nicobar Islands: The Ecological and Cultural Adaptations of the Various Ethnic Groups. In *Research Programmes on Cultural Anthropology and Allied Disciplines*. Ed. Surajit Sinha, Calcutta: Anthropological Survey of India.

Whitehead, G. 1924. *In the Nicobar Islands*. London: Seeley Service & Co.

18

The Sajolang Religion: A Study of Adoption, Continuation and Change

Sarit Kumar Chaudhuri

Anthropologists have defined religion in many ways. For instance, it is regarded as "any set of attitudes, beliefs and practices pertaining to supernatural powers, whether that power be forces, gods, spirits, ghosts or demons" (Bhagabati, 1998: 1). According to Yinger (1957), "Religion is the cultural knowledge that people use to cope with the ultimate problems of human existence." According to Spradley and McCurdy (1990: 359), "Belief in gods, spirits, ghosts and magical power often defines the supernatural, but the matter is complicated by cultural variation and the lack of a clear distinction in many societies between a natural and supernatural world. Ultimate problems, on the other hand, emerge from universal features of human life and include life's meaning, death, evil and transcendent values. People everywhere wonder why they are alive, why they must die and why evil strikes only some individuals and not others. In every society, people's personal desires and goals may conflict with the values of the larger group. But the religion provides a set of transcendent values that override differences and unify the group." Large number of concepts viz. animism, animatism, sacred and profane etc. have emerged in order to understand primitive or tribal religion (Lowie 1924, Tylor 1972, Durkheim 1961). Srinivas (1998) wrote about the significance of folk religion in order to understand the intricate social processes of Indian rural masses. He added that though the Indian anthropologists and sociologists have redressed the balance in favour of folk religion, they failed to create adequate space for such an important dimension of culture. It is generally agreed upon that religion is an all-pervading universal phenomena, which forms an essential part of human life. In anthropological parlance it is perceived as cultural system (Geertz, 1966) and it has a functional role to perform irrespective of types of the social formations. Signs of religious beliefs are traced even among the homo sapiens who lived at least 60,000 years ago (Bhagabati, 1998: 2). According to Cole (1982: 365), "The study of religions is complicated by the tremendous variety of beliefs and rituals. The variety is reflected in terms of who and what is considered a supernatural force, how many there are, how the supernatural is to be worshipped and placated, how individuals become religious specialists, the kinds of rituals they perform, how supernatural forces are communicated with, and so on."

With this backdrop, this paper discusses some of the basic elements of Sajolang religion, the process of adoption, and the nature of change which are integral to the present-day cultural system of the Sajolang. The data were collected from the Sajolang area (Nafra circle) during 1996--97 by using the conventional anthropological field tools.

The Sajolangs are one of the smallest tribes of Arunachal Pradesh and as per 1981 census they had a population of 4,085. The entire Sajolang belt is mountainous with deep gorges and covered with quite dense sub-tropical forest. The high hilly areas remain one of the most backward areas in terms of the indicators of development. The only road (60 kms long), which connects Bomdila with Nafra is mostly *katcha* and during rainy season is completely unuseable. At present, there are twenty-seven Sajolang villages under Nafra circle and twenty villages under Lada circle.

The Sajolang live in the valley of the Pakesa and Bichom rivers which lie in the middle belt of east and west Kameng district of Arunachal Pradesh. Like many other tribes of Arunachal, the Sajolangs are popularly known as Mijis. From the review of literature, it appears that they have been called as Miji, Dhammai, Nimmai, Sajolang, Giduku, etc. It is believed that the name 'Miji' was given by the Akas or Hrussos. In Aka language 'Mi' means fire and 'Ji' means giver, which literally means 'fire giver' or 'the man who gives fire'. It is believed that the Mijis were the first to demonstrate the use of fire in the locality. Again Dhammai means people of eastern region whereas Nimmai means people of western region. Jha (1994) mentioned that according to a legend the name Miji was first given by the Akas, their southern neighbour who exchanged their land for the habitation of the Sajolangs with fire in the remote past.

However, now the people prefer to call themselves Sajolangs from whom they descended on this earth.

The entire area is bounded by the Nyishi hills to the east, the Monpa area to the west, Tibet to the north and Aka hills to the south. The Sajolangs have multiple historical linkages with their neighbouring tribes (Dhar, 1995). Undoubtedly, cultivable land is their most valuable economic resource and shifting or hill cultivation is their dominant mode of agricultural production depending upon the geo-morphological nature of land under their possession. Surrounding hilly forestland also plays very crucial roles not only in the economic life but also in their sacred life. In fact with the establishment of Nafra chemical factory in 1982, their surrounding pine forest has emerged as their most important source of earning cash in variegated ways. Cattle especially mithuns, are also considered one of the valuable economic resources in Sajolang society. In comparison to these resources, water in the form of rivers and rivulets as economic resource play a trivial role as they practise fishing at a considerable scale. With the introduction of induced development, along with education, occupational mobility is initiated among the Sajolangs, but it remained insignificant in comparison to the total mass of Sajolang population. According to a survey conducted by the local administration in 1992, 95 per cent of the Sajolang families remain below the poverty line. The Sajolang society is stratified into three sections viz. Nyubu, Khianglin and Nyullu. These sections are clan specific and have multiple socio-economic implications.

The Sajolang Religion

Religion plays a very crucial role in multiple domains of the Sajolang society. At every stage of life, the conception of a baby to the death of an individual, many religious beliefs and intricate rituals are observed. Even in the spheres of economy and polity, we notice relevance of religion. In brief their whole social structure is regulated and controlled by religious considerations.

The Sajolangs like most tribes of Arunachal Pradesh, believe in a large number of deities and spirits, which are benevolent or malevolent in nature. They also worship natural objects like the earth, sky, moon, sun, water and hills. They consider Jang-Lang-Nui as the supreme god. Each and every Miji village has its own priest known as *givi* who mediates between the two worlds. The head priest of a village is known as *givi mukho* and the priest who assists him is known as *givi mineu*.

Both male and female priests are available in Nafra circle. The number of female priests is only two out of the existing twenty-seven of Sajolang villages. As per their belief, priesthood is not hereditary in nature, rather it depends on the possession of some unusual characteristics in an individual which may even be noticed since childhood. Naturally, as per their cognition anyone may become a priest. But if we carefully examine the class position or the location of priests within the stratified class ladder then it is revealed that all of them belong to the dominant Nyubbu and Khianglin sections and none is traceable from the lowest strata known as Nyullu.

It may be noteworthy to mention that their priests (*givi*) are also stratified into four categories according to their ability to sacrifice different animals which involves their religious power, which, they believe, is assigned supernaturally. The priests who belong to the highest strata or in other words, the most powerful sections of priests, are eligible for sacrificing cows; next to them are those eligible for sacrificing pigs and the lowest strata consists of the priests who can sacrifice only hens. However, it is interesting to note that mobility within these stratified ladders is evident. For instance, a priest who belongs to the lowest strata may find a place in the highest strata in course of time. However, this does not mean that each priest will be able to achieve such mobility, rather there are many instances where a priest remains at the lowest strata throughout his or her lifespan. This is because of the complex mechanism involved in such status mobility. According to their belief system, such mobility does not depend on one's efforts or willingness. Rather it is controlled by the complex magical-religious mechanisms performed by other priests. For example, if in any Sajolang family some serious illness or disease occurs then they call only their village priest as they believe in strong correlation between the disease and the local spirits or deities. It is only the priest who can mediate between the sufferer and those spirits or deities who are responsible for such misery, in the form of illness or disease. So the priest arrives and by examining chicken liver he or she not only identifies the spirit or deity but also prescribes the items, which need to be sacrificed to ward off that spirit or to appease the deity. More significantly, he or she also specifies who will be the most suitable priest to perform such worship as also necessary sacrifices. Here lie the clues for the upward mobility of a priest. For example, if the village priest announces that sacrifice of pigs is essential and the priest who is chosen for this task belongs to the lowest strata (which can only sacrifice hens), then after performing such worship and sacrifice he will be elevated into the next higher category of priesthood. It is evident that most of the priests who belong to the highest category of the strata, the Nyubbu, are the priests who are also associated with the second strata of their society (Khianlin) but hardly any one is traceable from Nyullu, the lowest strata of the Sajolang society. The Sajolang village has a sacred place called Phung-brung that is used for worshipping and sacrificing animals. It is reported that sometimes the Sajolang priests (*givi*) are invited by the neighbouring Akas, Khowas and Nyishis to perform rituals in their respective villages also. This shows a unique dimension of inter-religious blending and adoption.

Life Cycle Rituals

The Sajolang observe both pre-and post-delivery rituals and they also sacrifice animals to appease the deity for the welfare of the child and mother. In fact, when a child is due to be born, the members of the family must be on constant guard against evil spirits who always try to harm mankind. The moment of birth is considered as one of the most crucial periods in the life of a person and as soon as a baby is born, the grandmother and grandfather give it a name. A name can even be given by evil spirits in order to fulfill their mischievous motives. Generally, they prefer to give the name of a famous person who was well-recognized in their community. Just after the delivery, the child is given a bath and clothed; then the priest ties a woollen thread strung with a bead on each wrist and ankle with a blessing for good fortune and a prosperous life.

Simon reported (1977: 38) that after five days the child is bathed again and new clothes are put upon it. This is repeated after another five days. With this, all restrictions upon the movements of the parents are removed and both of them now emerge from the house, where they have been obliged to remain for ten long days. To further ensure the security of the child, as soon as it is born, a kind of creeper, believed to possess the power to keep evil spirits away, is stretched round the house and near the door. A dried piece of this 'ghost-chaser' creeper is burnt and stuck in the earth on its unburnt end, near the entrance of the house. The evil spirits are thus kept away from the child. Stillbirth or miscarriage is considered as a bad sign and during burial a few restricted close relatives come to attend where the priest worships evil spirits with the help of magico-religious supernatural devices. In case of barrenness also, the Sajolang take help of their priests to find a way out.

No ritual is observed when boys and girls attain puberty. Nevertheless, during menstruation of either a married or an unmarried girl, she has to stay in a separate chamber available in a traditional house.

She is not allowed to enter the main chamber of the house. She has to prepare her food within that specified chamber only. Even the firewood she collects during that period cannot be brought inside the main chamber and can only be used by her.

The death rites of the Sajolang are unique. To quote Simon again (1977:11) "When a person dies, the body is covered in a shroud ... a hole is dug near the house and the corpse is laid in it with the head to the west. The priest instructs the soul of the dead person the way it should take to go to the other world. Offerings of food are made before, and rest of the food is served to all the relations present. A bamboo pole is placed upright between the head and the exterior of the grave. Planks are then placed over the body and over them straw is placed after which the hole is covered up with earth and a pile of stones which are laid on top. When all this is done, food is laid on top of the pile... In order to frustrate evil spirits, a fire is kept constantly burning near the grave and every now and then during night the inmates go out of the house to shoot arrows around the graves to detonate green bamboos placed on the fire. This goes on for a five days for male and six days for a female and on the last day, the soul of the dead person is ready to leave the body, with the assistance of the priest who sends it off on its final journey".

The Sajolang are very afraid of any unnatural death and the funeral is generally attended by very limited persons and the procedure which a priest follows in such cases is quite lengthy. It may be mentioned here that the personal belongings of the deceased along with food and drinks are also kept in the grave (Narun). They also believe in the concept of rebirth and they are in possession of such prayers which let the soul take birth again in the same family (in case of natural death only).

At present Chindang is the most popular festival of the Sajolang. Chin means worship and Dang means offerings or sacrifices. During this festival they worship not only the Almighty God but also nature for the well-being of human beings, for production of better crops and also for warding off evil spirits. This is essentially a village-level festival which they started celebrating centrally in a particular spot located nearer to the Nafra circle headquarters. The origin and significance of this festival is related to their creation myth. In brief, according to their beliefs the creation of this universe is due to Abu Gophan Bomo (the male) and Ani digdyzien (the female) who came to live on this earth. In course of time, Ani digeyzien gave birth to eight sons namely Sangcho, Dongcho, Khanlo, Knanvoi, Chentai, Mialiu, Khanglong and Changthung. When they grew up, Sangcho and Dongcho left for Lhasa (Tibet) and

Khanplong and Changthung left for the plains to earn their living. The remaining four sons i.e. Khanlo, Khanvoi, Cheutai and Mialiu who started living in the mountain areas, are regarded as the ancestors of the Sajolang community.

It is further believed that the creator of this universe empowered them to pray to Him and offer sacrifices to Him as well as to the sun, the moon, mountains and rivers by chanting hymns for blessing. This is the reason for which Chindang festival is performed every year. Therefore, since long the ancestors of the Sajolang community had started observing Chindang puja and they advised their descendants to continue performing the Chidang puja after them. Accordingly, for generation after generation this puja has been celebrated by the Sajolang under the guidance of their priests. They strongly believe that if worship by sacrificing of animals is not done to mountains and rivers, then their field for cultivation will not be productive that year. This festival needs a very elaborate arrangement and continues for five days and on the last day when the sacrifice has to be done, many rituals are performed by the chief priest with the assistance of other priests. Several traditional songs, war dances, etc. are performed by the villagers dressed in their full traditional costumes. It is celebrated between October and December and actual date has to be fixed by the village priest through magico-religious devices (Chaudhuri, 1998).

Jha (1994: 62) reported that during 1870s, Khan was the most important festival of the Sajolang and was being organized on a community basis. This was basically after harvest celebration, when they beg for forgiveness from the creator, Janglangnoi, for killing various creatures while preparing *jhum* fields. They also pray to other gods and goddesses for a happy and prosperous life. Deuri in his several papers published in *Resarun* during 1982 and 1983 mentions that during worship, the priest wears a special ritual cap made of tiger skin and decorated with feathers of a hornbill. His ritual paraphernalia further consists of a snake tooth, a wolf tooth, a hornbill beak, a few pieces of white pebbles, etc., While celebrating the Khan festival, a number of worships and prayers are offered by slaughtering a *mithun*, a bull, an un-castrated goat, three cows and eight fowls... The period of festival varies from five to ten days depending on the type of animals to be sacrificed ... Generally a *mithun* is slaughtered in the name of the creator ... bull is slaughtered in the name of the gods of the hills (Phungringnoi - ramo), the god of water (Bhublyanoi-Sando), the god of the earth (Sulu-Khaitho and Dema-Khaiju) and the goddess of richness and prosperity (Buchiyang Bujoi). Other animals are also slaughtered in the name of different gods and goddesses. In Khan festival, the priest's costume also consists of a large bead (Thaichu), endi silk cloth (Orija) and a headgear (Utho). Apart from the above items, he is given meat from the chest portion and the left forelimbs of the animals that are slaughtered on the occasion. On the last day, the priest wraps a piece of wool around everybody's neck for well-being and then a feast is arranged for the villagers. On the day after the end of the festival no outsider is allowed to enter the village nor does anybody go out from the village. Like the Chindang festival, on the next day villagers proceed for community hunting. According to their belief, a good hunt can bring good fortune to the villagers, else there would be misery and famine in the village (*Resarun*, 1983:17–18).

Discussion

On account of long historical contacts with the surrounding Buddhist communities, and through gradual adoptions, many Sajolang villages under Nafra circle have started admitting Buddhist religious elements within their culture. During household surveys, many Sajolangs introduced themselves as followers of Buddhism, though after further cross-verification it was evident that they still practised their indigenous religious beliefs and rituals. However, celebration of Losar, one of the most important festivals of the Buddhist Monpas, depicting long flags with scripts and a newly constructed Gumpha (monastery) on a hill-top nearer to Nafra circle headquarters is one of the many signs of the growing Buddhist influence in the Sajolang society and culture. It may be noteworthy to mention that a big Siva temple was also recently constructed near the circle headquarters under the patronage of the Nafra chemical factory, a company mainly tapping resin from the pine forests. This temple was mainly constructed to cater to the needs of the non-tribal population that comes to stay in Nafra due to various official assignments. Since 1992, celebration of Durga Puja initiated within this temple and in areas nearer to the circle office has been a regular feature. Some of the Sajolangs are also taking part in such worships in multifarious ways. In Khellong village, one Sajolang family has constructed a temple-like structure by using boulders and kept some photographs of various Hindu gods and goddesses alongwith some symbolic elements associated with Hindu religion. This again exhibits the synthesis of the religious blending. Thus, we observe that culture-contact at two levels, with the Buddhist Monpas and the Hindus, has made a substantial impression in the religious life, whereby the Sajolangs have been selectively and consciously incorporating many religious beliefs and practices of their two neighbouring religious traditions. Christianity has not penetrated among the Sajolang of Nafra circle though many Sajolangs under Lada circle have accepted this alien religion. Apparently, there is no movement, which can be termed as revivalistic or reformist, to counter such emerging religious traits. However, the newly adopted strategy in this society has been to celebrate the traditional tribal Chindang festival on a community basis, this is gradually assuming great significance. This may be conceived as a conscious attempt to revive and promote their indigenous religious identity. Finally, it can be concluded that indigenous religion still plays a very crucial role in each aspect of the tribal society and culture of the Sajolang. Moreover, it is operating as a unifying force by promoting social solidarity and ensuring security. It has also crucially helped to sustain traditional social structure.

References

Bhagabati, C. (1998). Indigenous Faiths and Customs: Some Observation in *Indigenous Faith and Practices of the Tribes of Arunachal Pradesh,* (ed), M.C. Behera and S.K. Chaudhuri, New Delhi: Himalayan Publication.

Chaudhuri, S.K. (1998). Chindang: A Folk Festival of the Mijis (Sajolangs) of Arunachal Pradesh. *Dialogue,* Vol. III, pp. 100--114.

Cole, Johunetta. B.Ed. (1982). *Anthropology for the Eighties*, The Free Press: New York.

Dhar, B. (1995). Miji Trade: An Inter-Ethnic Interaction. *Resarun*, XXI: 1 & 2, pp. 12--15.

Durkheim, E. (1961). *The Elementary Forms of Religious Life*. London: Allen & Unwin.

Geertz, C. (1966). 'Religion as a Cultural System' in *Anthropological Approach to the of Religion*. Ed. Michal Banton, ASA Monograph. London: Troski.

Jha, B.N. (1994). The Religion and Festivals of the Sajolang: Continuity and Change. *Resarun, XX*, 1 & 2.

Lowie, R.H. (1924). *Primitive Religion.* New York: Free Press.

Simon, T.H. (1977). From Birth to Death among the Mijis. *Resarun*, 76, pp. 37--42.

Spradley, James, P. and David, W. McCurdy, Ed. (1990). *Conformity and Conflict: Readings in Cultural Anthropology*, London: Scott, Foresman and Company.

Srinivas, M.N. (1998). *Indian Society Through Personal Writings*, Delhi: Oxford University Press. 192–230.

Tylor, E.B. 1903 (1958, 1972). *Primitive Culture*. London: John Murray (Reprinted in 1958 and 1972).

Yinger, Milton (1957). *Religion, Society, and the Individual: An Introduction to the Sociology of Religion*, New York: Macmillan.

19

Buddhism, Lamaism and Bon Religion: Religious Synthesis among Monpas and Ladakhis

Bibhash Dhar

The Monpas of the highlands of western Arunachal Pradesh, northeast India, are widely recognized as a Buddhist tribe. There are many sub-groups of the Monpas with their habitats in the innumerable steep slopes in the altitudes ranging from 8,000 feet to 12,000 feet above the mean sea level in West Kameng and Tawang districts of the state of Arunachal Pradesh. Monpa is a generic term originally used by the Tibetans for the people of the lowlands. The 1981 census recorded the total Monpa population at 34,469. The community consists of Chug, Dirang, Lish, But, Kalaktang, Panehan and Tawang. Barring the But Monpas, all the Monpas belong to Lamaistic school of Tibetan Buddhism of the Mahayana sect (Singh, 1995:216). The Buddhism practised by the Monpas is akin to the Buddhism of Bhutan and Tibet. These people, however, also profess pre-Buddhist tribal religion and shamanism. The But Monpas have their own traditional faith, beliefs and festivals, though gradually they are also coming within the greater fold of Buddhism (Singh, 1995: 217). The Kalaktang Monpas belong to the Lamaistic sect of Buddhism. Their sacred place is called Goompha, which is adorned with the images of Buddha and Bodhistatva. The Lama is their priest whose services are sought during birth, marriage and death. Simultaneously they also practise pre-Buddhist tribal religion, including shamanism. The tribal priest, Phrame, also cures diseases and removes evil spirits (Barua and Ahmad, 1995). The Buddhism of Lish Monpas, according to Barua (1995), is a peculiar blend of tribal beliefs and shamanism. Their shaman is called Frimpa. They also practise witchcraft and sorcery to cure diseases and remove evil spirits. Besides Buddha, the Lishpas have a tribal deity, Phu, who is a hill deity.

According to the legends, the germ of the Tibetan-Lamaism form of Buddhism of the Mahayana division, was laid in the Monpa country of Tawang by no lesser a saint than Guru Padmasambhava himself, locally known as Lopon Rimpuche. It is believed that Lopon Rimpuche happened to visit the Monpa country as early as the fifth century from Tibet, and numerous places associated with his visit continue to preserve his hallowed memory. Such places are spread over different parts of the two districts. It may be mentioned that Guru Padmasmabhava was an Indian saint who happened to go to Tibet from Kashmir. Subsequently, the monastery at Tawang, the fountain head of the spiritual life of the Gelukpa sect of the Mahayana division, popularly known as the Tawang monastery, came to be regarded as Tawang Ganden Namgyal Lhatse Ling and is one of the largest monasteries of its kind in the world. The Dalai Lama from the Patola palace in Lhasa selected the Palden Lhamo (also regarded as goddess Kali) as the ruling deity of the monastery. Slowly most of the Monpas of the nearby and even far-off habitats adopted Buddhism and observed all the festivals and rites of the faith starting from Saga Dawa (Buddha purnima), Losar, and the different pantomime dances from time as notified by the Lamas of the monastery after consulting the Tibetan-Monpa lunar almanac. Thus the history of Buddhism among the Monpas is quite old and today they are better-known to the world as Buddhists. But, the religion of Bon as practised in Tibet before the advent of Buddhism was also the belief system of the Monpas in general. The believers of Bon used to propitiate a number of gods and spirits thought to be responsible for various calamities and disasters. The people used to appease the Bon spirits through many worships, sacrifices of animals and offering of eggs, fish and liquor. In this cult, there were several priests and shamans who were responsible for conducting the various rites and offerings. The shamans of the Bon faith are of both sexes and are known as Yumin. The Monpas still believe that the Bon deities reside in the highest peaks in the area and the priests and shamans still look at them with awe as they are thought to possess demonic powers.

The faith in Bon religious belief in the Monpa region continued unobstructed till the arrival of Lamaism, a branch of Buddhism from

Tibet with a greater force in the seventeenth century. It is, however, believed that Tibetan-Lamaism-Buddhism had already made its entry into the region even prior to the seventeenth century. Sarkar (1980:14), through his researches in the region, observed that the traditions linked to the known history of Buddhism show that the conversion of the Monpas to Buddhism was probably started by Padmasambhava himself in the eighth century.

The oral traditions suggest that the spread of Buddhism in the Monpa country was never a smooth affair. It faced tremendous opposition from the Bon priests and shamans. They were in the forefront in obstructing the spread of Buddhism. However, after offering the initial resistance the Bon priests had to relinquish and it is said that they were banished to some remote areas where they still survive. But the old Bon religious beliefs never died and people continued to pursue many practices associated with the old Bon religion. This author has observed that in the village Lhou, very close to Tawang, every year the Bon festivals are celebrated and the Monpas from near and far-off areas assemble there with religious fervour. Chhos-Kor is a Bon festival observed by the Monpas for the betterment of the community as a whole. Interestingly enough, this particular Tibetan festival has synthesized with the Tibetan-Lamaist form of Buddhism and thus during Chhos-Kor hymns are recited from the Buddhist holy books to get rid of disease, sufferings and also the pests and insects that damage the standing crops. In the context of Chhos-Kor and its synthesis with the Buddhist religion, this author (Dhar, 1982: 265, 267) has elsewhere observed that "Chhos-Kor is originally a Tibetan festival… During this festival the devotees come out in a procession from the local Gompa (monastery) and move around in all directions and go to such places where there are smaller Gompas… Two persons having put masks depicting human skulls lead the procession and they are known as the Kengpa. They go on dancing all the way and while dancing enact different obscene postures. Occasionally they go almost nude. They also put on a chain of phallus replicas on their waists and perform some profane actions when they dance. These actions are meant to give the evil-spirits a turn so that they might not do any harm to the participants as well as the community at large… Women who come out along with the procession carry loads of holy (Buddhist) books; the load of holy books being quite heavy, it is believed, helps the womenfolk in a way, expiate their sinful deeds." Thus we observe that an obvious tribal festival, Chhos-Kor, which has historical linkages with the

Tibetan religious system, has synthesized with the Lamaist form of Buddhism and thus the Buddhist hymns and Buddhist singing is blended with the tribal dancing tradition, which involves strong secular invocations.

Mann (1986:41) and other scholars have reported a similar synthesis of the Bon tradition, Lamaism and Buddhism among the Ladakhis. The Ladakhis, who are mainly Buddhists, are inhabitants of Leh and Zanskar regions, while the Muslims live mainly in Kargil region. The Buddhists populate the Indus valley. In Ladakh we witness the blending of various ethnic groups. The Aryans represented by the Dards and Mons have got assimilated with people of Mongoloid origin (Mann, 1986:10). Some Dards adopted Buddhist faith and came to be known as Dogpa or Brogpa. The Ladakhis came to Ladakh prior to the spread of Buddhism in the area. The Ladakhi language is similar to Tibetan language (Mann, 1986:12). The Ladakhis are involved in agriculture, animal husbandry, carpentry and masonry work.

Before Lamaism, two earlier religions had flourished in Ladakh, Bonchos and Buddhism, many features of both of these being embodied in the present-day Lamaism (Mann, 1986:142–143). The Bon religion is a very old religion of Tibet, which is described by Wadded as 'Animistic' and 'Shamanistic' with the devil dancing. Mann observed that "Buddhism in Ladakh is a mixture of Bon, the old religion of Tibet, Tantrism and Mahayana branch of the Buddhism. Some scholars have also referred to Lamaism as the religion of the Ladakhis... Demonology and idolatry are the other traits found in the religion of the Ladakhis and which are believed to be the outcome of Bon or Pon religion. Although Buddhism is the prevailing faith, the Ladakhis still worship and make offerings to some old divinities, such as gods of hills, fields, trees, water, etc.... The Tibetan Buddhism (Lamaism) which has largely influenced the Ladakhi Buddhism is, as stated by Sven Hedin (1910), only a corrupt form of Buddhism, and under an outward varnish of Buddhist symbolism has incorporated a number of Saivistic (Hindu) elements and has also retained the superstitions which in pre-Buddhist times found expression in wild Tantric devil dances, rites and sacrifices... In spite of the principle, 'not to kill', the monks eat meat and make use of goat's blood in certain religious rites. Lamaism has indeed absorbed many of the traits of Bon religion... Besides Buddhism, some Ladakhis have adopted Islam and Christianity. There is no serious community reaction to change of religion. In some families members with different religious backgrounds live together. The Buddhists have all along been tolerant" (Mann, 1986:142).

It may be concluded here that both Monpas and Ladakhis had strong religious links with Tibet in historical past from where they had first adopted the animistic Bon religion before their final acceptance of Buddhism. Bon religion retains tribal character with propitiation of several deities and spirits, alongside sacrifice of animals, offering of eggs, fish and liquor through priests and shamans of both sexes. In pre-Buddhist Bon festival of Chhos Kor among the Monpas hymns are recited from Buddhist holy book and animistic devil dances are blended with Buddhist singing. The Ladakhis too exhibit similar synthesis of Bon religion, Lamaism and Buddhism. In fact Lamaism of Ladakhis is a unique mixture of pre Buddhist Boncho religious tradition, Tantrism, Mahayan Buddhism, Demonology and idolatry. Ladakhis worship the water and hill deities too. Even Saivistic (Hindu) elements are part of syncretistic Ladakhi Religious tradition. We thus witness unique similarity of syncretistic traditions involving Bon religion, Lamaism and Buddhism in two mountainous communities living hundreds of miles apart.[1]

Note

1. Additional ethnographic information about Monpas and Ladakhis drawn from *Arunachal Preadsh, People of India* (1995, K.S. Singh, General Editor) and *The Ladakhis* (1986, R.S. Mann), some references (Barua 1995, Barua and Ahmad 1995, Singh 1995 and Hedin 1910) and a concluding paragraph are added by the Editor in this article in order to substantiate and emphasize the syncretistic dimension in the religious life of Monpas and Ladakhis from a comparative perspective.

References

Barua, S. 1995. The Lish Monpas. *Arunachal Pradesh, People of India*. K.S. Singh (General Editor), P. Dutta and S.I. Ahmad (Eds). Calcutta: ASI.

Barua, S. and S.I. Ahmad. 1995. The Kalaktang Monpa. *Arunachal Pradesh: People of India*. K.S. Singh (General Editor), P. Dutta and S.I. Ahmad (Eds). Calcutta: Anthropological Survey of India.

Dhar, Bibhash. 1982. Chhos-Kor: The Festival of the Monpas and the Shherdukpen. *Journal of the Indian Anthropological Society* Vol. 17 No. 3 November.

Hedin, Sven. 1910. *Trans-Himalayas.* London: MacMillan.

Mann, R.S. 1986. *The Ladakhis.* Calcutta: Anthropological Survey of India.

Sarkar, N. 1980. *Buddhism among the Monpas and Sherdukpen.* Government of Arunachal Pradesh, Shillong.

Singh, K.S. 1995. *Arunachal Pradesh, People of India*, K.S. Singh (General Editor), P. Dutta and S.I. Ahmad (Eds). Calcutta: Anthropological Survey of India.

20

Sufism in South India: A Study of the Shrine of Nagore-e-Sharif in Tamil Nadu

S.A.A. Saheb

Islam, stated to be the universal religion of mankind, has attracted millions of people from different strata owing to its egalitarian principles and undiscriminating social attitude. This religion is mainly built on the five pillars of creed (Kalima), prayer (Namaz), fasting (Roza), giving alms to the poor (Zakat) and pilgrimage to Mecca (Hajj). As generations passed, the mission of the prophet became less comprehensive and needed filling up of the gaps of the Prophet in spreading his message. It is believed that in due course of time this gap was filled by the Sufi saints (Aulia) and the associates of the Prophet (Sahaba), who followed the prophetic ideals and led a pious life. They not only transformed the beliefs and practices associated with the prophet but also worked as a prophetic intercession between man and god (Saheb, 1995). Curriee (1989) observes that as the cult of the prophet developed and passed from regular belief into respectable doctrines (Hadith), reverence for the places associated with him also increased in the same way, as the cult of Sufi saints also gathered its momentum. This led to the veneration of saints during their lifetime and even after their death. Thus the places associated with the saints became the pilgrimage centres (Ziaratgarh).

Sufism: Origin and Spread

According to one theory on account of the association of the Prophet and the saints of the early days of Islam with woollen clothing, the word 'Sufi' came to be used to refer to those, who led a pious and simple life. Thus 'Sufi' in general came to denote the saints of Islam. It is also believed that the term 'Sufi' is derived from the word 'Safa' (purity). Thus, Sufis are those spiritual beings purified from all the worldly impurities. In the Indian context, the Sufis are known as 'Fuqura' (plural of the Arabic word for 'Fhakir') and 'Darvish' (in Persian). Thus the word 'Fhakir' and 'Darvish' are also closely associated with the Sufis in India. In Arabic, Islamic mysticism is called 'Tasawwuf'—'the act of devotion' and 'adoption of the musical way of life'. But it is called 'Sufism' in most parts of the world, since the early 19th century. Sufism is defined as the mystic interpretation of religious life (Shariff, 1921). It mainly concentrates on the personal relationship between the believer and God. Thus in the Sufi Spirit is to be found an 'I—Thou' relationship (Lewis, 1984:145–60). Some schoars believe that Sufi doctrine and practices came to India from beyond the Northwestern Frontier Province and Iraq.

It is believed Sufism originated as a reaction to the monotheism of Islam by the Persian Musalmans in the ninth century (Shariff, 1921). Attempts were made by the theologians to study the synthesis between Sunni theology and Sufism. In due course, Sufism gained a significant place in puritanical Islam (Hastings, 1978). Thus, a difference of opinion arose between the Ullema, representatives of puritan Islam and the Sufis. The Sufis are regarded as less orthodox in nature compared to the puritan Musalmans who are considered to be more obstinate and unreasonable adherents of Islam (Raja, 1967). The liberal attitude of Sufism, and particularly its tolerance towards the other religions has enchanted many people. Within Sufism developed a new kind of master-disciple (Pir-Murid) relationship wherein the disciple accepts his master as his spiritual guide.

Through this practice of initiation of members, Sufism flourished into a big religious order having its branches or paths (Tarikats) spreading all over the globe in the 12th century (Hastings, 1978). The Sufi orders differed from each other in their path and recognition of their founders, i.e. spiritual guides. The residence of a Sufi founder became a place of reverence to the followers, and the devotees of all faiths were attracted towards the place. Thus, a kind of local cult in the form of a Sufi order developed in different places. Though the Sufi cult as such is not prescribed in Islam, this development is traced back to centuries, with its presence in several countries. It is observed that the degree of veneration differs from one area to another, but the central theme of Sufism centres around saint adoration. Despite anti-Sufi religious action such as the Wahabi movement, the saint cult is very much prevalent and more so among the Indian Muslims. Thus the Sufi cult has taken its stronger roots in religious spheres of India, particularly in such places where the followers of non-Islamic faiths like Hinduism, live close to Muslims.

The first Sufi religious order which came to Indian soil was that of Chistia, through Khawja Garib Nawaz, during the Sultanate era in the 12th century. Later, the Quadaria order entered the Indian subcontinent through Mohammed Ghouse Gwalior, who happened to be the spiritual guide of Syed Sahul Hameed Nagore Andawar of Tamil Nadu, south India, about whom we will discuss in this paper.

The cultural practices associated with the Sufi saints in India have distinct features. Instances from north India suggest that the Sufi shrines are worshipped by both Muslims and Hindus. A 'shrine' of a sufi saint is a place where a Sufi saint had preached and breathed his last, and where a tomb was built after his death and venerated as a sacred place. However, the members of Hindu and Muslim communities, in several instances, refer to the Sufi saints with different names. For example, the Saint Kanifnath's shrine located in Mahdhi village in Parthardi Taluka, Ahmad Nagar district, Maharastra, is regarded as a shrine of a Hindu saint Navnath, and thus the worship there is conducted by the pujari (Hindu priest). The Muslims call the same saint Shah Ramzan Moti Sarwar (Kanobaba) and the prayers are performed with the help of a Mujawar (Muslim priest). Thus, the Sufi saint in Ahmad Nagar district stands as a common saint for the Hindus as well as Muslims and his shrine becomes a common religious centre. This situation indeed helps in maintaining the communal amity among the believers of different faiths living in the locality (Hulbe *et al.*, 1994). Similar instances are observed in south India also. The study of Tinthin village shrine in Gulbarga district, Karnataka (Abdi, 1993), for example, also supports the above view and reveals further that the physical structures of the Sufi shrine combines the local pluralistic cultural traditions. The saints are believed to be powerful and answer the wishes of the devotees through supernatural acts (Karamat). In some places, the Sufi saints and their shrines are associated with sacred plants (Malhotra *et al.*, 1984:45) and sacred groves (Gadgil *et al.*, 1976:152). The shrines are often cleaned with water just like the pouring of libation water on the idols by the Hindus (Bhaumik, 1993:10).

Sufi Saint as a Hindu God

At Nagore, the Hindus worship the Sufi saint Sahul Hameed Nagore Andavar, as a presiding god. Although the existence of this Sufi saint's shrine is recorded, in the earlier Gazetteers, as Palli, in fact it actually refers to the Darga (shrine) of Sufi Saint. Even today, the Tamils address the Darga of a Sufi as Palli (Hemingway, 1906:315; Sharif, 1921:121). Darga or Dargah is a common place of veneration for devotees of religious faiths. In south India, it displays many common features in architectural style and motif, and the fusion of local rituals and customs. Though the practice of offering flowers, sweetmeats and food, the way of conducting worship, and playing of musical instruments are traditionally not allowed in Islam, yet all these practices are introduced in the Sufi shrine due to the strong influence of the local Hindu traditions. Because of the Hindu devotee's involvement and participation in the Darga activities, the Hindu customs began to be accepted in the Darga's sacred performances. Such cultural fusion is vividly seen in the Kanduri festival of the saint Sahul Hameed of Nagore-e-Sharif, which is celebrated in commemoration of the death anniversary of the saint.

The Legend of the Sufi Saint

It is said that the parents of the saint Syed Sahul Hameed, Syed Hassan Kuthos and Bibi Fathima, migrated from Bagdad in Iraq during the rule of Sultan Feroz Shah Thugluk of Delhi. They belonged to a small town of Manickpoor, in Pratapgarh district in Uttar Pradesh. He was a true Syed by descent, which can be proved by tracing his relationship to the prophet of Islam as a thirteenth lineal descendant and to the Sufi saint Syed Abdul Quadir Jeelani of Bagdad as a fifth lineal descendant. He was related through a mystic path to the foremost among Sufi saints, Syed Abdul Quadir Jeelani, who happened to be his great grandfather and the founder of the Quadaria order of Sufism.

Hagiological literature says that Sahul Hameed came to the material world though the divine message of Allah to his parents. He performed miracles (Karamat) even at the embryo stage when he was in his mother's womb. It is said that he was born on a Friday in the month of Jumathul Akhir, Hijiri, 1504 AD (Quddusi, 1991:2). The God's messenger Khilr named him Sahul Hameed. Sahul Hameed did his Islamic education at Gwalior, under the guidance of Hazarat Mohammad Ghouse. After his education, he declined the proposal of marriage and decided to spend his life in the service of Allah. He left home to preach his message. On his way to Mecca, through divine power he blessed the couple of Mufti Nooruddin and Bibi Zohara and desired a son be given to him as a disciple. They did so willingly and thus he got a spiritual son, named Yusuf Saheb, whom he fostered with affection. He went on a pilgrimage along with his foster son and the other followers to some places in south-west Asian and European countries. Later, he moved back in the direction of India. He visited Maldives, Sri Lanka and Tamil Nadu with his spiritual team. At last he came and settled down at Nagore, a small town located in Quaide Millat district of Tamil Nadu in AH 940 (1533–34 AD) (Quddusi, 1991:2). This place is nine kilometres away from the district headquarters. The town is situated on the Bay of Bengal coastal line of the country lying between $10^{0}51'$ North and longitude $79^{0}50'$ East. It is situated on the banks of the river Vettar, at the confluence of Bay of Bengal (Rahim, 1971). In the early 19th century, the port of Nagore played a more prominent role in the import and export business compared to the neighbouring port of Nagapatnam (Rahim, 1971). In due course, Nagore lost its significance as a port town, but flourished as the abode of the holy saint of Sahul Hameed Nagore Andavar (Saheb, 1998).

The Period of the Saint Sahul Hameed

The 'compiled record' of Nagore Kaifiat deals with the data collected from the elderly people who belonged to the period of 1817, and it was issued by the kings Chandra Sekhara and Jai Konda Chollan of Tanjore region. Sayyid (AH 1346:25--60) states that the saint reached and settled at Nagore in AH 940 (1533--34 AD). Quadir Hussain (1957) estimates Sahul Hameed's period as 1532 AD-1600 AD. The authenticity of Saints' birth on 18.11.1504 AD (910 Hijiri) and the death on 9.11.1570 AD (978 Hijiri), suggests that the saint belonged to the early 16th century (Quddusi, 1991:2; Hassan Saheb Quadhiri, 1980). The tradition and the historical records mention that the saint came to Nagore during the period of the Maratha king Achutappa Nayaka. It is recorded that the saint cured the illness of the king who endowed him with land as offerings for curing his treatment. The Hindu sage Sivananda (1966) while praising the healing powers of the saint, described Sahul Hameed as 'Nagore Andavar'. Since then, the Nagore saint has been popular as Nagore 'Andavar' (meaning 'God' in local Hindu religious parlance). The saint Sahul Hameed is therefore referred to as Nagore Andavar in the present paper to emphasize the dimension of cultural fusion in the Sufi cult.

The saint Nagore Andavar led a simple and pious life. The hagiological literature suggests that the saint was an adherent of the Shariat or the religious canons of Islam. The saint gained popularity by performing miracles, and thus fulfilling the material desires of the people.

The local people both Muslim as well as Hindus became his devotees and his residence soon came to be treated as a pilgrimage centre.

Nagore Andavar predicted his own death and conveyed it to his son, Yusuf Saheb. Telling him that he was going to leave the mundane world, the saint explained to him how to conduct the funeral rites and prayers and also showed the place of the burial. He advised Yusuf Saheb to visit his grave on the third day after his death and to greet him. He said that if he got a reply from him, i.e., from the saint's tomb, he should continue his stay at Nagore otherwise he could leave the place and go wherever he liked. On the 10th Jamathul Akhir AH 978 (9th November 1570 AD) (Quddusi, 1991:2), the saint's soul departed to the other world. The saint's funeral ceremonies and rituals were conducted by his son as per his father's instructions. Yusuf Saheb, according to his father's suggestions visited the grave on the 3rd day, conveyed his greeting and got a reply from his father's grave. He decided to stay at Nagore for the rest of his life. A tomb was made on the graveyard and people started venerating it. Thus the pilgrimage to Nagore Andavar's tomb was first initiated by his son, Yusuf Saheb, himself. Since then to the present day, his followers and devotees hold up the tradition of pilgrimage to Nagore-e-Sharif from different regions of the Indian sub-continent.

Even after the death of the saint Nagore Andavar, his miraculous powers had not disappeared. As soon as the tomb of the saint was consecrated, prayers to the tomb in the name of the saint Nagore Andavar continued to be made and the devotees continued to get some kind of relief and rectification of their personal problems. The saint's son, Yusuf Saheb, too had immense faith in his father's supernatural powers and used to advise his devotees to have faith and pray at the tomb with devotion, so that the individual devotees got their desires fulfilled by the grace of the Andavar.

There are strong sentiments among the Muslims that pilgrimage to a sacred centre gives religious merit to them after their death. This fact was attested by the prophet and the saints of the area. The pilgrimage to Mecca is obligatory on the part of those Muslims who can afford to make the journey to Mecca. It is believed that every step taken in the direction of pilgrimage to Mecca washes off a mortal sin (Hughes, 1975). The poor Muslims of the society developed a new kind of pilgrimage to the local tombs of the saints, thinking that their visits conveyed the same merit as a of pilgrimage to Mecca would. Thus saint Gesudaraj of Gulbarga, Karnataka, said that: "When, for good reason, people were unable to make the pilgrimage to Mecca, a visit once in their lives to his mausoleum (tomb) would convey the same merit" (Shariff, 1921:131). The statement of saint Sultanul Arfin of Baudan, Kolkata, also supports such a view: "Needy people should visit my grave for three days, and if their desires are not fulfilled they may demolish my grave on the fourth" (Raja, 1967:21). These statements of the two saints show that the saints possessed the supernatural power to solve the material problems of the people. There is a popular belief among the Muslims of north India, that: "Seven pilgrimages to Ajmer are equal to performing a Hajj (pilgrimage to Mecca)" (Sayyed, 1989:241). Similarly, there is belief among the Tamil-speaking Muslims of south India that: "Those who cannot afford to pay a visit to Mecca, seven visits to the shrine of Nagore-e-Sherif conveys the same merit of Hajj" (Rahim, 1971:21). Several other values are attached to Sufi shrines. More (1993:91) has observed that people visit the Sufi shrines like Nagore and Muthupet to wash away their sins. Thus the earlier hagiological writings and the popular beliefs support the view that pilgrimage to Sufi saints' shrines earns religious merit as well as material benefits for the people.

The Kanduri Festival of Nagore Andavar

The Kanduri festival of Nagore Andavar is the annual fair which is celebrated in conjunction with observance of the Saint's death anniversary at the Darga of Nagore-e-Sharif. Hence, the death anniversary of the saint Nagore Andavar is better known as the Kanduri festival. Pilgrims visit the Darga of Nagore-e-Sharif to participate in the rituals and witness the rites of the saint's death anniversary. The observance of such a death anniversary of the Sufi saint is called Urs in northern India. However, the Urs observance is termed as 'Kanduri' in South India and Sri Lanka by the Tamil-speaking Muslims. It may be stated that the word 'Kanduri' is derived from the Persian word for 'table covering'. In Indonesia, the same word denotes a feast or a commemorative meal (*Encyclopedia of Islam,* Leiden, 1978:540). The *New Royal Persian English Dictionary* (1932:336) states that 'Kanduri' means a feast or ceremony observed in honour of holy personages. The *Tamil Lexicon and Jubilee Tamil Dictionary* (1935:716) specifically explains that 'Kanduri' is the festival held at Nagore in honour of the holy saint Meera Saheb. The saint Sahul Hameed Nagore Andavar is also called Meera Saheb. In some places, the fairs are referred to as Jhande[4] (flag) festival. Thus, the *gyarmike* Jhande festival is celebrated in commemoration of the Sufi saint Syed Abdul Qyadir Jeelani of Bagadad. The saint Sahul Hameed's death anniversary is called Quadir Walike Jhande (flag) festival. The main attraction of the annual death anniversary of the saint is the hoisting and carrying out of these Jhande (flags) in a procession to honour Nagore Andavar. This festival demonstrates the fusion of Hindu as well as Islamic rituals. The Islamic rites include the recitation of Quranic verses, and observance of the Fathiha ritual is the common feature of this fair. The Hindu participation is another important feature of the festival.

The Kanduri festival of Nagore Andavar is performed for fourteen days starting from the first day to the fourteenth day of the Jamathul Akhir month of Muslim calendar year (Table 1). Just before the commencement of the Kanduri festival, the flag poles are erected on the five minarets of the shrine (Nagore-e-Sharif). The flags (Kodi) are traditionally received from the Nagapatnam Muslim Jamath. A devotee of Nagore Andavar traditionally sends the four flags from Singapore. While receiving the four flags, the fifth flag donated by the descendants of the then Maratha king of Tanjore, is added. After performing the Fathiha[5], the five flags are carried on the back of the elephant of Nagore-e-Sharif. Later the flags are displayed in the Mera Palli (mosque) at Nagapatnam. These flags contain the emblem of Zulfhikar which represents one shield and two swords of Ali (Prophet's son-in-law), who fought and died for the sake of Allah. The flags carry the words, "Ya Nagore Marade Hassil" which means Oh Lord Nagore ! My vows are fulfilled", and are also imprinted with the sandal paste palm prints of the devotee's hands. The devotees who desire to hoist the flag on the Darga minaret, have to pay a fee Kanikai of Rs.1001 as a gift to the Darga office. Such devotees' flags are hoisted daily in the evening on the big minaret at six p.m.

The special attraction of the saint Nagore Andavar's Kanduri is the presence of the Fakhir Jamas (mendicant priests), and the followers (disciples) of the saint who witness the festival. It is said that the saint had 404 disciples as his followers in his spiritual team. All these disciples are divided into four groups which consists of 100 members each with one headman for each group. These are Banwa, Malang, Mondal and Jalali groups. Since the inception of the saint Nagore Andavar's tomb, the saint's followers have been visiting the fair and paying homage to their spiritual master, Sahul Hameed Nagore Andavar. In due course the local mendicant associates, namely Rafai Jama was added to the earlier four mendicant groups of Yusuf Saheb. Thus at present five mendicant groups attend the Saint's Kanduri festival and observe the rituals of the Saint.

Table 1

Sacred Performances conducted at Nagpatnama and Nagore during Kanduri Festival of Saint Nagore Andavar

Day & Month as Per Muslim Calendar	*Time*	*Performance*	*Place where the ritual is conducted*
26th Jamathul Avval 1413 A.H.	2 p.m.	Erection of flag poles on the five minarets of the Nagore Andavar's Darga.	Nagore
30th Jamathul Avval 1413 A.H.	11 a.m.	Reception of Kodi (flags). Installation of the Iradum (car) in the Usimaam (chariot) for flag procession.	Nagapatnam
30th Jamathul Avval 1413 A.H.	8.30 p.m.	Display of crackers at the Iradam place.	Nagapatanam
1st Jamathul Akhir 1413 A.H.	8.30 p.m.	Reception of Fakhir Jamas (Nagore Andavar's disciples).	Nagore
1st Jamathul Akhir 1413 A.H.	12.30 p.m.	Procession of Kodi (Nagore Andavar's Darga flags).	Nagapatnam & Nagore
1st Jamathul Akhir 1413 A.H.	8.30 p.m.	Tuvaja Rohanam (flag–hoisting ceremony).	Nagore
8th Jamathul Akhir 1413 A.H.	8.30 p.m.	Vana Vedeke (display of Fireworks).	Nagore
9th Jamathul Akhir 1413 A.H.	8.00 a.m.	Installation of Sandana Koodu (Tabooth) in the Usimaram (chariot).	Nagapatnam
9th Jamathul Akhir 1413 A.H.	10 p.m.	Installation of Pir (Nagore Andavar's disciple's fasting ceremony).	Nagore
10th Jamathul Akhir 1413 A.H.	07 p.m.	Reception of Nagore Andavar's Rowla Sharif Chadar (shawl of sanctum) sanctorum.	Nagore
10th Jamathul Akhir 1413 A.H.	8.30 p.m.	Procession of Sandana Koodu at Nagapatnama and Nagore.	Nagapatnam & Nagore
11th Jamathul Akhir 1413 A.H.	4.30 p.m.	Annointment of Sandanam (sandal paste) to Rowla Sharif (Andavar's tomb).	Nagore
12th Jamathul Akhir 1413 A.H.	5 p.m.	Pir (Andavar's disciple) proceeds to sea-shore to break the fasting ceremony.	Nagore & Chilladi
14th Jamathul Akhir 1413 A.H.	8.30 p.m.	Tuvaja Avarohanam (flag–downing ceremony).	Nagore

The first mendicant group welcomed at the Kanduri festival of the saint Nagore Andavar by the Dargha management is Banwa at 8 a.m. Its members are honoured with garlands. While inviting them a cannon was fired in the past and musical pipes were played which marked the respect to them. A practice still prevalent is that they get their head tonsured. So, the local people refer to them as Mutte Fakhirs (tonsured mendicant priests). They claim that they belong to the Quadaria order, to which the saint Sahul Hameed Nagore Andavar belonged. Hence, they claim higher social status than the other four mendicant groups. The next group invited at 12 p.m. by the Darga management is Malang Jama. They usually grow their hair long. So, they are called by the people Jhata Fhakirs (long haired mendicant priests). The third group is the Mondal Fhakir, who enter the Darga precincts at 3 p.m. They used to play the Danka (drum) while going out for preaching. So, they are referred to as Danka Fhakhir Jama. The fourth group attending the Darga is Jalai Fhakhir, who carry along with them Kombu (horn). Hence, they are also known as Kombu Fhakhir Jama. The fifth Fhakhir group is Rafai Jama. They play the instrument Guruj (mace), during the festival to entertain the public. Hence, they got the local title Guruj Fhakhir Jama. Thus the five Jamas are welcomed to the Kanduri festival by the Darga management to perform Chilla (40 days meditation) at the Nagore-e-Sharif. The main duty of the five Jamas is to conduct the rituals of the saint's anniversary and to perform Ziarat (visit) to the saint's tomb twice a day, i.e. in the morning and evening, during their stay at the Darga premises.

On the first day of the Jamathul Akhir month the five minaret flags are taken out in procession. The procession starts at 12 p.m. from Nagapatnam Meerapalli mosque after performing the Fathiha ritual. The procession moves in the streets of Nagpatnam to sanctify the residential areas of the town. The procession consists of five big models of offerings such as big chariot (Peria Ratham), small chariot (Chinna Ratham), Mohammad Ghouse ship model Testa, Mohammad Gwalior ship model Testa and the palanquin model Chetti Pallaq offered by the merchant caste. They carry five flags to be hoisted on the five minarets of Nagore Andavar's Darga. The first minaret flag to be hoisted on the Talamattu Manora (minaret), located towards the head side of the saint's Darga, is placed in the big chariot model. The expenses of the chariot are borne by the Nagapatnam Muslim Jamath. The second minaret flag is placed in the Chettiar palanquin model and brought to the Darga. Later, it is hoisted on the Sahib minaret of the Darga. The expenses for this model are incurred by the Hindu merchant group. Hence, this model is known as Chettiar palanquin model. The third Muthubaq minaret flag, located at the north side of the saint's Darga, is placed in the Mohammed Ghouse ship model and then brought to the saint's Darga. Its management is done with the individual contributions of the devotees of the locality. The fourth Ottu minaret flag is placed and brought to the Darga. Its management is done by the devotees residing in Singapore. The fifth minaret flag is placed in the Mohammad Gwalior ship model and brought to the Darga. Thus the procession of five flags which contains five models are preceded by the individual models of devotees like small ships (Cuppal), boats (Padagai), ship engines, minarets (Manora), flower palanquin (Poopallaq) and fish model (Minu), belonging to the local area. These models which denote the fulfilment of the wishes of the devotees by Nagore Andavar are driven by the devotes. After the procession these are kept at home and used again only for the saint's annual fair. This tradition is being carried on from generation to generation by the descendants of the devotees. Following the flags procession an aloe woodcart (Ud-Vandi) is carried as a ritual tradition. The release of the smoke of the aloe-wood is an indication of worship of the Nagore Andavar flags (Kodi) and it is done for sanctifying the residential areas of the locality. Behind the flag procession, a Western music band plays; the double reed pipe instrument Nadaswaram is also played alongside.

Thus the aforesaid procession commences from the Meera Palli mosque and passes through streets like Abhiram Ammal Sannadi, Neena Dathachayani, Ammam West street, East Street, North Street, Nethaji Road and Hospital Road of Nagapatnam town. Later, the procession proceeds to Nagore town through streets such as Kunjali Mericar Street, Miya Street, Pandha Salai Street, Theru Palli Street, Sayyadu Palli Street and finally reaches the illuminated west gate of the Darga Alankara Vasal. The five flags are received with great honour by the Darga management and hoisted on the specified five minarets at 8 p.m., after performing the Fathiha. This ritual is known as Tuvajarohanam (flag hoisting). It is done with great devotion and immense faith witnessed by tens of thousands of pilgrims coming from different parts. The ritual is honoured by firing the cannon at the Darga. These flags remain flying on the minarets for 14 days till the completion of the saint's Kanduri ceremony. Several entertainment programmes are part of the saint's annual festival. There is a display of fireworks on the eight day of Jamathul Akhir month, from at 8 p.m. 10 p.m. which people enjoy. On the ninth day of Mahathul Akhir month, the Nagapatnama Jamath assembles at the shed of sandal anointed chariot (Sandanam Ratham). The Fathiha is conducted and the procession arrangements are made to carry out the chariot Tabooth.

Installation of Pir

On the 9th day of Jamathul Akhir month at 10 p.m. one disciple from the Malang Fhakhir Jama is chosen for spiritual exercise. This disciple is known as Pir[6] in the local parlance. Hence, the ritual is referred to as installation of Pir. It is performed at the place where the saint's body was offered the funeral prayer Janaze Kenamaz. It is rendered by the Malang Fhakhir Jama, who was one of the saint's disciples, and had followed the saint during preaching of the divine message of Allah. In the evening, all Darga trustees, Khalifa (spiritual successors of the Darga), the five Fhakhir Jamas and the pilgrims assemble near Pir Mandapam. The Fathiha is conducted and the toes of the two legs of the Pir are tied with a fine thread. It is believed that the thread should remain in a normal position for three days. The Pir during this period observes meditation, Zikr, reciting the names of God. While doing so, the Pir throws lemons at the crowd. There is a popular belief that the lemon thrown by the Pir has miraculous powers. The pilgrims believe that the one who gets the lemon is lucky and that his/her desires are going to be fulfilled by Nagore Andavar. The women believe that if a barren woman gets the lemon, it means that she will be blessed with an offspring. So, people of different faiths continuously stand before him during day and night, expecting to get a lemon. They do not mind standing even in the scorching heat of the sun or in rain. Their motive remains to get the blessings of Nagore Andavar in the shape of the lemon.

Shawl of Hindu Devotee at Nagore Andavar's Sanctum Sanctorum

In the past the shawl of Nagore Andavar's Rowla Sharif (sanctum sanctorium) used to be presented by the then Maratha king of Tanjore. Later, one Hindu devotee, Palaniandi Pillai, requested the Maratha king to allow him to present the shawl to the saint. Since then, the tradition has continued and even today the descendants of Palaniandi Pillai are privileged to offer the chadar. On the tenth day of Jamathul Akhir month, at 7 p.m. the Darga trustees and the descendants of the saint's son, Yusuf Sahib visit the family of Palaniandi Pillai's descendant, Karthikeyan, to receive the shawl. The shawl is displayed in the centre hall of the house of the devotee for the view of visitors. After performing the Fathiha, the shawl is carried on the back of the elephant of the Darga. Later on, the shawl is spread on the saint's Rowla Sharif, after anointing sandal paste over the tomb of the saint. This tradition is yet another example of Hindu-Muslim intermingling and communal amity witnessed in this part of India.

In the evening of the ninth day of Jamathul Akhir month, at 8 p.m. the tabooth chariot containing sandal paste is pulled by the pilgrims and devotees of the Nagore Andavar. The chariot is preceded by the aloe woodcart only. No models of the devotees are taken by them during the procession, but the procession includes a variety of musical instruments like drum (Tappu), a troupe of horns (Kombu), and the double reed musical instrument Nadaswaram, which is generally played in Hindu temples and a three-piece Western band troupe Sanai. It looks like a charming mela. The Tabooth while being pulled stops at different intervals. Wherever the chariot stops, the devotees including the Hindus offer prayer, by inviting the Muslims to their houses. They also offer the chariot-pullers tea, coffee, snacks etc. and honour them with a towel (Thundu) and distribute the Prasadam (sweatmeats) to the pilgrims following the chariot procession. The procession first moves from Nagapatnam town to Nagore to bestow the blessings of Andavar on the people of the area. Finally at 4 p.m. the Tabooth reaches the south gate of the Darga. The sandal paste (Sandanam) is received by the saint's descendants. The two pots of sandal paste earmarked for the ritual are taken inside the sanctum sanctorum of the Darga. The sandal paste is anointed on the Rowla Sharif of the saint by the spiritual successor (Khalifa) of the Darga after performing the Fathiha and reciting the genealogy, *Silsila*, of the saint. Then the shawl contributed by the Hindu descendant of Palaniandi Pillai is spread over the tomb of the saint. After the anointing ritual, the Darga gates are opened to the pilgrims and public.

On the 12th day of Jamathul Akhir month, at 5 p.m. the Darga Khalifa along with the Darga trustees and five Fhakhir Jamas assemble at the Pir Mandapam. After performing the Fathiha, the knot on the toes of the two legs of the Pir is removed by the Darga Khalifa. Then the Pir along with his headman Sarguru of the Malang Jama and the devotees moves towards the seashore, to break the fast (Roza). The Pir proceeds to the Chilladi Darga, where the saint Nagore Andavar had meditatid for 40 days. At that place, the Fathiha is conducted and the water from the dug pit is sipped ritually. People believe that the water which normally becomes sweet, thus reflecting the miraculous powers of the saint. Then the Pir visits the sea shore and pays tribute to the ocean god Khizr and later they all return to the Darga. On the evening of the 14th day of Jamathul Akhir month, the flags from the five minarets are downed, after performing Fathiha, amidst the gathering of the Darga trustees, Darga Khalifa and five Fhakhir Jamas. This ritual is known as Tuvaja Avarohanam (flag downing ritual). At night, the Quran is read and the

Silsila of the saint is read. This marks the completion of the saint's annual Kanduri festival which people attend in large numbers to witness the rituals and customs. Though this annual festival is of great importance, the daily and weekly rituals are also held at the Darga with great dedication and active participation of both the Hindus and Muslims.

The daily rituals such as cleaning the tomb and adorning it with flowers, lighting the lamps and offering Fathiha are performed by the sacred specialist Mujawar of the Darga. On weekdays, particularly on thursday, Zumekirat rituals have special significance. It is believed that if the devotees perform the rituals on that day their personal sufferings are heard and answered by the saint. The Darga is kept open daily for one hour after morning and evening prayers. On thursdays, the Darga remains open from afternoon to evening. Thus, the daily and weekly rituals too have great importance in the life of the common people, both Hindus and Muslims.

Multiple Modes of Reverence in Dargahs and the Bond of Hindu-Muslim Unity

People, both Hindus and Muslims, visit Dargahs all over India, with various kinds of motivations, including cessation of their pains such as sickness and insanity. There are also others with frustration in life, persons having high ambitions seeking success in examination, job, civil or criminal courts and barren women with the hope of offspring. All aims and expectations are placed before the saint of the Dargah for his blessings.

The customs and traditions of the shrines differ from one locality to another. Thus in the tomb of Khawja Garib Nawaz the offerings are made in the form of Chaddar (shawl) which is covered over the tomb of the saint. In some shrines, the practice of tying thread to the Dargah gate is noticed. After the fulfilment of the wish, the threads are offered to the saint along with Nazarana, a gift in the cash or kind. At the Darga of Sahul Hameed Nagore Andavar, however, the devotees follow the custom of offering Jhande flags in the name of the saint. This special feature is observed only in south India, particularly Tamil Nadu. These flag offerings are made depending upon the economic position of the devotees who can even offer cash, Kanikai, a gift to the Darga management. Generally, the offerings consist of puffed up dried sugar mixed with wheat cakes (Malleda) and a special variety of Jagi flowers. These offerings are presented to the descendants of the saint, i.e., Mujawar (priest of the Darga). After the Fathiha, a little portion of the offering is taken by the priest and the rest is returned to the devotees who will distribute the same among their friends and relatives. This sanctified offering is known as Tabarook. The thick layers of soot (Masi) in the sacred niches of the sanctum sanctorum is taken by the devotees as a sign of visit to the shrine. The ghee contained in the sacred lamp is touched and smeared on the face and hands as a token of blessings from the saint.

The Darga of Nagore Andavar is an essential resort especially for the insane. The poorer people strongly believe that insanity is the evil act of an evil spirit Jin. They do not treat it as a psychological affliction. The sufferers visit the tomb to seek cure. Thus the poor people, who cannot afford better treatment depend upon the supernatural treatment of the saint.

In front of saint Nagore Andavar's tomb, there is one iron chain hanging from the roof. There is a strong belief that the iron chain has miraculous powers. It is believed that the very first couple of mankind gave the chain to the saint, when he had visited Adam's Peak in Sri Lanka. Thus it is obvious that the Sufi saint has immense popularity. However, it is observed that greater support to the Sufi cult is received from the lower strata of the Muslim society. There is strict aversion to the saint cult among the puritan section of the Muslim society, though many secularist Muslims show respect to the saint.

To sum up, the saints practising Sufism express their broader vision of universal brotherhood among the people. The cult of the Sufi saints is widespread in India and it is congenial to the local surroundings, where it always helps to lessen the inter-religious hostility, which occasionally occurs. The number of shrines is increasing mainly owing to their inbuilt resilience and tolerance towards divergent religious orders. The high praise for the saintly mystic powers and veneration by way of offering flags and lighting ghee lamps at saint Nagore Andavar's tomb by the local people particularly the Hindus and their corroboration by the Muslims shows the importance of this Dargah as a great synthesizing shrine.

Glossary of Religious Terms

1. *Karamat*: It refers to the powers possessed by the Sufi saint (Wali) through which wishes are fulfilled. Due to these miraculous powers, they are regarded as nearer to God. The acts of miracles of the prophets are known as Mujizat while the acts of the Sufi saints are called Karamat.
2. *Andavar*: In Tamil vernacular Andavar means 'God'. The Sufi saint Sahul Hameed of Nagore-e-Sharif, is called Nagore Andavar because of his high degree of spiritual excellence and the power of fulfilling the material needs of the devotees. This title was given to him by the Hindu sage Shivananda in view of the high degree of miraculous acts of the saint. Thus the saint of Nagore is referred to as Nagore Andavar by the local people.
3. *Ziarat*: Traditionally a visit to the tomb of the prophet at Madina, Saudi Arabia, is known as Ziarat. The place of Ziarat is called Ziaratgarh or Dargah. It also indicates the Sufi saint's residence or burial place. In ordinary usage the burial place of an ordinary person is referred to as Kabar (grave); for the grave of dignitaries such as Ullema (Arabic scholars) the word 'Mazar' is used. For the graves the Sufi saints the word Dargah is used. 'Darga' is used for a Dargah in south India.
4. *Jhande*: The Dargah flag (carrying the sulphikar emblem) is ceremonially hoisted on a tall and imposing wooden pillar called Thuvajastambha. It is a late innovation. The Sanskrit word used for the flag is *thuvaja* and in Tamil 'Kodi' is used. The act of hoisting a flag connotes hope and desire. The raising of flags in the traditional context means a resolve to exert and a will to succeed.
5. *Fatiha:* It indicates the one time recitation of Sura fatiha (the first version of the holy text). The three times recitation is called the Sura Iklas. A Chapter that occurs in the daily prayer reads thus:

   He is God, the one and only God, the External,
   Absolute. He begetteth not, nor is
   He begotten, and there is none like unto him.

   Usually Muslims conduct this act before offering any thing in the name of Allah or to any Sufi saint.
6. *Pir*: It literally means spiritual mentor, who initiates the novices into the spiritual line of Sufism. In the present study, the word 'Pir' denotes the disciple of the saint Sahul Hameed Nagore Andavar, who attended to the traditional Kanduri festival of the saint. He acts as a 'ritual saint' and symbolizes the spiritual powers of the saint of Nagore.

References

Abdi, S.N.M., 1993, 'On the Sufi Trail' *The Illustrated Weekly of India*. June 5–II: 16–18.

Bhaumik, S.N., 1993, 'A Holy Mix' *India Today* November 7:8–10.

Chandrasekharan, T., 1817, *Nagore Kaifiayat: A Descriptive Catalogue: Marathi Modi Manuscripts D.No. 107. & 108* Madras: Government Oriental Manuscript Library.

Curriee, P.M., 1989, *The Shrine and Cult of Muin-a-al-Din Chisthi of Ajmer*, Delhi: Oxford University Press.

Cyril, G., 1978, *The Concise Encyclopedia of Islam*, London: Stancy International.

de Munick, Victor C., 1994, Sufi, Reformist and National Modles of Identity: The History of a Muslim Village Festival in Sri Lanka, *Contributions to Indian Sociology*, N S, 28, 2; 273--293.

Freitag, Sandria, B., 1988–89, *Collective Action and Community. Public Arenas and the Emergence of Communalism in North India* Berkley; University of California Press.

Gadgil, M. and V.D. Vartak, 1976, 'The Sacred Groves of the Western Ghats in India', *Economic Botany* 30: 152–160.

Gibb, H.A.R., and J.H. Karmers, 1981, *Shorter Encyclopedia of Islam* Karachi: South Asia Publishers.

Hastings, J., 1978, *Preaching of Islam*. In J. Hastings (ed) *Encyclopedia of Religion and Ethics*, Vol.9. New York: Charles Subscriber's and Sons.

Hemingway, F.R., 1906, *Madras District Gazetteer Records* Tanjore: Govt. Press, Madras.

Hughes, T.P., 1975, *Notes on Mohammadanism* Delhi, Idarahi-Adabiyat: 130–136.

Hulbe, S.K., T. Vetshere and S.B. Khomme, 1994, 'The Scared Complex at Madhi', *Man in India*, 55:237–253.

Hussain, S.S., 1963–64, *Annual Report on Indian Epigraphy* No. D-161--163: Nagpur: Archaeological Survey of India: 133.

Hussain, M.M.A., 1985, Karu Naikkadal Ajmer Haja Nayagam. Madras; Three Em Publications.

Lewis, I.M., 1984, *Sufism in Somaliland: A Study in Tribal Islam*: In Akbar, S. Ahamed and David. M. Harts (eds) *Islam in Tribal Societies*, London: Routledge and Kegan Paul.

Malhotra, K.C. and J. Basak, 1984, 'A Note on the Cultural Ecology of Husbanded Plants', *South Asian Anthropologist* 5, I: 45–47.

Malhotra, K.C. and S. Sah, 1993, 'Association of Pomegranate' (Punica Granatum) with the Sacred Complex at Madhi, Maharashtra', *Man in India* 73, 4:395--400.

Moini, S.L.H., 1932, *The New Royal Persian English Dictionary,* Vol.1, Madras: Madras University.

Moini, S.L.H., 1935, *The Tamil Lexicon and Jubilee Tamil Dictionary,* Vol. 2, part-1 Madras: Madras University.

More, J.B.P.L., 1993, 'Tamil Muslims and non-Brahmin Atheists -- 1925--1940', *Contributions to Indian Sociology* (N.S.) 27, I:83--104.

Qadhiri, S.H.S., 1980, *The Divine Light of Nagore.* Dargah Sharif; S.K. Publication.

Qadir Hussain, K., 1957, The South Indian Musalmans, Madras Christian College Magazine, 30:365 -369.

Quddusi, M.I., 1991, *A Bilingual Inscription of Pratap Singh from Nagore* (Tamil Nadu) paper presented at the 17th Annual Epigraphic Congress Tanjore: 2 (unpublished).

Rahim, M.A., 1971, *History of Nagapatnam and its Surroundings from the 16th Century* Madras: Madras University.

Raja, M., 1967, 'The Mazar Worship in Budaun', *Journal of Social Research* 10, 2: 27–36.

Rao, S., 1961--(1979), *The Temple: Its Meaning and Symbolism*, Bangalore. Theosophical Society Pub.

Saheb, AAA, 1995, 'A Festivals of Flags: Hindu-Muslim Devotion and Sacralising of Localism at the Shrine of Nagore-e-Sharif in Tamil Nadu' in Prina Werbner and Helene Basu (Eds.), *Embodying Charisma.* London: Routledge.

Sayyid, M., 1346 A.H., 'Manquibul Majid Pi Manaquib Sa H-al Hamid (Arabic)', Urdu Tr. By Hussain Alam, S.M. *Sawanth Hayati Hadrat Quadriwali*, Madras. (1379 A.H.) 251–60.

Shariff, J., 1921, *Islam in India: The Customs of the Musalmans of India* Tr. By G.A. Herklots, M.D. (1975): London: Curzon press.

Sivananda, V., 1966. *Release the Pigeon: Avert Death, Animal Citizen.* Madras: Animal Welfare Board.

21

Synthesis of Tribal Religion and Hindu Cults in Bastar

Samira Dasgupta and Amitabh Sarkar

Until recently, Bastar was the largest district of India. Now divided, it is part of the new state of Chhattisgarh. The tribes such as Abujh Maria, Dandami Maria, Muria, Bhatra, Halba, Dhurwa and Dorla predominantly inhabit Bastar. The first three tribes are regarded as the segments of the Gond tribe. Hajra (1970:79) has shown that the Dorla have some similarities with the Dandami Maria, and it may be regarded as an offshoot of the Gond tribe. Each of the tribal groups is an endogamous group, with its own religious beliefs and practices which in most cases have evolved in relation to the particular environmental background in which their habitat is located. In this tribal-dominated Bastar region the presence of the non-tribal people cannot be ignored. They have migrated to the region as businessmen or petty traders, service holders and also as refugee settlers. The kings of Bastar belonging to the Kakatiya dynasty had migrated to Bastar from the Warangal region of Andhra Pradesh. There are Brahmins, who have migrated from Orissa and Maharashtra and even from Andhra Pradesh. Rest of the non-tribal Hindu communities belong to the lower strata of Hindu caste hierarchy (Sarkar and Dasgupta, 1996: 21; Sunder, 1997:13–15). They are Panera, Painka Ghadwa and Mahara etc. Besides the followers of tribal religion, there are Hindus, Jains, Sikhs, Christians and Muslims living in Bastar.

Bastar is a region where people of various cultures lived together, often sharing each other's culture traits. Through their sharing and borrowing of culture traits of neighbouring communities, the Bastar people present a clear picture of cultural syncretism. This paper deals with the process of fusion of different religious beliefs and practices observed among the tribal and the non-tribal people of Bastar, in a historical perspective.

There exists a religious base through which one can trace that all the Maria and the Muria tribes have originated from a common stock—the Gond. The tribal deities of Bastar tribes live in the mountains, forests, land, rivers, wind, plants, animals and also in some stones. Most of the tribals believe that sun is the supreme deity and moon is his wife, and stars are their children. They worship them on specific occasions. Besides these deities, their ancestors hold a very important position in the religious and cultural spheres of tribal life. In each and every ritual and festival, offerings are made in honour of the ancestors. Their ancestors are believed to be their family deities who protect the families from all types of calamities, difficulties, diseases and hazards.[1] All tribes of Bastar practise ancestor worship. It is found that the tribals such as Abujh Maria, Dandami Maria, Muria and also Dorla have their own Pen deities. A Pen deity is the tribal clan deity. It is a guardian/governing deity of a particular clan or katta to which a person belongs. All these Pen deities of the celestial world are mythically connected with each other through the network of social relations (consisting of affinal and consanguineal ties among them). These deities have their own territory consisting of one, two or several villages. Some of the Pen deities are male and some are female. Wooden logs generally represent a male Pen deity. Grigson (1991:187–198) has referred to these wooden logs as log gods. It is a framework of three parallel saja logs held together by cross-pieces of bamboo or saja to which they are tied by cords of siyari creeper or twisted thongs to the outer ring of bamboos (Grigson, 1991). The Halbas of Bastar also have similar gods. When the Pen deity is a female then instead of logs it is represented through lat. A lat is a long bamboo stick with a piece of coloured cloth (which represents the flag of a particular deity) tied at the top and above that at the extreme top position there is a small conical or round bell metal piece in which the lat is inserted. This is known as gura. Just beneath the gura there are some very small musical bells which surround the lat. The log gods are commonly known as Anga Deo or Pat Deo. Anga Deo is the deity of the Muria community of Narayanpur area and Pat Deo is the deity of the communities living in Jagdalpur, Dantewada and Chhote Dongar areas. Thus, we see a close internal ethnic tie amongst the communities of Bastar. It is in the religious sphere that such inter-ethnic ties are sporadically invoked; these are culminated during the centralized Dashahra festival, about which we will discuss below.

It is observed that alongside their ancestors and Pen deities, the tribal people of Bastar venerate the earth goddess, Bhum. They believe that they all are her children as she feeds them by providing various types of crops and cereals. She is called Tallur Mutte by the Abujh Maria, and Tallin by the Dandami Maria and Dorla. Her husband's name is Kanga. They have seven children which are the cultivated crops and cereals of the locality. Tallur Mutte, an equivalent of Bhum, is also increasingly called Matti Deo by the local Hindu communities. Earth deity is prevalent among the Abujh Marias, Murias, Dandami Marias (or Bison-Horn Marias), Dhurwas, Dorlas, Bhatras and Halbas. These tribes constitute the main tribal population of Bastar. Each and every village has its own deity called Gaon Devi. Some of them are Jimmedarin Mata, Thakurain Mata, Jalni Mata, Mahamai Maa, Kankalin Mata, Maoli Mata and Danteswari Mata, the last one being the supreme among them. They are worshipped for the welfare of the village. The notion of Gaon Devi, the village deity, is prevalent among all tribes of Bastar. It may have been borrowed from Hindu neighbours in the plains. Besides all these deities, each and every village has its guard deity, who is generally established at the outskirts of the village. The deity exists as a guard deity and protects the village from all types of evils. These deities are also referred to as Dand Deo by most of the tribes of Bastar.

The tribes of Bastar being agriculturists, mostly depending on shifting cultivation, a large number of their festivals are centred on agrarian themes. It is observed that they perform several rituals and festivals such as Kaksar, Maria, etc. Kaksar is a festival celebrated by the Abujh Maria of the Abujh Marh hills. This is a pre-monsoon festival. After its performance, they start the agricultural operation. Marai is a harvest festival (during January-February) which is celebrated very elaborately in the villages. There are several other rituals and festivals, associated with various phases of cultivation starting from cutting, burning (in case of slash-and-burn cultivation), ploughing, seed sowing, transplantation, weeding, cutting, harvesting, threshing and storing. In each ritual, the Bastar tribals worship the earth goddess. Ritual offerings are also made to their deceased ancestors, clan deities, alongwith their village mother goddess. Kadrengal is regarded as the deity of forests. There are several other deities of the forest. Whenever they go hunting they worship all these deities. After getting a hunt they first offer some portion of the hunt to those deities and only after that arrange the feast.

The Hindus of Bastar also venerate a large number of deities. They worship all the major gods and goddesses of the Hindu pantheon such as Lord Vishnu, Siva, Parvati, Ganesha, Lakshmi, Sitala and also Hanuman. The Hindu communities of Bastar, however, simultaneously venerate the village mother goddess, the earth deity and many others deities of tribal origin. The earth deity is called Mati Deo (It is not clear how the earth deity of the tribals became Mati Deo of the non-tribals). Among the other deities of the Hindus of Bastar, we may mention Sitala Mata, normally called Mata. She holds the supreme position among all the deities. She has twenty-two sisters. Some of them are Danteswari Mata, Maoli Mata, Mahamai Mata, Kankalin Mata, etc. Each of these mother goddesses has one or more villages under her control. Danteswari Mata has a special position among the tribal and non-tribal people of Bastar. She is the tutelary deity of the kings of Bastar. She has her principal temple at Dantewada. She is also regarded as a form of Durga. During Dashahra she is worshipped elaborately. Dashahra festival is held in the month of Aswin (September-October). The Chariot procession during this festival gives special attraction to this festival. Dashahra is primarily the festival of the King's family in which both the Hindus and the tribals of Bastar traditionally participate together. Involvement of tribal people in Dashahra festival is prominently noticeable. Thus, we observe a clear fusion of Hindu and tribal cultures and religious practices in this pre-dominantly tribal region of Chhattisgarh.

In fact, the organization of the Dashahra festival begins in the month of Saon (July-August) when the selection of the site for collection of wood for chariot making is done. There are various phases and types of works associated with Dashahra festival. All these works have been historically allotted to different communities (including the Hindu and the tribal communities) and also different villages. Before the festival, on the day of the new moon of the month Aswin (September-October), the people of Bastar perform a ritual known as Kachin gadi. It is performed at a place named Kachin gadi, the place of worship of Kachin Mata. In fact, during this ritual the permission from the deity is taken to celebrate Dashahra. They select a virgin girl belonging to the ex-untouchable Mahara caste (scheduled caste).The girl is supposed to act as the representative of the deity. Through her the deity gives permission to celebrate Dashahra. Kachin Devi, though a deity of the ex-untouchable community, gained an important position among the king's deities due to some other historical reason. It is believed that in the Kachin gadi, at the time of ritual performance, Danteswari Mata herself comes there from her other temple, which is located at the king's palace. Kachin Mata gives her permission in front of Danteswari Mata when she visits the place. Interestingly, Pat Deo (a clan deity of the tribal Marias of Bastar) comes before her to purify the place and to drive out all the evils present there. Here it should be mentioned that Pat Deo, the clan deity of the Marias, has become a very important deity of all the Hindus also, as it has the power to locate evil, to punish it and to drive it out ultimately. Pat Deo's image is also kept in the Danteswari temple to ensure that no evil will be able to come and defile the place. In this way the tribal clan deity, Pat Deo is incorporated into the Hindu ritual arena and placed as one of the inevitable deities among the Hindu deities. Not only in Kachin gadi, as we observed above but also in other phases of the celebration of Dashahra festival and even during many other Hindu rituals, Pat Deo is installed and worshipped to ensure that there exists no malevolent spirit to harm the ritual and festivals.

After the conclusion of the Kachin gadi ritual, in the evening of next day a man from either the Jogi or the Halba community keeps a fast (known as Sanjam) on behalf of the king, during the Dashahra festival. Here we observe that there is also active participation of tribal Halba community in the Hindu festival of Dashahra. The fact remains that the Kakatiya kings of Bastar had historically incorporated the tribal people of their kingdom by allotting different works connected with the rituals and worship during Dashahra festival and ultimately it became a living tradition. Circumambulation of the chariot has been a very important feature of the Dashahra festival. The responsibility of drawing the chariot lies on the shoulders of the Dandami Maria tribe. At first the Dandami Maria people start to drive the chariot and then people of other communities assist them. There is a popular myth according to which some time in the past, during the circumambulation of the chariot, the people of another tribal group, the Bhatra, stole the chariot. Though initially it was stolen by the Bhatras but ultimately the Dandami Maria got priority in chariot drawing, which remains an important religious observance till this day. Even today symbolically, the Bhatra bring the chariot to a place named Kumrakot. Then the Dandami Maria boys go to that place in the temper of the warriors, with their weapons (bow, arrow, battle-axe, etc.). There, a symbolic fight takes place between the people of the two tribal communities (as part of the religious observance) and at last the Bhatras are defeated and the chariot is controlled by the Dandami Maria boys. After the war, the king's family members celebrate their Noakhani ritual of new rice eating. This again is an old ritual which has spread to the entire tribal and non-tribal region of central India. In the evening, the Dandami Maria boys again bring the chariot back to

Jagdalpur town, the place where the palace of the king is located. During Dashahra festival, the king of Bastar, on behalf of Danteswari Mata, used to invite all the deities of the tribal villages. The villagers even from far-off villages (both tribal and non-tribal) used to come with their deities to attend the festival. In a way not only the tribal people of entire Bastar but also all tribal deities of different communities were incorporated into what is a Hindu festival (Dashahra).

Danteswari Devi is an important and powerful deity of the Dandami Maria people. Their main concentration is in Dantewara area, which has now been declared a separate district within Bastar, where the deity's original temple is located. The temple had influenced the life and culture of the Maria tribe. Whenever they perform any of their tribal ritual and festivals, they offer puja to Dantewari Devi also. They collect the water with which the deity is given a ritual bath at the temple and keep it in their homes. It is regarded as holy and used during ritual purification. Not only in Dashahra, but in several other Hindu rituals and festivals also the tribal people of Bastar participate actively. Lakshmi Jagar is one such ritual. Lakshmi is regarded as the deity of wealth in the Hindu pantheon. In the month of Aghan or Paus (November-December) Lakshmi Jagar is performed. It is mainly the members of Dhakar caste, a peasant caste whose position is high in the local Hindu caste order who perform it. Jagar means service and in this ritual situation it means worship. It may be performed at the family level or several families may sometimes collectively perform this worship. This is an important festival celebrated in Jagdalpur and its neighbouring villages. These villages are in general multi-ethnic in nature where the tribals and the non-tribals live together. In such a close culture-contact situation, all the villagers perform Lakshmi Jagar. It is interesting to note that the priest performing Jagar puja generally belongs to one of the local tribal communities, especially Bhatra, Dhurwa or Halba.

Bali Mela is another festival in which the tribals and non-tribals (Hindus) of Bastar collectively participate. In this festival Bhima or Bhimul, the rain god, is propitiated. He is the god of rain whom the Hindus refer to as Varun Dev. The village priest officiates the ritual. He may belong to either a tribe or a Hindu caste; even a member from the lower strata of Hindu caste hierarchy may perform this ritual role. In fact, there are several religious events and annual rituals, sometimes village specific or community specific, either indigenous or imported, which have been gradually assimilated in the emerging composite culture of the people of Bastar amongst whom drawing a line of religious distinction will be very difficult today. Let us describe another example.

Mati-Teohar is a very important festival celebrated in and around Jagdalpur. Mati-Teohar very clearly shows how a tribal deity is modified and assimilated with a similar deity of the Hindus of the area. Among the tribals Bhum, the earth deity, is a female deity. She is regarded as the mother. She feeds the people producing crops. The Dandami Maria tribal people call this deity Bhum Tallin. The Abujh Maria call her Tallur Muttei, the Muria and the Dorla call her Tallin, but she is called Matti Deo (a male god) by the Hindus and those tribals who live in and around Jagdalpur town. This merging of the gender of the deity is indeed a unique phenomenon. He is worshipped at the village level and his ritual is known as Matti-Teohar. What is most significant about this festival is that this tribal festival which is supported by tribal priesthood is acceptable to Hindus. Throughout Bastar, in almost each village and town, a deity is worshipped collectively by the villagers, both tribals and Hindus. Pat Deo as discussed before, and Anga Deo, the tribal clan god, have special importance in the religious life of the Hindus. In Hindu rituals and festivals, their presence is needed as they are believed to protect them from all evils. There is a belief that they can guess, detect and drive out all the evil spirits and malevolent acts of persons. It may be mentioned here that there is a strong prevalence of sorcery in Bastar. The Sirha (sorcerer) belonging either to a Hindu or a tribal group is commonly found in Bastar. The Sirha drives out all the evil spirits. Whenever he works, all the villagers (both Hindu and tribal) assemble, contribute and take the consecrated food.

From time to time Bastar has witnessed various types of reformatory movements by Hindus religious preachers and social reformers (Das, 1982). These movements sought to re-orient the lives and cultures of both Hindu and tribal people of Bastar. Among these movements, mention may be made of Vihangam's movement and the Brahmakumari movement and Gayatri movements which have influenced people in the far-off places of Bastar. The Gayatri and Brahmakumari movements have a more dominant presence than Vihangam's movement. This movement is governed by Akhand Jyoti Sansthan of Mathura through their Shakti Peethas. Shakti Peethas are found to be working specially in Narayanpur, Dantewada and Patalkot regions of Bastar where people gather to listen to devotional songs, prayers and sermons, etc. A large number of tribal people are influenced by these religious activities. It is found that in the Orcha block, a place far-off from Jagdalpur, there is a Gayatri temple. The area is chiefly inhabited by the Abujh Maria tribe people who have their own religious beliefs and practices which are shaped and influenced by their hilly ecological niche; in such a physical environment they not only built a Gayatri temple but also popularized the alien deity. There are a few Abujh Maria disciples who now attend all the rituals and festivals held in the Gayatri temple. They compulsorily do prayers in the temple twice daily. The disciples of Gayatri have to follow vegetarianism and teetotalism very strictly. The fundamentals of the Gayatri movement are based on Vyaktitva Nirman (personality building), Parivar Nirman (family building) and Samaj Nirman (society building). Before reforming a society, one must primarily reform his personality. It is for this reason that there is a greater emphasis on personality building. Thus, one should follow strict rules of vegetarianism, abstinence from drinking liquor and lead a truthful honest life. One is also required to bring his/her family members to the same path and ultimately all the families will adhere to such rules and they will reshape the society to resemble the society of the Dev-Kul or heavenly father—a pious society with honesty, peace and happiness.

The entry of Baba Bihari Das into the landscape of Bastar stirred the people of the area. He spread the glow of light and happiness in the minds of the tribal people of Bastar. In fact, the people of Bastar were unsettled after the death of their most favourite king, Raja Pravir Chandra Bhanj Deo. Baba Bihari Das was thought by them to be reincarnation of their Raja (Das, 1982) and they have gladly accepted him as their reincarnated beloved king. Baba, having immigrated from Kalahandi in Orissa, appeared in Bastar in 1971. He established himself as a religious preacher and social reformer. He advised his disciples to wear *Kanthi*—a bead of the wood of tulsi plant as a garland around their necks. For this reason, he was also known as Kanthiwala Baba. He said that wearing of *Kanthi* will save the people of Bastar from all types of turmoil, diseases and destruction. He advised his disciples to leave the habit of eating non-vegetarian food and drinking liquor. He advised them not to keep any black domesticated animal as those are the bearers of evil spirits. Inspired by his religious teachings a large number of people belonging to both tribal and non-tribal (Hindu) communities became his disciples. Baba Bihari Das established his ashram in Chapka village. His tribal disciples mostly belong to the Halba, Bhatra, Muria and Dhurwa communities. The tribals who became the followers of Baba Bihari Das began wearing *Kanthi*. After wearing *Kanthi* it was taboo to eat any non-vegetarian food and drink alcoholic liquor. If there was breach of this restriction it was believed that a person will be punished by the heavenly father brutally. Animal sacrifice was one of the most important acts in each and every ritual of the tribal groups. Gradually they gave up those practices under the influence of Baba. At the same time they began to sell all their black domesticated animals. As they became vegetarian, domestication of animals lost its charm. They sold all their domesticated animals at cheaper rates. The businessmen from the neighbouring states, especially from Orissa, were the main buyers of those animals. In this way, an adverse impact was felt on the economic life of the people of Bastar. To save them from such economic crisis the local administration tried to stop them from selling their animals at a cheaper rate. There was a time when Baba could even influence the electoral results in Bastar (Das, 1982). His political successes and other privileges led the Baba to maximize his economic gains. Gradually, Baba Bihari Das began to lose his importance. There was severe dissent within his followers. Slowly, the old religious practices began to resurface. They stopped weaving their Kanthis. The beliefs of the new religion and respect for Baba gradually faded. The people of Bastar understood that though Baba initially acted as a religious preacher and social reformer, eventually, his main concern shifted to economic gains.

The Mahima sect which is a very popular sect of Orissa has made a strong impression among the tribal Bhatras of Bastar. This sect is called Alekh Dharam in Bastar. Among the Bhatras, there are two religious divisions, Jagatlok and Bhagatlok. The Jagatloks are those who follow their own tribal 'animistic' religious life. The Bhagatloks are those who have adopted the Alekh Dharam. Alekh Dharam is also known as Satya Mahima Dharam. Originally, this religious tradition was brought from Orissa by the religious preachers of Dhenkanal district. They influenced many adherents of Jagatlok through their rituals. The Bhagatlok Bhatras are advised to leave all their traditional religious beliefs and customs and worship only the formless heavenly father, the supreme authority—Alekh Niranjan Maha-Prabhu. It is found that though the number of Bhatras of Bhagatlok group is very less, those who have adopted Alekh Dharam follow the rules and regulations of the Satya Mahima Dharam very strictly. Everyday they get up before sunrise, bathe and pray to the supreme authority—Alekh Niranjan. They do it twice daily. In the morning they pray seven times facing east, and in the evening five times facing west. They take their meal before sunset. They are vegetarian and do not take liquor. The Bhagatlok Bhatras do not worship any of the tribal deities but they participate in the tribal festivals of Jagatlok. They do not worship any village deity, family deity or their deceased ancestors. They only worship Alekh Niranjan—the supreme authority. Because of religious transformation, the Bhagatlok section is also influenced in other spheres. Among these people, there exists a system of tribal stratification, involving three divisions—Bade Bhatra, Manjhla Bhatra and San Bhatra.

Table 1

Name of the Deities, Worships, Purpose and Level of Syncretism

	Name of the deity/ festival	*Month of worship/ season*	*Level of worship*	*Chief performer*	*Other performers*	*Locality*	*Purpose*	*Remarks*
1.	Pen deity (Clan deity of the tribals)	In all rituals and festivals	Community level	Tribals of Bastar (Abujh Maria, Dandami Maria, Muria, Dorla, etc.)	The non-tribal Hindu communities. They take the help of Anga Deo and Pat Deo the Pen deities of the tribals like the Dandami Marias, Abujh Marias and the Murias, during their important festivals to drive out all the evils and to keep the place safe and pure.	Pen-rawar (seat of Pen deity) and also the place where other rituals are performed.	Tribals worship their Pen deities to show reverence to the deity from whom they have originated. Again, both the tribals and non-tribal Hindus take help of those deities to get protection from all evils and also to detect evil if there is any.	
2.	Bhum/Matti Deo/Tallur Mutte/Talin Devi	In all rituals associated with agricultural operation. Special ritual is performed in Chait (March-April).	Village level/ Community level	All the tribals and non-tribal Hindu communities of Bastar.	—	Village sacred place meant particularly for the deity.	Welfare and especially to get a good harvest.	Bhum is called Matti Deo by the non-tribal Hindus and Tallur Matte by the Abujh Marias and Talin by the Dandami Marias and the Murias.

Contd...

Contd...

3.	Gaon Devi Puja	Anytime	Village level/ Community level	All the tribals and non-tribal Hindu communities of Bastar.	—	Village sacred place.	For the protection of the village.	
4.	Kaksar	Pre-monsoon	Community level	Abujh Maria	All the tribal communities such as Dandami Maria, Muria, etc. and all the non-tribal Hindu communities of Bastar.	Village sacred place especially at the Pen-rawar.	Before starting the agricultural operation, to get a successful harvest and also for the welfare of the village.	
5.	Bali Mela	Ashar (June-July)	Village level	Non-tribal Hindu communities of Bastar.	All the tribal communities of Bastar.	Village sacred place.	With a prayer to get rain which is needed for cultivation and which will give them bumper crop.	
6.	Dashahra	Aswin (September-October)	Whole of Bastar.	Non-tribal Hindu communities of Bastar.	All the tribal communities of Bastar, and also scheduled castes.	Jagdalpur and Dantewada.	Welfare	The deity is actually the tutelary deity of the kings of Bastar who belong to the Kakatiya Vans but ultimately the kings of Bastar gave different responsibilities of the rituals and functions to several tribal and non-tribal Hindu communities and it became the most important ritual of the district.

Contd...

Contd...

7.	Lakshmi Jagar	Aghan or Pand (November-December)	Village level/ Family level	Non-tribal Hindu communities (especially cultivating caste group—Dhakar, in the village).	Non-tribal Hindus and all the tribal communities of Bastar.	Household/ village sacred place.	Wealth, prosperity and welfare of the family/village.
8.	Marai	Paus (January-February)	Village level	Non-tribal Hindu communities.	All the non-tribal Hindus and tribals of Bastar.	Village sacred place.	Harvest festival

But the Bhagatlok Bhatras do not attach themselves to any tribal strata. They believe in equality of all human beings and ignore their traditional tribal status. However, they agree that there are two groups of people within Bhatra tribe, one the Jagatlok and another the Bhagatlok. They do not have any restrictions on marrying a Jagatlok girl provided the bride adopts the Bhagatlok religious order after her marriage but they never allow the marriage of their girls with persons belonging to the Jagatloks.

Compared to followers of Mahima cult, the followers of Christianity are many in Bastar. The Christian missionaries occupy a very important position among the people of Bastar. There are several churches belonging to diverse denominations such as Roman Catholic, Protestant, Lutherans and Pentecostal. There are schools, health centres and ashrams run by these missionaries. Through their social services and sympathetic attitude, they easily impose their faith on the simple tribal people. Many people, especially those belonging to the Dhurwa, Halba and migrant Oraon tribes and lower castes such as Mahara have been influenced and have adopted Christianity. They are taught to worship the heavenly father, the supreme authority, leaving all their religious beliefs and practices. Nevertheless, in practice it is observed that though these people have adopted the new religion, they could not leave all of their old religious beliefs and thoughts. Thus, after each harvest when the crops are collected, it is brought to the church to offer symbolically to the god and side by side they also offer the same crops to their own ancestral (tribal) deities. During the time of marriage and other life cycle rituals, the Christian people observe many of the traditional religious customs. In this way the people of Bastar have mingled the new religious beliefs and practices with old beliefs in their culture life (See Table 1 showing the distribution of deities and types of festivals and levels of religious synthesis).

Discussion

From time immemorial Bastar has been a stronghold of the Gond sub-tribes, who pursue tribal religious beliefs. The founder king of Bastar dynasty while coming from Warangal brought with him the tutelary goddess, Danteshwari, the mother goddess. Through this mother goddess cult the Bastar kings tried to unite all Bastar tribes who possessed a tribal 'Mata cult', in different names, in different villages, such as Sitala Mata, Maoli Mata, etc. The tribal deities who are genealogically related with each other and who are linked with Mata cult weaved the cultural fabric of the tribal communities who are spread in different villages of Bastar.

Keeping in view this religious background of the Bastar tribes, the kings of Bastar were able to exercise their political control mainly through imposition of a centralized Danteshwari Devi, a female religious cult and by assimilating many local female deities and tribal rituals also in propitiation of the Danteshwari Devi, which culminated in the annual celebration of Dashahra festival, involving Hindus, tribals and Dalits of the entire Bastar region. The reformatory movements, such as Baba cult and Mahima sect, which arose in different tribal pockets of Bastar, did have their influences in varied degrees, with their measures of the counter philosophy, but such movements could not eradicate the strong bases of tribal Mata cults buttressed by a tribal priesthood, though the tribals did amalgam their localized Matas with the centralized Brahmanical cult of Danteshwari, thus giving birth to a unique synthesized religious philosophy, which had the blessings of the Hindu Bastar kings.

Note

1. Part of data used in this paper are collected by Dr. (Miss.) Smira Dasgupta, and Dr. Amitabh Sarkar under the research project 'Fairs and Festivals of Tribal Bastar'. This paper with emphasis on religious synthesis is written specially for this volume. The authors had benefited from the ethnographic and editorial suggestions of Dr. N.K. Das during preparation of this paper.

References

Das, N.K., 1982, Tribal Unrest in Bastar. In *Tribal Development in India.* Ed. Buddhadeb Chaudhury. New Delhi: Inter-India Publications.

Firth, Raymond, 1996, *Religion: A Humanist Interpretation,* London: Routledge.

Grigson, Wilfred, 1991, *The Maria Gonds of Bastar.* Delhi: Oxford University Press (Reprint).

Hajra, D., 1970, *The Dorla of Bastar.* Memoir-17, Calcutta: Anthropological Survey of India.

Majumdar, D.N., 1944, *Races and Culture of India*, Lucknow: Universal Publishers Ltd.

Majumdar, D.N., 1948, *Matrix of Indian Culture,* Lucknow: Universal Published Ltd.

Sarkar, Amitabha and Samira Dasgupta, 1986, *Spectrum of Tribal Bastar* Delhi: Agam Kala Prakashan.

Sunder, Nandini, 1997, *Subalterns and Sovereigns: An Anthropological History of Bastar 1854--1996* New Delhi: Oxford University Press.

Vidyarthi, L.P., 1968, "Cultural Change in the tribes of Modern India", 55th Indian Science Congress, Varanasi; Presidential Address of Anthropology Section.

22

Religious Syncretism and Cultural Homogenization in North-East India

N.K. Das

The social formation and the cultural traditions observable in the north-east are archetype of pre-owned cultural traditions of Mongoloid tribes who came to India via the Burmese Pass and through other routes in historical past. The Kuki-Chin-Mizo, Naga, as also the Tai-Shan tribes such as the Ahom, Khamti, Khamyang, Turung, Aiton and Phakials entered through upper Burma (Bareh, 1993). The Bodos are regarded as the earliest settlers of North-East India. The Ahoms gradually expelled the Bodo-Kacharis from their fertile river valleys, virtually forcing them to change their habitation areas. In specific spheres of political identification and cultural mobilization, consequently the Bodoization process had been gradually replaced by the Ahomization process (Das, 1996), which had implications for the future course of cultural evolution in Assam.

The cultural charm of the tribes of North-East India, their social structures, their vibrant religious tenets and their harmonic relationship with the environment have demonstrated a rare capacity to survive. In different historical phases discrepant contacts with Buddhism, Hinduism and Christianity had caused transformation of tribal religious beliefs in this region, but this process may be characterized as sporadic. Known as Kamarupa, as also Pragjayotisha in historical past, Assam was regarded as the legendary home of magic, witchcraft and Tantra. The Kamakhya temple came to be recognized as the seat of Shakta tradition. The Bodo-Kachari tribe, before the advent of the Ahom era, had established itself over major parts of Assam, around the second millennium BC. The ruling clans of this tribe and rulers of several other tribal states such as the Meitei, Ahom, Tripuri, Kachari, Koch and Jaintia had adopted Hinduism, but there was a sluggish expansion of Hinduism among the common tribal people. The Sanskritization process in Assam plains had commenced in a methodic manner with the appearance of the Brahma movement that fascinated several Bodo tribes. Nevertheless, this process stopped short of the hills. In the north-east, unlike peninsular India, the Hinduization process never operated as an all-encompassing phenomenon. Gait has elucidated this process succinctly:

> In the Brahmaputra valley, large sections of population are still outside the pale of Hinduism at the beginning of this century, in the lower stages of conversion where their adopted religion still sits lightly on them and they have not yet learnt to resist the temptation to indulge in pork, fowls and other articles regarded by the orthodox as impure. The reason seems to be that in early days the Hindu settlers confined their attention to the king and his chief nobles. They would convert them, admit the nobles to Khastriya rank. They would not interfere with the tribal religious rites as to do so would call forth the active animosity of native priests; nor would they trouble about the beliefs of the common people who would continue to hold to their old religious notions. If the dynasty lasted long enough, the influence of Hindu ideas would gradually filter down—as actually happened in the case of Ahoms (1905).

The term Assam is derived from the term *Aham* (unequalled, peerless) which was given to the Ahoms, in admiration, by the local tribes (Gait, 1905:241). From the thirteenth to the sixteenth centuries and beyond, the Ahoms influenced and shaped the culture of Assam. The Ahom country, however, never became part of the Mugal empire. Hence, Islam had negligible presence in the region. The Ahoms established peace with various hill tribes though the Singphos and the Nagas remained most troublesome. Cultural contacts between the hills-people and the Ahoms were minimal. The cultural and religious traditions of the hills thus remained undiminished and unaltered to a great extent, till the arrival of the British, who blatantly encouraged the spread of Christianity in the hills, along with extension of education. Following the Ahom practice, the British also established peace with several hill peoples. The Inner Line Regulation (1873), introduced by the British, further isolated the tribes and severely constrained entry of plains-people into different hill areas and vice versa.

The religious traditions of the tribal people in colonial ethnographies are mentioned and characterized as animistic, which belittled the entire gamut of tribal religion. Tribal people of north-east indeed possess a wider world view and thus they believe in continuity amongst mankind, nature and supernatural forces. Thus a great deal of uniformity is observed among the Naga tribes with regard to the notions about the moon and the sun. The Naga tribes regard the rainbow as the heavenly bridge, the path of a god (Das, 1994a). Several Adi tribes of Arunachal Pradesh worship the sun and moon, Donyi Polo.

In Arunanchal Pradesh, we witness the existence of Buddhist tribes such as Sherdukpen, Monpa, Bugun, Aka, Dhammai, Khampti and Singpho. The adoption of Buddhism of the Tibetan variety by the Monpa and Sherdukpen of western Arunachal Pradesh, and of the South-East Asian variety of Buddhism by the Tai-Khampti and Singpho of eastern and southern Arunachal Pradesh, provides two examples of the differential adoption of religious traits in the region. In fact, besides the existence of Buddhism, we also witness the spread and continuation of Bon religion among the Monpas. In Tripura also the Buddhist Chakma people continue to profess and worship tribal deities, alongside Buddhism, in a syncretistic manner.

The phenomenal rise of Christianity in all north-east states, except Arunachal Pradesh, has accelerated cultural transformation considerably. The Naga, Mizo, Kuki, Khasi and Garo are the prominent Christian tribes. Christianity has introduced not only a new belief system but also a new identity. Our analysis of empirical evidences narrated below suggests that Christianity has not led to complete abandonment of original tribal religious convictions and practices. We thus notice a certain degree of cultural oscillation between opposed sets of ideals belonging to different religious traditions. There is least influence of Islam in North-East India. It has some influence in Assam, Manipur and Meghalaya. Hajo in Assam is a unique Muslim sacred centre. It is equated with Mecca symbolically and referred to as Pao Mecca. It has a Hindu temple and a Buddhist shrine at the same site, by the side of the mosque. Most people visiting any of these shrines invariably offer prayers in other shrines. Hajo thus epitomizes the inimitable tradition of cultural homogenization and religious fusion in the region.

We will discuss below, the dominant patterns of culture-change and religious transformation witnessed in different states of north-east India with special emphasis on culture-contact situations and adoption of new religious/sectarian beliefs and practices on part of the tribespeople who, as we will discuss, consistently pursued multiple religious traditions, in different historical periods.

Assam

Since AD 1126, Buddhist Tantriks, Sahajiyas and Naths from Bengal and Mahayana Buddhists of northern India had gradually penetrated into Assam. Shakti cult had established the ethos of indulgence in wine, meat and animal sacrifice and a variety of esoteric practices. Several branches of the Vajrayana and Sahajyana orders of Buddhism, mixed with magic and monistic philosophy had been merged. In such an environment of the fifteenth century, Sri Shankar Dev (1449–1569) introduced a neo-Vaishnavite sect. For both the tribal and non-tribal people of Assam, he was a preacher, philosopher, poet and social reformer. Following the Buddhist traditions, Sankara Dev designated his form of initiation as *Sarana,* and divided it into three categories, as *Nama-sarana, Guru-sarana,* and *Bhakta-sarana* corresponding to the Buddhists' Dharma-sarana, Buddha-sarana and Sangha-sarana. His congregational prayer house came to be called *Nama-ghara* where he installed the 'holy book' on a wooden pedestal and where the *kirtan* is held. Sri Shankar Deva preached the idea of salvation through faith and prayer rather than sacrifice. He discarded idol worship and established monotheism. The *Namaghara/Kirtana ghara* complex came to be known as Satra. The Mahapurushia Vaishnavism, however, got split into four schools soon after the death of Sri Shankar Dev (Brahma Samahati, Purusha Samahati, Kala Samahati and Nika Samahati). Kala Samahati contained the elements of the last phase of Tantrism of the Buddhist Vajrayana school (Dutta, 1978:250; Neog, 1976:240). Its followers came to be known as Rati Khowa (they had nocturnal dinner after performance of esoteric rites). They do not follow the orthodox system, hence they are called Aaritian (Athparia, 2000). In post-Shankar Deva period, however, what exists as Hinduism has developed through multiple processes of conflict, accommodation and syncretism.

Because of the Vaishnavite movement many plains' tribal societies had become members of different *satras*. For its own survival, however, the neo-Vasihnavism in Assam compromised with many pre-conversion cultural traditions of tribal adherents in different historical phases. The number of the neo-Vaishnavite monasteries-*satras* continued to grow and provided an outlet to the people to become *bhaktas*. In Assam, different segments of castes and tribes responded to Hinduism and neo-Vaishnavite faith and customs in various manner. In one example of cultural change, thus, we notice that while the entire Chapra section of the Koch substantially embraced the Hinduism, the Song Koch refused to set off the Chapra example of culture-change. Among the Rabha, the Rongdani segment was among the first to sanskritize its customs, but its acceptance into Hindu fold could hardly occur in the true sense. Some sections among the Lalung, Dalu, Karbi, Hajong and Garo transformed their cultural practices by resorting to ceremonial cleanliness, stern endogamy, taboo for eating 'unclean' animals, veneration of deities adopted from Hindu pantheon and employment of Brahman priests for life-cycle rituals, through adoption of neo-Vaishnavite Hinduism, but still many tribal rituals, and particularly the matrilineal customs and rules regulating property and kinship relations survived among them. The Koch community of Kamarupa was originally a tribe, like the Ahom (Das, 1994a). However, after the accomplishment of Hinduism process, the Koch came to provide a model of emulation to new 'Hinduized' Assamese tribes. Guha (1991) observed that to become Koch meant more than mere religious conversion. It meant the adoption of the plough in place of hoe, mud-plinth dwelling in place of pile-house dwelling and cremation of the dead. The tribes could progressively realize the caste status of the Koch through stages, and the process of promotion of the Bodo-Kachari, Mikir and other such tribes up the ladder of sanskritization had been continuous (Guha, 1991:19). The Hinduized sections of the Kachari, Lalung and Mikir/Karbi thus came to be called increasingly as Koch in some parts of Assam. In Assam-north Bengal area, however, the expression 'Koch' came to be regarded as dishonourable and hence it was abandoned in favour of the appellation Rajbanshi.

Culture change and religious transformation in tribal societies accelerated the process of ethnic boundary maintenance. Moreover, new ethnic labels were adopted increasingly. Thus followers of different religions not only distinguished themselves from each other deliberately; they also branded themselves differently. Chutiya and Deuri are thus today names of the Hinduized and non-Hindu sections of the Chutiya tribe. Vast populace of tribal tea garden labourers of Assam also adopted the Assamese language and festivals of Assam, such as Bihu, often ignoring their old folk dances.

Tribes of central and upper Assam were generally fascinated by diverse offshoot sects which grew often under the influence of *Eka Sarna-Nam-Dharma* such as Matak, Kalasmhati and Mayamara. These sects often advocated varied ideologies through their *Nama gharas*. With the introduction of the institutions of *Nam-ghara* and *Satra* the temple culture came to an end in Assam. While in Mayamara *Satra* (religious centre) a secular orientation is emphasized, the Mataks came to reject the Brahman priesthood and Brahmanical ritualism.

The Ahoms continued to perform their tribal religious beliefs and practices (Das and Gupta, 1982). There are villages in upper Assam inhabited by Ahom tribal priests (Mohans and Deodhais). With the adoption of Vaishnavism, the Ahoms lost their 'tribal' identity and acquired a Hindu caste-like identity, though there could never grow a viable caste system in Assam, as most occupational/professional castes (of *jajamani* system) never existed in Assam. There are family rituals like *damak diya* which resembles Hindu *sradha* ritual. There are some typical Ahom rituals such as Rik-Khvan (meant for Ahom god Leng dom) wherein several old deities are jointly worshipped. Umpha-puja is a community festival. They also worship the epical tribal ancestor during me-dam-me-phi ceremony. The Ahoms celebrate Janmashtami and Tithi of Sri Sankardev in the *namghara*. This is more common among Ahom sections such as Changmais, Bhuyans and Chetias. The Tai priestly sections of the Ahom tribe are least sanskritized, as they continue to have faith in supernatural powers and they also sacrifice pigs and fowls. Often the Ahom priests make utterances in Tai language (Das and Gupta, 1982).

Under the Ahoms the *khels*, groups of occupational families, existed and provided support to the Ahom kingdom. Some Hindu and Muslim artisan castes, Kumhar, Hira, Dhobis, Sonar, Kasai and Darji, immigrated. They had a low status in society. Towards the last phase of the Ahom rule the process of feudal consolidation in the valley had been established. Hussain (1993:30--33) has divided the pre-colonial Assamese society into two antagonistic categories---the ruling class and the toiling class. The Moamoria 'rebellion' (Sarmah, 1998), a peasant movement, shook the foundation of the Hinduized Ahom state. The followers of a neo-Vaishnavite monastery, called Moamara Satra provided the leadership to this armed struggle.

There has been a long tradition of cultural and religious revivalism among the Tai Ahoms of upper Assam (Das *et al.*, 1982). The All Assam Ahom Association, established in 1893, was the oldest cultural organization. The Ahom leaders propagated that Hinduism was not their original religion and it was introduced by the Ahom kings (Das, 1989). As a result of these movements the status and importance of Brahmanism gradually declined in upper Assam. In 1976, Ahom Tai Rajya Parishad came into existence in the wake of reorganization of Assam in 1967 and then a wider organization Ujani Asom Rajya Parishad came into existence. Through these efforts Ahoms have been able to revive many of their old religious customs. The fact remains that traditional Ahom religion had never died out and several families of Ahom priests such as Deva Dhai, Mohama and Bailong had never adopted Hinduism. These Ahom priests had always celebrated old Ahom ceremonies such as Umpha and Me-dam-me-phi regularly (Das *et al.*, 1982).

The Bodo-Kacharis, whom Endle (1911) described as 'animistic', constitute the largest tribal group of plains of Assam. According to Hira Charan Narjinari, (2002) what we know of the history of Assam is in fact the history of the Bodos. The Bodos believe in several gods and goddesses. Their chief god is Bathou. Hence their religion is called Bathou religion. Bathou was never represented in idol form. His living symbol is the Siju tree. The Baisagu festival of the Bodos has been adopted by the Assamese and is now called Bihu. The word Bihu is made up of two Bodo words—'Bi' meaning beg and 'Ho' meaning give (Narjinari, 2002).

Various cultural, linguistic, religious and political movements have been launched among them since Independence. A prime factor in development of cultural consciousness among the Bodo-Kachari has been the spread of Brahma sect among them. Kalicharan Mech, founder of Brahma sect, wrote a book *Saraniya Kriya*. The basic tenets of Brahmaism are contained in the phrase 'chandrama surjya narayane jyoti' (May the sunlight dispel all darkness and lead us to Brahma). A basic mantra of the new religion has been '*om sat guru*'. Some scholars have described Brahma religion as a cult (Saikia, 1982). According to the ethical dictums of the Brahma cult, neither idolatory nor sacrifice are permitted (Saikia, 1982). The followers of the Brahma religious traditions abstain from drinking rice beer and eating fish or meat.

The Rabhas are found in south Kamrup and south Goalpara districts of Assam and also in north Garo Hills districts of Meghalaya, where they have five distinct ethnic segments, Rongdani, Maitori, Pati, Dahori and Koch. The Rabhas are traditionally a matrilineal tribe but prolonged contacts with the Hindu communities have ushered in cultural change and thus some of the Rabha sub-tribes have adopted Hindu kinship traditions, though inheritance and descent rules continue to be matrilineal and the mother's property is inherited by the daughter and father's property by the son in many areas. The Pati and Dahori sub-tribes of Rabhas are Hinduized sections, but they continue to worship tribal deities too. Majumdar observed different degrees of sanskritization among different sections of the Rabha (Majumdar, 1968). Thus, the Pati Rabhas belonged to the top and the Rangdani Rabhas to the bottom of ritual order. In Garo Hills, the Rongdani Rabha have retained their traditional tribal deities. These Rabhas (Majumdar, 1968) have not been affected to any considerable extent by neighbouring Hinduized tribes. However, the Kachari neighbours have adopted two deities of the Rongdani Rabhas. The Rongdanis did not adopt any deity from the Hindu pantheon (Majumdar, 1969).

The Koch, Dalu, Hajong and some families of Garo have adopted Vaishnavism and they employ some professional castes, as barber, but in the same area, the Rongdani Rabhas adhere to 'traditional faith'. In certain respects however the Rongdani have imitated some cultural traits of the Hinduized tribals particularly their abstinence from beef and strict prohibition of inter-dining with 'beef-eating' non-Hindu peoples, such as Muslims and the Garo (Majumdar, 1968).

According to Mazumdar (1968), "If we compare religious practices as well as the social framework of the Rongdani with those of the Koch and the Hajong, we witness that there is a gradual infusion of more and more aspects of Hinduism as well as traditional Hindu social framework characterized by absence of matrilineal clans, adoption of Indo-Aryan kinship system (for example, treating the mother's brother's daughter as a sister). Thus we find the Rongdani in their pure tribal form, while the Hajong emerge as a purely Hindu caste, albeit at the lower end of the hierarchy, and the Koch occupy an intermediate position, because in them we find a good blending of traditional Hinduism with forms of pre-sanskritized religion and also aspects of a pre-sanskritized social framework represented by prevalence of matrilineal clan organization combined with a matching kinship terminology. So, here is a tribe which has aligned itself with the Hindus, though strictly speaking remains outside the sphere of Hinduism. In conclusion, it can safely be said that the Rongdani Rabha represent only the first stage (the incipient stage) of sanskritization—they are yet to enter the Hindu society. Here we witness the archetypal north-east mode of partial preservation of tribal religious traditions and partial adoption of certain Hindu traditions. This is indeed a unique example of religious syncretism (Das, 2002).

In his study of social movements among the Rajbanshis of Assam and north Bengal area who experienced only the fractional impact of Sri Sankar Dev's sect, Biman Das Gupta (1969) observed that, "The Koch tribe, on completion of Hinduization, took the honorific appellation of Rajbanshi ('men of royal race') to claim Kshatriya status." The first attempt towards re-designation of Rajbanshi as Rajbanshi-Kshatriya dates back to post-1901 census. Spread of Vaishnavism in the Rajbanshi area dates back to the 16th century when Sri Sankardeva held great sway in the area, as a result of which the Rajbanshi adopted Kirtan. The development of the Bhakti cult in Assam seems to be independent of the process of Kshatriyization.

An attempt was made around 1950 in Assam, especially in Goalpara district to establish the Sadau Assam Koch Rajbanshi Kshatriya Samiti, bringing 'thread-wearing' and 'non-thread-wearing' Koch and Rajbanshi under a common banner. This Samiti advocated the ethnic and cultural oneness of the Koch and Rajbanshi. Das Gupta (1969) wrote that, "in the same Rajbanshi area, where Sri Sankaradev preached his Vaishnavite ideas (in order that the ritual laden religion be replaced by a more simple, non-sacrificial method of ritual practice), we witness the existence of a very cruel and crude form of animal sacrifice, side by side with the usual method of sacrifice by one stroke".

The Song Kochs provide a unique example of coexistence of tribal religious practices and Hindu religious practices. In his study, Majumdar (1968) observed different stages of absorption of Hinduism among different groups of the Koch. Thus the Chapra section showed total transformation of tribal religion and adoption of Hinduism, while other sections showed adoption of only some deities from the Hindu pantheon. Among the Song Koch three types of mystical and supernatural beings are recognized: (1) Deities adopted from the Hindu pantheon, responsible for general well-being; (2) Tribal supernatural beings capable of doing harm to individuals; (3) Tribal-clan-deities, such as Nikini-wai, doing no harm to individuals.

For Hindu deities, a sacred place near the village known as *deothan* or *waithan* is established. Vaishnava Kirtan singers are invited for singing. For Kamakhya and Kali worship, the priests are selected from within the tribal community by the traditional Koch method (Majumdar, 1968). Bani Kanta Kakati (quoted in Majumdar, 1968) has traced the origin of Shib (Shiva) and Kamakhya worship in Assam to non-Aryan origin. According to Kakati (1960), worship of these deities was prevalent among the Kiratas, the Tibeto-Burman speaking predecessors of the Aryans. Majumdar suspects that the worship of these deities by the Koch tribals may be a continuance of their original religious practice. According to Gait (1905:58), in the Kirata form of the worship of these deities swine and cocks were sacrificed and rice beer was offered. Dance by a woman before the deity—*deodhani nach*—was a part of the rites. Further, the Song Koch do not associate *yoni* and *linga* with rites of Kamakhya and Shiva respectively (Majumdar, 1968; Das, 1989). We may surmise that among the Song Koch, Hinduism has had little influence. Brahman priesthood is generally rejected and tribal priests worship Hindu deities. Majumdar has rightly concluded that "the Song Koch are only half way in the adoption of Hinduism" (1968). The Song Koch term for priest is Deosi. The Deosis of Kali and Kamakhya and their Thengadhora Deosis refrain from taking pork and fowl meat as also rice beer. Among the Koch, tribal deity Balai continues to be worshipped along with Hindu deities, though only rich Koch households perform Balai worship involving a feast to all villagers... Women are not allowed to go near the place of his worship (1968).

The Assam plains tribals show no universal trend of religious change, though impact of Vaishanvism particularly through several distinct sects has been most visible trend. The Karbi, earlier called Mikirs, are one tribe who have strongly preserved their traditional cultural and religious traits, like mortuary practices, despite their adoption of the Lakhimon Sangha sect and also Christianity to a limited extent. Christianity made inroads into the Mikir area only in 1904 when the Gospel was translated into Karbi language as *Birta Keme*. But Christianity could hardly influence them as they remained very much tradition-bound (Parampanthi, 1978). The Karbis, like most tribes of Assam are pantheists. The Karbi religion is centred on 'Arnam Kethe' or Hemphu. On the basis of my data collected in Karbi villages, the religion of the Karbis may be described as 'ancestor worship' oriented. In view of excess reliance of Karbis on magic, cabalism and curing diseases through divination drew the attention of Lakhimon Dev, who initiated a new method of Vaishnavite faith (Parampanthi, 1978). Guru Lakhimon's discourse is a variation of Vaishnavism. He allowed followers to eat fish and said that through proper teaching, food and synchronized habit one can acquire *satvic* quality. The followers of Lakhimon Sangha maintain a private chapel 'guruthan', which resembles a 'naamghara'. Guru Lakhimon's initiation mantra is *Hare Hemphu*. It should be noted that Hemphu is original tribal god of the Karbis. They do not worship any image nor do they follow any rituals (Parampanthi, 1978).

The north Cachar area has been traditionally inhabited by the Bodo/Boro, Dimasa, Nepali/Gorkha and the Nagas, though Dimasa Cachari form the numerically most dominant population. The north Cachar tribal area of Assam has witnessed a strong wave of Hinduization. It has a hilly terrain and the people have least scope of culture contact, still 81 per cent local population, according to the 1961 census were Hindus. This increase may also be due to gradual emigration of non-tribal population during this period (Danda, 1994). Among the two major groups it is the Dimasa who have assimilated Hinduism without disturbing their value system (Danda, 1994). According to Danda, the process of Hinduization has been "a spontaneous process of assimilation. In this process they have never been drifted from their own culture, never got engulfed within Hindu social structure. Perhaps the tribes of North-East India present a unique case of becoming Hindu, being away from the Hindu hierarchical system" (1994). As observed among Hinduized sections of many plains tribes of north-east, the Hinduized tribespeople of north Cachar do not take services of the Brahmans.

The process of cultural transformation in north-east is often influenced by imitation of the cultural practices of allied ethnic groups. Thus, influenced and through their closer contact with the Christianized Nagas of Manipur, a section of Zemi Nagas in the neighbourhood of the Dimasa opted to become Christians. A section among them also opted to join the Naga religious cult, Heraka, introduced by Jadonang.

In the Udalguri area of Assam the tribals came to be influenced both by the Hindus and Christians. A section of Buddhists live at a distance of thirty kilometres from Udalguri. The original inhabitants of the area are the Bodo-Kacharis. The Santals and Nepalis were the first immigrants. After Udalguri was connected by railway line in 1932, Assamese traders came to this area. According to Goswami (1978), the Christian missionary activities started in 1926 and some Hinduized Bodos were converted. The main cause of conversion from Hinduism to Christianity on part of the tribals was a feeling of insecurity and subjugation experienced by the tribals. Most of the conversions were done by the Scottish Mission and as such majority of the converts were Protestants (1978). The Catholic Mission entered this part of Assam only after 1960. Christianity is prevalent mostly among the Bodos and Santals. There were a few Nepali Christians in the area. At the early stage of conversion to Christianity the Bodos gave up drinking country liquor but in course of time they resumed consumption of rice beer. According to Goswami (1978), the Christian missionaries worked hard among tribals—offered medical and even economic help to the victims of the Barpetia moneylenders. There are however some Bodos and Santals who refused to embrace 'foreign religion' (1978). Among the Hindus of the area there are several sects like neo-Vaishnavasim, Sahankari Dharma and Shakta sect. The Hindu Bodos continue to worship the tribal deity Bathou. Sometimes this deity is equated with Shiva (Goswami, 1978; Narjinari, 2002).

The Mishing of Lakhimpur, Dibrugarh, Sibsagar and Darang districts of Assam originally lived in hill ranges of Miri hills of Arunachal Pradesh.

According to Doley (1984) the Mishing religion is based on a belief in supernaturalism. The Mishing religion today is not a unified system based on tribal beliefs. After migration and coming in contact with other religions of the plains, the Mishings have adopted the *Bhakatiya-panth*, which refers to performing religious functions through the help of the Bhakatas. Despite great influence of Bhakatiya religion, the Mishing continue to worship some tribal deities such as Dobiurvie and celebrate tribal religious festivals. Bhakatiya functions are supervised by the *Sadhus*.

Thus the *Bhakatiya* cult as adopted and practised by the Mishings is a result of amalgamation of Mishing tribal religion, neo-Vaishnavism and Tantrik religious traditions. The Mishing Bhakatas recite religious verses, particularly the verses from Panthi holy books. The Bhakatiya sect has eroded the base of tribal religion considerably but at the same time the adopted Vaishnavite rituals have been influenced by the pre-existing Tantrik cults of the tribal Mishings. Thus the spirits are propitiated by offering *apong* (rice beer) and meat which are consumed by the Bhakatiyas themselves.

During thirteenth century the Kachari had a flourishing state. The Ahoms captured most of the Kachari state and thus the segments of Kachari settled in new areas. Thus the Sonowal came to adopt the profession of gold (*son*). Endle (1911) has described the Sonowal Kacharis as the earliest known inhabitants of Brahmaputra valley. This tribe is mainly distributed in Dibrugarh, Sibsagar, Lakhimpur and Tinsukia districts. Gradually, the Sonowal Kachari adopted two Vaishnavite sects called Sarania and Bhajania. The former have no restrictions but the Bhajaniyas have to follow certain food restrictions. Despite adoption of Vaishnavite Hinduism, the Sonowal Kachari follow their traditional religious, magical beliefs, customs and supernatural powers. They believe in magical powers of medicine-men such as Bez, who treats the sufferers. The belief that illness is a punishment for wrong doing is widespread among these tribes people (Barua and Phukan, 1998).

The Mataks are the followers of the Mayamara sect. They form a religious sect which has followers from different tribes (Dutta, 1985). The caste Hindus are also adherents of this sect. Thus the Kachari, Moran, Ahom, Chutiya, Barahis, Britials and Kaibarta are all followers of same homogenizing Matak sect. During the sixteenth century, Anuruddha Deva initiated a large number of tribals as his disciples and established the neo-Vaishnavite Mayamara sect, at Moamara. These disciples were called Mataks. The Mataks today are distributed in Dibrugarh, Darrang, Lakhimpur, Sibsagar and Nagaon districts of Assam. According to Sadou

Assam Matak Sanmilan, the Matak population is 1.2 million (Baruah, 1977, quoted in Bezbaruah, 1996). Mayamara Satra is the main religious centre of the Mataks. Though the Mayamara satra is based on the tenets of Sri Sankardev's *eka sarna-nam-dharma,* the Mataks subscribe to Kalasamhati philosophy, which is a religious philosophy. According to this religious philosophy, Guru himself occupies an exalted position like God. Hence, no idol worship is done in Mayamara satra. Worship of idols is forbidden among the followers of this sect, and it is substituted by simple observances of *Nama* (recitation of prayers) and *bhakti.* Main features of Kalasamhati philosophy are: supreme position of Guru (Guru is human incarnation of God), emphasis on egalitarianism, softening the vigour of caste-system and discarding of idol-worship. A strong emphasis is laid on equity and brotherhood among the followers.

The Mataks do not follow any Brahmanical ritual and the Brahmans have no roles in their religious performances. There is absence of use of flowers and basil leaves in the rituals. Only an earthen lamp of mustard oil is kindled in front of their holy book, *Bhakti Mangal.* All their festivities are sect-oriented.

Usually, the religious services and functions of the Mataks are performed in front of their sacred scriptures (the *Bhakti Mangal Sastra*). These are installed on the *asana* (the tray). The singing of hymns called *nama prosanga* and the chanting of prayers which are composed by Mayamara Gurus, with the accompaniment of Satra musical instruments, constitute the main features of devotional services of the Mayamaras. The Gayan-bayan, the Satra orchestra party, with music-cum-dance performance is the most distinctive feature of the Matak (Gogoi, 1977: 30–37, quoted in Bezbaruah, 1996). It is drastically different from the traditions of other Vaishnava Satras of Assam where the *kirtana* is performed by playing *khol* and *tal* in a rhythmic motion and in standing posture. They never clap their hands while singing. Another important feature of the Mayamara Satras is the conspicuous absence of *bhaona* (religious performance).

A secular orientation is always emphasized in the teachings and practices of the Mayamara Satra. The Satra regulates the Matak socio-cultural life at the community and village level. The Guru is the only preceptor and is considered as a divine embodiment of God. The Bhaktas are indispensable on all socio-religious occasions.

With passage of time, a strong Matak identity has been articulated and forcefully projected though occasionally original ethnic group affiliation is evoked. However, the multi-ethnic homogeneity of Matak identity has never been challenged.

The tea garden tribals who originally belong to eastern India have predominantly assimilated their culture, religion and language with Assamese culture. One Assamese scholar Saikia (1982) identifies these tribal labourers as Cha-Bagichar Assamiya—Assamese of Tea Gardens. The colonial British people had brought these tribal labourers from Jharkhand, Orissa and West Bengal to work in tea gardens of Assam. But a major section of them settled permanently in Assam (Kar, 1981; 2001), though as a peripheral disadvantaged community. They are demanding their recognition as a and insist to be called Adivasi. In Assam they are placed under 'Other Backward Classes' (Singh, 1982). This section of labourers are still called 'the ex-tea garden labour', and also as Bahaniya, Bonua, Mazdoor and Bongali. Though certain sections of migrant tribes even today speak in their own dialects, all of them share a new lingua-franca-Cha Bagichar Ahomiya-'Sadani'. This lingua-franca includes words from Assamese, Bengali, Oriya, Bhojpuri and Hindi.

Most of these tribespeople initially pursued their tribal religions, but the Christian Catholic and Protestant evangelization works among these people from the initial stage of their arrival prompted many to adopt Christianity (Becker, 1980). While more than ten per cent among them have become Christians, even bigger number of tribals have adopted local variants of Hinduism (Kar, 2001). Christianity has brought in a greater sense of unity even at the inter-tribal level involving Munda, Badaik, Oraon, Kharia, Savara, Santal, Bhumij, Kumar, Patir and Panika. Despite visible cultural transformation, most of these tribes have retained their original tribal institutions and cultural-religious traits.

Meghalaya

Christianity is widely practised by the tribes of Meghalaya alongwith tribal religion and Buddhism. The influence of the Ramkrishna mission and Brahmo Samaj has been marginal. The Man are the Buddhist tribe of Meghalaya. They pursue the Pali-Prakrit school of Hinayana Buddhism. They worship the image of Lord Buddha and observe *pancha shila*—five principles of Buddhism, as also *astha shila*. In most Man families,however, the Hindu goddess Laxmi and Saraswati are venerated (Barua, 1994). We witness the process of syncretism operative in this Meghalaya-Assam border.

The first church (a Presbyterian one) in Khasi area was established in Cherapunji area in 1841. Christianity was introduced in Garo Hills in 1863. Nag has based his study in a village called Mission Mairang and Shillong town. He observed that the Christian Khasi population is higher in urban areas and Christianity is slightly higher among the women than men. The greater inclination of the Khasis towards Christianity rather than towards Hinduism or Islam is perhaps also due to the fact that Christianity does not interfere in their habit of eating beef and pork. By analyzing demographic data, Nag (1965) concluded that the proportion of divorce/separation is higher among the non-Christian (for both males and females). Christianity thus seems to have some effect in stabilizing the Khasi marriage, although divorce/separation is not altogether absent among the Christian Khasis. Nag also observed that Christianity has not affected the matrilocal residence pattern of Khasi society. Christianity puts a heavier responsibility on the Khasi men to take care of their wives and children.

The development of Christianity in the Khasi Hills was seen as a challenge by certain Khasis who organized themselves initially under the banner of a young men's association in 1899. During the same period Khasi elders like Babu Jiban Roy and Radhon Singh Berry formed a cultural organization called Seng Khasi. By 1909, Seng Khasi movement had crystallized its objectives as: "to revive the true faith of forefathers, to understand the true meaning of conscience and truth as handed down by them and which were being neglected, misled and blinded by the teachings of the foreigners." Kynpham Singh had vigorously communicated the above objectives in his work *Where lies the Soul of our Race* (1982). The Seng Khasi leaders not only resisted large-scale schism by the Christian missionaries but they also made concerted efforts to codify tenets of Khasi religion (Das, 1989). Thus by 1915, even educated Christian Khasis had openly discussed the issues of virtues of Khasi religious heritage and matriliny through publication of articles in periodicals and newspapers. Even churches had started taking newer stands towards such issues, though the Catholics were more tolerant of Khasi culture than the Presbyterians (Natarajan, 1982:160; Das, 1989; Mukhopadhyay, 1994). By 1919, the Seng Khasi brought out its first non-Christian song book. Even a Christian poet U Soso Tham in his poem *Ki Hynniew Trep* (1937) described the divine origin of the Khasi people (Das, 1989).

The Garo believe in the existence of a supreme being, Tatara Rabuga and several spirits or Mite. The stars, moon and sun are associated with some Mite. The stars are called nonringro-nojingro. The Garos recognize fourteen stars. They believe in an abode of the spirits and that souls do not die. They also believe in re-birth of souls. No ancestor worship was ever practised. It was David Scott who initiated Christianity among the Garos in 1822. Around 1862, the American Baptist Mission began their work among the Garos. In 1870, the Lt. Governor and the Chief Commissioner recommended that Tura should be occupied as a mission station. The Roman Catholic Church Mission came to Garo Hills in 1932 and founded a church at Tura in 1933. The Seventh Day Adventists and the Church of north India are also working in Garo Hills. Before this period, in 1825, David Scott had written to the Secretary to Government of India about his "plan to civilize the Garos through missionary activities" (Majumdar, 1982). The spread of Christianity was coterminous with the spread of education.

The Hajong live in the plains of southern-western region of Garo Hills district. The material cultures and economic statuses of the Hajongs and their neighbours (Koch, Hindu castes, Muslim) are similar. The Hajong and Koch, however, possess good agricultural lands. The Hajong formerly had a strong matrilineal clan organization, which does not survive in totality but matriliny survives among the neighbouring Garo and Koch of Meghalaya. Clan is called *nikini* among the Hajong and Koch. Now the Hajongs trace both the paternal and maternal lines (three generations) for regulation of marriage. With reference to inheritance rule it may be stated that the Hajong are in a transition phase, pursuing both matrilineal and patrilineal rules. No social stigma thus is attached to the son-in-law residing in the bride's house.

The Hajongs, as a result of religious transformation, observe ceremonial defilement during birth, death and the menstrual period of women. In case of birth, the defilement period varies from five days to a month (Majumdar, 1972). Despite considerable degree of Hinduization, whereby patrilineal principles are introduced, the Hajong continue to propitiate a large number of tribal deities and spirits who are responsible for certain illness. Different animals are sacrificed to appease the spirits. Thus since Moila spirit may cause ill-health among children, so a she-goat, duck, cock, hen or pigeon is sacrificed. These rites are performed outside the village. The Hajong exemplify a unique case of religious fusion. Despite a considerable degree of Hinduization, the survival of the Deosi category of tribal priesthood in all Hajong villages is a unique facet of Hajong syncretism.

Elaborating on the Hinduization process, Majumdar (1972) wrote that the Hajongs have abandoned their matrilineal clan organization in the process of acculturation. They have adopted two of the most important elements of Hindu castes, namely, commensality and connubiality. Though both the Koch and the Hajong have adopted these two elements of Hindu castes, they are yet to form an hierarchy among themselves. The form of religion which emerged among the Hajongs does not belong to any particular cult. It can be described as a mixture of tribal beliefs and some elements of the Shakti cult. The influence of the Assamese neo-Vaishnavite movement has left its mark. The neo-Vaishnavites of the Brahmaputra valley have tried to do away with Brahmanical rituals. But even among them, after the death of Sri Sankaradeva, some sects have tried to revert to Brahmanical rites (Majumdar, 1972).

The occasional migration of the Muslims to the Khasi Hills continued over a long period. In course of time, they married Khasi women and adopted the Khasi traditional customs and practices (Mathur, 1975; Langstieh, 2001). Like all other Khasi sub-tribes, the Khasi Muslim have adopted the matrilineal clan title, which are often reflected with Muslim names, but all of them believe in and practise Islamic rites (Langstieh, 2001). The Khasi Muslim community, comprising of different ethnic stocks maintains their relationship with both the maternal and paternal relatives (Roy, 1994).

Nagaland

The Nagas represent a model of synthesis of tradition and modernity. The Nagas have adopted Christianity in large numbers, even though many traditional religious festivals and tribal customs survive among them and the Nagas continue to practise them vigorously (Das, 1993; 1994a; 1994b). The Nagas are highly conservative, traditionalist and orthodox (Das, 1985; 1987; 1993; 1994a; 1994b). In his book *The Angami Nagas*, J.H. Hutton (1921) has fittingly described the Christian members of the Nagas as 'pseudo-Christians'. In many of their writings the colonial ethnographers emphasized the absence of any definite idea about religion among the Nagas. Since Naga life was sought to be projected as bereft of any religion, it was considered an ideal field for success of the missions. Thus the annual report of the Baptist Mission in 1858 recorded the Nagas as "a heathen people whose speedy conversion was possible ...(for) they lack any distinctions of caste or priesthoods" (Pruett, 1974, Misra, 1998).

Christianity has a long tradition in Naga areas. The American Baptist Mission started work in 1836. Encouraged by E.W. Clark (1875--1911), Godhula Brown, an Assamese Christian, started missionary activity in 1842. By 1915, thirty-six churches had been established in Naga hills. Impur, in Ao Naga area of Naga Hills, received special attention ever since establishment of a church there in 1894. It remained an important centre not only of the Ao Nagas, but also of Semas, Lotha, Chang, Phom,

Sangtam and Angami. By 1930, the Naga membership had swelled to 60,000 (Barpujari, 1984). The Roman Catholic Church which started work after Independence made steady progress in evangelical, educational and social service. During 1961–71, Christians constituted 76.29 per cent of the total population. Since 1950, the Christian churches have become independent of foreign missionary support. Christianity has struck its root deep into the Naga Hills and has brought far-reaching changes in every domain of Naga culture and thought. School-work formed a very important part of the missionary programme. Initially the American Baptists used the Assamese language in both teaching and preaching. Gradually the missionaries learnt the important Naga dialects and translated Christian religious material including hymns using Roman script.

The earlier missionaries generally condemned the Naga food, festivals, dress, ornaments and mode of 'primitive living'. They prescribed teetotalism among the converts. They were persuaded to have only one wife. The Christian Naga refrained from participating in 'feasts' of villages, and boys and girls stopped going to *morungs* (dormitories). Christian hymns, Western songs and small tea parties replaced their folk music, war songs and elaborate feasts. Gradually the Nagas lost interest in woodcarving and textiles.

The early British colonial administrators were least concerned with Naga culture. They realized the political advantage of Christian hill tribes 'acting as buffers between Assam and Burma', and the Nagas were envisaged as 'a valuable prop to the state' (Johnston, 1971:25; see in Pruett, 1974; Misra, 1998). In the writings of later colonial authors like J.P. Mills and J.H. Hutton and even Elwin and Furer-Haimendorf, however, the adverse impact of Christianity was deplored. These authors brought to light several 'virtues of the Naga religion' (Mills, 1926). Elwin observed that the missionaries were responsible for the deterioration of the traditional culture, for bringing a dark night to tribal life (1961:78), and for "weakening the communal spirit of sharing" (1957:88). The fact remains that tribal religious specialists continue to exert influence in all Naga villages and even the Christian Nagas have not discarded tribal rituals associated with the agricultural calendar. During prolonged fieldwork (1975–1988) conducted in various parts of Nagaland, this author observed that great interest is shown towards resurgence and concern for their indigenous culture traits among the Nagas. It reflects, according to Pruett (1974), a rigorous programme of indigenous Christianity which has been persistently evident. The Angamis, Aos and other Nagas looked for a recovery of the best in their tradition. Most

Naga tribes even after acceptance of Christianity continued to observe scores of tribal rites and rituals. Among the Zounuo-Keyhonuo Naga (also known as southern Angamis), in Kohima district of Nagaland, the Christian and non-Christian sections equally associate themselves with the agricultural rituals conducted during 'first sowing' and 'first reaping'. They also collectively celebrate Sekrenyie, the major festival, which is celebrated by the whole village in the month of February (Das, 1993).

The Zeliangrong Naga movement among the Nagas was originally planned as an anti-Christian movement. It involved Nagas of Nagaland, Manipur and Assam (Mukherjee, Gupta and Das 1982; Das, 1989). Jadonang (1905--31) was the pioneer of this reformist religious movement. According to M. Kamson (1971) the first phase of this movement was purely religious and social as "the deceitful treatment of the Hindu neighbours towards the backward hillmen on the one hand and advance of proselytizing Christianity on the other hand had brought the darkest hour for the Zeliangrong Naga people to defend and preserve their tradition and religious beliefs" (Kamson, 1975). The Zeliangrong movement has passed through several stages. The initial religious programme was aimed at abolition of irrational customs and superstitions. Gaidinliu led the religious cult Heraka established by Zadonang, after the former was executed. The village of Jadonang, Kambiron slowly became a pilgrimage centre. Later Gaidinliu, who was said to have been installed as a goddess, headed the Heraka religious cult and was its high priestess (Rustomji, 1971: 103; Kabui, 1974). Jawaharlal Nehru recalled his feelings about his meeting with Gaidinliu in Assam prison cells and called her 'Rani' Gaidinliu (Nehru, 1948:187–88). Though ultimately political objectives were incorporated within the Zeliangrong movement, both Jadonang and Gaidinliu had been more religious leaders (Das, 1996). During the colonial period Jadonang started a new cult, Heraka. He preached that there is only one high God in place of many tribal gods. He prescribed ceremonies, which resembled the Hindu Tantrik cult practices (Singh, 1972). Synthesis of Hinduism and animism may be witnessed here.

Manipur

There are thirty-six communities in Manipur. The 1981 census recognized Naga and Kukis as two hill tribes. Manipur has three cultural groups—Meitei, Kuki and Naga. The Meitei, also called Manipuri, are divided into two major religious sections, the Gouriya (the Vaishnavite) and Sanamahi (the adherents of tribal faith). In traditional setting, only the Maharaja and some aristocratic royal families had adopted the

Ramanandi cult of Vaishnavism, particularly during the rule of Garib Nawaz (1709--48). The degraded Meitei were not allowed to embrace this religion, and thus the social distances within Meitei society became sharper. Further divisions were caused by ritual behaviour associated with different sections. Followers and non-followers of Vaishnavism came to be identified as *Asengba* (pure) and *Amangaba* (polluted). Many elements of Meitei tribal religion were, however, retained by the Meiteis. In fact the tribal religion, as observed by Saha (1994) "existed side by side with Vaishnavism". The religion of the Gouriyas indeed displays syncretistic religious features.

Through Vaishnavite Hinduism, the Meitei had sought to project a new ethnic identity and sought to re-establish their old Meitei tradition. Earlier, having been impressed with the alien religion, the people had modified their ethnic name and called the new adherents Gouriya Meitei. When the need to revive old religion was felt, a new name Sanamahi Meitei was accepted (Saha, 1994). Saha has refrained from making any 'religion centred' analysis of the ethnic situation in Manipur and has not spelled it clearly but the fact remains that the basic element of identity marker for the Manipuris in all historical phases has been their religious traits. Indeed their religious identity and ethnic base in the post-change phase had never been fixed; it was fluid in character and this fact is acknowledged by Saha (1994). It is this fluidity of religious domain that we prefer to identify as syncretistic phenomenon within which such characters as opposition, conflict, accommodation and replacement remain inherent and express themselves situationally.

According to Kabui (1977), the sanskritization in Manipur had blurred the cultural identity and self-consciousness of the Manipuris. The exactions of the Brahmans on the common people had made their life pretty miserable. It was a Kachar-based Meitei named Naorria Phullo who organized the anti-Brahman movement and founded the Apokpa Marrup in 1930 in Kachar. This movement also enthused the people of Manipur. Through this movement, the old religion of the Meitei was revived. An attempt was also made to use the original Meitei script which had been forgotten. In 1945, the Meiteei Phurup organization was established to revive the Sanamahi religion. Since the Hindu Manipuris had always worshipped all local deities, local Manipuri scholars, such as Kabui (1977), refuse to call Sanamahi movement a revivalist movement. According to Kabui (1977), the Christian missionaries had spread Western education among the hill people and widened their mental outlook. It also facilitated the penetration of Western ideas. William Pettigrew was the pioneer Christian missionary of Manipur. After joining the American Baptist Mission, he did religious as well as educational work (1977). Pettigrew arrived at Imphal on February 6, 1892 to start a school in the Tangkhul Naga area, in the hills, at Ukhrul. The foundation of the Baptist missionary movement was laid when, in 1907, the Church of Ukhrul was set up. Though the Tangkhul practise the Christian way of marriage, they observe traditional marriage customs to a great extent (Ruivah, 1993: 218). Extra-marital sex relations are regarded as crime for which the punishment of ex-communication, of both man and woman, is enforced. In order to establish their identities, the Christian and non-Christian villagers live in separate localities (Das, 1994b). If Hinduism had revolutionized the life of the Meiteis of the Imphal valley, Christianity had brought tremendous change in the life of the hill tribes of Manipur. Nevertheless, both communities have always shown strong syncretistic tendencies as they continue to observe several cultural and religious rituals of the past.

Arunachal Pradesh

The whole population of Arunachal Pradesh may be divided into three cultural groups on the basis of their social and religious affinities. The first group consists of Buddhists such as Monpas, Khamtis, etc. The second group consists of the Adis, Bangnis, Tagins, etc. They practise tribal religions, such as Donyi Polo. In the third group, the Wanchus and Noctes are included among whom we witness the spread of Vaishnavism to some extent. Many scholars have studied the cultural patterns of Arunachal in terms of Bodic and non-Bodic groups. The non-Bodic religion is based on tribal spirits and deities, oral tradition and absence of priesthood. The seventeenth century saw the rise of Buddhism in Arunachal. In the pre-British era, contact with Tibet had continued. The Lamaistic communities living in the border areas had holy contact with Tibet. They started turning more and more towards India, mainly for commerce (Dutta, 1989:3).

The Monpas follow Mahayana Buddhism, which centres around Tawang monastery. They also continue to follow the old Bon religion. The Sherdukpen religion is a blend of Mahayana Buddhism and tribal magicol-religious beliefs. The Mijis have also come under the influence of Buddhism, though tribal religion survives among them. The Sulung religion is a spirit-based religion. The Akas or Hrussos have come under the influence of both Hinduism and Buddhism. The Nishing, Khowa and the Apa Tani follow tribal religions. The Nishing believe that after death the spirit travels to the 'village of the ancestors'. The hill Miris had long contact with Assam plains. The Na are influenced by Buddhism, but many of their religious beliefs and practices are 'animistic'. The Khambas and Khamtis are Buddhist tribes. The Khamtis are also Buddhists but they also believe in a host of tribal deities. The Zakhrangs follow Buddhism of Hinayana sect, but tribal deities are also worshipped by them. The adopted religion of the several tribes included within the Adis is Donyi Polo. Thus, we observe that the religions of these tribes are strongly syncretistic in the true sense.

All religious systems of different tribes are based on a functional hierarchy of gods who exercise their supernatural control over humanity in varying orders. This religious pattern of the non-Buddhist tribes is called by different scholars "a blend of animism and animatism with naturalism" (Dutta, 1989). Dutta writes, "The duality of faiths that exists in the tribal societies has varied effect in the life of the people."

The Buddhist tribes have definite religious scriptures and places of worship. The seat of the Mahayana sect of Buddhism in Towang monastery is believed to be the largest in Asia (Dutta, 1989). The library of the monastery has more than 700 books in its stock. The main centre of the Hinayana sect of Buddhism is at Chwkham. A large number of religious books written in Khamti scripts are kept at Buddha Vihar, Chwkham.

The Sherdukpens combine their adherence to Mahayana Buddhism with the communal worship of tribal deities whose cult lies in the hands of priests, who are entirely distinct from the Lamas. The Lamas are in charge of the large *Gompa*, furnished and decorated in the style of Tibetan Gompa. Among the Monpas too elements of the ancient Bon religion coexist with the dominant Buddhist faith, and the parallel practice of both religions within the same community has not sparked off any conflict, though in a similar situation in Nishi society, the religious rivalries have threatened to destroy the social fabric of Nishi society (Furer-Haimendorf, 1985:308).

The Noctes of Arunachal have adopted a rudimentary form of Vaishnavism (Athparia, 2000). They are tied with the Sahri Chaliha Bareghar Satra of Nazira. The Vaishnavite Nocte villages have Namghars that serve as places of congregational worship. Mahanta (1996) has observed that Nocte Vaishnavite faith is conspicuous by the absence of any devotional song, dance and staging of religious drama such as *Bhavana,* the cardinal feature of Vaishanavism. The Sajolangs live in the valley of the Paksa. They are known as Mijis. They believe in several deities and spirits. They worship natural objects such as earth, sky, moon, sun, water and hills. They have a supreme god. Each village has a priest called Givi. Both male and female priests are present. They are selected based on their individual qualities (Chaudhuri, 2001). Chaudhuri has studied this tribe in the context of change. He says, "Due to historical contact with the surrounding Buddhist communities the Sajolangs have started imbibing Buddhist religious elements. Despite practising tribal religious rituals they identify themselves as Buddhists" (Chaudhuri, 2001).

Mizoram

Among all the states of North-East India, Mizoram is the most intimately associated with Christianity. The first Christian missionary reached Mizoram, then called Lushai Hills, way back in 1891. Many cults have also come into existence among the Christian Mizos. The first Christian missionary to land in Lushai Hills was William Williams. Others were J.H. Lorrain and F.W. Savidge. They mastered the Lushai language and opened schools for the villagers. Under these missionaries evangelization works also started.

Many cults are in existence among the Christian Mizos. Often elements from tribal religions are incorporated within these cults. Out of the Pentecostal movements sprang the Pawl cult (Zakia Pawl), according to which it is not worth worshiping God either in the Presbyterian Church or in the Pentecostal Church. What one needs is to sing only songs of joy. Another cult is called Khuangtua Pawl or Thaingzau. Followers of this cult believe in Christ, but they have no aversion towards many tribal cultural-religious customs including polygamy. The Christian Mizos regard them neither Christians nor traditionalists. The drinking of rice beer is common in the cult. The Thaingzaus regard sex relations (outside marriage) as normal behaviour and in fact, it is regarded as the command of God. Such a couple is called Khurbing. There is another cult of the Mizos, whose members believed that they (Mizos) are 'one of the lost tribes' of Israel (Goswami, 1979).

Tripura

The rulers of Tripura originally belonged to the tribal Tripuri community. The original tribes of Tripura are the Tripuri, Riang, Noatia, Jamatia and Halam with sub-tribes. The Riang of Tripura had migrated from Burma through Chittagong hill tracts and settled in Tripura in historical past. These tribes profess tribal religions, Hinduism, Buddhism and Christianity. Hinduism has immense influence on the tribes of Tripura. On account of large scale influx of Hindu refugees from then

East Pakistan present Bangladesh, Tripura witnessed an abnormal rise of population (Mukherjee, 1973). Increasing penetration of Bengali Hindu refugees into tribal territories of Tripura gave rise to tribal unrest, leading to several tribal separatist organizations. Because of immigration of vast populations, mostly Hindus, many local tribal communities came to be affected.

The Noatia tribe were the first to have come under the influence of Vaishnavite Hinduism. The Riang started imbibing some traits of Hinduism, though they continued to stick to tribal religion simultaneously. On the other hand, the Mag and Riang tribes had influenced each other's cultural and religious life to some extent. Thus the Riang adopted also from the Mag certain cultural items, including the use of amulet (ang). Some other changes which took place in Riang society are as follows. Out of sixty-six tribal rituals, about thirty-eight rituals became obsolete and sacrifice of buffalo was no longer in practise (Mukherjee, 1959: 101). The Riang tribals had been exposed to Hinduism through their interactions with the ruling families of Tripura, who had become Hindus. The Riang also encountered a Buddhist tribe Mag, from whom they learnt the technique of plough cultivation (Mukherjee, 1959). Mukherjee observed that in the mist of all round cultural change and religious transformation, the concepts of sacred (*kaham*) and profane (*haia* or *snuk*) among the Riang tribals remained well guarded (Mukherjee, 1959:69). Because of contact with the incoming Hindus, according to Mukherjee (1959), the Riang came to "equate their deities with those of the Hindus and add new elements in ritual offerings". We witness here certain elements of religious syncretism.

Among the Buddhist Chakma tribe of Tripura, as observed by Maitra (2002), several pre-change tribal deities are worshipped. The most important tribal deity is Goojen, the supreme deity, which consists of Chumlang and Paramaswari, with the male and female features respectively. The Chakma also believe in *tumbru* (magic). Baidya conducts magical performances. There are also some Tantrik hermits known as Fagir. Among the Chakma, there are two categories of Buddhist preachers, the Lori and Vikhu. Any person may become a Lori by observing ten preachings of Buddha. They wear *gerua* (ochre) cloth. They were called Prateyk Buddha. A Vikhu has to observe 223 principles of Buddha. During her era, Kalindi Rani, the Chakma queen, propagated the expansion of Buddha Vikkhus instead of Lori. She adopted the Hinayana Buddhism, and propagated the same among her people. There is yet another category of religious specialists called Genkuli. They read sacred texts and performed funeral rites. They are musicians also. The

Chakma tribal Ojhas (sorcerers) practise Tantrism, perform tribal religious rituals and cure patients through incantation method. We thus notice that alongside Buddhism, Tantrik Ojhaism with tribal religious trait, survives in Chakma society.

A Recapitulation

North-East India's cultural image, its regional cultures and tribal religions, with their local variants, stand out distinctly. On account of multi-pronged culture contact, the regional cultures and native religions have been influenced, but the indigenous cultures and religions of North-East India, as we recorded above, are too strong to be obliterated easily. Dogmatic ideologies of divergent faiths have not been able to deeply influence the native value systems and tribal religious orientations, despite a long tradition of sweeping cultural transformation over a long time. We have noted above not only diverse instances of cultural fusion, but also examples of reform and revivalism in the domains of culture and religion of tribal people of North-East India. Shankar Dev provided a fresh elucidation of *bhakti* and set the pace of anti-Brahmanism, chiefly in the Brahmaputra valley. His procedures buttressed and prompted growth of numerous syncretistic cults, which flourished in tribal areas without injuring the basic cultural ethos of the tribal people. Shankar Dev bestowed a new cultural identity upon Assam by initiating a process of homogenization. His was a bold attempt at synthesis of tribal religions and alien cultures. Further, there are several cases of adoption of Buddhism, Christianity and even Islam among the tribes of this region, but we noted that merely through the pace of imposed changes deep-seated tribal religious beliefs could not be done away with. Drastic cultural transformation and religious conversions never eroded the essential tribal religious convictions and moral principles, and thus what we witness is a syncretistic coexistence of multiple religious traditions in the region.

References

Athparia, R.P. 2000. Impact of Alien Culture on the Noctes. In *Tribal Religion.* Ed. M.C. Behera. New Delhi: Commonwealth Publishers.

Banerjee, S., 1964. Residence Pattern among the Pnar *Bulletin of the Anthropological Survey of India* 13(1--2) 107–110.

Barpujari, H.K., 1970. *Problems of the Hill Tribes of the North-East Frontier* Volume 1, 1822--42, Guwahati: Spectra.

Barpujari, S.K., 1984. Christianity and its Impact on the Nagas. In *Tribes of North-East India.* Ed. Karotemprel. Calcutta; Pharma KLM Mukhopadhyay.

Bareh, H., 1993. India's North-east and her Ethnic Character during the British and Contemporary Set Up, in *Regionalism in India.* B. Pakem (Ed.), pp. 196--226, New Delhi: Har-Anand Publications.

Barpujari, S.K., 2001. Beginning of Educational Attempts in Lushai Hills *Journal of North-East India Council for Social Science Research.* 25 (2)1–6.

Barua, Indira and Rupa Phukan, 1998. Socio-Religious Aspects of Health among the Sonowal Kachari, *The Eastern Anthropologist* Vol. 51 (4) 351–362.

Barua, Indira, 1981. The Ahoms of Assam. *Varia.* Acta Ethnographica academiae Scientiarum Hungaricaae, Tomus 30(3--4) 407--426.

Barua, S., 1994. Man, Meghalya. Vol. 32. Eds. B. Pakem, Shibani Roy and Arbinda Basu. Calcutta; Anthropological Survey of India.

Becker, C., 1980. *History of Catholic Missions in North-East India (1890--1915).* Shillong: Y.M. Institute.

Bezbaruah, B., 1996. The Mataks as an Ethno-Religious Sect. In *Communities of North-East India.* Eds. Farida A. Das and Indira Barua. New Delhi: Mittal Publications.

Chaudhuri, Sarit, K. 2001. The Sajolang Religion. Mimeographed.

Danda, Dipali, G., 1994. Method of Hinduisation in North Cachar. *Journal of Indian Anthropological Society.* 29(1--2): 143--150.

Das Gupta, Biman, 1969. A Note on the Rajbanshi of Eastern India with a Special Reference to Social Movements, *Bulletin of the Anthropological Survey of India.* Vol XVIII, 1; 1–44.

Das, N.K., 1982 (a) The Naga Movement in *Tribal Movements in India.* Volume I Ed. K.S. Singh, Delhi: Manohar.

Das, N.K., 1982 (b), Review of the Works on Social Structures of Some Matrilineal Tribes of North-east India and Observations Thereon. *Journal of Indian Anthropological Society.* 17 (3):199–214.

Das, N.K. and P. Gupta, 1982, 'The Ahom Movement' in *Tribal Movements in India* Volume I Ed. K.S. Singh, Delhi: Manohar.

Das, N.K., 1985, "The Politico-Jural Aspects of the Segmentary Social System of the Zounuo-Kjeyhonuo Naga" Ph.D. Thesis. Gauhati; Gauhati University.

Das, N.K., 1989. *Ethnic Identity, Ethnicity and Social Stratification in North-East India.* New Delhi: Inter-India Publications.

Das, N.K., 1993. *Kinship, Politics and Law in Naga Society*. Memoir No.96. Calcutta: Anthropological Survey of India.

Das, N.K., 1994 (a). Ethno--Historical Processes and Ethnicity in North-East India, *Journal of Indian Anthropological Society*, 29 (1–2) 3--35.

Das, N.K., 1994 (b). Review of Social Change among the Nagas (Tangkhul). By K.Ruivah. *Journal of Indian Anthropological Society*, Vol. I.

Das, N.K., 1996. Cultural Identity and Tribal Heritage of North-East. In *Tribal Identity in India: Extinction and Adaptation*. Ed. Kalyan Kumar Chakravarty. Bhopal: Indira Gandhi Rashtriya Manav Sangrahalaya.

Das, N.K., 2002. *Religious Transformation and Culture-Change among the Tribes of North East India*. Project Report of Centre for Studies in Civilization. New Delhi: Indian Council of Philosophical Studies. General Ed. D.P. Chattopadhyaya.

Doley, D., 1984. The Religious Beliefs and Practices among the Mishings of Asdsam in *The Tribes of North-East India* Ed. S. Karotmprel and D. Danda. Calcutta: Firma KLM Pvt. Ltd.

Downs, F.S., 1971. *The Mighty Works of God*. Gauhati: Christian Literature Centre.

Dutta, P., 1978. *The Noctes*. Shillong: Directorate of Research: Government of Arunachal.

Dutta, P., 1989. *Tribes of Arunachal Pradesh*. Itanagar: Arunachal Pradesh Administration.

Dutta, S.K., 1985. *The Mataks and their Kingdom*. Allahabad: Chugh Publication.

Elwin, Verrier, 1957. *A Philosophy for NEFA*. Shillong: NEFA Administration.

Elwin, Verrier, 1961. *Nagaland* Shillong: Advviser's Secratariat.

Endle, S., 1911. *The Kacharis*. London: MacMillan.

Furer-Haimendorf. C.Von. 1985. *Tribes of India* New Delhi: Oxford University Press.

Gait, E., 1905. *History of Assam*. Calcutta: Thackeres Spink and Co.

Goswami, B.B., 1979. By-Product of Christianity on Hill Tribes of North-East India *Review of Anthropology* Vol-7/1–9. Vienna.

Goswami, M.C., 1978. Tribal Unrest and Inter Ethnic Tensions in North-East India *Bulletin of the Anthroplogical Survey of India*. Vol. xxvii, No. 3–4:1--24.

Guha, A. 1991. *Medieval and Early Colonial Assam*. Calcutta: K.P. Bagchi and Co.

Hussain, M., 1993. *The Assam Movement*. Delhi: Manak Publications.

Hutton, J.H., 1921. *The Angami Nagas*, London: McMillan & Co. 1969, Second Edition, Bombay: Oxford University Press.

Kamson, M., 1975. Jadonang as a Social and Religious Reformer. *Jadonang Volume*, Imphal.

Kabui, G., 1974. *Social and Religious Reforms Movements in Manipur*. Mimeographed, Shillong, N.E.H.U.

Kabui, Gangmumei, 1977. Social Reforms and Religious Movements in Manipur: Nineteenth and Twentieth Centuries. *North Eastern Spectrum*. Gauhati. January.

Kakati, Bani Kanta, 1960. 'The Mother Goddess Kamakhya' or Studies in Fusion of Aryan and Primitive Beliefs of Assam', sec. 15, p. 17ff. Gauhati: Author.

Kakoti, B.K., 1949. Assam through the Ages. *Assam Tribune*. Independence Number. Gauhati.

Kar, R.K., 1981. *The Savaras of Manakta*. New Delhi: Intra-India Publications.

Kar, R., 2001, Presidential Address. *Anthropo-Historical Appraisal of Migrant Population in Assam, North-East India*. Anthropology and Archaeology Section. Indian Science Congress, 88th. Session (2000--2001).

Langstieh, B.T., 2001. Demographic Structure of the Khasi Muslim of Shillong, Meghalaya *Jr. H.Ecol*, 12(2): 121--125.

Mahanta, K.C., 1996. Vaishanavism among the Noctes' in People of North-East India. S. Sengupta. Ed. New Delhi: Gyan.

Mahanta, K.C., 1997. 'Shamanistic Dance and Treatment of Disease in Assam' in *Contemporary Society: Tribal Studies*. Vol. I. Eds. G. Pfeffer and D.K. Behera. New Delhi: Concept.

Maitra, S.R., 2002. *The Cakma of Tripura* Calcutta: Anthropological Survey of India.

Majumdar, D.N., 1968. An Account of Magico-Religious Rites and Beliefs of the Rongdani Rabha *Bulletin of the Anthropological Survey of India*. Vol XVII, No.3.

Majumdar, D.N., 1969. A Study of Religious Practices among the Song Koch of Garo Hills. *Bulletin of the Anthropological Survey of India*. Vol XVII, 3.

Majumdar, D.N., 1972. Acculturation among the Hajong of Meghalaya *Man in India* 52(1) 46--63.

Majumdar, D.N., 1982. The Garo National Council in *Tribal Movements in India* Volume I Ed. K.S. Singh Delhi: Manohar.

Mathur, P.R.G., 1979. *The Khasis of Meghalaya*. New Delhi: Cosmo Publications.

Mathur, P.R.G., 1975. The Muslim Khasi of Meghalaya: Perspective of Tribal Development and Administration. ICSSR Hyderabad.

Mills, J.P., 1926. *The Ao Nagas* London: McMillan Co.

Mills, J.P., 1927. Some Aspects of Anthropology *Man in India* Vol. 7, No. 1.

Misra, S., 1998. The Nature of Colonial Intervention in the Naga Hills, 1840--80, *Economic and Political Weekly*, December 19, 1998.

Mukherjee, B., 1959. The Riang *Bulletin of the Anthropological Survey of India* VIII (2).

Mukherjee, B., 1959. Trends of Changes in the Riang Culture Since Independence, *Bulletin of the Anthropological Survey of India* VIII(2).

Mukherjee, B., 1973. Tribal Situation and Development Problems in Tripura Culture, *Bulletin of the Anthropological Survey of India* XXII (3–4) 16--31.

Mukherjee D.P., P. Gupta and N.K. Das, 1982. The Zeliangrong or Haomei Movement in *Tribal Movements in India*, Volume I Ed. K.S. Singh, Delhi: Manohar.

Mukhopadhyay, Kanchan, 1994. Dynamics of Ethnic Identity Maintenance among the Khasis of North-East India. *Journal of the Indian Anthropological Society*. 29(3)209--220.

Nag, M.K., 1965. Effect of Christianity on a Few Aspects of Khasi Culture, *Bulletin of the Anthropological Survey of India* 14 (1–2) 1--34.

Narjinari, Hira Charan, 2002. The Religion of the Bodes. Mimeographed.

Natarajan, Nalini. 1977. The Missionary among the Khasis. New Delhi: Sterling Publications.

Natarajan, Nalini. 1982. Cultural Change among the Khasis in *Tribal Movements in India* Volume I Ed. K.S. Singh. New Delhi: Manohar.

Nehru, Jawaharlal, 1948. *Unity of India*. London.

Neog, M., 1976. Arunachal, My Hills So Strong. Jorhat; Assam Sahitya Saabha.

Parampanthi, 1978. The Lakhimon Sangh Movement among the Karbis, in *North East India*. Ed. S.M. Dubey. New Delhi: Concept.

Pruett, Gordon E., 1974. Christianity, History and Culture in Nagaland *Contributions to Indian Sociology* No. 8: 51–66.

Roy, Shibani, 1994. Khasi Muslim in Meghalya. Vol. 32. Eds. B. Pakem, Shibani Roy and Arbinda Basu. Calcutta; Anthropological Survey of India.

Ruivah, K., 1993. *Social Change among the Nagas (Tangkhul)*. Delhi, Cosmo Publications.

Rustomji, N.K., 1971. *Enchanted Frontiers*. London, Oxford University Press.

Saha, R.K., 1994. Ethnic Identity of the Meitei: A Contextual Analysis. *Journal of the Indian Anthropological Society*. 29(3) 269--276.

Saikia, M.C., 1982. The Brahma Movement among the Bodo Kaachaaris in *Tribal Movements in India* Volume I Ed. K.S. Singh, Delhi: Manohar.

Saikia, N., 1982. Cha Mazdoor Assamiya Samaj in *Nibandha Niryas*. Ed. N. Ghotowar Jorhat: Assamiya Sahitya Sabha.

Sarmah, Bhupen, 1998. The Pre-Colonial Agrarian Scenario of Assam in *North-East India: The Human Interface*. Eds. M.K. Raha and A.K. Ghosh. New Delhi: Gyan Publishers.

Singh, K.S., 1982. *Tribal Movements in India*. Volume I. New Delhi: Manohar Publishers.

Singh, Prakash, 1972 *Nagaland.* New Delhi, National Book Trust.

23

Cult of Bongaism, Linguistic Synthesis and Religious Syncretism in Ho Society

Basanta Kumar Mohanta

According to *Encyclopaedia Britannica* any attempt to combine or unite different principles pertain to syncretizing process. The term syncretism is defined as different systems of beliefs/fusion or blending of religions/selection of whatever seems best in each. According to the *Oxford Dictionary of Current English*, any attempt towards unifying or reconciling different schools of thought belongs to the syncretic process. From this perspective, the Ho situation presents an ideal example of religious and linguistic syncretism, which this paper intends to elucidate in cross-cultural and cross-regional perspectives. This paper deals with the Ho tribe spread in two contiguous locations of Saraikella-Kharsuan district of Jharkhand state and Mayurbhanj district of Orissa state. Eastern India consists of states such as Jharkhand, Orissa and West Bengal. The states of Jharkhand and Orissa have large congregations of tribal populations, while only a few pockets in West Bengal have tribal concentration. These three states being contiguous many tribal communities have spread in all the three states, such as Santal, Munda and Ho. Of the two principal Ho villages from where the data are mainly collected, Rabankocha, in Jharkhand is a uni-ethnic Ho village and Badhatnabeda, the village located in Orissa, is a multi-ethnic village. While the Orissa village is exposed to urban and mining environment, the Jharkhand village is comparatively interior and less exposed to urban influences. The Hos of these two villages have many similarities in terms of cultural and religious beliefs, and practices, though linguistically they are drastically influenced by the dominant languages and prevalent scripts of the respective regions. Thus in Jharkhand the Hos, besides speaking Ho language at community level are oriented towards Hindi because being part of the Hindi speaking state of Bihar till recently, Jharkhand continues to retain Hindi at state level. Accordingly, the Hos of Jharkhand use Devnagri script. On the other hand, the Orissa Hos continue to retain their tribal language at the community level but are oriented towards Oriya language for communication outside their home. They have adopted the Oriya script. In this diverse cultural and linguistic backdrop, the Hos have succeeded largely in protecting their basic linguistic and cultural traits, with little outside intervention. This paper mainly deals with the survival course adopted by the Hos of these areas in the spheres of linguistic and cultural (religious, political) traditions, and their reconciliation and accommodation with the dominant linguistic and religious patterns of respective zones. It is proposed to describe the basic cultural system of the Hos which centres around the cult of Bongaism and then to comparatively assess the level of linguistic synthesis and religious syncretism among the Hos of these two locations keeping in view their different cultural contexts, using first-hand and secondary source materials, both historically and anthropologically.

I have used data collected from several villages of Jharkhand and Orissa, particularly from the Saraikella-Kharsuan (then west Singbhum) district of Jharkhand and Mayurbhanj district of Orissa. West Singhbhum, situated at the southern part of the state, covers an area of 9,90,700 sq.kms. The three district boundaries of the Jharkhand and boundaries of Orissa and West Bengal surround it. Both the rural and urban settlements are found in this district and its 3,23,487 sq.kms. are covered with forest, which is 32.65 per cent of the total area of the district. The forest area of the district is divided into three types, namely, dry, semi-evergreen and moist tropical deciduous type. Mayurbhanj is one of the biggest revenue districts of Orissa. It covers an area of 10,418 sq.kms. It is bordered by the districts of Balasore in the south, Keonjhar in the west, west Singhbhum of Jharkhand in north-west, east Singhbhum of Jharkhand in the north and Medinipur district of West Bengal in the east. For better administration, this Mayurbhanj district is again divided into Baripada Sadar, Bamaghaty (Badhatnabeda lies in it), Kaptipada and Panchpir. The Simlipal forest ecological zone is situated at the core of the district, covering an area of 2,750 sq.kms, which divides the whole district into two parts—eastern and western. The eastern flank includes the Baripada Sadar and Kaptipada sub-divisions which possess many similar geomorphic features of coastal Orissa, whereas the western flank of the district covers the areas of Bamanghaty and Panchpir sub-divisions, possessing geomorphic features similar to those of Chotanagpur plateau.

The total population of the Hos, as per 1981 census, is 5,86,221, i.e., 53,6,523 in Bihar (including Jharkhand), 46,496 in Orissa and 3,202 in West Bengal. The district of Saraikella-Kharsuan till recently was part of west Singhbhum district. According to the 1991 census the total population of undivided west Singhbhum district is 17,87,955 (8.19 per cent of the total state population) of which 9,09,796 (51.52 per cent) are male and 8,78,159 (48.48 per cent) are female. The density of the scheduled tribe population in the district is very high. There are 9,78,069 scheduled tribe people living in the 23 blocks and they constitute 54.70 per cent of the total district population. Similarly, there are 18,84,000 people living in Mayurbhanj district, which is 5.95 per cent of the total state population. This total number includes both tribal and non-tribal people. According to the above report 1,32,000 (7.01 per cent) belong to the scheduled caste and 10,91,000 (57.91 per cent) belong to the scheduled tribe. The major scheduled tribes of the district are Santal, Ho, Bhumij, Bhatudi, Bhuyian, Gond, Saunti and Munda. Kharia and Birhor are the two backward tribes living inside the dense region of Simlipal forest ecological zone.

The Hos of Jharkhand and Orissa: Ethnonym, Material Culture and Political System

The Ho are also known as Kol, Kolha and Kol-Lohara (Majumdar, 1950:18). The existence of multiple nomenclatures of the Ho tribe creates a great problem for proper identification of the tribe. In several areas of Jharkhand and Orissa however, they identify themselves as Ho as well as Kohl. In the Ho language the word 'Ho' means a man and hence as per their language any human being can theoretically be designated as a Ho. The term 'Ho' is used only by this community to identify themselves, whereas the other neighbouring communities address them by the term 'Kolha'. Following Dalton's view, Majumdar (1950:18) has mentioned that the generic term 'Ho' has been derived either from the Sanskrit word 'Kola', meaning 'pig' or from the word 'Horo', which has different forms, viz, 'Koro', 'Kolo' and 'Kol'.

The west Singhbhum district of Jharkhand state in the past was known as Kol-Sthan (land of Kols) or Kolhan area (the homeland/ heartland of Kols), where the people of Kol or Ho tribe have been living since long past. As per historical evidence, all the tribal communities of

Chotanagpur plateau have emigrated from the Gangetic plains during the Aryan invasion of north India (Roy, 1918). Some scholars have also opined that Munda and Ho (Kol) belonged to the same ancestral stock and in course of time they got separated from each other. After coming in contact with the neighbouring Hindu caste communities Munda people became more Hinduized whereas on the other hand the people of Ho (Kol) tribe kept considerable distance with the other neighbouring people and tried to stay in isolation. Though nowadays many of the Hos have changed their attitude yet the traditional Hos do not allow outsiders to hold land near their village. This west Singhbhum district of Jharkhand is a core place of Ho and in course of time they migrated to the different parts of neighbouring areas of Jharkhand, Orissa and west Singhbhum (Roy, 1918; Mishra, 1987:10–12).The Ho belong to the Proto-Australoid group. They are short statureed dark complexioned with a broad and flat nose. The hair is usually black and straight and wavy with a tendency to curl, the beard scanty and the eyes dark-brown. Usually, the Hos possess narrow chins. The Hos possess neither strong muscles nor broad shoulders (Kar, 1961).

In most of the cases, the typical Ho villages are situated either on the foothill of the jungle or on the slopy land close to the water source. Among the two villages studied, the first village is Rabankocha, situated on the foothill of the Hataburu, whereas the second village is Badhatnabeda which is situated on the slopy land close to the Jolpa river. Except for a few, all the Ho huts of the villages are very simple and traditional in form. In both the villages, houses are divided into a number of hamlet. All the Ho houses are generally constructed on either sides of the street facing each other. Ho houses are built very neatly having a rectangular ground plan. The sizes of the house vary from family to family as per their requirement. Majority of the Ho houses contain either one multi-purpose room or three to four rooms at the most. In case of a multi-purpose room house, the total room is divided into two to three small chambers by a temporary thin and small wall and then each chamber is used for separate purpose like cooking, storing grains, bedroom, etc. Sometimes a small chamber is also used for various purposes. If the house contains more than one room then each room is used for separate work. Generally, the inner chamber of the house or *aading* is used for cooking purposes. The ancestral spirits are also worshipped in this room. The Hos have exploited the locally available natural resources for constructing their houses. The traditional Ho hut is generally built on mud or framed with wood, bamboo and a local shrub and plastered with a mixture of mud, cow dung, etc. The Hos do not follow any strict rule about the direction of the door. The main entrance of their house is always faced towards the village street. The Hos decorate their house walls with different types of locally available mud colours. All the traditional Ho huts are thatched either with Kher (a type of grass), paddy straw or *khappra* (locally made half-circled mud tile). Paddy is the major crop cultivated in this part of the area. Rice is the major food item of the Hos. During free time, some of the Hos go to the jungle for hunting different wild animals and birds. Although there is no objection to eating beef and pork when it is available, presently the Hinduized Ho do not like to eat these. *Deing* or rice beer is an important drink of Ho. Irrespective of age and sex everybody consumes this rice beer. The Hos drink everyday in their house, and out of the family they call it as their morning tea. In Ho society *Deing* is considered a very prestigious drink. It is such a basic item that without this the guest cannot be entertained. *Deing* is prepared from half-boiled rice. For the preparation some white tablets, locally known as Ranu which are prepared from the roots of jungle shrubs, are mixed with the half boiled rice and kept for three or four days for fermentation after which they add the required amount of water to it to prepare to drink. *Mahuli*, country made beer, prepared from the Mahua (*Modhuca latifolia*) flower is also another favourite drink of the Hos. The adult males and some females also smoke *ficca* or *bidi.* The practice of chewing tobacco is also noticed among the adult Hos.

As the Hos are settled agriculturists, they use different types of wooden as well as iron implements for their agricultural activities. The agricultural implements consist mainly of wooden plough with iron blade, yoke, Moi (a long wooden field-levelling implement), shovel, crowbar, knife, sickle, bullock cart, etc. The Hos use very simple dress to cover their body, which are very similar to the dress pattern of their neighbouring tribes like Santal, Munda, Bathudi, etc. Traditionally, the male members wore a handwoven coarse and narrow striped dhoti (Botoi) around their waist, which rarely reached their knees. The lower corner of the dhoti was tucked at the back. Presently shirt, pant, trouser and *lungi* are frequently worn by the younger generation. The women folk use a locally made coarse *sari* (*lagna/lagia*) in their village. One end of this *sari* is used to cover the waist to knee portion whereas the rest covers the chest and left shoulder reaching under the right armpit. The village women rarely use the undergarment and blouse. However, due to the regular contact with the other communities and frequent visit to the nearby town and market, their dress pattern is gradually changing. Presently most of the women are wearing *sari* and other dresses and material like their neighbouring communities; also, some school going girls wear frock, shirt and ribbon as their school dress. The practice of both individual and ceremonial hunting, is noticed among the Hos. There is no fixed time for individual hunting whereas ceremonial or communal hunting is done only once a year. This annual ceremonial hunting expedition is very important among the Hos. It is observed in the month of *Baisakha* (April-May). The long bow and arrow are the major hunting implements of the Hos. The bow is usually made of broad, pliant sticks of bamboo with the ends tied with a thin bamboo string. The Hos use two types of arrows—the sharp and the blunt arrow.

The Hos of Jharkhand and Orissa have an elaborate tribal political system, which is based on a well-defined territorial system, with corresponding political offices to maintain social control. Thus, the Hos of Jharkhand at the lowest level have been placed under Pirs, which are under a Manki (a divisional headman). Each Ho village has its own headman called Munda. The whole Kolhan area was divided into 73 Pirs. Normally, the Mundas and the Mankis are descendants of original reclaimers of land, such as the Khuntkatti headmen found among the Oraons and Mundas. The office of the Munda is generally hereditary but the administration recognizes it. At different levels, the councils of headmen look after the internal affairs of the tribe, and their decisions which are based on customary laws are accepted by all. For different wrong doings, different punishments are recognized as per the customs. It may be mentioned that recognizing the great political and judicial rules of the Ho headman in maintenance of law and orders in their respective regions, the state government has granted certain official privileges to these informal tribal headmen with suitable monthly remuneration (Dhan, 1961: 74–80). Similarly, in Orissa an elaborate political system based on Pirhas (Garhas) at the maximal level is recognized. Every Pirha is divided into Parganas and then into revenue villages. In the past, Sarbarakars were the chiefs of the Pirhas. People still remember the names of Pirhas. In 1829, Tahasildar replaced the post of the Sarbarakar, by the king. A post of Sardar was created in 1853, and was under a Tahasildar. At the minimal level of the Ho village, Pradhan is the head of the local political system. This is a hereditary position. Pradhan is responsible for regulating the village affairs strictly in terms of customary laws.

Linguistic Syncretism

The traditional dialect of the Hos is known as Ho; it belongs to the Munda branch of Austro-Asiatic languages and is allied to Santali and

Mundari dialects in certain respects. The inflection system of the Ho dialect is very peculiar in nature. Like the Turkish language, the Ho dialect is also known as the agglutinative language, where the inflections have lost their meaning as separate entities by the process of 'phonetic decay'. The vocabulary of the Ho dialect is also very peculiar, where a number of words are used to indicate individual things and ideas but there are no such words used for general and abstract terms (Prasad, 1961:1). It is interesting to note that the younger generation is trying to discard the regional language of their locality and are speaking a mixture of Hindi, Oriya and Ho languages. In Jharkhand (as it belonged to the erstwhile Hindi-speaking state of Bihar until recently) the Hindi language based on Devnagri script is used for inter-community communication whereas among themselves they speak the Ho dialect. The Hos of Orissa use both Hindi and Oriya languages and the Oriya script. The Hos, who reside in West Bengal, follow both Bengali language as well as Bengali script for communication among themselves and their neighbouring communities, though their number is very small. As per the 1961 census there were 6,48,066 people in all the areas who spoke the Ho language of which 1,41,856 were bilingual. Out of those bilinguals 91,611 (64.58 per cent) used Oriya as their secondary language while 44,242 (31.19 per cent) used Hindi and only 6,003 (4.23 per cent) used other languages as their secondary language (Singh, 1994:404--405).

In various spheres of cultural life, linguistic syncretism is noticed in both the voluntary adaptation and sometimes imposition of Hindu-centric nomenclature, particularly observable in changing personal names, mainly of students, village names, place names, etc. The most common change observable is in personal names of individuals, such as Ghanashyam, Durga, Ramchandra, Janaki, Kamal, Rabindra, Brajamohan, Krishna, Renuka, etc., though typical tribal names also continue to survive such as Jaklo, Chandu, Rode, Jhingi, Dumbi, Joba, Budni, Kisun, Koda, Mangi, etc. Often in many families it is observed that old tribal names and adopted Sanskritic names simultaneously prevail. It is observed that teachers in the schools, failing to spell the tribal names, often provide Sanskritic names to tribal students though such students are called at home and in the community by tribal names only. Such coexistence of dual markers of identities in terms of nomenclature is seen in other areas also. Then we have such personal names as Lily, and English month-based names such as January, August, etc. Those families having the history of sending labourers to tea gardens in Assam have given the name Assami to their children. Then we have a large number of Sanskrit names which have either been linguistically corrupted or phonetically distorted such as Site (Sita), Janke (for Janaki), Gite (fot Gita), Lokon (for Laxman), Jabuna (Jamuna), Routu (for Rout), Mokta (for Mukta), Chandoboni (Chandramani), etc. Besides, some of the Hos are also using the surnames of prominent Oriya communities as their first name along with their tribal surname, such as Mohanty Deogam and Rout Deogam, etc., whereby synthesis is noticed in a single name.

The etymology of one of the studied villages, i.e., Badhatnabeda is quite interesting. It is a combination of three separate words namely '*Bad*', '*Haitian*' and '*Beda*'. The original name of the village is '*Hatnabeda*' that is derived from Ho language and the Oriya word '*Bad*' has been added later to it. In Ho language, '*Hatu*' means village and '*Beda*' means open field including both cultivated and non-cultivated areas. The word '*Hatna*' is probably derived from the original word '*Hatu*'. Thus '*Hatnabeda*' means the village within an open field or land. There were two villages of the same name (i.e. Hatnabeda) in the same locality and close to each other. This created a lot of confusion and hence to distinguish the villages from one another the Oriya words '*Bad*' (big) and '*San*' (small) were prefixed to the original names of the villages as per the area and size of the population of each village. Both these prefixes have been given by the local Oriya-speaking people. The complete meaning of the word '*Badhatnabeda*' is thus a big village within/having an open field or land. But according to Abhiram Tiriya of the same village, the ancestors (particularly the ancestors of Tiriya clanspeople who first settled down in the village) had migrated from Kolhan area seven generations back. He has prepared a genealogical chart of the Tiriya clan of their village. As per his knowledge their ancestors were first residing in Moudi, Jetia and Danko (Danguaposi) villages near Chaibasa. In due course of time, they migrated to village Kalaia and then to Kulbei and Kulbai to Dhobadhabini and finally from Dhabadhabini to Badhatnabeda. Presently some of the Hos of Dhabadhabini and Badhatnabeda villages are migrating to villages Doyaposi and Dhodihua. Regarding the etymology of the village home, he stated that when their ancestors had come to this village the entire area was covered with dense jungle. Arjun (Terminalia Arjuna) was the dominant flora of that jungle. Gradually they cleaned the jungle and converted it into large-sized cultivable land. In Ho language, this Arjun is called *Hatma* and the large sized-low cultivable land is known as *Beda*. Thus, the two combined to give the original name of the village. The term '*Bad*' was added to it later.

Because of the fast spread of electronic media, the younger generation is very fond of Hindi and Oriya film songs which is reflected in many areas of Ho tribal life. It is more particularly evident during their different life-cycle rituals as well as in their annual festivals. In these celebrations, they sometimes also arrange video shows along with their traditional dances. Some TV serials like Ramayana, Mahabharata, Jay Hanuman, Om Namah Shivaya and Vishnu Puran were/are very popular among the Hos of exposed villages. At show time they gather near the TV or at the house of the TV owner and enjoy the serials.

We also notice the insertion of the dominant linguistic tradition in certain other areas of traditional Ho life. In case of death of respected persons like Munda and Manki of the village the Hos erect an additional vertical memorial stone/pillar (menhir) locally called *Sasandhiri* on which they engrave the deceased's name, place of birth and achievements. Generally these types of engraved vertical memorial stones/pillars are found at the entrance of the village, centre of the village, sides of the village streets, near religious places or close to any public place like pond, well, tube-well, etc. After placing the memorial stones/pillars on the selected spot, they engrave on the plain surface of the stone the details of the deceased either in Devnagri or in Oriya script. English is very rarely used along with the above scripts. The Hos traditionally did not have their own script and at the same time, they did not have the expertise to engrave. Hence they depend on the neighbouring communities to engrave their pillars. When engraving on the memorial stones/pillars, care needs to be taken about the size, type and spelling of the words. They do not like to take any risk and therefore they engage the services of a professional engraver from outside their community because if something is written on the memorial stone, it is not possible to change it. If the Ho writer makes some mistakes during his writing, it looks ugly and creates a bad impression. Also, the Hos regard it as a dishonour to the deceased person. In some of the villages like Rabankocha, people are neither well-educated nor expert in stone carving. Therefore, the epitaph on the memorial stones/pillars is written not by the Ho, but by professional Hindu-caste engravers of neighbouring villages. For this particular work, the stone carvers are paid well by the Hos. Often the phrase "*Om Ganesaya Nomoh*" is now found engraved at the top of the epitaph, which is actually inserted by the Hindu-caste engravers on their own, though the rest of the text of the epitaph remains that of the Hos. But the Hos do not show strong resentment towards such accretion to their identification marker, though the opening line and the text indeed have no correlation whatsoever from the perspective of the Hos, since the epitaph is very much an essential part of the indigenous tribal religious ethics which has nothing to do with the 'Great Hindu Tradition'.

Religious Syncretism

The 1981 census in Bihar (including present Jharkhand) returned 81.65 per cent of Hos under 'other religion' implying thereby a majority of their population as followers of a tribal religion. In the same census, the religious status of the Hos is: 16.52 per cent are Hindus, 1.43 per cent are Christians and the rest are Muslims, Sikhs and others, whereas in Orissa 81.49 per cent Hos Hindus, 0.87 per cent Christians and 3.70 per cent others. Similarly in West Bengal, 97.69 per cent are followers of Hinduism, 0.87 per cent of Christianity, 0.22 per cent of Islam and 1.22 per cent 'other religions'. From the comparison of 1961–1981 census data it is evident that the population of adherents of traditional tribal religion in Bihar (including present Jharkhand) has increased from 73.30 per cent to 81.65 per cent. The number of Hos who follow Hinduism decreased from 26.15 per cent to 16.52 per cent while in the case of Christians it has increased from 0.55 per cent to 1.43 per cent. Similarly in Orissa 13.94 per cent tribals have returned as adherents of 'other religions'. From the comparison of the above census data it is also evident that the population of Hindus is on the decrease from 99.97 per cent (1961) to 81.49 per cent (1981). As per the 1971 census 12.79 per cent Hos have been returned under 'other religions' which also includes their traditional tribal religion. Here we noticed a slow resurgence of tribal faith (Singh, 1994: 406–408).

Like the other tribes of Jharkhand and some tribes of Orissa, the nature worshipping Hos also believe in Sarna religion. The word 'Sarna' is derived from the word 'Sar' (arrow). The worship place of the Hos as well as other tribes of Chotanagpur is known as Sarnasthal or Jahera, which is nothing but a sacred grove, where a set of old Sal trees grow. This Sarnasthal is usually, but not necessarily, at a little distance from the village. In his first monumental work *Munda and Their Country*, S.C. Roy (1918) has mentioned that "Although the greater portion of the primeval forest, in clearings of which the Munda villages were originally established, have since disappeared under the axe or under the jara-fire, many a Munda villages still retain a portion or portions of the original forest to serve as Sarnas or sacred groves. In some Mundari villages, only a small clump of ancient trees now represents the original forest and serves as the village-Sarna. These Sarnas are the only temples the Mundas know. Here the village-gods reside, and are periodically worshipped and propitiated with sacrifices" (1918:242). To describe Sarna religion, Dalton (1872:56–57) and Dehon (1906:124) have mentioned that it is a composite in nature but to Roy (1918:1) it is an organized system of spiritism set on a background of vague animism which institutionally recognizes the deities and ancestral spirits.

The Hos call all their deities and spirits Bongas, which are non-anthropomorphic. Thus, Bonga is the generic term which is used to signify both the power and spirits. The Hos believe in a number of gods and goddesses as well as some benevolent and malevolent spirits who reside in and around the hills, forests, agricultural lands and village premises. They also worship their Bura Buri (ancestral spirits) inside their aading (kitchen). Like the Hos, the same term (Bonga) is also used by the Santals and Mundas of the region. According to Bodding (1942), "All the spirits worshipped by the Santhals are called Bonga." Similarly, Mital (1986:69) has mentioned that, "The Bongas among the Santhals are not bound by temporal bodies. The Bonga world of the Santhals includes the benevolent ancestral Bongas as well as the malevolent demons, which are worshipped and appeased out of fear. The major element of Santhal religion is the belief that they are totally under the control of the Bongas and also surrounded by Bongas. These Bongas reside in the house, village, forest and even on the mountains." Similarly, Roy (1918) has mentioned that the Munda worship Manita-Bonga and the spirit. While describing the Bongas of Ho, Majumdar (1950:264--267) has mentioned that

> "the word Bonga is a generic name, and is applied indiscriminately to refer to gods and spirits. The real meaning of Bonga is power, force, and therefore the religion of the Hos may be called the religion based on 'Bongaism'. The power, which is called Bonga, is possessed by every individual, animal, plant, stream, rivulet, tank, rock, tree, forest, field and mountain. It is possessed in greater or lesser degree by a person. When a man possesses a personality and wields authority over others, he is a Bongaleka, i.e., a man like a Bonga. The Bongas have no specific shape. They can take any form. Although the Hos believe in the beneficence of their Bongas, they also know that these Bongas can, and do, punish or chastise them. Earthly failures, bodily afflictions and material losses are accounted for by the fact that they often disregard the traditional rules of conduct and fail to follow the mode of life which alone can ensure a peaceful and happy existence on earth. Whenever they fall victim to a disease or an epidemic, when their crops fail, or their dexterity in hunting and fishing are of no avail, they first blame themselves and not the Bongas."

From this discussion, it is evident that the Hos believe both in benevolent and malevolent spirits. Some of the important Bongas of Hos are Marang Bonga, Singh Bonga and Dessauli.

The religious head of Ho is known as Dehuri/Deuri, who is a mediator between Hor (man) and Bongas. He works as a priest and officiates in all the village or community level worships. The source of diseases, illness, drought and any other calamity are traced only by him through dreams. He is not able to know about the role of a Bonga directly in his day-to-day life, but it gets revealed to him through dreams.The Hos worship these Bongas during the different festivals as well as at the time of their life-cycle rituals. As per the hierarchy or position of the Bongas they offer them flowers, arua rice, *bel sakam*, *tulsi sakam* and *illi* or *diang* and sacrifice *sim* (chicken), *boda/merom* (unsterile he-goat), etc. Serious illness is thought to be due to Bonga. The Hos worship them and sacrifice different types of birds/animals to get relief from it. According to Prasad (1961:107–108) and Duary (2000:184) the size/type or grade of sacrifice varies as per the diseases. Initially they sacrifice a *sim* chicken but if it does not give a good result then a *merom* is sacrificed. If this sacrifice fails to provide relief then the sacrifice is increased one one by one and a sheep or even a calf, cow or buffalo may then be sacrificed. They worship both their regional, village and clan Bongas like Sing Bonga, Garam, Basuki, etc., along with the Bongas of the Hindu pantheon like Saraswati and Laxmi, etc. They take help of different sacred specialists from their own tribe as well as from other communities like Gunia, Jyotish and Brahman priest, etc., (Singh, 1994: 406--408).

As they are a settled agricultural community, most of Ho festivals are associated with their agricultural activities. Their festivals may be divided into two types, namely, traditional and adopted. Apart from their domestic traditional rituals, they also worship their different Bongas communally, either at the clan or village levels, in different festivals. The traditional Ho festivals are communal in nature where the social-religious as well as the recreational activities are performed simultaneously. After coming in regular contact with the wider Hindu pantheon, some of Hos adopted several festivals, but they do not neglect their traditional ones. Though the process of syncretism in the ritual sphere of religion is noticed among Hos, the level of syncretism varies in different areas depending on their different social-cultural contact and ecological environment. The Hos of Kolhan area (west Singhbhum district of Jharkhand) are more traditionalists as compared to Hos of Orissa. Further., Hos of boarding area of Kolhan area are not much exposed like Hos of other parts of Orissa and because of this the level of syncretism varies according to their exposure. For example, the level of syncretism is less among Hos of Jharkhand as compared to the Hos of Orissa. Similarly it is less among the Hos of Bamanghaty and Panchpir sub-division of Mayurbhanj district and Champua sub-division of Keonjhar district of

Orissa, which are located in the immediate neighbourhood of Kolhan area, as compared to Hos of other parts of Orissa. Because of this, Hos of the above mentioned areas of Mayurbhanj and Keonjhar districts of Orissa participate in or celebrate very limited Hindu festivals like Durga puja, Biswakarma puja, Ganesh puja, Saraswati puja and Ratha yatra (car festival), etc., whereas the Hos of other parts of Orissa are more Hinduized and participate directly or indirectly in most of the Hindu festivals and sometimes give less importance to their traditional festivals. Similarly, some of the Hos particularly those who work in different towns with different people of wider pantheon celebrate the Hindu festivals at their working place and also take part in their traditional festivals in their village.

In some cases, it is also observed that some of the educated/service-retired Hos who are living in their native village worship their traditional Bongas like Singh Bonga, Marang Bonga, Dessauli, etc., and during their festive occasions also simultaneously worship the Hindu deities both at the family and village levels. An example may be cited of Mr Satrughan Bari, a forty year old man of village Sunamara of Jamda block of Mayurbhanj district, who is an retired army person who believes in and worships his traditional deities at his village but when he purchased a Bajaj Kawasaki motorcycle in 1999 he took it to his nearest Hindu temple to take the blessings of the Hindu deity. Also, before starting his motorcycle he uttered the name of a Hindu deity. Similarly, Lord Ganesh and devi Saraswati are being worshipped each year regularly in the village school officiated by a Hindu priest. Another example may be cited of Subasini Singh, a thirty-five year old Ho, who is working as a nurse in village Kulgi, is highly qualified and has been living with the adherents of the wider Hindu pantheon for a long time. She speaks and writes Oriya and worships Hindu deities like Lord Ganesh, devi Saraswati and devi Laxmi, etc., each day in her house. She participates in celebration of Saraswati puja and performs Sonipuja. Once she was also worshipping Santoshimata continuously for fourteen Fridays for fulfilling some of her wishes. We may also surmise that women folk in simple tribal societies are more prone to adoption of multifarious religious traditions seeking fulfilment of their desires. Duary has studied Hos of Chaibasa area where also we notice the synthesis of dual religious beliefs. Duary has observed that, "many Ho people go to the local temple twice or thrice a week to make offerings of fruit, flower and incense like their Hindu brethren. Likewise whenever they purchase a new vehicle they visit a Hindu temple, preferably the Kali temple, to seek her blessings" (2000: 187).

Tusu Vasani is the main attraction of the Makar Sakranti or Makar parab which is celebrated basically by the Hindu caste people in almost all parts of south Jharkhand and north Orissa in the month of January. This festival is also popularly known as Tusu parab. During this festival the villagers prepare an image of Tusu devi and worship her. On the fixed date the villagers from all neighbouring villages gather their Tusus in a common place near any water source, where they sing Tusu songs and dance and finally immerse their images. The Hos of Mayurbhanj district in general and the Hos of Bahalda, Tiring, Jharadihi, Jamda, Gorumahisani, Rairangpur and Badampahar area in particular also take part in this Tusu parab directly or indirectly. They go to their nearby Tusu Vasani centres like Ranibandh, Satikudar (Rairangpur), Ghumal, Gambharia, Kulgi, Bahalda, Basingi, Mahulpani, Paharpur, etc., on different fixed dates and enjoy the festival. The use of different types of colour papers, ribbons, flags, plastic flowers, colour powders is also evident during their different pujas and festivals. "In some cases the Ho people also use mango leaves, tulsi sakam (basil leaves) and da (water). It is probably borrowed from the neighbouring Hindu society" (Duary, 2000).

According to Majumdar most of the malevolent Bongas of the Hos are not their own and seem to have come from some Hindu equivalent deities found among the neighbouring Oriyas. Gara Satamai of Ho is none other than the devi Nai Bhagawati of the Oriya, which is perhaps a name for that spirit who presides over tanks and ponds. Satamai is the distorted form of Sat-ma, the stepmother, and the actual mother being Nage-Bonga or the river goddess. At the time of analyzing the Kar-bongako like, the Suni kar, Rahu kar, Dinda kar and Chuhar kar he argued that "Kar is not a Ho word, it is the same word as Kal, the destroyer, and is associated with 'time'. The word Kali that signifies the goddess of that name in popular Hinduism is derived from the same word Kal. Suni kar, Rahu kar are none other than the planets Sani (Saturn) and Rahu, known to the Hindus as Kal... The word Chandi (another name for Kali) is taken from the Hindus, particularly from the Oriyas, for example, Bisai Chandi (poisonous), Ranga Chandi (bloodthirsty or red); Chinta Dain and Kaltud (a corrupion of Kalketu), Jugini-bonga is none other than Jugini, who with her counterpart Dakini is said to accompany Kali or Chandi" (Majumdar, 1950:255–256). From this statement of Majumdar, it is clear that most of the deities worshipped by Hos during different festivals are not their own, but are borrowed from their neighbouring Hindus. We see here a long process of adoption of several deities from the dominant community through culture-contact.

The popularity of Manasa devi (a Hindu goddess, believed to be the daughter of Lord Shiva who presides over snakes) is not limited to the Hindus; she is equally popular among the tribes (particularly Hos) of the region. The entire Kolhan area as well as its neighbouring areas is covered with hills and forests and people move in and around the dense jungle in search of games and other forest products. As different types of poisonous snakes are abundant in this forest, there is high possibility of snakebite. Therefore, the Hindus of the region worship devi Manasa for protection. In the earlier days, the Hos tried to cure the victims of such accidents with their own traditional method. However, sometimes they were unable to protect the lives of the victims. The insufficiency of their own method and fear encouraged a number of Hos to adopt worship of this Hindu goddess. Thus the Hos of the region adopted this alien goddess and started worshipping her, which gradually got assimilated in their culture. According to Chatterjee and Das (1927:59) the people of Purti khili (of Ho tribe) of village Nohadi, which is situated near the town of Saraikella, worship goddess Manasa to whom they offer sweets and flowers and before whom they also sacrifice fowls and goats. Religious syncretism is noticed in several instances of Ho life. There are many Akharas (training centres) functioning in different parts of the region where a number of tribal and non-tribal people are learning incantations (mantras) from their Gurus or teachers. According to Majumdar, "a number of young men have learnt the spells and prayers to this goddess as a protection against snake-bite, and as a method of driving the poison from the system. The Guru or teacher is usually an Oriya Ojha, who teaches spectacular methods of invoking the goddess. Mantras which are nothing but names of Hindu gods and goddesses with their modes of worship, the details of the offerings which they are fond of and stories of the assistance they have rendered to this or that individual in times of calamity are muttered and sung in such a sing-song tune that very few could understand that they were mostly in Bengali, spoken in Oriya style" (1950: 360–361). According to Majumdar, every fortnight, two days before the Amabashya or the new moon the Guru sits in meditation under a tamarind tree. He decorates his forehead with vermilion and places plates of *Arua* rice and banana cut into small pieces on his sides. Besides these offerings he (Guru) also keeps a few leaf cups of illi (rice beer). If we analyze these offerings it will be evident that though the tribals adopted alien deities, they worshipped them with their own methods which includes Hinduized methods of worship along with their tribal method of worship.

All the tribal communities of the studied region have a very strong belief in witchcraft. Continuation of any kind of disease for a long time is regarded as the action of Dian (witch) or evil Bongas. These Dians are generally elderly women members of their society. Though some of the aged women are generally treated as Dian irrespective of age they can learn the Dian bidya (the technique of witch craft). On the night of Amabashya, the Dians go to their nearby Shamshan (burial place) where they change their clothes and wear broom sticks at their waist and dance around the trees. Sometimes, they are supposed to have intercourse with the malevolent Bongas or spirits so as to have the power to bring any type of natural calamity in their region or to harm their enemies or to kill. Ojha or Deonwa is the traditional medicine man among the tribes who finds out the causes of disease of the people and their solutions. According to Das Gupta, the belief in Dian among the Hos is due to culture contact with Hindus where the belief in their Bongas (both benevolent and malevolent), as well as sacrifice to them through Dehuri to get rid of the problems are their indigenous procedures. He further stated that the Deonwas cult is not originally of the Hos and is borrowed from the neighbouring 'low' caste Hindu people. Most of these Deonwas belong to Gouda (milkman) caste of Hindus. The Guru of these Deonwas is again from the Hindu community, who train the Deonwas in their Akhara. As mentioned above, the mantras are nothing but the names of different Hindu gods and goddesses rearranged with some Hindi words. It shows a clear-cut influence of Hindu cultural elements in Ho community (1978:86–90).

Whenever a Ho suffers from a serious disease he usually takes the help of a Deonwa, who tries to detect the causes, whether it has happened due to some evil Bongas or Dian or some other causes. Sometimes, he first gives some herbal medicines and if that is unsuccessful, he tries to detect its actual cause. He usually follows two types of methods for identifying the causes. Firstly, he checks the pulse rate on the hand; where a high pulse rate signifies the influence of unnatural causes. Secondly, he grinds some Arua rice along with sindur, either in a *sarjom sakam* or on *a hata*. Failure of the traditional method of treatment forces them to bring the patient to a nearby hospital. Thus, it is noticed that they continue their traditional methods of treatment simultaneously with the modern medicines.

The Bonga-Centred Tribal Rituals

The following are the traditional rituals of the Hos where their Bongas are worshipped at both family and village/community levels. These are mostly agriculture-related festivals.

Maghe Parab

It is the principal festival of Hos, which is celebrated in the month of Magh (January-February), when their granaries are full of paddy. For the welfare of the villagers, Hos worship the Singh Bonga and Dessauli along with some other Bongas of lesser importance during this festival. Different villagers celebrate this festival on different dates, but at one place/village, it is celebrated for six days. The village Dehuri with the help of other village headmen fixes the date for the festival which are declared in different public places and weekly market centres. Sometimes, they also send special messengers to different villages to invite their relatives. During the fixing of dates, they always take care of the date of the same festival of their neighbouring/relatives' villages. They always try to give an opportunity to the people of their neighbouring villages and relatives to come and attend their village festival and vice versa. During this festival Hos take illi or diang, sing Maghe songs and dance. "Songs with high dose of sex themes are sung by boys and girls from the Marang parav day onwards" (Mishra, 1987). The youth of both sexes visit village by village and participate in their Maghe festival, which also provides them a scope to get acquainted with one another which ultimately helps them to select their life partner. "In spite of this folk belief, the festival is otherwise thought to be recreational and smoothens the process of selecting life partners" (Mishra, 1987: 60). According to the nature of Maghe festival each day of the festival is named separately like Gawamara or Gawal, Ote Illi or Ate Ili, Loyo or Sange Ili, Marang parab or Marang Musing, Basi parab, Maghe Basi or Basi Musig and, Hanr Maghe or Hanr Bonga or Har Bagia which are described briefly below. It is interesting to note that though the Hindu month of Magh has been internalized here, they continue to refer to each day of the festival in their own language. The fact remains however that they have some tribal names to identify the months.

Gawamara / Gawal

The first day of Maghe parab is known as the Gawamara or Gawal. On this day, Hos worship their ancestral Bongas in their house for betterment of their cattle. Besides this, no such communal worship is made. In the morning they gather at the house of Dehuri with grass, saim ba, pulses, illi and busumhasa (soil from white-ant mound) which are placed on a spot rinsed with cowdung solution. A cowboy, who imitates or symbolically represents a cow, takes seven rounds of the spot after uttering some incarnations and takes a little amount of illi from the spot.

Thereafter, the villagers take some grass from the spot of the ritual for keeping it in their cattle shed.

Ote Illi / Ate Illi

On this particular day, Hos offer illi (rice beer) to their Bongas. For this offering one member, preferably the headman, from each family carries a potful of illi to Dehuri's house, where Dehuri and his wife sit on *machila/gandu* each holding a puh (sal leaf cup). The villagers give their illi to Jomsim (assitant of Dehuri), who pours a little in the puh of Dehuri. Dehuri utters prayers in his mind and offers it to different Bongas like Singh Bonga, Dessauli and Maghe Bonga. Then Dehuri and his wife take a little illi from the pot followed by other villagers present, after which dancing and singing continues till late night.

Loyo / Sange Illi

This is the day of purification when Hos clean their courtyard, houses, granaries and plaster them with cowdung solution. They also sprinkle this cowdung solution over all their utensils, agricultural implements as well as the other daily-use artefacts. The Jomsim cleans the jahera (the sacred grove generally located on the outskirts of the village which is believed to be the place of their village Bonga---Dessauli) along with the courtyard of Dehuri. Besides this, the Hos do not do any kind of work and spend their time on dining, drinking, singing and dancing.

Marang parab / Marang Musing

This is the main day of the festival, when Hos sacrifice some sim (chicken) to their Bongas and observe other rituals. On this day Dehuri observes fast. Also, he is not allowed to have sex with his wife the night before. The village youth decorate the place of worship in the morning, and at mid-day the Dehuri goes to their nearest water source for having a purificatory bath. The Jomsim and the other villagers accompany him along with different musical instruments. After the bath they all come to the worship place in a procession. They bring along with them some dried rice, sims, puh, illi, da (water) and a weapon to sacrifice sim. Dehuri scatters some sun-dried rice on the ground for the sim. It is believed to be auspicious if the sim swallow this rice freely. Then Dehuri sacrifices these sims to different Bongas. The white sim is sacrificed to Singh Bongas, red to Dessauli and black to Nage bonga. The first two sims are sacrificed but the last one, i.e., the black sim is not killed but freed and stoned to death by the villagers. At the time of worship both the Jomsim and villagers assist the Dehuri in different aspects while the female members watch from a little distance. Then the villager cook these sacrificed sims at Dehuri's house and eat with illi. Dancing and singing obscene songs describing the different organs of both sexes or inviting each other for sexual relations follows and continues till the late hours of the night.

Basi parab / Basi Musing / Maghe Basi

This is the day when Hos say goodbye to their invited Bongas. They offer the cooked food and illi to their ancestral Bongas at their *aading*. On this day Deonwa (the diviner or medicine man) worships at his courtyard and sacrifices sim.

Hanr Maghe / Hanr Bonga / Har Bagia

On this day of the festival the malignant Bongas are driven out from the village. At noon, the village boys come out in groups and hit the roof and wall of houses with sticks with the belief that it expels all types of diseases and misery from the village. They collect some rice, vegetables and sims from villagers and finally all gather at the outskirts of the village, where they sacrifice sims and have a feast. Thus, they finish their Maghe parab.

Baha / Baha parab

In Ho language 'Ba' means flower and from the name of the festival it is clear that this festival is related to flowers, particularly indigenous flowers like Sarjom ba or Sal flower. This festival is also known as Phulbhanguni and is celebrated in the month of Chaitra (February-March) in honour of the village deity Dessauli. It continues for four days and each day has a separate name. The first day is known as He sakam diang, second day as Marang musing, third day as Basi musing and the last day as Bala badni. The Hos collect Sarjom sakam, Sarjom ba, Tila ba and Icha ba, etc., from their nearby jungle on the first day of the festival, whereas on the second day the Dehuri worships the Dessauli, Gram siri and Singh Bonga as well as sacrifices sims and boda/merom to these Bongas. He offers some ba to the Bongas and distributes others to the villagers. On the third day the Hos worship their ancestral Bongas at their aading, while the last day is meant for the expulsion of the invited Bongas. Eating, drinking of illi, singing and dancing are the other major part of this festival. Irrespective of age and sex every Ho enjoys this festival. In brief, it is a traditional flower festival when nature is worshipped at the village level to invoke good flowering.

Rajasala / Raja parab

It is a regional festival of enjoyment which falls during the Yethe chandu/Yoisthya (May-June) month. The Hos celebrate it at the family level for two days. No sacrifice is offered nor any worship done in this festival. It is the time of rest and during this festive period, any kind of agricultural work is strictly prohibited. Group dancing, singing and taking of illi is the major feature of this festival.

Hero parab

It is essentially related to the agricultural activities and is celebrated for three days during the Hero chandu/Ashar (June-July) for sufficient rains and bumper crops. On the first day of the festival Hos collect Sarjom sakam from jungle and clean their houses and courtyard. On the second day, Dehuri worships Dessauli Bonga either at the paddy field or at the Kolom or threshing ground or at their courtyard. He offers arua rice and bel sakam (wood apple leaves) and sacrifices a sim or a boda/merom to her. The other villagers follow the Dehuri; sometimes even those who do not have any landed property worship the Bonga in the same manner. In the evening they offer cooked food and illi to their ancestral Bongas at their *aading* and then the recreational part of the festival starts. On the last day Dehuri worships their Bongas and initiates seed sowing on the land which is followed by the villagers.

Bahtauli parab

This festival is connected with the activities which happen during the Bahare chandu or Sravana (July-August). In this festival, Dehuri worships the Dessauli Bonga at Jahera for protecting the paddy fields from insects and pests as well as for yielding bumper crops. There is no particular date for this festival. Before its celebration Dehuri worships the Dessauli Bonga at Jahera and fixes a date which is accepted by all the villagers. On the day of the festival the Hos offer a tiril sakam (Kendu leaves) and sacrifice a sim at Jahera. On the preceding day each family erects a twig of tiril (Kendu) tree in its own paddy field.

Jamnawa parab

During this festival, the main crop (paddy) matures and the Hos communally offer it to their Bongas. On this day, the Hos consume their new rice first. This festival is equivalent to the Nua Khai or Nua Khia parab of the Oriyas, which is celebrated in the month of Aswina

(September-October) of each year. It also has no fixed date, and the time is fixed by the Dehuri, Munda or any other headman of the village as per their convenience. On the fixed day, Dehuri worships the Dessauli Bonga along with some other Bongas and sacrifices sim for them. Sometimes, some other headman of village can also perform this worship. The villagers worship their ancestral Bongas at their aading and offer taben (flattened rice prepared from new paddy crop) along with illi. The time of the rest of the festival is spent eating, drinking, singing and dancing, which continues till late night.

Kakamontanri / Kalam parab

It is also an agriculture-based festival which is celebrated prior to threshing of paddy, during the Kalam chandu (December-January) of each year. It is a family level festival where Dessauli Bonga, Singh Bonga and Marang Bonga are worshipped. In this festival, Hos worship the Bongas at their threshing ground for the purification of paddy straw. During this worship Hos place all of their agriculture-related implements like Siu (plough), Moi (long wooden field levelling implement), sickle, etc., at their threshing place and spray turmeric mixed water on these as well as on the paddy with tulsi (basil) sakam and mango twigs for purification. At the end they sacrifice three red sims, one white sim and a black sim to their Bongas. As Hos live close to the hills and jungles, they spend their maximum time moving around the jungles in search of game and different types of forest products. While moving inside the jungles there is every possibility of attack by wild animals and being killed by accident. Therefore, Hos worship the jungle god (Marangburu Bonga) and pray for protection.

Partial Adoption of Hindu traits in Ho Life-Cycle Rituals

Partial adoption of Hindu traits is observed in the life-cycle rituals of Hos of Jharkhand and Orissa. We will discuss this process below.

Birth

Birth is considered an important landmark in Ho life-cycle. Though they now believe that a father plays an important role in the procreation of a child, it is also believed that a child is a gift of Sing Bonga. Maternity is considered an important event. They always promptly try to fulfill the needs of an expectant mother and give her proper attention. There are some strict rules and regulations observed by a woman during her pregnancy. The stoppage of menstruation is considered the first sign of conception. When this first symptom is noticed a sacrifice of a fowl in the name of Churing Bonga (a mischievous spirit) is made by the family to protect the foetus and the mother from the evil eye. Although at the early stage of the pregnancy, a Ho woman does almost all house work to help her family, she is not allowed to go to the tank or river to fetch water. Besides, she is always accompanied, preferably by a female family member, when she comes out from her house after dusk. During this period, she is allowed to neither sit nor stand on the Sasandhiri (memorial stone placed on the burial pit) nor is she allowed to go to their clan burial place. She is also not permitted to cook and offer anything to any family ancestors in festivals or any special occasions. A pregnant woman usually does not prepare the illi. Apart from this, she cannot touch the hunting and fishing implements; she cannot eat some specific portion (head) of the fish and animals. Walking under any string/rope and neem/jojo tree is strictly prohibited and she is restricted from using oolee (mango) wood as firewood. Though these rules and regulations are strictly followed during the first pregnancy, they do not follow these restrictions so strictly in successive pregnancies. The Hos do not perform any special type of ceremony during the childbearing period. They are very open-minded people and a Ho woman tells everything about her pregnancy to her husband and parents. Though, nowadays, the Hos are taking the help of a midwife or a trained nurse, in the earlier days they did not take such help. During the time of childbirth, a female relative or mother-in-law or even the husband helps the expectant mother. In case of severe labour pain the expectant mother is attended by a Ghasi woman, a lower caste Hindu woman who generally performs the work related to delivery (Chatterje and Das, 1927: 23; Das Patnaik, 1990: 116). As most of Hos live in single-room house, one portion of their hut is temporarily partitioned for a labour room. The inner wall of the room is decorated with cowries (conch shell) and different types of fishing and hunting implements, whereas the outer wall is covered with thorny bushes and Sotas made of branches of pipal tree. Each of these items have significance related to childbirth. The cowries and Sotas signify fertility while the fishing and hunting implements protect both the mother and child from evil spirits. It is interesting to note that if a woman gets prolonged labour pain, some traditional magical treatments are performed. If they do not succeed then finally they consult doctors of their nearby health centre. Immediately after the birth of the child, either the father or the present female member or midwife cuts the umbilical cord with a sharp edged sheath of the maize plant. Nowadays steel blades and sharp knife are also used for this purpose. The placenta and cord are kept in a new earthen pot and placed in a corner in the labour room for two days. Finally, they bury it in their courtyard only after getting a sign of sound health of the child. During this period, they carefully watch the health of the child. Though the period of Bisi (pollution) varies among Hos from place to place, generally it is observed for eight days and during that time the father of the newborn child prepares food for himself and the mother. On the morning of the eight day, both father and child shave their hair and then the father offers illi to all their ancestral spirits and clan members.

Name giving

In Ho language, the name giving event is called Numutupuria, which is usually held on the 21st day of the birth of a child, but some of Hos observe it on the eight day after the birth. On that day, the father gets shaved and the whole family takes bath prior to the beginning of the name giving. At the end of the event, a feast is given to all the Khili (clan) members as well as other close relatives. The act of shaving is performed only by a Ho man of another clan. There are mainly three methods adopted for giving a name to a newborn child. In each method, they drop sun-dried rice into a potful of water one after another uttering the proposed name of the child. If the rice floats for sometime and finally touches the bottom of the pot the proposed name is considered to be auspicious for the child and is accepted. If this does not happen they try again uttering another name and the process is continued until a name is selected. For this purpose, Hos usually prefer the name of a grandparent. In the earlier days, they also gave the name of the weekdays such as Sambari, Bhudhbari and Gurubari to babies born on Monday, Wednesday and Thursday respectively. But now they are giving new names, especially names borrowed from their Hindu neighbours (Majumdar, 1950:177–189; Mishra, 1987:53--55; Duary, 1995:38–40).

Puberty

The Ho Kui (girl) usually attains puberty when she is ten to fourteen years old. There is no special socio-religious ceremony observed with the onset of the first menstruation. The Hos believe that if a girl touches any male member during the first seven days of her first menstruation period, she sucks all his blood and ultimately the male member faces death. Because of this, Hos try to keep the girl in a separate room for seven days if possible. After completion of these days, she smears mustard oil mixed with turmeric paste and takes a bath in a nearby pond or river. With this bathing her pollution period ends and she leads a normal life. If the first menstruation is a sunday, tuesday or thursday it is considered inauspicious, which creates problems during and after her andi (marriage). In such cases they take help of the village Dehuri who sacrifices some chickens and worships Singh Bonga to control this inauspiciousness (Mishra, 1987:53–54).

Marriage

Marriage is a happy and joyous moment in the life of a Ho; it not only regulates their economic life but also continues their family line. The Hos believe that marriage is essential to lead a normal life. They practise tribe endogamy and clan exogamy. Marriage within the clan is strictly prohibited and the offenders are expelled from their society. They usually prefer monogamy but in some cases polygamy is also found, but only very rarely. In polygamy, a man may be allowed to marry two sisters but in such cases he must marry the elder sister first. There are mainly six types of marriages found among the Hos, which includes: (a) andi, (b) Diku andi (marriage by negotiation), (c) Opertipi andi (marriage by capture), (d) Raji Khusi andi (marriage by elopement), (e) Anader andi (marriage by instrusion), (f) Gardi jamai andi (marriage by adoption) and (g) Badal andi (marriage by exchange). They prefer that the proposal of marriage come from the boy's side. According to Majumdar (1950:134), in Kolhan area a girl may remain a spinster throughout her life, but her parents or guardian do not propose her marriage as it may degrade family pride and social status. The proposal must come from the other side. In their traditional andi, a Dutam (mediator) is sent by the groom's family to girl's communicate the proposal. If he gets a positive signal, a date is fixed for the formal visit of the groom and his relatives to the bride's house. On the fixed day, the groom and his relatives visit the brides house along with rice beer, rice, dal, he-goats etc. At bride's house, the groom offers the rice beer to the bride in a sal-leaf cup and her acceptance gives the symbolic consent. In the evening, the groom's relatives prepare food at the bride's house and after eating they sing and dance with the villagers at night. In a similar way, the bride's relatives pay a visit to the groom's house. The amount of bride price and the date of marriage is fixed during this visit. On the day of marriage, a team including the groom's family and relatives proceeds to the bride's village. In the afternoon, they come back to their village with the bride and her relatives. Before entering the outskirts of the village, a mock fight begins between these two parties and then the groom's party welcomes the bride's party to their house. In the evening, both bride and groom sit on the platform where the sacred rice is cooked for the ancestral spirits. The Dehuri worships the Singh Bonga and other deities and officiates the marriage. After worshipping the deities, both the bride and groom touch the sacred rice. The Hos believe that the bride gets converted into the groom's clan only after touching this sacred rice. Finally, the groom takes vermilion in his left hand and marks it on the forehead of the bride. The bride repeats the process, but she takes the vermilion in her right hand. Following this, feasting and dancing continue throughout the night (Mishra, 1987:56–57). There is no doubt that several life-cycle related rituals of Hos, the concept of pollution and use of vermilion, as noted above, have been influenced by contact with Oriya Hindu neighbours. Despite persistence of Bongaism, syncretistic involvement of several Hindu rituals in the cultural-religious life of the Ho society is a unique characteristic.

In the Kolhan and Mayurbhanj areas, the term Diku refers to aliens or outsiders. Hence, Diku andi is a borrowed form of marriage in the Ho society. In this form of marriage some specific Hindu rites are observed along with the rites of tribal andi. This type of marriage is noticed among those Hos of Mayurbhanj area who are economically sound as well as living in closer vicinity of the Hindu caste people. In this Diku form of andi, Hos take help of a Hindu Brahman who officiates the marriage before whom both the bride and groom take a vow of mutual protection and fidelity. In Kolhan area, according to Majumdar,

> "The replacement of the indigenous priest by the Oriya Brahman has not been complete even in those families who have introduced him to officiate in their marriage ceremonies, for the essential rites in accordance with tribal prescriptions are still observed by these families simultaneously with the introduced rites. Nor is it a case of a change in beliefs or in the attitude of Hos to their tribal spirits and their importance in their social life. It is mostly due to a false idea of prestige attached to the adoption of Hindu prescriptions which make them conscious of their superiority to their tribesmen that has favoured the formation of classes..." (1950:134).

These observations of a senior anthropologist made five decades ago are very pertinent with reference to our discussion on syncretism studied through comparative method. It is interesting that Oriya Brahmans in the past had entered the Ho stronghold of Kolhan area and influenced the tribals, though the impact of such influence, as Majumdar observed, remained incomplete.

In the Opertipi form of marriage, a groom forcibly carries away the bride from the market centre or any other place. Sometimes when a girl is not happy in her house, she forces her acquaintance to marry her quickly and in such cases this Opertipi form of marriage occurs. In Ho society, there is no objection to the Raji Khusi andi. This form of marriage is done when both the bride and groom give their consent. In this Raji Khusi andi neither is any marriage ceremony observed nor bride price given to the bride's family. Sometimes the parents of the groom are unwilling and unhappy with this marriage and in such cases both bride and groom elope and live away from their villages. In some cases they go to their relative or friend's house and live there until the parents change their mind and allow them to come. But in case of Anader form of marriage, a girl forces herself into the house of her lover and tries to motivate the members of her lover's family to accept her. Both divorce and widow remarriages are found in Ho society. In case of divorce, a woman can have a second marriage in the form of Sangha. In case of widow marriage, the youngest brother of the deceased husband is given the first chance to marry her widowed sister-in-law. If he is unwilling to marry, the widow is allowed to marry any other younger brother of her deceased's husband.

Death

The Hos believe in black magic as well as other spiritual powers which are supposed to be mainly responsible for the death of a person. They also believe that the birth and death of a person totally depend upon Singh Bonga. They believe that he has given a particular time and work to each creature, and within that period they have to perform their work in a proper way. If somebody does not perform his work properly he will be punished. The concept of rebirth is also noticed among Hos. They believe that if a person dies without doing the given work properly or dies by performing some bad deeds during his/her life period he/she will be born again to complete his/her work. This rebirth is totally dependent on a person's deeds in his/her previous life. Nowadays, a few educated Hos believe that death does not occur due to magical or spiritual powers, but due to old age, disease, accidents and other cause. If anybody suffers from serious diseases and comes into the last stage, then Hos take help of a Dehuri (the traditional priest) or a spirit doctor. They perform some religious activities and offer some chicken to ward off the bad effects. Besides, Hos also take the help of the local Baidyas (local medicine men) for curing their diseases. When all their curing abilities fail they go to the hospital. The neighbours and villagers, on getting the news of death, gather at the deceased's house. The closest relatives living in the nearby villages are informed quickly by sending special messengers. After gathering all the members, they arrange for burial or cremation.

The Hos follow both practices of cremation and burial. Before going to the burial/cremation ground, the family members of the deceased carry the dead body from the house and place it in the courtyard for the final bathing. As per Ho belief, sometimes the evil spirits hovering outside their house bring some harm on the dead body. In such cases the family members take some help from the priest. To protect the dead body the Dehuri chants some incantations and casts some Arua rice on the dead body as well as the courtyard of the house. The female members of the family wash the corpse very carefully with mild water, anoint it with turmeric paste mixed with mustard oil and again wash the corpse. Though the female members are engaged in the final ritualistic bathing of the corpse, who will bathe whom, depends on her social relation with the deceased.

After the completion of the final bathing at the courtyard and before the funeral procession, the family members change the old clothes of the corpse and keep the dead body on a wooden cot. The *khili* members who are present sprinkle some water mixed with basil leaves on the face of the deceased. The face of the corpse is decorated with a paste prepared from lime, vermilion and sandalwood. For preparation of this paste, female members of the family grind these three ingredients separately in 3:2:1 proportion and mix it in a leaf-cup. In case of death of a wife, the deceased's husband puts the final vermilion on the forehead of the corpse, after her face has been decorated. Finally, the corpse is covered with a new (preferably white) cloth. Some Hos, particularly the female members, possess tattoo marks on the hands, legs and around the necks. On death of such persons they take care to expose that part of the body. The Hos believe that all the property that a person accumulates during his/her lifetime gets left behind after death; the only thing a person does take along are the tattoo marks which are body decorations symbolic of jewellery. According to a person from Badhatna beda these marks cannot leave a person even after his/her death. Therefore, they always take care to expose these tattoo marks.

After the ritual bathing of the corpse, the deceased's family prepares for the funeral procession. Both male and female participate in the funeral procession. There are no restrictions on children to participate in this procession. The presence of widows is very essential in this funeral procession. According to Majumdar (1950:40), "The custom of hiring two widows for this purpose is found in Kolhan." Traditionally, the female members of the deceased's family carried the dead body on a wooden cot. According to Chatterjee and Das (1927:28), "The pall-bearers are the women of the same Khili as the deceased. They carry the dead on the bedstead on which he expired... The men follow the procession at a distance. They don't take part in any of the rites..." It is found that nowadays the system of the female pall-bearer dose not exist among Hos of any part of Kolhan as well as its neighbouring areas. Nowadays they simply touch the bier and then it is lifted by the male members. Generally, the sons and nephews of the deceased carry the dead body. In case of absence of the above, the khili members and relatives are invited for this purpose. The female members who follow the procession nowadays carry a plate of rice, a small brass basin, rice beer, a pot of water, a turmeric paste mixed with mustard oil, coins and a small quantity of salt in a winnowing fan.

In Kolhan area, some aged widows, particularly those who have no child are treated as Dians. Therefore, the villagers are very careful about them. If by chance she comes face to face with them at any place, they try to please her. But during the funeral procession the presence of widows is as essential as a Diwas or medicine-women who protect the corpse as well as the bereaved family from the evil spirits. The Ho widows play an active role at the burial ground. They decorate the wooden planks inside the burial pit with turmeric paste and mustard oil. These widows stay with the bereaved family up to the Jongtopa day and they are paid well for this. As Hos are a settled agriculturist tribe, the widows are always paid in kind (mainly paddy) not in cash. Though there is no fixed amount for their service, as per tradition they should be paid well by the deceased's family. If the deceased's family is poor then they only give the widows the daily wages that they earn as daily labourers. Also, during their stay they take food at the deceased's house. In some cases, the widows are not paid any amount for their service if they belong to deceased's own house or are very close relatives.

In Ho society, the spirit or soul of a departed person is treated as a Bonga (god) who resides at (or close to) their house and look after their welfare. Because of this, Hos bury or cremate dead bodies close to their habitation area. Each clan (khili) has a separate burial ground close to their house where Hos usually bury or cremate their dead. Before the burial or cremation of the dead bodies the male members of the deceased's family sit together and decide where they should bury or cremate their dead relative. Sometimes, they also take suggestions from their elder clan members as well as the female members. If a woman dies during her pregnancy she becomes a ghost. Therefore, the dead body of a pregnant woman is normally buried far from their general clan burial place. In case of death of a mother and newborn child, both are buried side by side but in separate burial pits.

It is interesting to note that Hos perform different types of mortuary practices for different types of deaths. Persons dying an unnatural death from snakebite, small pox, lighting, etc., are usually buried outside their clan or family burial places. In case of accidental death, the deceased's family members try to bring the dead body from the accident site. Sometimes, if they cannot find the dead body they simply collect a small amount of earth from that accident site and bury it at their clan burial place. This buried earth represents the deceased person. After the selection of a burial pit, the male members of the deceased's village and some relatives from the neighbouring villages present on the spot, dig a stepped burial pit in north-south direction. Sometimes, expert pit diggers from other villages are specially invited for this purpose. Shovel (kulam), crowbar (sabal) and spade (kankua) are the major digging implements used for this work. All the excavated earth is deposited on either side of the pit and is later used for refilling the pit. The burial pit contains two chambers—outer and inner. The outer chamber is always dug on the surface of the selected spot, whereas the inner chamber is dug at the centre of the floor of the outer chamber.

In case of burial, the dead body is kept in a wooden box placed inside the inner chamber of the burial pit. This wooden box is prepared inside the burial pit by an expert carpenter of their tribe. The deceased's family provides the wooden planks to the carpenters. If these wooden planks are not readily available in the deceased's house then the other khili members help them. They always use a small piece of the wooden plank to cover one end of the inner chamber. Before placing these end planks a horse's head is engraved on a wooden plank and placed at the southern end of the wooden box. As per Ho belief, the ancestors of Hos were very powerful and used to cross hill tracts by horse. Nowadays, though they do not possess any horse, in memory of the association of horses with their ancestors, they engrave a horse's head at the southern side of the wooden box. As per their belief, this symbolic horse, will carry the deceased person upto the house of their Singh Bonga during his/her journey after death.

The engraving of a horse's head on the wooden box is not the practice in each village; it varies from place to place. It is only found in the first studied village (i.e. Rabankocha) which is very traditional in nature. In the second village, instead of a horse's head Hos engrave a deer's head (Murum-bo-gando). According to people from Badhatnabeda, in earlier times they had the practice of hunting deer and other wild animals from their nearby jungles and eating their meat. In memory of earlier hunting activity, the present Hos of Badhatnabeda engrave this Murum-bo-gando on both ends of the box. During the preparation of this wooden box Hos prefer to use a single wooden plank on one side of the inner chamber to avoid the unnecessary entry of soil. If such wooden planks are not available to them, then they tightly join the small sized wooden planks. After the wooden box inside the inner chamber of the pit is ready, a widow decorates the wooden planks with some turmeric paste mixed with mustard oil. Immediately after the decoration of the wooden planks, some female members present on the spot shoulder the cot of the corpse, move around the pit seven times from right to left and carefully replace the dead body inside the wooden box. During the placing of the dead body, care is taken of the direction of the head, which always points south because Hos believe that they have migrated from northern going towards the south. If they place the dead body horizontally pointing the head towards south it will be easier for him to go to the south as well as to go to the place of Bonga. After placing the dead body inside the wooden box, some essential items are placed by the side of the corpse, such as a water pot, rice, rice beer, salt, oil, coins and new clothes. After the death of the person, he/she is detached from the relatives and goes to the Singh Bonga's place.

In case of cremation, after the ritualistic bathing and face decoration of the corpse, the dead body is placed in a wooden coffin known as Chapla. In such cases, the expert carpenters prepare this Chapla at the deceased's house. The usual size of this Chapla is about 1.50 x 0.60 x 0.45 mts. in length, breadth and height respectively. However, the size of the Chapla may vary depending on the stature of the corpse. The carpenters first prepare the base portion of the Chapla, which is known as Ganati, by joining two or three wooden planks with iron nails. Later, the side planks (Kanati) and the end planks (Aanr) of the box are attached with the Ganati. For preparing the Kanati, they usually prefer long wooden planks whereas small, wooden pieces are used for Aanr. Like the burial, at village Badhatnabeda, Hos engrave the Murum-bo-gando on the either ends of the Chapla. When it is prepared completely, the dead body is placed inside it very carefully pointing the head towards south. The items to be buried with the deceased are placed in a similar position inside the Chapla and then closed with a Temen (wooden lid). Finally, the entire Chapla is covered with a new cloth, as per the gender of the deceased. The Hos cremate their dead at either their clan graveyard or family burial place. Besides these, they have no special or separate place for cremating their dead.

The Hos follow a similar type of funeral procession in both burial and cremation. In case of cremation, some relatives prepare a funeral pyre on the selected spot of cremation. The Hos follow a typical pattern for setting fire to the pyre. Generally, two male members of the deceased's family, preferably the two sons of the deceased, set fire to the corpse. In case of absence of a pair of sons one of the daughters (preferably the elder and unmarried one) of the deceased is allowed to assist her brother. In case the deceased has no son and he/she has only daughter(s), one of the deceased's nephews along with his/her daughter perform this work. In case of cremation of a child, the father and mother of the deceased set fire to the pyre. After completion of the cremation work all members go to the nearest pond or river to take a bath. Sometimes, some female members of the family also take bath on the next day during the time of Jongpokhari.

The Jongpokhari or the packing up of mortal remains ceremony usually takes place a day after the cremation. For this Jongpokhari, a group of women go to the cremation ground with a new winnowing fan, new pot and water in a big pot. They pour the water on the site of cremation and collect the charred remains in the winnowing fan. After washing it properly they keep the remains in a white cotton cloth and then keep it in a new earthern pot which is anointed with Arua rice paste. On return, they halt in front of each clan member's house, where the clan members light a Dip (lamp) and pray for the peace of the deceased's soul. After going to all the clan members they reach the deceased's house where they temporarily hang the pot under the thatch of the Aading or place it inside the Aading. After placing this pot all the team members proceed towards the pond or river for bathing. This bone-keeping ceremony is known as Jongpokhari. In some exceptional cases, if time permits, this Jongpokhari is done on the same day of the cremation. The word 'Jangtopa' is a combination of two Ho words 'Jang' (bone) and 'topa' (bury) which means to bury the bone. In case of cremation, the Jangtopa is a part of Pathalghari or final purificatory ceremony. During this Jongtopa, the Hos bury earlier collected mortal remains, which were kept in a decorated pot and placed at the Aading on the day of Jangpokhari. Customarily this Jangtopa is held on the ninth day after Jangpokhari, i.e., tenth day after cremation. If the mourner's family is unable to perform the Pathalghari ceremony on the customary day then they postpone it as per their convenience. But according to a person from village Rabankocha, the Jangtopa is done on the same day of the Jongpokhari. Jangtopa is not an occasion of sorrow or grief. All the members present enjoy it like a festival. They carry these remains in a procession in which the female members sing marriage songs relating to the dead and the male members accompany them with beating of drums, and then both dance.

The Pathalghari or the final purificatory ritual is a communal ceremony of the Hos; it is observed at the deceased's house. Presence of all the agnates and cognates is essential during this Pathalghari ceremony. On a fixed day, a huge memorial stone is placed at the site by them after cutting/shaving of their hair and beards and clipping of their nails, after which a feast is given to all present as well as to villagers. According to late Suika Deogam of village Rabankocha and Abhiram Triya of village Badhatnabeda, this ceremony needs heavy expenditure and it sometimes becomes a burden on the deceased's family. The expenditure at a Pathalghari ceremony sometimes exceeds the total half-year's expenditure of the family. The Pathalghari ceremony of an adult person is customarily held on the tenth day after the death or ninth day after the Jongpokhari ceremony, but in case of a child it is held on the seventh day after the death. As the Pathalghari ceremony needs heavy expenditure, sometimes the ceremony is postponed upto the next harvesting period, so that the family can bear the expenses. However, in emergency, a deceased family can also finish it on the fourth day after the death. If the date of the Pathalghari ceremony falls during a dark fortnight then all the work is finished immediately but not on the fourth day after death. In such a case, the Pathalghari ceremony is held on the sixth or seventh day after the new moon.

Except for a few well-to-do families, Hos usually prefer to postpone the Pathalghari ceremony until the next harvesting period (i.e. December-January). There are three main reasons for postponement of the ceremony. Firstly, Hos are settled agriculturalists and they depend upon the seasonal agricultural produce. They mainly cultivate paddy, in which they remain usually busy from July to December, which is the peak agricultural season. During this period, they have to invest a lot of money for different types of agricultural activities. Therefore, Hos are financially not in a position to perform these rituals. Secondly, Pathalghari is a communal ceremony of Hos where the presence of all kith and kin is very essential. The Hos perform it just like a ceremony. No sign of grief or sorrow is noticed among Hos. Thirdly, the Sasandhiri (memorial stone) is generally collected from their nearby jungles and hills. On the day of the final purificatory ceremony, the placement of Sasandhiri on the buried site is very essential. It is very difficult to transport a huge Sasandhiri through the hilly tracts during the monsoons. This needs a lot of manual power for its transportation. During this agricultural period, it is very difficult to gather such manpower for transporting this Sasandhiri. Because of the above reasons Hos usually do not prefer to do the final purificatory ceremony within their agricultural period and postpone it until the finishing of the harvesting period. If the final purificatory ceremony is to be done on the tenth day after the death, it is fixed immediately after the burial or cremation. If it is postponed until the harvesting period or to some other date, the tentative date and month is fixed after the burial/cremation. In such cases, a final date is fixed immediately after the completion of harvesting. It is always decided about one month before the final date for the purificatory ceremony so that it will be easy to invite all relatives and they can get sufficient time to purchase and collect all the necessary items.

After fixing of the date for the Pathalghari both the family members of the deceased as well as the invitees prepare themselves for the ceremony. The family members of the deceased prepare/collect these items before the day of the Pathalghari. The items include rice, fried rice, flattened rice, rice beer, oils, vegetables and other cooking materials, big sized cooking utensils, water drums, new pots, new winnowing fans, new bamboo baskets, chicken, he-goat, ghee, vermilion, honey, new clothes for offering and for family members as well as close relatives, Sal-sakam or leaf-plates and leaf-cups, fire wood, etc. A temporary rest shed is prepared with leaves and branches. Then the most important item is Sasandhiri or the memorial stone. Tonsuring is one of the major rituals of the final purificatory ceremony, which takes place on the forenoon of the tenth day of the death or on a pre-decided day. On this day, male members of the deceased's family including some male members from the deceased's clan also shave their head, beards and moustaches. The female members of the deceased's family as well as some other clan members clip their nails. Sasangmandi is a type of turmeric mixed rice, which is specially cooked on the day of the final purificatory ceremony. After clipping their nails, the female members cook this rice in a new pot and place it in their courtyard, and then they go for final purificatory bath. After returning from the bath, they rub this rice on their legs.

As soon as the shaving ceremony is over, all the male members go to the nearest pond or river to bathe, and apply mustard oil on their body and dried black mud on their head. A Bame (a relative from another village or khili who sprinkles ritual water over them), also bathes along with the members and collects water in his lota. In a similar manner, the female members of the deceased's family along with some other female clan members also go to another ghat of the pond or river where they take bath. A female member from another khili goes up to the bathing place with a water pot to collect some water. After the bath, the female members return to the deceased's house. While returning, they check the Rum Sakam packet, earlier kept near their bathing ghat on the day of the death of the deceased. The elder female member of the family usually checks it. After opening the packet, she minutely checks the quantity of rice, black gram, coins, ghee, jaggery and cow dung. If there is any change in the colour of the contents in the packet or if any of the ingredients is missing it is a bad signal for the deceased's family. The Hos believe that the loss of rice or black gram indicates the possibility of another death in the family. After checking, they throw these materials into the water. Then they return to the house where they invoke the deceased person at regular intervals in the following way:

Gel ma re,
Dilit yate miyan,
Tising pure yena,
Pire chamin dinem tayaina,
Renga geya Rabang geya,
Sikim, Molmoli Koya.
Hebe aagume kayam aagu tanko.
Oah te duar te kayam
aagu ye pe elabo.

(Tenth day of the Death is fixed to bring you back. It is complete today. How many days you will stay outside? You might be feeling hungry and cold. There are ants and insects. Dear ancestors bring him/her in your arms.) After each invocation, the female member puts some drops of water on the ground. Then the whole group proceeds towards the house. While returning, the male members follow the female members. One or two members who had not gone for the bath arrange the following articles at the courtyard of the deceased's house for burning of Sang. The articles are Sasangmandi Subdhiri (a stone piece), Hati sedam (an earthen image of an elephant), a pot of Mera, Sangbidah (a bunch of sang sticks), a cotton wick and a match box. After coming to the house, all members stand near these articles. The female member who carries the water pot places it near the Sasangmandi Subdhiri. The Bame puts either some holy basil or a mango twig inside this water pot. One of the sons of the deceased (preferably the youngest one) ties one end of the three sang sticks with the cotton wick. The other ends of the sticks are spread outward and form a conical stand. The extra portion of the wick hangs down inside this conical sang stand. Then the fire is lit. Immediately after the burning of the wick and sang sticks, he places his left foot on the Sasangmandi Subdhiri and besmears the Sasangmandi on it with three fingers (ring, middle and forefinger) of his left hand. Mera is also besmeared on this in a similar way. Later he washes his feet with water and besmeares these Sasangmandi and Mera on the right foot. After this, all the female members who have returned after taking bath besmear the Sasangmandi and Mera on their feet and go inside the house.

All the relatives present purify themselves by besmearing the Mera on their feet. The Bame sprinkles some holy basil or mango leaf water over all those present and purifies them. After this, the Sang burning ceremony is complete. In Ho language, the term 'Ambul Aadel' means calling back the soul of the deceased. Like the other tribes and Hindu caste people, the Hos also believe in rebirth. According to Surendra Tiriya from village Badhatnabeda, "Death means the transportation of the soul from one body to another body through a new birth... After a death of a person or animal, his/her soul never dies; it only changes the body." Here one may infer that during the course of prolonged contact with the dominant Hindu neighbours, some of the Hindu notions related to soul and rebirth may have been internalized by the tribal cosmologies of people such as Ho, Munda, Oraon and Juang as also Santal. In Ho society, the death of a person is considered as a loss to the entire community. According to their beliefs, after death, the departed person becomes a Bonga for them and Hos pay regards accordingly. The Hos are always interested in knowing about the departed soul and its next rebirth. They do not like to leave it alone outside their house and hence the Ambul Aadel or calling back the soul. According to their belief, during its (soul's) entry into the Aading, the foot impressions of deceased's next birth are depicted on the ashes on the floor on either sides of the door. For this ceremony, a minimum of six to seven persons (including one or two family members, one maidservant and one servant) are required. They arrange a sickle, a ploughshare, a straw torch, few mango twigs and a water pot and then proceed towards the grave of deceased. After calling the deceased the woman carrying the water pot sprinkles some water on the ground with the mango twigs and then other team members strike the plough share and sickle against each other to produce a sound. In this way, they move thrice around the burial pit and call the name of the dead person. After this act they proceed towards the deceased's house. In the meantime, the female members collect some fine ashes in a Hata (winnowing fan) from the hearth and carefully spread it at either sides of the threshold. Usually, three family members (one male and two females) from the deceased's house stay inside the Aading to watch the deceased's foot impression. These two female members are preferably the younger and elder sisters-in-law of the male member. For Bonga Aadel they bring rice beer and khichidi rice from the mourner's house and offer it to the ancestors at the burial ground. First, the priest offers khichidi rice on four Siali leaves. Each Siali patta contains a small quantity of khichidi rice in four places; then rice beer is offered in two leaf-cups. It is a common belief among Hos that after the Bonga Aadel the deceased soul becomes happy and easily enters the Aading. Based on the impression on the ashes, Hos determine the probable causes of the death. The second day of Pathalghari ceremony starts with the placing of the Sasandhiri on the grave of the deceased.

Erection of Memorial Stones and Pillars

Before its placement, the Sasandhiri (Memorial Stone) is washed properly with water and then placed over the grave slowly by a group of male members. Like the direction of the dead body, it is also placed in north-south direction. As mentioned earlier, Hos fill the pit with earth after the burial of the dead body. Placing of *Sasandhiri* suggests the completion of the final purificatory ceremony of the deceased. Nowadays Hos, under the influence of dominant communities, start preparing a concrete platform on the grave after the final purificatory ceremony. As mentioned before, several elements of Hindu religious rites have been gradually integrated into the purificatory ceremony which is essentially a Bonga-based tribal ritual. After the placing of the *Sasandhiri* some *sims* and *boda* are sacrificed on the grave in the name of the departed soul which is known as *Mal*. The deceased's maternal uncle performs the sacrificial work. He sacrifices and sprinkles blood over the newly placed *Sasandhiri*. He also sprinkles the blood over the other *Sasandhiris.* Sacrifice of at least one *boda* from the deceased's family is essential. The sacrifice by the different invitees during the *Pathalghari* ceremony symbolizes unity of the clan and lineage members. The Dhiridulsunum or the oil giving ceremony is held on the second day of the Pathalghari ceremony. After taking the leftover rice beer of Ambul-Aader is observed on the previous night, a group of female member go to the graveyard for Dhiridulsunum with some fried rice and sunum (oil). Generally, they keep this sunum in a leaf-cup and the fried rice is taken in a leaf-plate.

They put some drops of oil and water over the Sasandhiri; this is known as Dhiridulsunum. After performing the ritual on the new memorial stone, other ancestral memorial stones of their family and clan graveyards are also anointed with oil and water. After completion of this ritual, they take a bath. All the family members and relatives who were present during the Sang burning ceremony on the previous day take rice beer after the completion of the ritual. No other members are allowed to take this rice beer during this period.

During the *Pathalghari* ceremony, the deceased family invites all the kinsmen and other members. Almost all the invitees come with their family members either on the first day of the *Pathalghari* ceremony or on the second day when a feast is given to all the cognates and agnates. The invitees bring some dal, rice, oil and other food stuffs in a bamboo basket and deposit it with the head of the deceased family. The quantity of material varies as per their closeness. The closest relatives bring a quantity of food materials in a big basket whereas others bring a small basket. On arrival of these guests they are offered *illi* and fried rice, whereas some take boiled rice and curry. In the evening, after the *Ambul-Aader*, all guests and family members take vegetarian food, but sometimes, they are also served fish curry. On the second day of the *Pathalghari* ceremony, a feast is given to all the invitees. There are mainly three methods adopted for this feast, namely, (1) the headman of the deceased family collects all the sacrificed chicken and he-goats, and cooks in a common place, (2) on the basis of the number of villages all the invited guests are divided into different groups, then the collected meat of chicken and he-goats are equally distributed among them and (3) the relatives of each village dress up their sacrificed *sim* and *meroms* in a common place, then they distribute some to the head of the deceased's family and other groups, and rest of the meat is prepared for them. After cooking, the food is first received by the deceased's family and then the whole group takes the prepared food in a common place. With this feast, the *Pathalghari* ceremony comes to an end. The Hos use different sizes of memorial stones for covering the mortal remains of their deceased relatives. It depends on their social status, financial condition of the deceased's family, time of the purificatory ceremony and the availability of suitable stone in the nearby jungle or hills.

In case of death of a reputed person, all the villagers, including the people from other neighbouring villages, help to search for a huge memorial stone. The economically weaker Hos prefer to place a small memorial stone. Some well-to-do Hos construct a concrete platform on the grave covering the whole memorial stone or sometimes erect a concrete memorial pillar either on the grave or close to the roadside or any public place. The size of the concrete memorial platform/pillars are comparatively bigger than the memorial stones. The detailed measurement (i.e. maximum length, maximum breadth and maximum thickness) of each memorial stone/pillar is taken separately. As mentioned earlier, the maximum number of Ho villages are situated either on the foothills of the jungle or hills or are close to it and they are dependent upon these jungles and hills for various purposes. The hills and jungles of the region are very rich in hard granite stones. These granite stones of different sizes and shapes are found in abundance in these jungles and hills, and are preferred for *Sasandhiri*. The selection of Sasandhiri is usually done three to four days before the Pathalghari ceremony or the final purificatory ceremony. For the selection of the Sasandhiri a team of minimum of a three persons go to the nearby jungle or hill where they choose a stone slab. During the selection of Sasandhiri care is taken of its shape, size and location. They usually prefer a flat rectangular stone at the foothill region of the jungle/hills or close to the jungle path, as it will be easier to transport them. Sometimes these Sasandhiris are selected in advance during their movement in the jungle for various purposes. Transportation of the Sasandhiri is one of the important parts of Ho mortuary practice, which is usually done on the previous day of the Pathalghari ceremony. To bring a huge Sasandhiri, the Dhiriarko (a group of villagers who transport the Sasandhiri) go to the selected spot in the early part of the day where they worship the hill god and offer a red coloured chicken. They pray for the easy transportation of the Sasandhiri as well as for protection from evil spirits during the transportation. Traditionally, Hos transported the Sasandhiri by two methods—in a Dhirijangi (in a non-wheeled cart pulled by a group of people) or in a Koali (a palanquin made with four wooden rods). Presently, the use of bullock cart for this purpose is also noticed. As Hos consider the deceased's soul as their well-wisher they do not fear to move freely in and around the burial place. They also use the memorial stones of different burial places for various purposes. In village Rabankocha, a cattleshed is constructed on a clan burial place. Besides, some Hos provide shelter for goats on the memorial stones in the daytime. In a Ho village, these burial places are suitable places for recreation, where the memorial stones are used as platforms while playing board-games, cards, etc. In village Badhatnabeda many villagers used these horizontal memorial stones as a platform for crushing oilseeds whereas at Rabankocha a memorial stone is used for grinding turmeric and different herbal medicines. Almost all the horizontal memorial stones of roadsides,

Table 1

The Ho Bongas: Nature of Worship and Hindu Equivalence

Name of the Bonga	*Its nature/ place of existence*	*Time of worship*	*Reason of worship*	*Offerings and sacrifices*	*Corresponding name in Hindu pantheon*
Singh-Bonga	The supreme deity, creator	Prior to every worship, but specially during Maghe parab	Expression of devotedness	White sim (chicken)	Sun god
Marang-Bonga*	Clan deity	Irregular interval	To protect respective clan/clans from disease, drought, etc.	Sunned rice, sindur (vermilion) and areca nut and sometimes a boda (unsterilized he-goat) is sacrificed	Mahadev
Buru Bonga** (Buru means hill)	The deity of hill. Responsible for different types of danger in forest/hills	Akhari parab	To protect them from evil sprits, accidents and other sorts of danger in forest/hills		
Bura buri	Ancestor spirits	Sarhul parab			
Goram	Village deity	Every month	To protect the village and its inhabitants	Sindur, rice,flower and red sim	
Dessauli Bonga(Desh means country/place)	Village deity, protector against diseases	Maghe parab, Baha parab, Haro parab and Jomnawa parab	To protect the villagers from small pox, cholera and other epidemics	Sarjom blossoms, red sim, merom, etc.	
Bagia Bonga **	The deity of tiger and other wild animal	Akhari parab	To drive away hazards from forest/hills		

Contd...

Contd...

Nage Bonga	The river goddess (supposed to be the wife of Singbonga)		To protect from the diseases of ear and hydrocele	Pig, egg, haldi (turmeric powder)	
Gara satamia**					Nai Bhagawati
Suni kar**					Shani (Saturn) Kal
Rahu kar**					Rahu Kal
Chandi**					Chandi/Kali
Juguni Bonga**					Juguni

* According to some scholars, the Marang Bonga and Buru Bonga are two different names of the same deity but as per the field information both are different from each other.

** Malevolent Bongas

Table 2

Names of Important Hindu Deities Meagrely Worshipped by the Hos

Name of the deity	*Status and power*	*Time of worship**	*Presided by***	*Offerings*	*Place of worship*	*Symbol, form of deity*
Ganesh	Supreme protector	Fourth day of bright fortnight in the month of Bhadrab	Brahmin priest	Coconut, sweets, flower, banana, etc.	On specific day celebrated at home, teaching institutions, club, etc.	Clay idol and photo
Biswakarma	Divine architect	Kanya sankranti tithi in the month of Bhadrab	Brahmin priest	Coconut, sweets, flower, banana, etc.	Cycle/motor cycle garage, mills, industries, etc.	Clay idol and photo
Durga	Symbol of great strength and power	Sasthi-ekadashi tithis of the bright fortnight of Aswin	Brahmin priest	Coconut, sweets, flower, banana, etc. along with sacrifice	House,public places, clubs, etc.	Clay idol and photo
Laxmi	Goddess of wealth	Full moon day of Aswin	Brahmin priest	Paddy, coconut, sweets, milk,flower, banana, etc.	Family and village levels	Clay idol and photo
Kali	Symbolizes the benign, gracefulness, and the most powerful form of the Matrusakti, the supreme mother goddess.	New moon day of the dark fortnight of Kartik	Brahmin priest	Coconut, sweets, flowers, banana etc along with sacrifice.	Generally in public places	Clay idol
Saraswati	The goddess of learning	Sri panchami or Basanta panchami (Panchami tithi of bright fortnight of Magha)	Brahmin priest	Coconut, sweets, flower, milk, banana, etc.	Educational institutions, houses, clubs, etc.	Clay idol and photo

Contd...

Contd...

Manasa	Believed as a daughter of Lord Shiva, presiding over snakes	September-November	Brahmin priest	Sacrifice along with other offerings	Clubs and public places	Clay idol and photo
Kichakeswari	Local goddess of Mayurbhanj	Tuesday and Saturday	Brahmin priest	Sacrifice along with other offerings	Temple	Clay idol and photo
Tarini	Local goddess of northern Orissa	Tuesday and Saturday	Brahmin priest and dehuri	Coconut, sweets, flower, banana, etc. (coconut is liked by this goddess)	Temple and house	Idol (symbolic stone) and photo
Jagannath	Main deity of Orissa	Ratha-yatra and other festivals	Brahmin priest	Coconut, sweets, flower, banana, etc. (this deity is very fond of coconut)	Temple and house	Idol and photo
Shiva	Saviour god	Shiva ratri, Sravan month, Raja sankranti, etc.	Brahmin priest	Ganja, coconut, sweets, flower, banana, etc.	Temple and house	

*Though it is the special day of worship these deities are worshipped every day by some people at their house and people pay visit to the temple both on the special days as well as on the other normal days as per their convenience.

** Officiate on special occasions, but the family members also participate.

located under the shadow of the tree, are used as resting platforms, where not only Hos but also non-Ho villagers and travellers, who pass by, use them. Sometimes, Hos prepare structures just like a Hindu temple on the memorial stone along with a trident on its top, which shows the impact of Hinduism. Similarly, sometimes the concrete horizontal platform prepared on the memorial stone, placed on the grave, shows the influence of Christianity. Although Hos have adopted these cultural elements of their neighbouring communities in more recent years, they have not withdrawn fully from their Bonga-centred original core culture.

Discussion

The Bonga cult, as we discussed, is the central power which controls all domains of Ho tribal culture. In fact, Bongaism is crucial in the maintenance of social solidarity, and in enforcing, what Das (1993:147, 2002) has termed, the 'jural order', in Ho society. The Ho society recognizes various kinds of ritual sanctions for the violence of social norms. Strict adherence to such sanctions ensures smooth functioning of Ho society, which is well-knit and neatly integrated like many other tribal societies in Orissa and elsewhere (Mishra, 1987:45). Ritual sanctions indeed help in maintaining social integrity and regulate action as per the perpetual norms of the society. Crop failure, disease and death, natural calamities, etc., are said to occur due to failure in proper propitiation of the ancestors or the Bongas (Ho gods and goddesses). Any such outbreak culminates in elaborate sacrifice before the Bongas, both at family and at communal levels (Mishra, 1987:45).

There are several instances of the blending of tribal and Hindu religious traditions, as we discussed above. The popularity of Manasa devi (a Hindu goddess who presides over snakes) is not limited to the Hindus. It is equally popular among the tribes (particularly the Hos) of the region. The entire Kolhan area, which is the original home of the Hos, as well as its neighbouring areas, covered with hills and forests, is full of different types of poisonous snakes and cases of snakebite in the region are plenty. Since the Hindus of the region worship Manasa devi for protection from the snakes, the Hos were prompted to adopt worship of this Hindu goddess when their own religious procedure of protection from the snakes failed. Thus, an alien religious ritual was gradually assimilated into their culture. Being tribals, the Hos worship goddess Manasa by sacrificing fowls and goats as also by offering sweets and flowers. If we analyze these offerings it will be evident that though the tribals have adopted this and some other alien deities, as we discussed above, they worship them both by the local Hindu methods of worship and their tribal method of worship, which invariably includes animal sacrifices and offering of ricebeer.

We also observed a strong trend of linguistic syncretism among the Hos of Jharkhand and Orissa, whose major languages have had deep impact upon both cultural and religious lives of Hos of both regions. Thus in Orissa, the younger generation is trying to discard the tribal language of their locality and is speaking a mixture of Hindi, Oriya and Ho language. In Jharkhand (as it belonged to erstwhile Hindi state of Bihar until recently) Hindi continues to be used for inter-community communication whereas among themselves Hos speak Ho dialect. In various spheres of cultural life, linguistic synthesis is noticed in terms of both the voluntary adaptation and imposition of Hindu-centric attributes. In case of death of respected persons like Munda and Manki of the village, Hos erect an additional vertical memorial stone/pillar (menhir) locally called Sasandhiri on which they engrave the deceased's name, place of birth and his achievements, either in Devnagri or Oriya script. The Hos do not have the expertise to engrave. Hence, they engage the services of a professional Hindu engraver from outside their community because if something is once written on the memorial stone it is not possible to change it. Most often the phrase "*Om Ganesaya Nomoh*" is now found engraved at the top of the epitaph of Hos, which is actually inserted by the Hindu Caste engraver, though the rest of the text of the epitaph remains that of the Hos. But Hos do not show any strong resentment for such accretion to their identification marker, though the opening line with a Hindu tilt and the tribal text have no correlation whatsoever, since the epitaph is a component of the indigenous tribal religious ethics which has nothing to do with the 'Great Hindu Tradition'.

There are instances when Hinduized names are almost imposed though such impositions hardly make deep intrusion into the tribal linguistic sphere. This we observed particularly in alteration of personal names, mainly of students, village names, place names, etc. It is observed that teachers in the schools failing to spell the tribal names, often provide Sanskritic names to tribal students though such students are called at home and in their community by tribal names only. Such coexistence of dual markers of identities in terms of nomenclature is seen in other areas also. Then we have such personal names as Lily, and English month-based names such as January August, etc. Those families that send labourers to tea gardens in Assam have given the name Assami to their children. Then we have a large number of Sanskrit names which have either been linguistically corrupted or phonetically distorted such as Site (Sita), Janke (Janaki), Gite (Gita), Lokon (Laxman), Jabuna (Jamuna), Routu (Rout), Mokta (Mukta), Chandoboni (Chandramani), etc. Besides, some Hos are also using the surnames of prominent Oriya communities as their first name along with their tribal surname, such as Mohanty Deogam and Rout Deogam whereby linguistic synthesis is noticed in a single name. Most often, it is observed that old tribal names and adopted Sanskritic names simultaneously prevail in many families.

Modernization and profound linguistic-religious contacts in both Jharkhand and Orissa have had a great impact on tribal value systems and thus an enormous blending of religious elements of the dominant Hindu communities with Ho religious beliefs and practices is noticed. Though Bongaism may have started losing its charisma and authority, the Hos have never disregarded the capability of the Bongas, and thus even today all major rituals associated with life-cycle events, including elaborate mortuary rites and agriculture related rituals essentially involve propitiation of the main Bongas, though the Hindu procedures of veneration and idolatry have increased in this tribal society of eastern India.

Acknowledgement

The author is grateful to Dr. N.K. Das, the editor of this volume for his persistent guidance and particularly for motivating and reorienting this author to rearrange and reinterpret the entire firsthand and secondary source material used in this paper from the analytic perspective of religious and linguistic syncretism. The author is also indebted to him for suggesting several modifications during the preparation of this paper, for thoroughly editing and improving the analytical depth of this paper. The author also acknowledges his gratitude to the many authors whose works on Jharkhand and Orissa are extensively referred to, particularly with reference to the cult of Bongaism. The author had submitted a report to the Anthropological Survey of India titled *Mortuary Practices of Hos: An Ethno- Archaeological Study,* as a senior research fellow (1999–2002). A small portion from this report with modification is referred to in this paper. The author is thankful to the authorities of the Anthropological Survey of India for the grant of fellowship. In order to prepare this paper however, the author revisited the previously-studied Ho villages, during July- August, 2002, mainly to collect fresh data from the viewpoint of linguistic and religious syncretism, under the guidance of Dr.Das. The views expressed in the paper, however, are those of the author alone.

References

Bodding, P.O., 1942, *Traditions and Institutions of Santhal*. Oslo: D.W. Broggers Boktrykheri.

Chatterjee, A.N. and T.C. Das, 1927, *The Hos of Sareikella*. Calcutta: Calcutta University.

Datton, E.T., 1872, *Descriptive Ethnology of Bengal*. Calcutta: Asiatic Society.

Das, N.K., 1993, *Kinship Politics and Law in Naga Society*. Calcutta: Anthropological Survey of India

Das. N.K., 2002, Kinship, Headmanship and Jural Order in Naga Society, in *Studies in Anthropology in India*. Ed. P.K. Misra. Mysore: Anthropological Association.

Das Gupta, P.K., 1978, *Impact of Industrialization on a Tribe in South Bihar*. Calcutta; Anthropological Survey of India.

Das Patnaik, P.S., 1990, Ho. In *Tribes of Orissa*. Ed. R.M. Senapati, Bhubaneswar: Harijan and Tribal Welfare Department, Government of Orissa: 114–118.

Dehon, P., 1906, *The Religion and Customs of the Oraon*. Calcutta; Asiatic Society.

Dhan, R.O., 1961, The Hos of Saranda: An Ethnographic Study. *Bulletin of the Bihar Tribal Research Institute*. Vol.-III (I): 37–114.

Duary, Nabakumar, 1995, Continuity and Change in Political System of Hos in Two Different Settings: A Micro Study in Two Bihar-Bengal Villages. *Journal of the Indian Anthropological Society*, Vol-30:145–51.

Duary, Nabakumar, 2000, Change and Continuity in Ho Religion: An Impact Study in South Bihar. In *Tribal Religion: Change and Continuity*. Ed. M.C. Behera. New Delhi; Commonwealth Publishers.

Kar, S.B., 1961, The Intelligence of the Hos. *Bulletin of the Bihar Tribal Research Institute*. Vol.-III (I): 167–179.

Majumdar, D.N., 1950, *The Affairs of a Tribes: A Study in Tribal Dynamics*. Lucknow; Universal Press Ltd.

Midya, Dipak. K., 1996, A Study on Ritual Action in Hos Festivals. *Journal of the Indian Anthropological Society*, Vol-31: 161–170.

Mishra, K.K., 1987, *Social Structure and Change among the Ho of Orissa*. Delhi; Gian Publishing House.

Mital, K., 1986, *Tribal Identity in Changing Industrial Environment: The Santhal Case*. New Delhi; Metropolitan Book Co. Pvt Ltd.

Mohanta, Basanta Kumar, 2002, *Mortuary Practices of Hos: An Ethno Archaeological Study*. A report submitted to the Anthropological Survey of India, Mimeographed.

Mohanty, Bijaylaxmi, 1997, Festivals of Orissa. In *Comparative History and Culture of Orissa*, Ed. P.K. Mishra Vol. 2: 657--705. New Delhi; Kaveri Books.

Prasad, N., 1961, *Land and People of Tribal Bihar*. Ranchi: Bihar Tribal Research Institute.

Prasad, S., 1961, A Study of Ho Dialect. *Bulletin of the Bihar Tribal Research Institute*, Vol. III(I):1–36.

Roy, S.C., 1918, *Oraon Religion and Customs*. Calcutta: The Industry Press.

Senapati, N. and N.K. Sahu, 1967, *Orissa District Gazetteers, Mayurbhanj*. Cuttack: Orissa Government Press.

Singh, K.S., 1994, *The Scheduled Tribes, National Series, People of India*, Vol. III. Calcutta; Anthropological Survey of India.

Contributors

Bijayananda Kar, Professor, U.G.C. Emeritus Fellow, Department of Philosophy, Utkal University, Bhubaneswar.

Suniti Kumar Pathak, former Professor, Department of Indo-Tibetan Studies, Visva-Bharati University, Santiniketan, West Bengal.

Anoop Chandola, Professor, Department of East Asian Studies, The University of Arizona, Tucson, Arizona, U.S.A.
E-Mail: chandola@u.arizona.edu

Mathieu Boisvert, C/o Barre Centre for Buddhist Studies, Universit du Qubec Montral, Montreal, Canada.
E-Mail: boisvert.mathievu@uqam.ca

K.S. Singh, Former Director General, Anthropological Survey of India, New Delhi.

T. Madhava Menon, Senior Fellow, International School of Dravidian Linguistics, Tiruvananthapuram.
E-Mail: tmadhavamenon@hotmail.com

K.G. Gurumurthy, former Professor of Cultural Anthropology, Karnataka University, Dharwad, Karnataka.

P. Venkata Rao, Professor, Department of Anthropology, University of Hyderabad, Hyderabad.
E-Mail: pvrss@uohyd.ernet.in

Rajat Shubhra Mukhopadhyay, Professor, Department of Sociology, University of North Bengal, Siligudi, District Darjeeling.
E-Mail: rajatsocio@rediffmail.com

Tamo Mibang, Pro-Vice-Chancellor, Arunachal Pradesh University, Itanagar, Arunachal Pradesh.

M.K. Raha, Former Joint Director, Anthropological Survey of India, Kolkata.

Sarit Kumar Chaudhuri, Department of Tribal Studies, Arunachal Pradesh University, Itanagar, Arunachal Pradesh.

Shibani Roy, Superintending Anthropologist, Anthropological Survey of India, Central Regional Centre, Nagpur.

S.H.M. Rizvi, Anthropologist, Anthropological Survey of India, Central Regional Centre, Nagpur.

Suresh Patil, Superintending Anthropologist, Anthropological Survey of India, Southern Regional Centre, Mysore.
E-Mail: sureshpatilmys@ rediffmail.com

B. Francis Kulirani, Superintending Anthropologist, Anthropological Survey of India, North East Regional Centre, Shillong.
E-Mail: fkulirani@yahoo.com

Deimaphishisha Sun, Anthropological Survey of India, North East Regional Centre, Shillong.

A. Justin, Anthropologist, Anthropological Survey of India, Andaman and Nicobar Regional Centre, Port Blair.
E-Mail: ansticejustin@ rediffmail.com

R.K. Sinha, Anthropological Survey of India, Southern Regional Centre, Mysore.

S.A.A. Saheb, Anthropologist, Anthropological Survey of India, Southern Regional Centre, Mysore.

Amitabh Sarkar, Anthropologist, Anthropological Survey of India, Eastern Regional Centre, Kolkata.

Samira Das Gupta, Anthropological Survey of India, Kolkata.

William Ekka, Former Anthropologist, Anthropological Survey of India, Ranchi.

Bibhash Dhar, Anthropologist, Anthropological Survey of India, North East Regional Centre, Shillong.

Basant Kumar Mohanta, Ph.D. Research Scholar, Department of Anthropology, Utkal University, Bhubaneswar.
E-Mail: basanta_mohanta2002@yahoo.co.in

N.K. Das, Superintending Anthropologist, Anthropological Survey of India, Kolkata.
E-Mail: nkdas49@rediffmail.com